Susan Henning

Test Bank

for

Baron
ESSENTIALS OF PSYCHOLOGY

Second Edition

Thomas T. Jackson
Fort Hays State University

Allyn and Bacon
Boston London Toronto Sydney Tokyo Singapore

Copyright © 1999 by Allyn & Bacon
A Viacom Company
160 Gould Street
Needham Heights, Massachusetts 02194

Internet: www.abacon.com
America Online: keyword: College Online

All rights reserved. The contents, or parts thereof, may be reproduced for use
with *Essentials of Psychology,* Second Edition, by Robert A. Baron, provided
such reproductions bear copyright notice, but may not be reproduced in any form
for any other purpose without written permission from the copyright owner.

ISBN 0-205-28846-4

Printed in the United States of America

10 9 8 7 6 5 4 3 2 1   03 02 01 00 99 98

TABLE OF CONTENTS

INTRODUCTION

EXAM CONSTRUCTION FORM ii

Chapter 1: Psychology: A Science ... and a Perspective 1

Chapter 2: Biological Bases of Behavior: A Look Beneath the Surface 23

Chapter 3: Sensation and Perception: Making Contact with the World around Us 47

Chapter 4: States of Consciousness 68

Chapter 5: Learning: How We're Changed by Experience 86

Chapter 6: Memory: Of Things Remembered ... and Forgotten 107

Chapter 7: Cognition and Intelligence 123

Chapter 8: Human Development 147

Chapter 9: Motivation and Emotion 174

Chapter 10: Personality: Uniqueness and Consistency in the Behavior of Individuals . . . 194

Chapter 11: Health, Stress, and Coping 218

Chapter 12: Psychological Disorders: Their Nature and Causes 239

Chapter 13: Therapy: Diminishing the Pain of Psychological Disorders 262

Chapter 14: Social Thought and Social Behavior 282

INTRODUCTION

This testbank is to accompany *ESSENTIALS OF PSYCHOLOGY (Second Edition)* by Robert A. Baron. The testbank provides a total of 2489 multiple choice questions that address the content in the chapters of the textbook. The following is a list of the features of this testbank:

1. Each chapter has between 126 and 225 multiple-choice questions.
2. This testbank has the names of the chapters listed in the Table of Contents, in addition to the chapter name being in the running head. The inclusion of the chapter names is a convenience for the professor.
3. There are no "all of the above," or "none of the above," type of answers in this testbank.
4. Each multiple choice question has specific information at the left of the item. The following question illustrates this information:

1.21	Your response to an elderly person in a grocery line illustrates
b	a. the impact of ecological variables.
p. 5	b. the impact of the actions and characteristics of others.
Applied	c. the impact of perceptual variables.
M	d. the impact of biological variables.
PT/OLSG	

   In this item, the first line lists the chapter and number of the question (Chapter 1, item 21). The second line contains the correct answer to the question and will be a **bold** typed small letter (**b** in this example). I have used small letters in the information line for consistency with the small letters in the question. The third line contains the page number of the text on which the relevant material is presented (page 5 in this example). When the material covers two pages of the text, I have <u>usually</u> used the first page number. The fourth line contains the type of question, either Applied, Concept, Fact, or Study (Applied in this example). The fifth line contains a subjective estimate of the item difficulty (M in the example). There are three categories of difficulty, Easy (E), Medium (M), or Challenging (C). The assignment of difficulty level is based upon several considerations. The type of item (Applied, Concept, Fact, Study) was considered, with Concept and Fact questions usually being easier than Applied and Study questions. The wording and specificity of the question was also considered. However, the difficulty rating is still highly subjective. The fifth line on selected questions (20 from each chapter) is labeled PT/OLSG, meaning that these questions have been used in the Practice Test Manual and in the OnLine Study Guide.

5. I have also included a sheet titled, "EXAM CONSTRUCTION FORM" in the front of this testbank. This sheet is a convenient form that could be used when making up an exam. The headings for the various columns correspond to the information items at the left of each question in the testbank. This form provides an easy way to see the mix of types of questions on the exam, what parts of the chapter have been covered by the exam, and the mix of difficulty level of questions on the exam. The last column could be used to write a brief comment about the topic of a question, or it could be used as a place to record performance data after the exam. I have found that using this form reduces my time in preparing an exam, makes it much easier for a secretary to prepare the exam, and provides me with an organized record of each exam.

Many of the questions from this testbank were taken from the testbank that I prepared for *Psychology* (4th Edition) by Baron. Accordingly, I thank the many individuals who prepared questions that were used in that testbank.

I again thank my wife, Nancy, and my son, Bret for their understanding and cooperation.

If you have modifications of the testbank you would like to see, or suggestions for improvement of this testbank, please send this information to me at the address listed below.

Thomas T. Jackson, PhD
Department of Psychology
Fort Hays State University
Hays, Kansas 67601
pstj@fhsuvm.fhsu.edu

EXAM CONSTRUCTION FORM
Essentials of Psychology (2nd Edition)

Chapter_____   Form _____   Date _____

Item	Question Number	Answer	Type	Page Number	Difficulty	Comments

Question Types   Difficulty
A = Applied   F = Fact   E = Easy
C = Concept   S = Study   M = Medium   C = Challenging

Chapter 1 - Psychology: A Science ... and a Perspective

CHAPTER 1

Multiple-Choice Questions

Modern Psychology: What It Is and Where It Came From

1.1 The view that knowledge can be gained through careful observation is referred to as
d
p. 4
Concept
E
a. phenomenology.
b. rationalism.
c. evolutionary psychology.
d. empiricism.

1.2 The view that knowledge can be gained through logic and careful reasoning is
a
p. 4
Fact
E
a. rationalism.
b. empiricism.
c. functionalism.
d. behaviorism.

1.3 Logic and careful reasoning is to careful observation as
c
p. 4
Concept
M
a. functionalism is to structuralism.
b. structuralism is to functionalism.
c. rationalism is to empiricism.
d. empiricism is to rationalism.

1.4 The branch of biology that studies the functions of living organisms is called
c
p. 4
Fact
E
a. psychology.
b. physiognomy.
c. physiology.
d. physiological psychology.

1.5 Muller, Fechner, and von Helmholtz were important in the development of psychology in that their research
d
p. 4
Fact
M
a. indicated that the structure of the individual was capable of measurement.
b. revealed that measurement was a crucial component for the advancement of psychology.
c. indicated that it was not possible to measure functions of the human body.
d. revealed that the scientific method could be used to study human behavior.

1.6 The individual usually credited with selling his colleagues on the idea of an independent science of psychology is
d
p. 4
Fact
M
PT/OLSG
a. Gustav Fechner.
b. Hermann von Helmholtz.
c. Johannes Muller.
d. Wilhelm Wundt.

1.7 The first laboratory of psychology was established by
b
p. 4
Fact
M
a. Gustav Fechner.
b. Wilhelm Wundt.
c. Johannes Muller.
d. Hermann von Helmholtz.

1.8 Wilhelm Wundt believed that psychologists should study _____.
a
p. 4
Fact
E
a. consciousness
b. behavior
c. physiology
d. perception

1.9   Wundt focused his attention on analyzing sensations, feelings, and images into their basic components, because he believed that psychologists should discover the
b
p. 4
Concept
M
a. structure of the human body.
b. structure of the human mind.
c. structure of the basis of human perception.
d. structure of the basis of human sensation.

1.10   Which of the following argued that the study of psychology should be to identify the basic parts of the consciousness?
b
p. 4
Concept
E
a. behaviorists
b. structuralists
c. functionalists
d. rationalists

1.11   The method in which individuals describe what is going on in their minds is called _____.
c
p. 4
Fact
M
a. structuralism
b. operationalism
c. introspection
d. retrospection

1.12   Introspection is a scientific methodology in which
a
p. 4
Fact
M
a. individuals describe what is going on in their own minds.
b. individuals carefully calculate the basic processes of sensation.
c. individuals measure the physiological reactions they are having a stimulus.
d. individuals report the response they are having to a physiological stimulus.

1.13   Which of the following argued that psychology should only involve the study of observable events?
d
p. 4
Fact
E
a. rationalists
b. structuralists
c. functionalists
d. behaviorists

1.14   Psychologists who felt that psychology should study only observable activities were the
c
p. 4
Fact
E
PT/OLSG
a. functionalists.
b. structuralists.
c. behaviorists.
d. experimentalists.

1.15   Observable behavior is to conscious behavior as
d
p. 4
Concept
M
PT/OLSG
a. structuralism is to behaviorism.
b. structuralism is to psychoanalysis.
c. behaviorism is to psychoanalysis.
d. behaviorism is to structuralism.

1.16   The founder of Behaviorism was
c
p. 4
Fact
E
a. Wilhelm Wundt.
b. William James.
c. John B. Watson.
d. James McKeen Cattell.

Chapter 1 - Psychology: A Science ... and a Perspective

1.17
a
p. 4
Concept
M

In the following,
a. Watson is to behavior as Wundt is to consciousness.
b. Watson is to consciousness as Wundt is to behavior.
c. Watson is to consciousness as Fechner is to consciousness.
d. Watson is to behavior as Fechner is to consciousness.

1.18
c
p. 4
Fact
M

For almost 40 years, psychology was defined as the science of
a. the mind.
b. human beings.
c. behavior.
d. mind and behavior.

1.19
b
p. 5
Concept
C

The inclusion of computers in experimental research gave psychologists the ability to
a. calculate their results with minute precision.
b. expose individuals to specific stimuli and measure the speed of their reactions, both with great precision.
c. expose individuals to carefully planned measurements of their behavior.
d. manipulate variables graphically, while at the same time measuring with great precision.

1.20
c
p. 5
Concept
C

While the Behaviorists limited the study of psychology to behavior, there was a developing, but contrasting, interest in _____.
a. physiological processes
b. social processes
c. mental processes
d. individual processes

1.21
a
p. 5
Concept
M
PT/OLSG

The _____ was the result of combining new research techniques with a growing interest in mental processes.
a. cognitive revolution
b. artistic revolution
c. experimental revolution
d. behavioral revolution

1.22
b
p. 5
Concept
E

Psychologists tend to refer to mental events as
a. mental processes.
b. cognitive processes.
c. mind processes.
d. behavioral processes.

1.23
d
p. 5
Fact
M

In your textbook, psychology is defined as
a. the science of the mind.
b. the science of behavior processes and mind processes.
c. the science of mind processes and cognitive processes.
d. the science of behavior and cognitive processes.

1.24
b
p. 5
Fact
M

Your textbook uses the phrase, "Science of behavior and cognitive processes" to define
a. physiology.
b. psychology.
c. psychoanalysis.
d. physiognomy.

1.25
d
p. 5
Concept
M

Cognitive processes are included in the definition of psychology because
a. the mind is still an object of curiosity.
b. these processes utilize the findings of many individual observations of mental life.
c. these processes are more explanatory than the term behavior.
d. the concept of behavior does not fully represent every aspect of mental life.

4   Test Bank - Essentials of Psychology (2nd Edition)

1.26
a
p. 6
Concept
M

One of the "grand issues" in psychology involves the question of
a. stability versus change.
b. behavior versus cognitive processes.
c. science versus applied.
d. physiological versus philosophical.

1.27
b
p. 6
Concept
M

The question of "stability versus change" involves
a. the extent to which psychology's experimental findings remain stable or change over time.
b. the extent to which characteristics and behavior of individuals remain stable or change over time.
c. the extent to which behavior in experiments remains stable over a long period of time or change over this period.
d. the extent to which IQ measures stay the same or change over time.

1.28
a
p. 6
Concept
M

Trying to determine the extent to which behavior remains constant over time or changes over time involves the question of
a. stability versus change.
b. rationality versus irrationality.
c. nature versus nurture.
d. determinism versus free will.

1.29
c
p. 6
Concept
M

Trying to determine the extent to which behavior is influenced by heredity or by learning involves the question of
a. stability versus change.
b. rationality versus irrationality.
c. nature versus nurture.
d. determinism versus free will.

1.30
c
p. 6
Concept
M

The answer to the nature-nurture question involves complex _____ between the environment and heredity.
a. measurements
b. enhancements
c. interactions
d. confounds

1.31
d
p. 7
Concept
M

Not wanting to eat a piece of cake shaped like a spider is an example of which "grand theme" of psychology?
a. nature versus nurture
b. stability versus change
c. continuous versus discontinuous
d. rationality versus irrationality

1.32
b
p. 7
Concept
M

The grand issue of _____ involves the fact that sometimes humans just do not behave as they would be expected to based on logic.
a. nature versus nurture
b. rationality versus irrationality
c. determinism versus free will
d. stability versus change

1.33
b
p. 7
Concept
M

Trying to determine the extent to which behavior is influenced by logic or by emotion involves the question of
a. stability versus change.
b. rationality versus irrationality.
c. nature versus nurture.
d. determinism versus free will.

Chapter 1 - Psychology: A Science ... and a Perspective

1.34 Emphasis on objective observation and measurement characterizes the
b
p. 7   a. cognitive perspective.
Concept   b. behavioral perspective.
M   c. psychodynamic perspective.
    d. biological perspective.

1.35 Manipulating factory work conditions and observing how performance changes reflects a _____ perspective.
c
p. 7   a. social and cultural
Concept   b. biological
M   c. behavioral
    d. evolutionary

1.36 The perspective emphasizing the study of thinking, remembering, decision making, etc. is called the
c
p. 7   a. psychodynamic perspective.
Concept   b. behavioral perspective.
M   c. cognitive perspective.
    d. evolutionary perspective.

1.37 A psychologist interested in how young children think when learning how to play games is probably a _____ psychologist.
d
p. 7   a. psychodynamic
Concept   b. environmental
M   c. behavioral
    d. cognitive

1.38 Psychologists who try to understand how we think and remember are taking a _____ perspective.
d
p. 7   a. physiological
Concept   b. psychodynamic
M   c. social-cultural
PT/OLSG   d. cognitive

1.39 Lisa is facing a charging bull and her heart rate and blood pressure increased. The _____ perspective would be appropriate to study these reactions.
b
p. 7   a. evolutionary
Applied   b. biological
M   c. cognitive
    d. social

1.40 The biological perspective would emphasize which of the following reactions to a charging bull?
a
p. 7   a. increased heart rate when avoiding the bull
Concept   b. movements to avoid the bull
M   c. thinking about how to avoid the bull
    d. dreaming about avoiding the bull

1.41 A psychologist was investigating the popularity of bullfighting. This psychologist was probably interested in
c
p. 7   a. the biological perspective.
Concept   b. the evolutionary perspective.
M   c. the social-cultural perspective.
    d. the behavioral perspective.

1.42   Psychologists who focus on unconscious processes in their study of human behavior take a perspective
b   known as
p. 7
    a. evolutionary.
Concept
    b. psychodynamic.
M
    c. social-cultural.
    d. cognitive.

1.43   Ralph started riding a horse when he was two years old. A psychologist who was interested in this
d   fact would be using the _____ perspective.
p. 7
    a. cognitive
Concept
    b. social-cultural
M
    c. behavioral
    d. evolutionary

1.44   Which of the following perspectives is least likely to use mental processes as a explanation for
c   behavior?
p. 7
    a. cognitive
Concept
    b. psychodynamic
M
    c. evolutionary
    d. social-cultural

1.45   In psychology, the multicultural perspective represents a focus on issues relating to
c
    a. the problems of blending different neural structures in the brain.
p. 9
    b. the ways people change as they grow older or experience new things.
Concept
    c. the effects of ethnic and cultural factors on behavior.
C
    d. how people interact with many different types of information.

1.46   The relatively recent emphasis in psychology on the multicultural perspective is partly a result of
c   which social trend?
p. 9
    a. Improvements in health care mean that there are more and more elderly Americans.
Concept
    b. An increasingly technological society makes higher education more and more important.
C
    c. Widespread immigration is bringing together people with differing ethnic backgrounds.
PT/OLSG
    d. Television has created a generation of children who think visually and often can't read.

1.47   Lisa is interviewing a client who seems to be suffering from depression. If she is strongly influenced
b   by the multicultural perspective, which question is she most likely to ask?
p. 9
    a. "Are you allergic to any medications?"
Applied
    b. "To what ethnic group does your family belong?"
E
    c. "Do you ever remember any of your dreams?"
    d. "What score did you get on your last IQ test?"

1.48   One result of the growing multicultural perspective in psychology has been the development of
a
    a. guidelines for serving people with different ethnic backgrounds.
p. 10
    b. rules for the most efficient ways to memorize lists of words.
Fact
    c. maps that show the functions of many key areas of the brain.
M
    d. a better understanding of the importance of personal growth.

1.49   In psychology, the multicultural perspective has had an impact on
b
    a. primarily the application of psychological principles.
p. 10
    b. primarily the investigation of psychological principles.
Concept
    c. primarily the applied and the research approaches to behavior.
C
    d. both the applied and the social approaches to behavior.

Chapter 1 - Psychology: A Science ... and a Perspective

1.50 One criticism of psychology concerning the level of adoption of the multicultural perspective is that
b a. most practicing psychologists do not address ethnic issues.
p. 10 b. most research still ignores minority groups.
Applied c. most graduate psychology programs have gone to the extreme in hiring faculty members of color.
C d. most psychologists are simply racially prejudiced.

Psychologists: Who They Are and What They Do

1.51 MD is to PhD as
a a. psychiatrist is to psychologist.
p. 10 b. psychologist is to psychiatrist.
Fact c. neuroscientist is to biopsychologist.
M d. biopsychologist is to neuroscientist.

1.52 Individuals who specialize in the diagnosis, study, and treatment of psychological disorders include
b a. only psychiatrists.
p. 10 b. both psychiatrists and psychologists.
Fact c. only psychologists.
M d. both psychologists and podiatrists.

1.53 Which is the following is the biggest difference between psychologists and psychiatrists?
c a. diagnostic procedures
p. 10 b. treatments
Concept c. training
E d. view of mental disorders

1.54 Roughly what percent of graduate students in psychology today are women?
c a. 10%
p. 11 b. 30%
Fact c. 50%
E d. 70%

1.55 A clinical psychologist typically has a _____ degree in the field of _____.
a a. doctoral, psychology
p. 11 b. medical, psychiatry
Fact c. bachelor's, social science
M d. legal, mental deficiency

1.56 An applied psychologist is one who
b a. prescribes and monitors the effects of medications.
p. 11 b. does research and uses it to solve practical problems.
Fact c. conducts research that is purely theoretical and abstract.
M d. explores the subconscious through dream analysis.

1.57 The greatest number of psychologists are in the subfields of
a a. clinical and counseling psychology.
p. 12 b. developmental and educational psychology.
Fact c. cognitive and industrial psychology.
M d. social and organizational psychology.

1.58 An experimental psychologist is one whose work focuses primarily on
a a. using research to understand basic psychological processes.
p. 12 b. conducting experiments designed to find out the best way to help people.
Fact c. creating psychological tests to better diagnose psychological disorders.
M d. understanding how to organize a workplace so that workers will be more efficient.

8 Test Bank - Essentials of Psychology (2nd Edition)

1.59 Psychologists who study all aspects of behavior in work settings are called _____ psychologists.
c
p. 12   a. career/educational
Fact   b. clinical/counseling
E   c. industrial/organizational
    d. social/occupational

1.60 Psychologists who study aspects of basic psychological processes such as perception, learning, and motivation are called _____ psychologists.
d
p. 12   a. social
Fact   b. cognitive
E   c. phenomenological
    d. experimental

1.61 A developmental psychologist would be most interested in which of these issues?
c
p. 12   a. Which areas of the brain are involved in using language?
Applied   b. How does a judge's instructions affect a jury's deliberations?
M   c. How do children understand their own thought processes?
    d. What sorts of control panels reduce accidents in factories?

1.62 A cognitive psychologist is most likely to be interested in which of the following questions?
d
p. 12   a. Do different parts of the brain have different functions?
Applied   b. How can we reduce the amount of violence in our schools?
M   c. What causes someone to develop a psychological disorder?
    d. What can we do to remember more of what we read?

Psychology and the Scientific Method

1.63 The knowledge gathered by psychologists is _____ than knowledge provided by intuition.
c
p. 13   a. more related
Concept   b. more tangential
M   c. more accurate
    d. more common sense

1.64 The scientific method is a
c
p. 13   a. complex mathematical analysis procedure.
Fact   b. set of rules for how to conduct good experiments.
M   c. systematic method for gathering information.
    d. technique that guarantees the result will be true.

1.65 A technique that involves systematically following a series of steps to acquire knowledge about something is called the
d
p. 13   a. functional process.
Fact   b. skeptical inquiry.
M   c. structural system.
    d. scientific method.

1.66 Scientific accuracy means
d
p. 13   a. considering only observations that fit a scientific theory.
Fact   b. ignoring the scientist's own biases and prejudices.
M   c. observing only observable, measurable behaviors.
    d. gathering data in careful, precise, error-free ways.

Chapter 1 - Psychology: A Science ... and a Perspective

1.67
c
p. 13
Applied
M
PT/OLSG

Suppose Ralph tries out a new intelligence test, but the first two or three people who use it complain that it is too hard. If Ralph concludes from this information that the test is bad, it would violate the principle of scientific
a. open-mindedness.
b. functionality.
c. accuracy.
d. empiricism.

1.68
b
p. 13
Fact
M

Scientists should be very cautious about accepting claims until these claims have been tested over and over again under many different circumstances. This operation is the principle of
a. scientific accuracy.
b. scientific skepticism.
c. scientific bias.
d. scientific functionality.

1.69
b
p. 13
Fact
M

Scientific objectivity means
a. studying only observable, overt behaviors, not invisible internal processes.
b. evaluating ideas on the basis of research evidence, without bias.
c. refusing to consider ideas that don't agree with accepted scientific principles.
d. only collecting data, never drawing unnecessary conclusions from the data.

1.70
b
p. 13
Applied
M

Suppose a psychologist learned of a series of well-designed studies that supported an idea the psychologist did not believe. If the psychologist refuses to accept the results, it would violate the principle of scientific
a. accuracy.
b. open-mindedness.
c. skepticism.
d. objectivity.

1.71
a
p. 14
Fact
M

The field of psychology is committed to objectivity, accuracy, skepticism, and open-mindedness, which means that
a. psychology is a science.
b. psychologists must have graduate degrees.
c. feelings and dreams aren't part of psychology.
d. psychology only studies overt behaviors.

1.72
a
p. 14
Fact
E
PT/OLSG

The main purpose of theories is to
a. explain.
b. postdict.
c. evaluate.
d. summarize.

1.73
b
p. 14
Fact
M
PT/OLSG

An important sources of ideas for studies in psychology is
a. literature.
b. theory.
c. common sense.
d. mathematics.

1.74
c
p. 14
Concept
M

The primary purpose of psychological theories is to
a. summarize research results.
b. relate various fields of psychology to each other.
c. explain behavior and cognitive processes.
d. understand behavior and cognitive processes.

1.75 The two major parts of a theory are
b
p. 14 a. basic concepts and common sense ideas.
Fact b. basic concepts and relationships between concepts.
C c. detailed observations and relationships between concepts.
d. detailed observations and logical reasoning.

1.76 If a psychologist claims to be able to explain some phenomenon, then the psychologist must have a
c
p. 14 a. set of detailed observations of the phenomenon.
Fact b. common sense understanding of how it works.
M c. theory describing its basic concepts and how they are related.
d. statistical meta-analysis of all the related research.

1.77 As described in your text, predictions derived from theory are called
d
p. 14 a. statements.
Fact b. axioms.
E c. propositions.
d. hypotheses.

1.78 Hypotheses are
a
p. 14 a. testable predictions derived from a theory.
Fact b. statistical analyses of the probability of a given result.
E c. common sense beliefs about how a certain system works.
d. scientific statements that have been proved true.

1.79 After a psychologist has developed a theory, the psychologist then uses the theory to develop a
d specific prediction to be tested, which is called a(n)
p. 14
Fact a. structural loop.
M b. statistical test.
c. observation.
d. hypothesis.

1.80 A hypothesis is a statement that specifies
c
p. 14 a. how the results of an experiment will be analyzed.
Concept b. exactly what will be measured and how.
C c. what a theory predicts in certain circumstances.
d. the problem that a scientist is studying.

1.81 The statement, "throwing good money after bad" is an illustration of the process of
b
p. 14 a. poor fiscal management.
Applied b. escalation of commitment.
M c. commitment with no financial backing.
d. having more money than necessary.

1.82 Lisa made a commitment to buy an exercise bike and told Ralph that she was going to buy this bike.
c She then found that the bike needed some gadgets to make it work effectively. The bike was going
p. 14 to cost her much more than she originally thought, but she bought it anyway. This situation
Applied illustrates
C a. caveat emptor.
b. lack of consumer savvy.
c. escalation of commitment.
d. advertising compliance.

Chapter 1 - Psychology: A Science ... and a Perspective

1.83
a
p. 14
Concept
M
If the results of a research project support the original predictions of a theory, the
a. confidence in the theory's predictions increases.
b. confidence in the theory's predictions decreases.
c. confidence in the researcher's abilities increases.
d. confidence in the stability of the variables increases.

1.84
a
p. 14
Concept
M
If the predictions of a theory are not confirmed by research, the
a. confidence in the theory is decreased.
b. confidence in the theory is increased.
c. confidence in the researcher is decreased.
d. confidence in the researcher is increased.

1.85
d
p. 15
Concept
M
Common sense provides us with
a. accurate explanations of behavior.
b. complex explanations of behavior.
c. unacceptable explanations of behavior.
d. contradictory explanations of behavior.

1.86
b
p. 15
Concept
M
PT/OLSG
The common sense approach to psychology is often characterized by
a. objective evaluations.
b. contradictory statements.
c. direct experimentation.
d. systematic observation.

1.87
b
p. 16
Applied
C
"Birds of a feather flock together" and "Opposites attract" are
a. complex statements of the same behavior.
b. common sense explanations of the same behavior.
c. common sense explanations of different behaviors.
d. simple explanations of different behaviors.

1.88
d
p. 16
Applied
M
Ralph has just purchased a new car. He feels he got a good deal, but read in one consumer magazine that this car has a tendency to "tip over." He rejects the conclusions from this magazine. This scenario is an example of
a. illusory correlation.
b. fundamental attribution error.
c. availability heuristic.
d. confirmation bias.

1.89
c
p. 16
Concept
C
The tendency to perceive that just because something is easy to remember it must be important represents
a. the confirmation bias.
b. the representative heuristic.
c. the availability heuristic.
d. the holistic bias.

1.90
c
p. 16
Concept
M
Which of the following is mentioned in your textbook as a tendency that can influence our judgment concerning human behavior?
a. representative heuristic
b. illusory correlation
c. mood effects
d. conceptual bias

12   Test Bank - Essentials of Psychology (2ⁿᵈ Edition)

1.91 We cannot rely on informal observation as a basis for valid conclusions about behavior because
a
p. 16   a. such observation is subject to many potential sources of bias.
Concept b. such observation is reducible to one subjective statement.
C   c. such observation has no basis in reality.
        d. such observation gets its validity from many independent confirmations.

The Scientific Method in Everyday Life: Thinking Critically about Human Behavior

1.92 Being skeptical, keeping an open mind, and not jumping to conclusions are characteristics of
c
p. 17   a. a negative approach to life.
Concept b. dispositional attribute.
M   c. critical thinking.
        d. analytical thinking.

1.93 To evaluate carefully all aspects of a piece of research and question exactly how it was conducted and
c   what it really means is to use
p. 17   a. statistical analysis.
Concept b. demand characteristics.
M   c. critical thinking.
        d. observational definitions.

1.94 Which of the following statements best reflects an attitude of critical thinking with respect to the
d   report of a research project?
p. 17   a. I don't care what they say, I won't believe it.
Applied b. Of course, I've always known that was true.
C   c. I really like what these people are saying.
PT/OLSG d. I wonder how they measured that variable.

1.95 Lisa is considered a critical thinker, therefore she would have which of the following characteristics?
b
p. 17   a. jumps to conclusions
Applied b. keeps an open mind
E   c. is easily persuaded
        d. has a negative slant on things

1.96 Practice in critical thinking will help you
a
p. 18   a. think in a more sophisticated way.
Concept b. think in a more elongated way.
M   c. think in a more convoluted way.
        d. think in a more constricted way.

1.97 Ralph read an advertisement that said, "Four out of five dentists use this product!" He decided to
d   buy the product based on this claim. Ralph is characteristic of
p. 18   a. a sophisticated consumer.
Applied b. an evaluative consumer.
M   c. a convoluted consumer.
        d. an unsophisticated consumer.

1.98 Being a critical thinker implies that you will be a
b
p. 18   a. negative voter.
Concept b. sophisticated voter.
M   c. convoluted voter.
        d. emotional voter.

Chapter 1 - Psychology: A Science ... and a Perspective

Research Methods in Psychology: How Psychologists Answer Questions about Behavior

1.99
a
p. 20
Concept
M

Studying behavior by recording what a subject is doing while in its normal habitat is called the
a. naturalistic observation method.
b. case method.
c. experimental observation method.
d. normal correlation method.

1.100
b
p. 20
Concept
M

Some psychologists observed people saying good-bye to each other at airports in order to study the types of behaviors displayed during these emotional situations. The method they used is best described as the
a. case method.
b. naturalistic observation method.
c. experimental manipulation method.
d. correlational method.

1.101
c
p. 20
Concept
M

The systematic study of behavior in real-life situations is called the
a. real world science method.
b. case method.
c. naturalistic observation method.
d. nonscientific observation method.

1.102
b
p. 20
Concept
M

Which of the following research methods is most likely to be useful to a psychologist who wants to find out how people typically behave in a certain fairly common situation?
a. surveys
b. naturalistic observation
c. case methods
d. experimentation

1.103
d
p. 20
Applied
M

In order to examine play behavior in wolves, a comparative psychologist spent three weeks observing wolves in the northwest regions of the United States. The method used was most likely
a. the case method.
b. the real world observation method.
c. the pseudo-scientific method.
d. the naturalistic observation method.

1.104
a
p. 20
Concept
M

A method of research in which detailed information about individuals is used to develop general principles about behavior is called the
a. case method.
b. naturalistic observation method.
c. interview method.
d. experimental method.

1.105
b
p. 20
Applied
M

Jean Piaget carefully observed his children as they developed. On the basis of these observations made with just his children, he formulated some very important hypotheses about cognitive development. His approach can best be classified as
a. the experimental method.
b. the case method.
c. the retrospective study method.
d. the natural survey method.

14 Test Bank - Essentials of Psychology (2nd Edition)

1.106
c
p. 21
Applied
C
PT/OLSG

Freud based many of his ideas about personality on extensive interviews with his clients. He had them tell him about their lives, especially their early childhood experiences. Freud's method of obtaining information is referred to as
a. naturalistic observation.
b. systematic desensitization.
c. case method.
d. meta-analysis.

1.107
b
p. 21
Concept
M

The major advantage of the case method is
a. how objective and scientific it is.
b. the amount of detailed information available.
c. the ability to generalize to many other people.
d. how quickly the data can be collected.

1.108
a
p. 21
Concept
M

The major disadvantage of the case method is
a. the possibility of the researcher losing scientific objectivity because of repeated contact.
b. the lack of clearly defined goals of the researcher.
c. the involvement of a very few number of participants.
d. the uniqueness of each individual participant.

1.109
c
p. 21
Concept
M

Self-report is to normal habitat as
a. case method is to experiment.
b. experiment is to case method.
c. survey is to naturalistic observation.
d. naturalistic observation is to survey.

1.110
b
p. 21
Concept
M

A method that involves asking a large number of individuals to complete questionnaires designed to yield information on specific aspects of their behavior or attitudes is called the
a. naturalistic observation method.
b. survey method.
c. real-world assessment method.
d. case method.

1.111
d
p. 21
Applied
M

Polls taken asking college-age individuals about the current use of alcohol are examples of the
a. naturalistic observation method.
b. case method.
c. real-world assessment method.
d. survey method.

1.112
b
p. 21
Concept
E

A research method that can be used to gain a large amount of relatively simple information from a large group of people is
a. naturalistic observation.
b. survey.
c. experiment.
d. case method.

1.113
a
p. 21
Applied
M
PT/OLSG

Your high school guidance counselor sends you a questionnaire to complete about many of your high school experiences. The counselor indicates that the questionnaire has been sent to all graduates within the last ten years. In all likelihood, your counselor is using which of the following methods?
a. survey method
b. double-blind method
c. naturalistic observation method
d. case method

Chapter 1 - Psychology: A Science ... and a Perspective

1.114
d
p. 21
Concept
M

Which of the following methods has the advantage of allowing the investigator to collect large amounts of information and detect changes in behavior and attitudes over time?
a. independent variable method
b. case method
c. naturalistic observation method
d. survey method

1.115
a
p. 21
Concept
M

One of the difficulties with the survey method is
a. that wording of questions may influence responses.
b. an inability to examine changes over time.
c. the relatively small number of subjects used.
d. the lack of cooperation of participants.

1.116
c
p. 21
Concept
M

In a piece of research, the sample is the group of people who
a. have the usual value of the independent variable.
b. have the manipulated value of the independent variable.
c. are assumed to represent the rest of the population.
d. give the researcher the expected pattern of results.

1.117
b
p. 22
Fact
E

A research method in which two or more variables are observed to determine whether changes in one are related to changes in the other is called the
a. prediction method.
b. correlational method.
c. case method.
d. natural tendency method.

1.118
d
p. 22
Fact
E

The extent to which changes in one factor are associated with changes in another can best be determined using the
a. naturalistic observation method.
b. real-world science method.
c. case method.
d. correlational method.

1.119
d
p. 22
Concept
E

Which of the following is true concerning a correlational study?
a. It is a very inefficient design.
b. It allows for the determination of cause-and-effect relationships.
c. It requires the manipulation of an independent variable.
d. It can be used to study behavior in real-life situations.

1.120
b
p. 22
Fact
E

Values for correlation coefficients can range between which of the following values?
a. 0.00 to +1.00
b. -1.00 to +1.00
c. 0.00 to 100.00
d. -1.00 to 0.00

1.121
c
p. 22
Concept
M

If large values of one variable are associated with small values of another variable, the correlation between the two is probably
a. zero.
b. positive.
c. negative.
d. greater than +1.00.

1.122 For which of the following correlation coefficients is the degree of relationship the strongest?
c
p. 22   a.   +.55
Concept   b.   +.10
M   c.   -.60
            d.   -.30

1.123 As the strength of a negative correlation increases, the ability to predict the value of one variable
a   from another
p. 22   a.   increases.
Concept   b.   decreases.
M   c.   stays the same.
PT/OLSG   d.   cannot be determined.

1.124 The major usefulness of a correlation is that it allows us to
a   a.   predict one variable when we know the other.
p. 22   b.   find out what caused something to happen.
Concept   c.   know how people really act in some situation.
M   d.   understand why someone is good in school.

1.125 Research in natural settings is to _____ as research in special settings is to _____.
c   a.   laboratory research: special research
p. 23   b.   field research: special research
Concept   c.   field research: laboratory research
M   d.   laboratory research: field research

1.126 Suppose there is a strong correlation between how often mothers smile at their babies and the
c   number of friends the children have at age 6 years. The main reason why we cannot draw the
p. 23 conclusion that the mothers' smiles cause the children to make more friends is that
Applied   a.   it is impossible to accurately measure smiling.
C   b.   all mothers and all children are different.
            c.   correlations cannot prove causal relationships.
            d.   psychologists know no reason why this should be true.

1.127 The major strength of the experimental method is that it allows us to
b   a.   measure more than one variable at a time.
p. 25   b.   draw cause-and-effect conclusions.
Fact   c.   calculate positive and negative correlations.
M   d.   measure variables more objectively.

1.128 An experiment is a procedure in which the researcher
d   a.   uses complex statistical analyses to interpret observations.
p. 25   b.   collects information from a very large number of people.
Fact   c.   observes people acting naturally in their normal environment.
C   d.   systematically manipulates and observes a situation.

1.129 In order to explain a cause-and-effect relationship between two or more variables, the method used
d   most often by psychologists is the
p. 25   a.   correlational method.
Concept   b.   case method.
M   c.   naturalistic observation method.
            d.   experimental method.

Chapter 1 - Psychology: A Science ... and a Perspective

1.130   If one wants to know the cause of behavior, one should use
c
p. 25   a. observation.
Concept   b. correlation.
M   c. experimentation.
    d. surveys.

1.131   The method used to determine if variables are related to each other by systematically changing one
a   and observing the effects of these changes on another variable is called the
p. 25   a. experimental method.
Fact   b. correlational method.
E   c. naturalistic observation method.
    d. pseudoscience.

1.132   Relationship is to cause-and-effect as
c
p. 25   a. case method is to naturalistic observation.
Concept   b. naturalistic observation is to case study.
M   c. correlation is to experiment.
    d. experiment is to correlation.

1.133   The factor that is systematically varied in an experiment is the
a
p. 25   a. independent variable.
Fact   b. dependent variable.
E   c. operational variable.
    d. correlational variable.

1.134   In an experiment, the factor that is varied is called the _____ variable.
c
p. 25   a. control
Fact   b. dependent
E   c. independent
PT/OLSG   d. stimulus

1.135   In an experiment, the independent variable is the variable that is
b
p. 25   a. predicted by the experimenter.
Fact   b. directly controlled by the experimenter.
M   c. measured to see if it shows any effect.
    d. correlated with the experimenter variable.

1.136   In an experiment, the dependent variable is the variable that is
c
p. 25   a. directly controlled by the experimenter.
Fact   b. supposed to have an effect on something else.
M   c. measured to see if it shows any effect.
    d. randomly assigned to groups.

1.137   An experiment can be considered a way to tell whether manipulations of the _____ variable have an
a   effect on measurements of the _____ variable.
p. 25   a. independent: dependent
Fact   b. dependent: independent
M   c. correlational: control
    d. control: correlational

18   Test Bank - Essentials of Psychology (2nd Edition)

1.138
d
p. 25
Applied
C

In an experiment on how seating affects grades, a researcher had students sit in randomly assigned seats for a lecture and then take a test. The researcher found that those sitting in front got higher test scores. In this experiment, the independent variable would be
   a.   the test scores.
   b.   the lecture.
   c.   the college students.
   d.   the seating location.

1.139
c
p. 25
Concept
M

Careful measurement is to systematic variation as
   a.   correlation is to survey.
   b.   survey is to correlation.
   c.   dependent variable is to independent variable.
   d.   independent variable is to dependent variable.

1.140
b
p. 25
Applied
M

In an experiment on the effects of tutoring on the grades of college students, the condition in which students do not receive tutoring is called the
   a.   experimental condition.
   b.   control condition.
   c.   bypassed condition.
   d.   uncontrolled condition.

1.141
b
p. 26
Fact
M

The procedure used to assure that all research participants have an equal chance of being assigned to each of the experimental conditions is called
   a.   experimental assignment.
   b.   random assignment.
   c.   control manipulation.
   d.   confound assignment.

1.142
c
p. 26
Concept
M

The procedure used to reduce the possibility that differences in experimental participants' performance are due to the differences that participants brought with them into the experiment is
   a.   confound assessment.
   b.   experimental assignment.
   c.   random assignment.
   d.   bias reduction.

1.143
d
p. 27
Concept
M

If another variable besides that which is systematically manipulated by the experimenter can affect the measured behaviors in an experiment, a _____ is said to exist in the experiment.
   a.   deception
   b.   bias
   c.   meta-analysis
   d.   confound

1.144
b
p. 27
Applied
M
PT/OLSG

In an experiment, all participants in a noisy condition are tested on Mondays and those in the no noise condition are tested on Wednesdays. The noise and day of week variables are
   a.   implicated.
   b.   confounded.
   c.   contrived.
   d.   interactive.

1.145
a
p. 27
Fact
M

When an experimenter's expectations differentially influence participants' behavior, these effects are called
   a.   experimenter effects.
   b.   dependent variable effects.
   c.   deception effects.
   d.   statistically significant effects.

Chapter 1 - Psychology: A Science ... and a Perspective

1.146
d
p. 27
Fact
M

Procedures in which neither the persons collecting data nor research participants have knowledge of the experimental conditions to which they have been assigned are called
a. arbitrary assignment procedures.
b. demand characteristic procedures.
c. naturalistic observations procedures.
d. double-blind procedures.

1.147
b
p. 27
Concept
M

Who is aware of which participants are in which condition when using the double-blind procedure?
a. only the researcher collecting the data
b. neither the researcher collecting the data nor the participants
c. only the participants
d. both the researcher collecting the data and the participants

1.148
d
p. 29
Concept
M

A special form of mathematics designed, in part, to evaluate the likelihood that a given pattern of findings is due to chance is called _____ statistics.
a. descriptive
b. confirmation
c. random
d. inferential

1.149
a
p. 29
Fact
M

If statistical analyses suggest that the likelihood of obtaining the observed findings by chance is low, the results are described as being
a. significant.
b. meaningful.
c. meaningless.
d. not interpretable.

1.150
b
p. 29
Concept
M
PT/OLSG

If the likelihood by chance of obtained results is less than or equal to .05, the results are described as being
a. meaningful.
b. significant.
c. meaningless.
d. not interpretable.

1.151
d
p. 29
Fact
C

The probability that a given pattern of findings is a chance event is
a. dependent on the number of participants.
b. always zero.
c. due to random events.
d. never zero.

1.152
c
p. 29
Fact
M

Repeating an experiment over and over to verify the result is called
a. hypothesis.
b. functionalism.
c. replication.
d. denial.

1.153
b
p. 29
Fact
M

Replication is the process of
a. generating several hypotheses from one theory.
b. repeating an experiment to verify the results.
c. testing a result with statistical analyses.
d. inserting extraneous variables into an experiment.

Ethical Issues in Psychological Research

1.154
b
p. 29
Fact
M

Ethical standards designed to assure the safety, privacy, and well-being of research participants have been developed by the
a. American Philosophical Association.
b. American Psychological Association.
c. American Philological Association.
d. American Philanthropic Association.

1.155
b
p. 30
Fact
M

Deception in psychology experiments usually involves
a. adjusting experimental findings so that they can be published.
b. withholding information from participants so that their behavior is not affected.
c. statistically insignificant results.
d. changing an experimental condition so that the subject does not become aware of the intent.

1.156
a
p. 30
Concept
E
PT/OLSG

Because it is often necessary to conceal certain aspects of an experiment, experimental psychologists may use the technique of
a. deception.
b. projection.
c. subliminal stimulation.
d. conversion.

1.157
b
p. 30
Fact
M

The technique of informed consent involves giving the participants in a study
a. therapy, if needed, to deal with the experience.
b. complete information about the research beforehand.
c. complete information about the research after it is over.
d. an adequate payment in return for their services.

1.158
b
p. 30
Concept
M

When a researcher uses deception as part of a research project, it is especially important that there should be
a. no animals or children used in the research.
b. both informed consent and debriefing.
c. a second piece of research that does not use deception.
d. a careful record of all responses.

1.159
a
p. 30
Fact
M

The technique of debriefing involves giving the participants in a study
a. complete information about the research after it is over.
b. complete information about the research beforehand.
c. the training they will need to participate effectively.
d. an environment in which they can operate comfortably.

1.160
a
p. 30
Concept
M

Pre-experiment is to post-experiment as
a. informed consent is to debriefing.
b. debriefing is to informed consent.
c. meta-analysis is to statistical significance.
d. statistical significance is to meta-analysis.

1.161
d
p. 30
Fact
E
PT/OLSG

Giving a participant full information about all aspects of an experiment after the participant has fulfilled his or her role in an experiment is referred to as
a. confounding.
b. deception.
c. informed consent.
d. debriefing.

Chapter 1 - Psychology: A Science ... and a Perspective

1.162   The view of most psychologists on using deception in psychological research can be summarized as
c
p. 30   a.   deception is always acceptable as long as no one is hurt.
Concept   b.   deception is never acceptable under any circumstances.
M   c.   deception must be used carefully, and avoided if possible.
           d.   deception can be used as long as debriefing is eliminated.

1.163   Which of the following is an important reason for using animals as research subjects in psychology?
c
p. 31   a.   There are no ethical rules that limit what research can be performed with animals.
Fact   b.   All important human psychological abilities can be found in animals.
M   c.   Some kinds of research are allowed with animals but not with humans.
           d.   Nothing: there are no important, ethically justified reasons for using animals in research.

1.164   Most psychological research using animals
d
p. 31   a.   involves some harm or discomfort.
Fact   b.   is unnecessary.
M   c.   involves drugs that have psychopharmacological properties.
           d.   provides information not available from humans.

1.165   As opposed to the ethical issues involved in research with human and animal subjects, ethical issues
d   in the practice of psychology have to do with
p. 32   a.   whether or not people are deceived about what the research is about.
Concept   b.   forming meaningful, important theories and developing testable predictions.
C   c.   making allowances for the effects of people's differing ethnic backgrounds.
           d.   dilemmas therapists face while providing psychological services to clients.

1.166   The most common ethical problem psychologists face in the practice of psychology is
a
p. 32   a.   protecting their clients' confidentiality.
Fact   b.   deceiving their research participants.
M   c.   causing stress to laboratory animals.
           d.   avoiding sexual relations with their clients.

1.167   Which of these scenes reflects the most common type of ethical problem that occurs in the practice
c   of psychology?
p. 32   a.   A researcher deliberately falsifies the results of an experiment.
Applied   b.   A doctor prescribes medication that addicts a client.
C   c.   A therapist learns that a client has committed a crime.
PT/OLSG   d.   A counselor falls in love with a client.

1.168   A school psychologist conducting therapy sessions with a disturbed child learns that the child's father
c   works in the same office as the psychologist's wife. This situation reflects an ethical dilemma related to
p. 32   a.   protecting the client's confidentiality.
Applied   b.   deceiving the research subject.
C   c.   conflicting relationships with the client.
           d.   falsifying data in scientific research.

1.169   One important ethical principle that psychologists hold to in the practice of psychology is
b
p. 32   a.   try not to cause unnecessary harm to research animals.
Concept   b.   sexual relations between therapists and clients are forbidden.
M   c.   any illegal activities a client admits must be reported immediately.
           d.   only report statistically significant results if they are important.

1.170 A psychologist who engages in sexual relations with a client has violated ethical guidelines adopted by the
b
p. 32 a. American Philosophical Association.
Fact   b. American Psychological Association.
E   c. American Philological Association.
       d. American Philanthropic Association.

Using This Book: A Review of Its Special Features

1.171 Which of the following is not one of the features in your textbook?
c
p. 33   a. Ideas to Take with You
Fact   b. Exploring Gender and Diversity
E   c. Knowing the Researchers
        d. Research Methods: How Psychologists Study

1.172 Which of the following is not good advice for effective studying?
b
p. 34   a. minimize distraction
Fact   b. save all of your studying for one long session
E   c. reward yourself for attaining selected goals
        d. use active rather than passive studying techniques

1.173 One of the first things a student should do when preparing to study is
a
p. 34   a. overview the chapter.
Applied   b. get a comfortable chair.
E   c. read the entire chapter first.
          d. turn on the radio.

1.174 In order to study effectively, a student should
c
p. 34   a. eliminate rewards.
Applied   b. read the entire chapter first.
E   c. minimize distractions.
          d. study all at once.

1.175 One technique for effective studying is to
a
p. 35   a. provide rewards for accomplishing study goals.
Applied   b. listening to a lecture without taking notes.
E   c. having a radio tuned to enjoyable music.
          d. read each chapter straight through.

1.176 Which of the following is an example of an active studying technique?
b
p. 35   a. reading each chapter straight through
Applied   b. visualizing an example of a concept after reading about it in the text
M   c. listening to a lecture without taking notes
          d. having your favorite music playing when you study

Chapter 2 - Biological Bases of Behavior: A Look Beneath the Surface

CHAPTER 2

Multiple-Choice Questions

Neurons: Building Blocks of the Nervous System

2.1
a
p. 40
Fact
E

The term used to refer to the field concerned with the relationship between biology and behavior is called
a. biopsychology.
b. biocognition.
c. cognitive science.
d. neuropsychology.

2.2
b
p. 40
Fact
M

Which of the following is likely to study how our brains store memories?
a. evolutionary psychologist
b. biopsychologist
c. psychiatrist
d. physiologist

2.3
c
p. 41
Concept
M

Cells within our bodies that are specialized for the tasks of receiving, moving, and processing information are called
a. endocrine cells.
b. ganglion cells.
c. neurons.
d. glial cells.

2.4
d
p. 41
Concept
M
C

Which of the following are specialized for the task of interpreting the environment with regard to activity?
a. endocrine cells
b. astrocytes
c. glial cells
d. neurons

2.5
c
p. 41
Fact
M
PT/OLSG

The three basic parts of the neuron are
a. vesicles, gray matter, and the synapse.
b. telodendria, nodes of Ranvier, and synaptic terminals.
c. cell body, axon, and dendrites.
d. myelin sheath, cell body, and dendrites.

2.6
c
p. 41
Fact
M

Which of the following carries information toward the cell body of a nerve cell?
a. axon
b. astrocyte
c. dendrite
d. myelin

2.7
d
p. 41
Fact
M

Which of the following carries information away from the cell body of a nerve cell?
a. dendrite
b. astrocyte
c. glial cells
d. axon

24   Test Bank - Essentials of Psychology (2nd Edition)

2.8   Input is to output as
a
p. 41   a. dendrite is to axon.
Concept   b. axon is to dendrite.
M   c. axon terminal is to astrocyte.
    d. astrocyte is to axon terminal.

2.9   Dendrites are structures in a neuron that
d
p. 41   a. carry signals out to other neurons.
Fact   b. make signals travel more quickly.
M   c. nourish and support the other neurons.
    d. carry signals in from other neurons.

2.10   The long slim fiber that extends from a neuron and that carries its message out to other
d   neurons is called the
p. 41   a. dendrite.
Concept   b. glial.
C   c. myelin.
    d. axon.

2.11   An axon is a structure in a neuron that
c
p. 41   a. speeds up the transmission of the nerve signals.
Concept   b. crosses the gap separating one neuron from the next.
M   c. carries messages out of the cell to the next neuron.
    d. nourishes and supports the other neurons in the brain.

2.12   An individual nerve cell is called a(n)
b
p. 41   a. gamete.
Fact   b. neuron.
E   c. chromosome.
    d. neurotransmitter.

2.13   A sheath of fatty material that covers the axon of many nerve cells and plays a role in the
b   transmission of information is called
p. 42   a. glial.
Concept   b. myelin.
M   c. acetylcholine.
PT/OLSG   d. ion membrane.

2.14   Myelin is a fatty substance that is used in the nervous system to
b
p. 42   a. provide nourishment to the nerve cells.
Concept   b. speed up the conduction of neural signals.
M   c. prevent the buildup of excess glial cells.
    d. carry signals from the brain to the muscles.

2.15   Small cells in the nervous system that are ten times as numerous as neurons
c   and that flourish and support the neurons are called
p. 42   a. interneurons.
Concept   b. neurotransmitters.
M   c. glial cells.
    d. dendrites.

2.16   Protection is to communication as
a
p. 42   a. glial is to neuron.
Concept   b. neuron is to glial.
M   c. axon is to dendrite.
    d. dendrite is to axon.

Chapter 2 - Biological Bases of Behavior: A Look Beneath the Surface 25

2.17 What would happen if glial cells were damaged?
c
p. 42 a. Acetylcholine could not be produced.
Concept b. The pituitary would produce epinephrine.
M c. Myelin would not be formed.
 d. Neurotransmitter substances would be inhibited.

2.18 Glial cells help form the _____, a structure that prevents certain substances from
d reaching the brain.
p. 42 a. neurotransmitter
Concept b. myelin sheath
C c. synaptic transmitter
 d. blood-brain barrier

2.19 The round structures that make up the ends of axon terminals are called
a
p. 42 a. axon terminals.
Concept b. end points.
M c. glial swellings.
 d. myelin nodes.

2.20 The region at which the ends of axons closely approach other cells is known as the
b
p. 42 a. antagonist.
Fact b. synapse.
M c. action potential.
 d. sensitive area.

2.21 The state at which information is not being transmitted from a nerve cell, and there are more
c negatively charged particles within the cell than outside, is referred to as the
p. 42 a. synaptic potential.
Fact b. quiet potential.
M c. resting potential.
 d. action potential.

2.22 When not transmitting information, the inside of a nerve cell, in comparison to the outside, is
d
p. 42 a. largely positive.
Fact b. slightly positive.
M c. largely negative.
 d. slightly negative.

2.23 The stage at which the neuron has a slightly negative charge is called the
d
p. 42 a. dynamic state.
Fact b. steady-state stage.
M c. action potential.
 d. resting potential.
PT/OLSG

2.24 The normal state of a nerve cell, when it is resting, is to have
d
p. 42 a. its myelin stored in a small vesicle in the axon.
Fact b. the synapse leading to the next cell closed completely.
C c. electrical charges equalized inside and out.
 d. a negative charge inside and a positive charge outside.

2.25 External physical stimulation of the dendrite or cell body of a neuron produces _____.
c
p. 42 a. resting potentials
Fact b. action potentials
C c. graded potentials
 d. synaptic potentials

2.26 A graded potential is a basic type of signal _____ neurons.
b
p. 42   a. between
Fact   b. within
M   c. supporting
         d. protecting

2.27 The _____ of a graded potential is proportional to the strength of the stimulus.
c
p. 42   a. duration
Fact   b. modality
C   c. magnitude
         d. complexity

2.28 One characteristic of graded potentials is that they tend to
a
p. 42   a. weaken quickly.
Concept b. convey information over long distances.
C   c. have a short delay before "firing."
         d. have a low threshold level.

2.29 What will happen if the level of excitation inside a neuron goes higher than the cell's threshold?
c
p. 42   a. It will become polarized.
Concept b. It will break down and stop functioning.
M   c. It will trigger an action potential.
         d. It will produce extra myelin.

2.30 The electrochemical process that produces an action potential can be described as
c
p. 43   a. direct current electricity.
Concept b. chemical bonding any hydrolysis.
M   c. exchange of ions through ion channels.
         d. creation of chemical neurotransmitters.

2.31 A swing in electric charge, from negative to positive and back again, that constitutes a basic
b   information signal within our nervous system is called the
p. 43   a. resting potential.
Concept b. action potential.
M   c. ion channel.
         d. current transmission.

2.32 Each time a neuron fires, it fires at full strength. This activity is referred to as
d
p. 43   a. Ranvier movement.
Fact   b. discrete.
E   c. potentiation.
         d. all-or-none.

2.33 The action potential is a(n)
b
p. 43   a. chemical used to transmit nerve messages.
Fact   b. all-or-none electrical signal inside a nerve.
M   c. level of activation each cell tries to maintain.
         d. type of nerve cell that carries muscle commands.

2.34 The electrical signal that travels down the axon of a neuron toward the next cell is called the
a
p. 43   a. action potential.
Fact   b. glial message.
M   c. threshold.
PT/OLSG d. myelin sheath.

Chapter 2 - Biological Bases of Behavior: A Look Beneath the Surface

2.35   Which of these statements best characterizes how a nerve cell sends its messages?
a
p. 43   a. They fire either full strength or not at all.
Fact   b. A stronger message has a larger electrical range.
C   c. A stronger message will travel more quickly.
   d. They require gradual shifts in electrical charge.

2.36   The speed of conduction on an axon is fastest if the axon is
a
p. 43   a. myelinated.
Concept   b. hyperpolarized.
M   c. sensitized.
   d. lacking nodes of Ranvier.

2.37   Damage to myelin would result in
a
p. 43   a. slower transmission of action potentials.
Concept   b. increased nodes of Ranvier.
M   c. decreased ion channels.
   d. faster transmission of action potentials.

2.38   In neurons possessing a myelin sheath, the action potential
a
p. 43   a. jumps from gap to gap along the sheath.
Concept   b. travels continuously down the axon.
M   c. only uses negative ion exchange.
   d. only uses positive ion exchange.

2.39   Gaps in the myelin sheath are called
b
p. 43   a. ion channels.
Fact   b. nodes of Ranvier.
E   c. axon terminals.
   d. synaptic vesicles.

2.40   Structures located in the axon terminals that contain chemicals used in nerve cell communication are
c   called
p. 44   a. neuron containers.
Fact   b. chemical vesicles.
M   c. synaptic vesicles.
PT/OLSG   d. ion pouches.

2.41   When an electrical impulse travels to the end of an axon, it produces
b
p. 44   a. electrical resistance in the next cell.
Fact   b. the release of a neurotransmitter chemical.
M   c. a sensation of pain in the nerve ending.
   d. the growth of a new synaptic vesicle.

2.42   Information is transmitted from one cell to the next using
a
p. 44   a. neurotransmitters.
Fact   b. myelin sheaths.
M   c. electrical signals.
   d. glial cells.

2.43   Chemicals released from nerve cells that play an important role in nerve cell communication are
d   called
p. 44   a. neurovesicles.
Concept   b. communication chemicals.
M   c. transmission ions.
   d. neurotransmitters.

28   Test Bank - Essentials of Psychology (2nd Edition)

2.44
b
p. 44
Concept
M

Communication between neurons is initiated by
a. ion exchange across the synapse.
b. neurotransmitters being released into the synapse.
c. action potentials along the dendrites.
d. release of negative ions.

2.45
a
p. 44
Fact
M

Neural receptor sites appear to be composed of
a. complex protein molecules.
b. simple lipids.
c. synaptic vesicles.
d. nodes of Ranvier.

2.46
b
p. 44
Fact
C

The "chemical keys" that fit into the structure of the receptor sites are called
a. protein molecules.
b. neurotransmitters.
c. glial cells.
d. ion particles.

2.47
c
p. 44
Concept
C

In addition to being released into synapses, neurotransmitters can also be released into
a. nearby neurons.
b. ion particles.
c. body fluids.
d. axons.

2.48
a
p. 44
Fact
M

Excitatory is to _____ as inhibitory is to _____.
a. depolarize, polarize
b. polarize, depolarize
c. uptake, reuptake
d. reuptake, uptake

2.49
a
p. 44
Fact
M

A decrease in the negative charge of a neuron makes it
a. more likely to fire.
b. less likely to fire.
c. receptive to protein molecules from another neuron.
d. non-receptive to protein molecules from another neuron.

2.50
d
p. 45
Fact
M

Which of these will make a cell less likely to fire?
a. A myelin sheath on its axon.
b. Neurotransmitter reuptake.
c. An excitatory postsynaptic effect.
d. An inhibitory postsynaptic effect.

2.51
c
p. 45
Fact
C

When a postsynaptic potential is received by a cell, if it is excitatory it will _____, if it is inhibitory it will _____.
a. trigger the release of neurotransmitters; trigger the absorption of neurotransmitters
b. trigger the absorption of neurotransmitters; trigger the release of neurotransmitters
c. make the cell fire more easily; make the cell fire less easily
d. make the cell fire less easily; make the cell fire more easily

2.52
b
p. 45
Concept
C
PT/OLSG

Since neurons only fire when the right pattern of information reaches them, they can be conceived of as
a. small modular transmitters.
b. tiny decision-making mechanisms.
c. tiny modular receivers.
d. small information mechanisms.

Chapter 2 - Biological Bases of Behavior: A Look Beneath the Surface

2.53
b
p. 45
Concept
M

Reuptake is a process associated with
a. initiating a neural transmission.
b. ending a neural transmission.
c. restoring the action potential.
d. releasing myelin.

2.54
c
p. 46
Fact
M

A neurotransmitter that is crucial in exciting skeletal muscles, and is necessary for movement, is
a. GABA.
b. serotonin.
c. acetylcholine.
d. endorphin.

2.55
d
p. 46
Concept
M

The neurotransmitter believed to play a role in attention, arousal, memory processing, and possibly Alzheimer's disease is
a. endorphin.
b. dopamine.
c. epinephrine.
d. acetylcholine.

2.56
b
p. 46
Applied
M

Curare is a drug that causes paralysis of the voluntary muscles in the body by blocking the effect of the neurotransmitter
a. dopamine.
b. acetylcholine.
c. serotonin.
d. opioid peptide.

2.57
b
p. 46
Study
M

Some research indicates that severe memory loss from Alzheimer's disease results from the _____ that produce acetylcholine.
a. enhancement of cells
b. degeneration of cells
c. limitation of cells
d. acquisition of cells

2.58
c
p. 47
Fact
M

High levels of the neurotransmitter _____ have been found in individuals with schizophrenia.
a. epinephrine
b. acetylcholine
c. dopamine
d. endorphin

2.59
b
p. 47
Fact
M

Low levels of the neurotransmitter dopamine have been found in individuals with
a. schizophrenia.
b. Parkinson's disease.
c. Alzheimer's disease.
d. depression.

2.60
c
p. 47
Fact
M

Endorphins seem to be produced in response to
a. pain.
b. laughter.
c. cognitive activity.
d. emotional highs.

2.61　　Endorphins are chemicals in the brain that produce effects similar to
d
p. 47　　a. caffeine.
Concept　　b. marijuana.
M　　c. LSD.
　　d. morphine.

2.62　　Which of the following are substances produced in the brain that seem to moderate
a　　unpleasant sensations and magnify pleasant sensations?
p. 47　　a. endorphins
Concept　　b. acetylcholine
M　　c. myelin
　　d. negative ions

2.63　　Drugs alter our feeling or behaviors by
b　　a. increasing the number of nodes of Ranvier.
p. 47　　b. altering the process of synaptic transmission.
Concept　　c. decreasing myelin production.
M　　d. producing carrier activity in synaptic transmission.

2.64　　Drugs seem to affect our behavior and cognitive processes primarily by changing
b　　a. thalamic structures.
p. 47　　b. synaptic transmission.
Concept　　c. the shape of the axons.
E　　d. the number of axon terminals.
PT/OLSG

2.65　　Mimicry is to inhibition as
c　　a. endorphin is to acetylcholine.
p. 47　　b. acetylcholine is to endorphin.
Concept　　c. agonist is to antagonist.
M　　d. antagonist is to agonist.

2.66　　A drug that stimulates or imitates the action of a neurotransmitter is called an _____,
b　　while a drug that reduces or blocks neurotransmitter action is called an _____.
p. 49　　a. antagonist; agonist
Fact　　b. agonist; antagonist
M　　c. endorphin; opiate
　　d. opiate; endorphin

2.67　　Drugs such as cocaine and amphetamine seem to inhibit reuptake of dopamine and norepinephrine.
d　　Thus, cocaine and amphetamine would be considered _____ of dopamine and norepinephrine.
p. 49　　a. depressants
Concept　　b. naltrexones
C　　c. antagonists
　　d. agonists

2.68　　A new procedure called _____ has been used to investigate brain stimulation in rats.
b　　a. parasympathetic brain stimulation
p. 50　　b. intracranial self-stimulation
Concept　　c. self-controlled brain stimulation
C　　d. hemispheric self-stimulation

Chapter 2 - Biological Bases of Behavior: A Look Beneath the Surface   31

2.69 Damage to what system of the brain greatly reduces self-stimulation in rats?
c
p. 50 a. hypothalamic nerve center
Concept b. posterior midbrain circuit
M c. medial forebrain bundle
  d. lateral forebrain transmitter

2.70 The rewarding effect of cocaine and amphetamines are related to the fact that they
d
p. 50 a. inhibit the impact of dopamine.
Applied b. inhibit the impact of naltrexone.
C c. enhance the impact of naltrexone.
  d. enhance the impact of dopamine.

2.71 The drug naltrexone is used to reduce pleasurable effects associated with MDMA. Naltrexone would thus
b be classified as
p. 50 a. an agonist.
Concept b. an antagonist.
M c. a mimic.
  d. a PET.

The Nervous System: Its Basic Structure and Functions

2.72 The major divisions of the nervous system are the
c
p. 51 a. somatic and autonomic.
Fact b. central and subcentral.
E c. central and peripheral.
  d. brain and somatic.

2.73 The brain and spinal cord make up the
d
p. 52 a. autonomic nervous system.
Fact b. parasympathetic nervous system.
E c. entire nervous system.
  d. central nervous system.

2.74 Sensory is to motor as
a
p. 52 a. afferent is to efferent.
Concept b. efferent is to afferent.
M c. sympathetic is to parasympathetic.
  d. parasympathetic is to sympathetic.

2.75 Which of the following consists of the major afferent and efferent fibers running between
b the brain and the rest of our body?
p. 52 a. interneuron complex
Fact b. spinal cord
M c. cerebral cortex
  d. cerebellum

2.76 Which of the following is not one of the functions of the spinal cord?
d
p. 52 a. regulates reflexes
Concept b. conducts information from receptors to the brain
M c. conducts information from the brain to the muscles
  d. connects the central nervous system to the involuntary muscles
PT/OLSG

32   Test Bank - Essentials of Psychology (2nd Edition)

2.77　　　　　　　　Destruction of all the nerves that connect the central nervous system with our sense organs,
c　　　　　　　　　muscles, and glands would amount to destroying the
p. 52　　　　　　　a.　spinal cord.
Concept　　　　　　b.　thalamus.
M　　　　　　　　c.　peripheral nervous system.
　　　　　　　　　d.　somatic nervous system.

2.78　　　　　　　　The nerves that serve all of the body below the neck are called the
a　　　　　　　　　a.　spinal nerves.
p. 52　　　　　　　b.　cranial nerves.
Concept　　　　　　c.　monosynaptic nerves.
M　　　　　　　　d.　polysynaptic nerves.

2.79　　　　　　　　The nerves that extend from the brain are called
b　　　　　　　　　a.　spinal nerves.
p. 52　　　　　　　b.　cranial nerves.
Concept　　　　　　c.　interneural nerves.
M　　　　　　　　d.　monosynaptic nerves.

2.80　　　　　　　　Ralph is having difficulty moving his limbs due to nervous system dysfunction. The system most likely at
b　　　　　　　　　fault would be the
p. 52　　　　　　　a.　parasympathetic nervous system.
Applied　　　　　　b.　somatic nervous system.
M　　　　　　　　c.　sympathetic nervous system.
　　　　　　　　　d.　afferent nervous system.

2.81　　　　　　　　The part of the peripheral nervous system that connects the central nervous system to
d　　　　　　　　　the voluntary muscles is the _____ nervous system.
p. 52　　　　　　　a.　central
Fact　　　　　　　b.　sympathetic
M　　　　　　　　c.　parasympathetic
PT/OLSG　　　　　d.　somatic

2.82　　　　　　　　Voluntary is to involuntary as
c　　　　　　　　　a.　afferent is to efferent.
p. 52　　　　　　　b.　efferent is to afferent.
Concept　　　　　　c.　somatic is to autonomic.
M　　　　　　　　d.　autonomic is to somatic.

2.83　　　　　　　　Which of the following activities is largely an autonomic nervous system function?
d　　　　　　　　　a.　typing a take home test
p. 52　　　　　　　b.　watching a televised lecture
Applied　　　　　　c.　studying for your exam
M　　　　　　　　d.　sweating during an exam

2.84　　　　　　　　Which of the following is a subdivision of the autonomic nervous system?
a　　　　　　　　　a.　both the sympathetic and parasympathetic nervous systems
p. 52　　　　　　　b.　only the sympathetic nervous system
Fact　　　　　　　c.　only the parasympathetic nervous system
M　　　　　　　　d.　neither the sympathetic nor the parasympathetic nervous system

2.85　　　　　　　　Using energy is to conserving energy as
a　　　　　　　　　a.　sympathetic is to parasympathetic.
p. 52　　　　　　　b.　parasympathetic is to sympathetic.
Concept　　　　　　c.　somatic is to autonomic.
M　　　　　　　　d.　autonomic is to somatic.

Chapter 2 - Biological Bases of Behavior: A Look Beneath the Surface

2.86
c
p. 52
Fact
M

Which of these body organs is most directly related to the functioning of the autonomic nervous system?
a. the eyes
b. the skeletal muscles
c. the heart
d. the ears

2.87
b
p. 52
Applied
M

"Wow," said Lisa, "that movie was really scary. I can't believe how much it activated my _____ nervous system."
a. parasympathetic
b. sympathetic
c. somatic
d. frontal

2.88
c
p. 52
Applied
C

The teacher looked out at the class full of students who were either sleeping or very sleepy, and wondered why their _____ nervous systems should be so active.
a. somatic
b. sympathetic
c. parasympathetic
d. central

2.89
d
p. 54
Applied
M

The damage to Phineas Gage's brain clearly illustrates the close relationship between the
a. neurons and the nervous system.
b. temporal region of the brain and cognition.
c. emotions and genetics.
d. brain and behavior.

2.90
a
p. 54
Fact
M

Researchers sometimes destroy portions of the brains of animals in order to
a. study the effects of the damage on their behavior.
b. punish the animals for failing to behave as they should.
c. look for the effects of certain drugs on their behavior.
d. record the distribution of radioactive glucose in their brains.

2.91
b
p. 54
Concept
M

If you wanted to determine which areas of the brain are active when an animal is sleeping, which of the following techniques should you use?
a. electrical stimulation
b. electrical recording
c. lesion, that is, systematic destruction of brain areas
d. MRI scans

2.92
d
p. 54
Fact
M

Electroencephalography is obtained with
a. magnetic resonance imaging (MRI).
b. positron emission tomography (PET).
c. electrical stimulation methods.
d. electrical recording methods.

2.93
d
p. 54
Fact
M
PT/OLSG

A procedure for measuring the electrical activity of the entire brain is called
a. superconducting quantum interference device or SQUID.
b. positron emission tomography or PET.
c. high-tech snooper or HTS.
d. electroencephalography or EEG.

34   Test Bank - Essentials of Psychology (2nd Edition)

2.94   If you wanted to initiate activity in a specific group of nerve cells, which of the following
c   techniques should you use?
p. 54
    a. magnetic resonance imaging (MRI)
Concept
    b. positron emission tomography (PET)
M
    c. electrical stimulation
    d. resonance event timing (RET)

2.95   Scientists can use an _____ to measure the location and timing of brain activity while someone performs a
b   cognitive task.
p. 54
    a. EEG (electroencephalography)
Fact
    b. ERP (event-related potential)
M
    c. EGR (electrogalvanic response)
    d. EPA (event-potential action)

2.96   Which of the following research techniques provides the least detailed information
c   about the specific structures of an entire human brain?
p. 54
    a. PET
Concept
    b. MRI
C
    c. EEG
    d. SQUID

2.97   Brain imagery is to brain metabolic activity as
a
    a. MRI is to PET.
p. 54
    b. PET is to MRI.
Concept
    c. EEG is to PKU.
M
    d. PKU is to EEG.

2.98   All living tissue contain hydrogen atoms, which emit energy when exposed to strong
b   magnetic fields. Measuring this energy is the basis of which research technique?
p. 54
    a. PET
Fact
    b. MRI
M
    c. EEG
    d. ~~SQUID~~ PKU

2.99   An imaging technique that captures images of the brain through its ability to detect
b   tiny changes in magnetic fields in the brain is referred to as
p. 55
    a. PET.
Concept
    b. SQUID.
M
    c. CAT.
    d. BMF.

2.100   Positron emission tomography (PET) scans allow researchers to
b
    a. record the precise electrical activity of a small group of cells.
p. 55
    b. observe how active different brain areas are at a given moment.
Fact
    c. measure the response of the brain to strong magnetic fields.
M
    d. stimulate specific individual cells and monitor the effect.

2.101   PET scans indicate that increased activity to the frontal lobes of the cerebral cortex is
d   related to
p. 56
    a. signing one's name.
Applied
    b. listening to music.
C
    c. depression.
    d. obsessive-compulsive disorder.

Chapter 2 - Biological Bases of Behavior: A Look Beneath the Surface   35

2.102
c
p. 56
Concept
M

Results of PET scans suggest that the obsessive-compulsive disorder may be related to increased activity in the
a. cerebellum.
b. hypothalamus.
c. frontal lobes.
d. reticular activity system.

2.103
a
p. 56
Applied
M

When Lisa signed her name with her dominant hand, a PET scan of her brain showed high activity in her _____ and low activity in her _____.
a. basal ganglia; cortex
b. cortex; basal ganglia
c. hypothalamus; thalamus
d. thalamus; hypothalamus

2.104
b
p. 56
Applied
M

When Ralph signed his name with his nondominant hand, a PET scan of his brain showed high activity in his _____ and low activity in his _____.
a. basal ganglia; cortex
b. cortex; basal ganglia
c. hypothalamus; thalamus
d. thalamus; hypothalamus

2.105
d
p. 56
Concept
C
PT/OLSG

Results of PET scans suggest that as we become more familiar with a task or problem, neural activity is
a. always processed in the same area as it was first processed.
b. processed first on the left side and then on the right side of the brain.
c. delegated to different areas of the brain as a result of hypothalamic activity.
d. shifted from the cortex to more automatic brain regions.

2.106
d
p. 56
Concept
M

PET scans indicate that as we become familiar with a task, neural activity shifts from _____ of the brain to _____.
a. frontal regions; temporal regions
b. temporal regions; frontal regions
c. more automatic regions; the cortex
d. the cortex; more automatic regions

2.107
a
p. 56
Applied
C

The first time you are asked to perform some new task you've never done before, a PET scan of your brain is likely to show
a. increased activity in the cerebral cortex.
b. decreased activity in the cerebral cortex.
c. increased activity in the midbrain.
d. decreased activity in the midbrain.

2.108
c
p. 56
Applied
C

Lisa's band is learning a new song that involves precise timing between the various instruments. After enough practice, a PET scan of Lisa's brain would probably show decreased activity in the
a. hypothalamus.
b. corpus callosum.
c. cerebral cortex.
d. cerebellum.

The Brain: Where Consciousness Is Manifest

2.109
d
p. 57
Fact
M

The brain structure that controls the body's activity level, including sleep and wakefulness, is the
a. cerebellum.
b. pons.
c. midbrain.
d. reticular activating system.

2.110
b
p. 57
Applied
M

If a patient has suffered a small injury to the brain and, as a result, is generally asleep and has great difficulty waking up, the damage is most likely to be in the
a. cerebellum.
b. reticular activating system.
c. corpus callosum.
d. hypothalamus.

2.111
a
p. 57
Concept
M

An accomplished dancer must rely most heavily on activity in
a. the cerebellum.
b. Broca's area.
c. the hypothalamus.
d. the amygdala.

2.112
b
p. 57
Concept
M

An area primarily concerned with the regulation of motor activities serving to orchestrate muscular activities so that they occur in a synchronized fashion is
a. the amygdala.
b. the cerebellum.
c. the hypothalamus.
d. Wernicke's area.

2.113
b
p. 58
Concept
M

One of the portions of the midbrain is responsible for
a. regulating emotional responses to events.
b. control of muscle movements.
c. controlling hunger and thirst.
d. communicating between the two hemispheres.

2.114
c
p. 58
Fact
E

Which of the following areas is located above the brain stem, and contains some of the processing centers dealing with vision and hearing?
a. hindbrain
b. cerebellum
c. midbrain
d. forebrain

2.115
b
p. 58
Fact
E

Primitive centers for vision and hearing are in the
a. brain stem.
b. midbrain.
c. cerebellum.
d. pons.

2.116
c
p. 58
Fact
M
PT/OLSG

Which of the following structures regulates the autonomic nervous system?
a. thalamus
b. cerebellum
c. hypothalamus
d. medulla

Chapter 2 - Biological Bases of Behavior: A Look Beneath the Surface   37

2.117 This part of the brain plays a key role in homeostasis.
a
p. 58 a. hypothalamus
Fact   b. thalamus
E   c. midbrain
       d. medulla

2.118 Homeostasis is to attention as
b
p. 58   a. reticular activating system is to hypothalamus.
Concept   b. hypothalamus is to reticular activating system.
M   c. cerebellum is to Broca's area.
           d. Broca's area is to cerebellum.

2.119 Which of the following structures plays a role in regulating the autonomic nervous
d system and the pituitary gland?
p. 58 a. corpus callosum
Fact   b. basal ganglia
M   c. pons
       d. hypothalamus

2.120 The hypothalamus is a brain structure that acts to coordinate communication between
b parts of the brain that regulate and monitor the body's internal states and the
p. 59   a. cerebellum.
Concept   b. frontal cortex.
C   c. reticular activating system.
           d. pons.

2.121 A patient who has suffered a small, localized injury to the brain and who, as a result,
d never feels hungry and must be forced to eat has probably sustained damage to the
p. 59   a. cerebellum.
Applied   b. reticular activating system.
M   c. thalamus.
           d. hypothalamus.

2.122 The structure called the "great relay station" that receives input from all senses
d except olfaction is the
p. 59   a. cortex.
Fact   b. hypothalamus.
M   c. cerebellum.
           d. thalamus.

2.123 The thalamus handles the
d
p. 59   a. coordination of muscle movements.
Fact   b. regulation of body temperature.
M   c. control of eating and sex.
           d. inputs from every sense but smell.

2.124 Damage to the thalamus is most likely to cause
b
p. 59   a. clumsiness and lack of coordination.
Applied   b. difficulty seeing or hearing.
M   c. an inability to stay awake.
           d. complete loss of appetite.
PT/OLSG

2.125 The limbic system is a complex part of the forebrain that is involved in
b
p. 59 a. coordination and balance.
Fact b. emotions and memory.
M c. sensory information processing.
d. sleep and wakefulness.

2.126 Which of the following parts of the brain is most heavily involved in regulating emotions?
c
p. 59 a. cerebellum
Fact b. reticular activating system
M c. limbic system
d. corpus callosum

2.127 The hippocampus is a part of the _____ system.
a
p. 59 a. limbic
Fact b. autonomic nervous
C c. reticular activating
d. medulla oblongata

2.128 The limbic system seems to be important for regulating
b
p. 59 a. motor coordination and movement.
Fact b. fear, aggressiveness, and pleasure.
C c. sleep, dreams, and wakefulness.
d. the flow of information from the senses.

2.129 The outer covering of the brain most responsible for reasoning, planning, and
c remembering is the
p. 59 a. cerebellum.
Fact b. corpus callosum.
M c. cerebral cortex.
d. reticular activating system.

2.130 Your ability to read and understand this item is controlled, in part, by the
d
p. 59 a. amygdala.
Applied b. medulla.
M c. inferior colliculi.
d. cerebral cortex.

2.131 The outer surface of the two hemispheres of the brain is called the
d
p. 59 a. corpus callosum.
Fact b. medulla.
E c. pons.
d. cortex.

2.132 The outer surface of the human brain is deeply wrinkled or folded, most likely because
b
p. 59 a. the corpus callosum is so much larger in humans.
Concept b. it creates more surface area for the human cortex.
M c. it helps in the regulation of the basic bodily processes.
d. of the greater activation of the human nervous system.

2.133 One sign of the greater capacity of the human brain for thought, reasoning, and other
c abilities that make us human is
p. 59 a. the greater size of the cerebellum.
Concept b. a large number of nuclei in the hindbrain.
C c. the many deep folds in the cortex.
d. the complex interconnections in the thalamus.

Chapter 2 - Biological Bases of Behavior: A Look Beneath the Surface   39

2.134　　　　　　The frontal lobes, the parietal lobes, the temporal lobes, and the occipital lobes
d　　　　　　　together make up the
p. 60　　　　　　a.　cerebellum.
Fact　　　　　　b.　hypothalamus.
M　　　　　　　c.　medulla.
PT/OLSG　　　　d.　cerebral hemispheres.

2.135　　　　　　The lobes of the cerebral hemispheres are separated by
a　　　　　　　a.　fissures.
p. 60　　　　　　b.　glial cells.
Fact　　　　　　c.　basal ganglia.
E　　　　　　　d.　astrocytes.

2.136　　　　　　Which of the following is NOT a cerebral lobe?
b　　　　　　　a.　frontal
p. 60　　　　　　b.　central
Fact　　　　　　c.　parietal
E　　　　　　　d.　temporal

2.137　　　　　　The part of the brain located behind the forehead above the eyes is called the
a　　　　　　　a.　frontal lobes.
p. 60　　　　　　b.　parietal lobes.
Fact　　　　　　c.　occipital lobes.
M　　　　　　　d.　temporal lobes.

2.138　　　　　　Loss of fine motor control due to head injury is most likely the result of damage to
c　　　　　　　the _____ lobe.
p. 60　　　　　　a.　temporal
Applied　　　　　b.　occipital
M　　　　　　　c.　frontal
　　　　　　　　d.　parietal

2.139　　　　　　Damage to the motor cortex leads to
a　　　　　　　a.　loss of fine motor control.
p. 60　　　　　　b.　complete paralysis.
Fact　　　　　　c.　motor hyperactivity.
M　　　　　　　d.　reduced plasticity.

2.140　　　　　　The brain's ability to retrain an area to compensate for damage to another area refers to
d　　　　　　　a.　differentiation.
p. 60　　　　　　b.　specialization.
Fact　　　　　　c.　contralateralization.
M　　　　　　　d.　plasticity.

2.141　　　　　　The somatosensory cortex is located in the
b　　　　　　　a.　frontal lobe.
p. 60　　　　　　b.　parietal lobe.
Fact　　　　　　c.　temporal lobe.
M　　　　　　　d.　occipital lobe.

2.142　　　　　　If you lose feeling in your left arm yet can still move it, then you probably had a mild
a　　　　　　　stroke in the
p. 60　　　　　　a.　right parietal lobe.
Concept　　　　　b.　left parietal lobe.
M　　　　　　　c.　right occipital lobe.
　　　　　　　　d.　left occipital lobe.

2.143　　　　Vision is to audition as
c
p. 60　　　　a.　frontal lobe is to parietal lobe.
Fact　　　　b.　parietal lobe is to frontal lobe.
M　　　　　c.　occipital lobe is to temporal lobe.
　　　　　　d.　temporal lobe is to occipital lobe.

2.144　　　　The lobe concerned with vision is
a
p. 60　　　　a.　occipital.
Fact　　　　b.　temporal.
E　　　　　c.　frontal.
PT/OLSG　　d.　parietal.

2.145　　　　The part of the brain located at the sides of the head near the ears is called the
c
p. 60　　　　a.　occipital lobes.
Fact　　　　b.　parietal lobes.
M　　　　　c.　temporal lobes.
　　　　　　d.　frontal lobes.

2.146　　　　The lobe concerned with hearing is
b
p. 60　　　　a.　occipital.
Fact　　　　b.　temporal.
E　　　　　c.　frontal.
　　　　　　d.　parietal.

2.147　　　　Speech comprehension is to recognition of tones and melodies as
a
p. 60　　　　a.　left temporal lobe is to right temporal lobe.
Concept　　 b.　right temporal lobe is to left temporal lobe.
C　　　　　c.　right occipital lobe is to left occipital lobe.
　　　　　　d.　left occipital lobe is to right occipital lobe.

2.148　　　　Neurons that play a role in integrating activities of sensory systems and translating
d　　　　　 sensory input into motor information are referred to as
p. 61　　　　a.　limbic cortex.
Concept　　 b.　plasticity cells.
C　　　　　c.　somatosensory neurons.
　　　　　　d.　association cortex.

2.149　　　　As societies around the world change to provide equality of opportunity to men and
c　　　　　 women, the gender differences in abilities that psychologists measure
p. 62　　　　a.　are becoming a more serious social problem.
Concept　　 b.　have been shown to be a myth, based on no reality.
M　　　　　c.　are growing smaller and smaller over the years.
　　　　　　d.　have been shown to relate to hormone swings in men and women.

2.150　　　　A study by Hines and her colleagues (1992) found a significant _____ relationship
b　　　　　 between women's scores on a verbal test and the size of a region in the corpus
p. 62　　　　callosum reported to be larger in women.
Study　　　 a.　negative
C　　　　　b.　positive
　　　　　　c.　neutral
　　　　　　d.　curvilinear

Chapter 2 - Biological Bases of Behavior: A Look Beneath the Surface   41

2.151   When studying differences in how the brains of men and women process information,
b   it is important to remember that
p. 62   a.   hormone levels before birth have strong effects on how the brains are organized.
Concept   b.   all the observed differences between men and women are extremely small.
C   c.   men use the left sides of their brains more heavily, women the right sides.
            d.   differences in brain function are affected only by biology, not social factors.

2.152   Most research indicates that the range of performance _____ greatly exceeds the range of performance
b   _____.
p. 62   a.   between the genders, within the genders
Study   b.   within the genders, between the genders
C   c.   between males, between females
            d.   within males, within females

2.153   According to the Wernicke-Geschwind theory, which of the following areas would
d   disrupt speech comprehension if damaged?
p. 63   a.   Broca's area
Concept   b.   medulla oblongata
M   c.   left frontal lobe
PT/OLSG   d.   Wernicke's area

2.154   The Wernicke-Geschwind model of language processing in the brain
b   a.   is strongly supported by modern evidence.
p. 63   b.   is not strongly supported by modern evidence.
Concept   c.   concentrates on brain stem functions.
M   d.   concentrates on midbrain functions.

2.155   Why is it that researchers today are less convinced of the accuracy of the
d   Wernicke-Geschwind model of language processing in the brain?
p. 63   a.   It contradicts modern theories about the functions of the left hemisphere.
Concept   b.   It has never been tested in humans, but only in the brains of animals.
C   c.   Detailed theories about the functions of specific structures are no longer useful.
            d.   Evidence from brain surgery and autopsies contradicts this theory.

Lateralization of the Cerebral Cortex: Two Minds in One Body?

2.156   The fact that the cerebral hemispheres specialize in different activities such as speech
d   versus spatial comprehension is referred to as
p. 64   a.   bi-function dimensionality.
Fact   b.   task specialization.
M   c.   hemispheric regionality.
            d.   lateralization of function.

2.157   The phrase "lateralization of function" refers to the fact that
a   a.   the two hemispheres function differently.
p. 64   b.   men are better than women at some things.
Fact   c.   children learn language faster than adults.
E   d.   the brain cortex is wrinkled and folded.

2.158   Speech is to emotion as
a   a.   left hemisphere is to right hemisphere.
p. 64   b.   right hemisphere is to left hemisphere.
Concept   c.   Broca is to Wernicke.
M   d.   Wernicke is to Broca.

2.159 Which is a function generally controlled by the left hemisphere?
b
p. 64   a. motor movements
Concept   b. logical thought
M   c. communication of emotion
            d. comprehension of emotion

2.160 If a patient has been given the drug sodium amytal and can not recite letters of the
d   alphabet or days of the week, which of the following is an appropriate deduction?
p. 64   a. The reticular activating system is disrupted.
Concept   b. The brain stem is not functioning properly.
M   c. The right hemisphere is anesthetized.
            d. The left hemisphere is anesthetized.

2.161 Results of research done with PET scans indicate that work on perceptual tasks results
a   in increased activity in the
p. 64   a. right hemisphere.
Concept   b. left hemisphere.
M   c. occipital lobe.
            d. frontal lobe motor strip.

2.162 Research has found that during the making of a decision, the _____ hemisphere is
b   active; once the decision is made, the _____ hemisphere is active.
p. 64   a. left; left
Concept   b. left; right
M   c. right; right
PT/OLSG   d. right; left

2.163 Which function is most strongly associated with the left cerebral hemisphere?
c
p. 65   a. The ability to express emotions
Fact   b. The ability to recognize emotions
M   c. Positive emotions
            d. Negative emotions

2.164 People suffering from depression typically show increased activity in
a
p. 65   a. the right cerebral hemisphere.
Concept   b. the left cerebral hemisphere.
M   c. the pons and medulla.
            d. the occipital lobe.

2.165 The two hemispheres of the brain communicate with each other primarily through a
b   wide band of nerve fibers that pass between them called the
p. 65   a. hemispheric channel.
Fact   b. corpus callosum.
E   c. tomographic connection.
            d. myelin sheath.

2.166 A split brain patient is shown the name of an object so that it stimulates only the right
b   cerebral hemisphere. Which of the following can this patient do?
p. 65   a. name the object
Applied   b. select the object with the left hand
M   c. select the object with the right hand
            d. recognize but not name nor select the object

Chapter 2 - Biological Bases of Behavior: A Look Beneath the Surface   43

2.167
b
p. 65
Concept
M

When the name of an object is presented to the left hemisphere only, split-brain individuals can usually
a. draw a picture of the object.
b. point to the object with the right hand.
c. point to the object with the left hand.
d. do nothing to identify the object.

2.168
c
p. 65
Applied
M

The word CARGO is shown to a split-brain individual so that the first three letters go to the right hemisphere and the last two to the left hemisphere. When asked to point to the related picture with his left hand, the person would most likely point to the picture of
a. a green traffic light.
b. a stack of boxes being loaded on a truck.
c. an automobile.
d. an arrow.

2.169
d
p. 65
Study
C

In the research that had split-brain patients view pictures of faces they had seen before and pictures of similar faces (composites of the original faces) they had not seen before, the results indicated that
a. the right hemisphere correctly identified the composite pictures as ones they had seen before.
b. the left hemisphere correctly identified the composite pictures as ones they had seen before.
c. the right hemisphere incorrectly identified the composite pictures as ones they had seen before.
d. the left hemisphere incorrectly identified the composite pictures as ones they had seen before.

The Endocrine System: Chemical Regulators of Bodily Processes

2.170
b
p. 66
Fact
M

Structures that secrete hormones directly into the bloodstream are called
a. basal ganglia.
b. endocrine glands.
c. limbic glands.
d. secretion glands.

2.171
c
p. 66
Concept
M

Hormones are to neurotransmitters as
a. endorphins are to opiates.
b. opiates are to endorphins.
c. endocrine glands are to neurons.
d. neurons are to endocrine glands.

2.172
b
p. 67
Fact
E

Neurohormones are produced by
a. neurons.
b. endocrine glands.
c. the corpus callosum.
d. superior colliculi.

2.173
d
p. 67
Concept
M
PT/OLSG

The brain structure that regulates many basic body functions is the _____. It regulates these functions through the action of the "master gland," the _____.
a. left hemisphere; thyroid
b. right hemisphere; parathyroid
c. cerebellum; adrenal gland
d. hypothalamus; pituitary

44 Test Bank - Essentials of Psychology (2nd Edition)

2.174 Regulation of water reabsorption is to regulation of endocrine glands as
c
p. 67   a. acetylcholine is to norepinephrine.
Concept b. norepinephrine is to acetylcholine.
C   c. posterior pituitary is to anterior pituitary.
        d. anterior pituitary is to posterior pituitary.

2.175 In the congenital adrenogenital syndrome (CAS), there is an
c
p. 68   a. incomplete development of the adrenal gland.
Fact   b. enlargement of the adrenal gland.
M   c. excessive level of adrenal androgens.
        d. insufficient level of adrenal androgens.

2.176 The disorder where cells of genetic males lack receptors for androgens causing them
d   to be born with female genitalia and to develop as normal females is called
p. 68   a. congenital adrenogenital syndrome.
Concept b. hypoadrenalism.
M   c. androgyny.
        d. androgen insensitivity syndrome.

2.177 The pancreas produces hormones that regulate
b
p. 68   a. movement.
Fact   b. metabolism.
M   c. sexual growth.
        d. secondary sex characteristics.

2.178 Epinephrine and norepinephrine are hormones that play important roles in reactions to
a
p. 68   a. stress.
Fact   b. pregnancy.
M   c. sexual development.
        d. metabolism.

Heredity and Behavior

2.179 Strand-like structures of DNA found in the nuclei of all cells are called
b
p. 69   a. gametes.
Fact   b. chromosomes.
E   c. gonads.
        d. genes.

2.180 The basic units of heredity that are only segments of DNA are called
c
p. 69   a. gametes.
Fact   b. homoloques.
M   c. genes.
        d. messenger proteins.

2.181 Which statement is not true about genes?
c
p. 69   a. They contain thousands of segments of DNA.
Concept b. Most human traits are determined by more than one gene.
M   c. Genes influence behavior directly.
PT/OLSG d. There is evidence for genetic involvement in a variety of physical and mental disorders.

Chapter 2 - Biological Bases of Behavior: A Look Beneath the Surface   45

2.182   Sperm and ova are referred to as
a
p. 70   a.   gametes.
Fact   b.   gonads.
E   c.   chromosomes.
          d.   astrocytes.

2.183   Most cells contain _____ chromosomes.
b
p. 70   a.   23
Fact   b.   46
E   c.   31
PT/OLSG   d.   43

2.184   Identical is to similar as
b
p. 70   a.   fraternal is to monozygotic.
Concept   b.   monozygotic is to fraternal.
M   c.   ova is to sperm.
          d.   sperm is to ova.

2.185   Phenylketonuria (PKU) is an example of a genetically-based disorder in which
d
p. 70   a.   mental retardation is produced exclusively as a result of specific genes.
Concept   b.   the nature of sex-related biological disorders is demonstrated.
M   c.   the notion of biologically determined sexual preferences is supported.
          d.   the notion that behavior can be influenced both by one's genetic make-up and environmental experiences is revealed.

2.186   Bailey and Pillard (1991), in their examination of concordance rates in a group of gay men each having an
b   identical twin, found results implying that there is
p. 71   a.   an interaction between environmental and genetic components in homosexuality.
Study   b.   a genetic component to homosexuality.
C   c.   an environmental component to homosexuality.
          d.   no relationship between environmental and genetic components in homosexuality.

2.187   When Hamer and colleagues performed an analysis of family histories of pairs of homosexual
a   males, they discovered
p. 71   a.   many pairs indicated having mothers who had male relatives who were homosexual.
Study   b.   they all shared an identical chromosome in pair 21.
M   c.   they had an extra female X chromosome in pair 23.
          d.   there were no genetic similarities at all.

2.188   When the childhood and adolescent experiences of homosexual adults were compared
d   with those of heterosexual adults, the strongest difference was that
p. 71   a.   homosexuals reported engaging in sexual behavior at a much younger age.
Concept   b.   homosexuals were much more likely to have been sexually abused.
C   c.   homosexuals reported more older homosexual friends as children.
          d.   homosexuals reported knowing at an early age that they were different from others.

2.189   A research strategy frequently used to assess the relative importance of genetic and
c   environmental factors in human behavior
p. 72   a.   requires manipulation of strands of DNA.
Concept   b.   relies on comparisons of differences of behaviors between grandparents and their
M   grandchildren.
          c.   compares similarities and differences of monozygotic twins raised apart.
          d.   requires that a longitudinal method be used.

2.190　　　　　If identical twins who were separated at birth and raised in different environments show
b　　　　　marked similarities in behavior, it is probably because
p. 72　　　　　a.　their adoptive parents are very similar to their birth parents.
Concept　　　b.　their behavior is being affected by their biological, genetic inheritance.
C　　　　　　c.　twins have a subconscious telepathic link that makes them similar.
　　　　　　　d.　all children are very similar, no matter how they are raised or by whom.

2.191　　　　　Traumatic brain injury refers to brain damage as a result of
b　　　　　a.　drug induced neural damage.
p. 73　　　　　b.　head injury from force applied to the skull.
Fact　　　　　c.　alcohol induced brain damage.
M　　　　　　d.　inherited structural malformations of the brain causing trauma.

2.192　　　　　One of the most important aspects of rehabilitation for TBI seems to be
c　　　　　a.　variety.
p. 74　　　　　b.　exercise.
Fact　　　　　c.　structure.
M　　　　　　d.　verbalization.

CHAPTER 3

Multiple-Choice Questions

Sensation: The Raw Materials of Understanding

3.1
a
p. 80
Fact
E

The study of the relationship between various forms of stimulation such as sound waves and how these inputs are registered by organs such as the ears refers to
a. sensation.
b. perception.
c. cognition.
d. consciousness.

3.2
b
p. 80
Fact
E

The study of the processes through which we interpret and organize various forms of stimulation such as sound waves and how these inputs produce our conscious experiences refers to
a. sensation.
b. perception.
c. cognition.
d. consciousness.

3.3
c
p. 80
Concept
M

Detection is to interpretation as
a. difference threshold is to absolute threshold.
b. absolute threshold is to difference threshold.
c. sensation is to perception.
d. perception is to sensation.

3.4
d
p. 80
Concept
M

Imagine you have your eyes closed and you smell a very unusual odor. After a few seconds, you recognize it to be the deodorant of a good friend that you have not seen in several years. Your ability to recognize and interpret this odor refers to
a. opponent processing.
b. anosmia.
c. sensation.
d. perception.

3.5
a
p. 80
Concept
M

The study of _____ is concerned with how sensory stimulation is organized and interpreted.
a. perception
b. sensation
c. consciousness
d. threshold

3.6
b
p. 80
Fact
E
PT/OLSG

The definition of perception involves
a. transduction.
b. interpretation.
c. simplicity.
d. direct sensation.

3.7
d
p. 80
Fact
E
PT/OLSG

The definition of sensation involves
a. knowledge.
b. interpretation.
c. simplicity.
d. the senses.

3.8
c
p. 80
Applied
M

When a chemical stimulates the taste buds in your tongue, that is _____; when you recognize the flavor as your favorite dessert, that is _____.
a. opponent processing; transduction
b. transduction; opponent processing
c. sensation; perception
d. perception; sensation

3.9
a
p. 80
Applied
M

Which of these is an example of sensation?
a. Hair cells in the cochlea responding to sound waves.
b. A small child reacting to a stranger with fear.
c. Recognizing a familiar word when reading a book.
d. A smell from your childhood triggering vivid memories.

3.10
d
p. 80
Applied
M

Which of these is an example of perception?
a. Free nerve endings sending pain signals to the brain.
b. Receptive fields in the retina reacting to spots of light.
c. Hairs cells in the cochlea responding to sound waves.
d. Recognizing the face of someone in your family.

3.11
b
p. 80
Fact
M

A process in which physical properties of stimuli are converted into neural signals is called
a. telekinesis.
b. transduction.
c. perception.
d. convergence.

3.12
d
p. 80
Concept
M

The process by which electromagnetic energy is converted into nerve cell activity is referred to as
a. anosmia.
b. conduction.
c. electromechanical transposition.
d. transduction.

3.13
b
p. 81
Concept
M

When put in a prolonged state of sensory deprivation we are likely to
a. become extremely relaxed.
b. produce hallucinations.
c. decrease saccadic movements.
d. respond only to prototypes and not exemplars.

3.14
a
p. 81
Fact
M

The smallest magnitude of a stimulus that can be reliably discriminated from no stimulus at all 50% of the time is called
a. absolute threshold.
b. extrasensory threshold.
c. difference threshold.
d. petite threshold.

3.15
c
p. 81
Fact
M
PT/OLSG

The absolute threshold is usually defined as the magnitude of physical energy one can detect _____% of the time.
a. 10
b. 30
c. 50
d. 70

Chapter 3 - Sensation and Perception: Making Contact with the World around Us 49

3.16
b
p. 82
Applied
M

Determining the minimal level of sound that can be heard 50% of the time is an example of determining a(n) _____ threshold.
a. petite
b. absolute
c. difference
d. phi

3.17
c
p. 82
Applied
M

Determining the lowest level of illumination that can be detected at least half of the time a light is presented is an example of determining a(n) _____ threshold.
a. psi
b. petite
c. absolute
d. difference

3.18
a
p. 82
Fact
M

The state in which our body's internal environment is maintained at optimal level is called
a. homeostasis.
b. threshold.
c. psychophysics.
d. sensitivity.

3.19
d
p. 82
Fact
M

Which of the following theories takes into consideration that rewards and costs affect our ability to detect environmental stimulation?
a. discrimination theory
b. threshold analysis
c. place theory
d. signal detection theory

3.20
a
p. 82
Fact
M

The theory that suggests that detection of stimuli depends upon their physical energy and upon external factors such as the relative costs and benefits associated with detecting the presence of these stimuli is called
a. signal detection theory.
b. absolute threshold theory.
c. subliminal perception theory.
d. opponent process theory.

3.21
b
p. 82
Fact
M

The amount of change in a stimulus required for a person to detect the change is called
a. absolute threshold.
b. difference threshold.
c. two-point threshold.
d. frequency threshold.

3.22
c
p. 82
Applied
M
PT/OLSG

An experimenter has you compare the temperature of water in two different containers. She asks you if they feel the same or different. She is probably trying to determine your
a. subliminal threshold.
b. absolute threshold.
c. difference threshold.
d. frequency threshold.

3.23 a p. 82 Concept M

The amount of change in a physical stimulus necessary for an individual to notice a difference in the intensity of a stimulus is called the
a. just noticeable difference.
b. absolute threshold.
c. boundary threshold.
d. kinesthetic difference.

3.24 b p. 82 Concept M

Which of the following statements correctly describes our abilities to detect differences in stimulus intensity?
a. The amount of change needed to detect differences in weak stimuli and strong stimuli is constant.
b. Larger changes in strong stimuli are needed to detect changes than are needed for weak stimuli.
c. Larger changes in weak stimuli are needed to detect changes than are needed for strong stimuli.
d. Amount of change needed to detect differences in stimuli is identical for each sense.

3.25 d p. 82 Fact M

Subliminal perception is perception that takes place
a. when there is no physical stimulus.
b. automatically, without conscious intention.
c. in the highest levels of the brain.
d. below the level of conscious awareness.

3.26 c p. 82 Concept M

The presumed influence on behavior of a stimulus that is below the threshold for conscious experience is called
a. absolute threshold.
b. just noticeable difference.
c. subliminal perception.
d. prosopagnosia.

3.27 d p. 83 Applied M

Some people believe that there are films that contain subliminal messages that are not consciously visible yet affect our behavior. The term for these sub-threshold messages is
a. j.n.d.
b. synesthesia.
c. prosopagnosia.
d. subliminal.

3.28 c p. 83 Concept M

On the subject of subliminal perception, most cognitive psychologists today would agree with the statement that
a. it has never been scientifically demonstrated.
b. it is not possible for human perceptual systems.
c. it is possible but does not have strong effects.
d. it presents a real danger of mind control.

3.29 a p. 83 Concept M

The fact that our sensitivity to an unchanging stimulus tends to decrease over time is referred to as
a. sensory adaptation.
b. sensory perception.
c. sensory deprivation.
d. sensory stimulation.

Chapter 3 - Sensation and Perception: Making Contact with the World around Us

3.30
b
p. 83
Applied
M

Which of the following concepts best explains why you first feel hot when you get into a rather warm bath but after a few minutes feel just right?
a. sensory deprivation.
b. sensory adaptation.
c. sensory perception.
d. sensory stimulation.

3.31
d
p. 83
Applied
M

Sensory adaptation refers to which common perceptual experience?
a. Being affected by hidden messages in advertising.
b. Seeing flashes of light at night in a dark room.
c. Hearing whistling sounds in the ear that aren't real.
d. Not noticing a bad smell after a few minutes.

3.32
c
p. 83
Applied
M

Without sensory adaptation, which of the following would be the most likely result?
a. An extreme tendency to overreact to even the slightest stimulation.
b. Difficulty interpreting the meaning of socially important stimuli like faces.
c. An inability to get used to such constant stimuli as the pressure of our shoes.
d. Problems with balance and motor coordination, particularly in children.

3.33
c
p. 84
Applied
C

In which of the following situations might sensory adaptation be dangerous?
a. Trying to concentrate on driving while the radio is on.
b. Experiencing sudden mild symptoms of illness.
c. When smoke gradually builds up in the house.
d. When the baby cries in the middle of the night.

Vision

3.34
d
p. 84
Fact
M

The order in which light moves toward the visual receptors is
a. lens, cornea, iris.
b. iris, lens, cornea.
c. iris, cornea, lens.
d. cornea, pupil, lens.

3.35
c
p. 84
Fact
E

The amount of light that enters the eye is controlled by the
a. pupil.
b. photoreceptor.
c. iris.
d. cornea.

3.36
a
p. 84
Fact
E
PT/OLSG

The sensory receptors in the eye are found in the
a. retina.
b. cochlea.
c. ganglion cells.
d. cornea.

3.37
d
p. 84
Concept
M

Day vision is to night vision as
a. passive perception is to sensory adaptation.
b. sensory adaptation is to passive perception.
c. rod is to cone.
d. cone is to rod.

3.38 The cones in the retina are photoreceptors used primarily for
b
p. 84 a. vision under conditions of very dim lighting.
Fact b. color vision and fine discriminations in daylight.
M c. focusing the image accurately on the retina.
 d. detecting movement in the corner of the eye.

3.39 The rods in the retina are photoreceptors used primarily for
c
p. 84 a. distinguishing different colors in daylight.
Fact b. focusing the image accurately on the retina.
M c. night vision under conditions of dim lighting.
 d. fine discriminations in the center of the eye.

3.40 Axons from the ganglion cells form the
c
p. 86 a. bipolar cells.
Fact b. fovea.
M c. optic nerve.
 d. retina.

3.41 The image on the retina is
c
p. 86 a. weakest at the fovea.
Fact b. strongest where the optic nerve exits the eye.
M c. upside down and reversed.
 d. longer on the periphery than in the center.

3.42 Wavelength is to intensity as
b
p. 86 a. brightness is to hue.
Concept b. hue is to brightness.
M c. saturation is to complexity.
 d. complexity is to saturation.

3.43 The difference in the number of wavelengths is related to the perception of
a
p. 86 a. saturation.
Concept b. brightness.
M c. hue.
 d. complexity.

3.44 An artist who decides a color is too garish and mixes in a little gray to tone it down
a is having the most direct effect on which psychological dimension of color?
p. 86 a. saturation
Applied b. hue
C c. brightness
 d. complexity

3.45 Static visual acuity is to dynamic visual acuity as
a
p. 87 a. stationary is to moving.
Concept b. moving is to stationary.
M c. nearsightedness is to farsightedness.
 d. farsightedness is to nearsightedness.

3.46 The visual feature most important for your dog to catch frisbees in the air is
c
p. 87 a. angular velocity.
Applied b. static visual acuity.
M c. dynamic visual acuity.
 d. saccadic movements.

PT/OLSG

Chapter 3 - Sensation and Perception: Making Contact with the World around Us

3.47　　What is it that makes someone unable to focus on objects that are too near or too far?
b
p. 87　　a. a missing or damaged retina
Fact　　b. eyeballs that are too long or too short
M　　　c. pupils that are too tightly constricted
　　　　d. a lens that is too large or too small

3.48　　Dark adaptation results in
b
p. 87　　a. decreased sensitivity to light.
Concept　b. increased sensitivity to light.
M　　　c. increased abilities to perceive feature detectors.
　　　　d. decreased abilities to perceive feature detectors.

3.49　　The eye movements necessary to read this question are called _____ movements.
d
p. 88　　a. random
Applied　b. arbitrary
M　　　c. pursuit
　　　　d. saccadic

3.50　　To watch the ball move back and forth during a professional tennis match requires
a　　_____ eye movements.
p. 88　　a. pursuit
Applied　b. saccadic
M　　　c. involuntary
　　　　d. staccato

3.51　　Which of the following theories suggests that color vision can be explained on
b　　the basis of unique receptors sensitive to red, green, or blue?
p. 88　　a. opponent process theory
Fact　　b. trichromatic theory
M　　　c. signal detection theory
　　　　d. dark adaptation theory

3.52　　After staring at a yellow stimulus you may sense the color blue if you gaze at a
d　　neutral background. This is an example of
p. 88　　a. clairvoyance.
Applied　b. a difference threshold.
M　　　c. passive perception.
　　　　d. a negative afterimage.

3.53　　Which of the following theories can best explain the phenomena of negative afterimages?
a　　a. opponent process theory
p. 89　　b. trichromatic theory
Concept　c. signal detection theory
M　　　d. dark adaptation theory

3.54　　The theory that holds that there are six cells that play a role in color vision is
b
p. 89　　a. trichromatic theory.
Concept　b. opponent process theory.
M　　　c. signal detection theory.
PT/OLSG　d. dark adaptation theory.

3.55 a
p. 89
Fact
C

In the opponent process theory of color, our experience of a color is controlled by
a. its position on three dimensions (red-green, blue-yellow, black-white).
b. the relative activations of three different kinds of cones (red, green, blue).
c. the frequency of firing in the optic nerve, corresponding to the frequency of the light.
d. an automatic process that triggers the opposite color for any wavelength of light.

3.56 c
p. 90
Concept
C

The conflict between the trichromatic and the opponent process theories of color vision seems to be resolved in what way?
a. The trichromatic theory has been supported and the opponent process theory has been shown to be invalid.
b. The opponent process theory has been supported and the trichromatic theory has been shown to be invalid.
c. The trichromatic theory applies in the retina, the opponent process theory applies at higher levels.
d. The opponent process theory applies in the retina, the trichromatic theory applies at higher levels.

3.57 b
p. 90
Fact
E

Which of the following are examples of feature detectors?
a. rods and cones
b. simple, complex, and hypercomplex cells
c. cochlea and hair cells
d. monocular and binocular cues

3.58 c
p. 90
Concept
M

Neurons that respond to the orientation of lines are called _____, and neurons that respond to movement are called _____.
a. complex cells, simple cells
b. hypercomplex cells, simple cells
c. simple cells, complex cells
d. complex cells, hypercomplex cells

3.59 a
p. 90
Fact
M

As described by Hubel and Wiesel, cells that respond to length, width, and certain aspects of shape, such as corners and angles are called
a. hypercomplex.
b. simple.
c. complex.
d. exemplars.

3.60 d
p. 90
Concept
C

How does our visual system hierarchically process the scenes presented to our eyes?
a. Piece by piece, analyzing each area of the scene separately from the others.
b. By sending all the information from the eyes to the brain for processing.
c. By extracting all the important information from the scene inside the eye.
d. Step by step, working from simple to more and more complex information.

3.61 b
p. 90
Fact
M

Individuals who report being blind, yet are able to respond to aspects of visual stimuli as if they can see are suffering from
a. pinna distortion.
b. blindsight.
c. kinetic amnesia.
d. negative imagery.

Chapter 3 - Sensation and Perception: Making Contact with the World around Us

3.62
a
p. 91
Fact
M

A condition in which a person can no longer recognize faces, but still retains relatively normal vision is called
a. prosopagnosia.
b. negative imagery.
c. expressionless syndrome.
d. kinesthesia.

Hearing

3.63
c
p. 91
Fact
M

The _____ is the technical term for the visible part of our hearing organ.
a. cochlea
b. malleus
c. pinna
d. incus

3.64
c
p. 92
Concept
M

The sensory receptors that are responsible for transforming sound stimuli into neural messages are the
a. ganglion cells.
b. bipolar cells.
c. hair cells.
d. hypercomplex cells.

3.65
b
p. 92
Concept
M

Frequency is to amplitude as
a. loudness is to pitch.
b. pitch is to loudness.
c. timbre is to saturation.
d. saturation is to timbre.

3.66
c
p. 93
Fact
M

The quality of a sound resulting from the complexity of a sound wave that helps us to distinguish the sound of a trumpet from a saxophone is called
a. saturation.
b. pitch.
c. timbre.
d. prosopagnosia.

3.67
d
p. 93
Concept
M

Theories of hearing that emphasize differential displacement of the basilar membrane are called
a. field theories.
b. membrane theories.
c. frequency theories.
d. place theories.

3.68
a
p. 94
Concept
M
PT/OLSG

Which of the following theories suggests that sounds of different pitch cause different rates of neural firing?
a. frequency theory
b. place theory
c. opponent process theory
d. field theory

3.69
b
p. 94
Concept
C

Place theory does not adequately explain the ability to detect
a. large differences in frequencies.
b. low frequencies and small frequency differences.
c. high frequencies and large frequency differences.
d. large differences in amplitude.

3.70 Low frequency is to high frequency as
c
p. 94 a. trichromatic theory is to opponent process theory.
Concept b. opponent process theory is to trichromatic theory.
C c. frequency theory is to place theory.
 d. place theory is to frequency theory.

3.71 If someone can distinguish high frequency sounds quite accurately, but has
b difficulty tell low frequency sounds apart, you might conclude that the person
p. 94 is relying mostly on which theory of pitch perception?
Applied a. frequency theory
M b. place theory
 c. amplitude theory
 d. opponent process theory

3.72 Which of the following perceptions is based upon differences in the time at which
a a sound reaches the two ears and differences in the intensity of a sound going to
p. 94 your ear?
Concept a. localization
M b. timbre
 c. pitch
 d. loudness

3.73 A "sound shadow" is created when some barrier blocks sound waves, so that the
d waves are weaker on the other side of the barrier. The sound shadow that helps
p. 94 localize sounds is created by
Concept a. the cochlea.
M b. the tympanic membrane.
 c. the oval window.
 d. our heads.

3.74 For which of the following sounds would it be most difficult to identify where
c the sound is coming from?
p. 94 a. a sound located on your left side
Applied b. a sound located on your right side
M c. a sound located directly behind you
 d. a sound located lower than your eyes

Touch and Other Skin Senses

3.75 How do the different types of skin receptors function in our perception of touch,
d warmth, and cold?
p. 95 a. There are three different receptors, one for each type of sensation.
Fact b. One type exists on the hands and feet, another on the arms and legs, and the
M third on the face.
 c. There is actually only one type of skin receptor, but it responds differently to
 different sensations.
 d. The total pattern of responses of all the receptors determines our experience

3.76 Which part of the body contains the most skin receptors for touch?
c a. The bottom of the foot.
p. 95 b. The front of the knee.
Fact c. The tips of the fingers.
E d. The forehead.
PT/OLSG

Chapter 3 - Sensation and Perception: Making Contact with the World around Us   57

3.77   If we touch an object, _____ is involved. If an object touches us, _____ is involved.
b
p. 95   a. passive touch, active touch
Concept b. active touch, passive touch
M   c. expressive touch, receptive touch
         d. receptive touch, expressive touch

3.78   We are considerably more accurate in identifying objects when we use _____.
d
p. 95   a. expressive touch
Concept b. receptive touch
M   c. passive touch
         d. active touch

3.79   When the power goes out, we are best able to identify objects by touch in the dark
a   when we
p. 96   a. actively explore them with our fingertips.
Applied b. concentrate on one type of skin receptor.
M   c. press them deeply and firmly into our skin.
         d. use unusual skin surfaces, such as our elbows.

3.80   Free nerve endings throughout the body seem to be the source of
a
p. 96   a. sensations of pain.
Fact   b. perception of objects through touch.
M   c. feelings of warmth or cold.
         d. hallucinations.

3.81   Sharp pain, such as from the prick of a needle, is transmitted to the brain through
b
p. 96   a. small, unmyelinated nerve fibers.
Applied b. large, myelinated nerve fibers.
M   c. small, myelinated nerve fibers.
         d. large unmyelinated nerve fibers.

3.82   Sharp pain is to dull pain as
b
p. 96   a. small nerve fiber is to large nerve fiber.
Concept b. large nerve fiber is to small nerve fiber.
M   c. simple cell is to complex cell.
         d. complex cell is to simple cell.

3.83   Someone who is following gate-control theory would make which suggestion to a
a   person who has just scraped a finger?
p. 96   a. Rub the back of the hand vigorously.
Applied b. Take two aspirin and call me later.
M   c. Close your eyes and concentrate on the pain.
         d. Let me hypnotize you into feeling no pain.

3.84   Which of the following theories suggests that there are neural mechanisms in the
c   spinal cord that sometimes close, thus preventing pain messages from reaching the
p. 96   brain?
Concept a. pain inhibition theory
M   b. Substance P theory
         c. gate-control theory
         d. signal detection theory

3.85   If a society puts a high value on the quality of stoicism, then people in that society
b
p. 97
Applied
M
- a. have very low pain thresholds.
- b. have very high pain thresholds.
- c. can discuss pain in great detail.
- d. enjoy inflicting and feeling pain.

3.86
c
p. 97
Concept
M
PT/OLSG
When a person's culture emphasizes the stoical acceptance of pain, a person is likely to respond by
- a. overacting and responding excessively to pain.
- b. enjoying pain, and inflicting it on others.
- c. becoming able to tolerate high levels of pain silently.
- d. making no change; this will not affect one's perception of pain.

3.87
d
p. 98
Study
C
In a study by Montgomery and Kirsch (1996), the introduction of a placebo before subjects were exposed to painful pressure in their fingers resulted in
- a. an increase in the perception of pain by the subjects.
- b. an increase in the enjoyment of the pain by the subjects.
- c. a decrease in the enjoyment of the pain by the subjects.
- d. a decrease in the perception of pain by the subjects.

3.88
c
p. 98
Applied
C
A person who is a catastrophizer will more than likely
- a. engage in increased negative thought, thereby reducing the perception of pain.
- b. engage in decreased negative thought, thereby increasing the perception of pain.
- c. engage in increased negative thought, thereby increasing the perception of pain.
- d. engage in decreased negative thought, thereby reducing the perception of pain.

Smell and Taste: The Chemical Senses

3.89
c
p. 99
Fact
E
The chemical senses include
- a. touch and taste.
- b. pain and temperature.
- c. smell and taste.
- d. vision and hearing.

3.90
d
p. 99
Fact
E
The receptors for odors are located in the
- a. cochlea.
- b. vestibular membrane.
- c. papillae.
- d. olfactory epithelium.

3.91
a
p. 99
Concept
M
A critical physical dimension of olfactory stimuli that determines the range of smells we are capable of detecting is
- a. molecular weight.
- b. ion distribution.
- c. molecular bonding.
- d. ion concentration.

3.92
b
p. 100
Fact
M
PT/OLSG
The theory put forth to explain how we detect odors based on different molecular shapes is the
- a. opponent process theory.
- b. stereochemical theory.
- c. electromagnetic theory.
- d. malodorous detection theory.

Chapter 3 - Sensation and Perception: Making Contact with the World around Us   59

3.93 The sensory receptors for taste are located inside
c   a. olfactory epithelium.
p. 100 b. hypercomplex cells.
Fact   c. papillae.
M   d. ganglion cells.

3.94 Olfactory epithelium is to papillae as
d   a. prototype is to exemplar.
p. 100 b. exemplar is to prototype.
Concept c. taste is to smell.
M   d. smell is to taste.

3.95 Which of the following is not a basic taste for humans?
a   a. mint
p. 100 b. bitter
Fact   c. salt
E   d. sweet

3.96 Flavors are distinguished on the basis of
b   a. tastes and smells only.
p. 101 b. tastes, smells, texture, and temperature.
Concept c. tastes and temperatures only.
M   d. tastes, smells, humidity, and resonance.

3.97 Our ability to identify specific odors is _____; our ability to remember odors
a   from the past is _____.
p. 101 a. poor; good
Concept b. good; poor
M   c. good; good
        d. poor; poor

3.98 Which of the following is false with regard to smell?
b   a. We are poor at identifying odors.
p. 101 b. Linguistic processing plays a central role in our ability to recognize odors.
Concept c. Memory of past odors is quite accurate.
C   d. Task performance can be enhanced by pleasant fragrances.

3.99 When presented with common odors such as smoke and mint, the most common
c   reaction people had was to
p. 101 a. correctly identify the smell.
Concept b. fail to realize the odor is familiar at all.
M   c. recognize the smell but be unable to name it.
        d. fail to notice the presence of the smell.

3.100 One reason why we seem able to remember odors very well is that
d   a. we are better than most animals at detecting and processing odors.
p. 101 b. we are good at giving verbal labels to the smell we experience.
Concept c. we seldom notice the smells that are all around us in daily life.
C   d. we encode memories for odors with memories of the events we experience.

3.101 Which of the following is true with respect to the use of fragrances by companies?
d   a. Certain scents can cure some psychological illnesses.
p. 101 b. It is impossible for aromas to affect human behavior.
Concept c. They have proven that lemon scent helps people relax.
C   d. There is little scientific evidence to support the claims of companies.

3.102   The author of your textbook and a colleague (1996) found that lemon fragrance
a
p. 102   a. enhanced the performance on a simulated driving task.
Study   b. inhibited the performance on a simulated driving task.
M   c. enhanced the detection of the aroma during a simulated driving task.
          d. inhibited the detection of the aroma during a simulated driving task.

Kinesthesia and Vestibular Sense

3.103   When a police officer asks a suspected drunk driver "How many fingers do you
a   see?" it is a test of vision. When the officer asks the driver to touch his finger to
p. 102   the tip of his nose with his eyes closed, which sense is being tested?
Applied   a. kinesthesia
M   b. olfaction
          c. gustation
          d. orientation

3.104   The sense that gives us information about the location of our body parts with respect
c   to each other and allows us to perform movements is called
p. 102   a. vestibular.
Fact   b. prosopagnosia.
M   c. kinesthesia.
PT/OLSG   d. gustation.

3.105   When performing, gymnasts rely heavily on
a   a. kinesthesia and vestibular senses.
p. 102   b. prosopagnosia and anosmia.
Applied   c. olfaction and gustation senses.
M   d. cognition and orientation.

3.106   The sense most used by ballet dancers to stay balanced while standing on their toes is
a   a. the vestibular sense.
p. 102   b. kinesthesia.
Applied   c. the proprioceptive sense.
M   d. gustation.

3.107   Which of the following are critical components of the sensory system used to
b   maintain our sense of balance?
p. 102   a. papillae and epithelium
Applied   b. vestibular sacs and semi-circular canals
M   c. simplex and complex cells
          d. prototypes and exemplars

3.108   Lisa is riding a bus with her eyes closed. She can very easily determine when the bus is accelerating or
d   stopping because of the movement of hair cells in her
p. 102   a. semicircular canals.
Applied   b. cochlea.
M   c. mandibula.
          d. vestibular sacs.

3.109   Changes in linear acceleration are to changes in rotational acceleration as
c   a. simplex cells are to complex cells.
p. 102   b. complex cells are to simplex cells.
Concept   c. vestibular sacs are to semicircular canals.
M   d. semicircular canals are to vestibular sacs.

Chapter 3 - Sensation and Perception: Making Contact with the World around Us

Perception: Putting It All Together

3.110
d
p. 105
Fact
M

Which of the following is important in alerting us to immediate natural dangers in the environment?
a. parallel processing
b. prosopagnosia
c. kinesthesia
d. selective attention

3.111
a
p. 105
Fact
E

The fact that we typically are aware of only a small fraction of the stimuli that are available to us at any one time is the result of the process of
a. selective attention.
b. prosopagnosia.
c. Gestalt analysis.
d. good continuation.

3.112
b
p. 105
Concept
M
PT/OLSG

The tendency to shift the focus of our attention toward meaningful, unattended information is known as the
a. risky-shift effect.
b. cocktail party phenomenon.
c. template matching effect.
d. prototype matching phenomenon.

3.113
c
p. 105
Concept
M

What aspects of a stimulus will cause it to receive our selective attention?
a. Persistence, in which a stimulus lasts a long time.
b. Depth, in which a stimulus shows how far away it is.
c. Change, in which something about the stimulus changes.
d. Congruence, in which a stimulus matches what we expect.

3.114
c
p. 106
Applied
M

Which one of the following does not meet the criteria for a warning?
a. The warning must be conspicuous relative to their surroundings.
b. The warning must be understood by those to whom it is directed.
c. The warning must specify the consequences of disobeying the warning.
d. The warning must be designed to motivate people to engage in safe behavior.

3.115
c
p. 107
Study
M

A study of warnings by Wogalter and Young (1991) found that warnings were most effective when presented
a. only in oral form.
b. only in printed form.
c. both in oral and printed form.
d. neither oral nor printed, verbal form was most effective.

3.116
b
p. 107
Fact
M

Which of the following groups of psychologists first studied perceptual organization?
a. Behaviorists
b. Gestaltists
c. Psychophysiologists
d. Psychoanalysts

3.117
c
p. 108
Concept
C

The tendency to divide the visual world into two parts, one having a definite shape and location in space and the other having no shape that seems to have no definite location is called
a. volley principle.
b. law of closure.
c. figure-ground relationship.
d. phi phenomenon.

3.118 Which statement describes a limitation of the figure-ground relationship in perception?
a
p. 108   a. We cannot see the same shape as both figure and ground at the same time.
Concept b. We are frequently unable to see any figures at all in a complex visual
M   representation.
         c. In many situations we perceive figures that have no definite shape or boundaries.
         d. When we become tired or confused everything begins to look like a figure.

3.119 When worn in a forest area, green camouflage clothing makes it harder to perceive
d
p. 108   a. closure.
Applied b. stereoscopic cues.
M   c. perceptual constancies.
         d. figure-ground relationships.

3.120 Basic ways in which we group items together perceptually are known as the
d
p. 108   a. proximity principle.
Fact   b. good continuation rule.
E   c. closure laws.
PT/OLSG d. laws of grouping.

3.121 The tendency to perceive items located close together as a group is known as the
a
p. 109   a. law of proximity.
Concept b. law of similarity.
M   c. law of closure.
         d. law of simplicity.

3.122 The tendency to perceive objects as whole entities, even when they are incomplete is known as the
d
p. 109   a. law of simplicity.
Concept b. law of continuation.
M   c. law of proximity.
         d. law of closure.

3.123 The ability to perceive stability in the face of change defines
b
p. 110   a. perceptual illusions.
Concept b. perceptual constancies.
M   c. closure orientation.
PT/OLSG d. laws of grouping.

3.124 Size-distance invariance and the use of relative size are used to explain
c
p. 110   a. the law of proximity.
Concept b. shape constancy.
M   c. size constancy.
         d. closure.

3.125 The fact that you perceive the shape of a door as a rectangle regardless of whether
d   it is completely closed or open at various degrees is due to
p. 110   a. size constancy.
Applied b. closure.
M   c. size-distance invariance.
         d. shape constancy.

Chapter 3 - Sensation and Perception: Making Contact with the World around Us

3.126
a
p. 110
Concept
M

Brightness constancy breaks down when
a. changes in lighting are different for an object and its surroundings.
b. lighting is the same for both the object and its surroundings.
c. red colors are contrasted with blue colors.
d. red colors are contrasted with yellow colors.

3.127
c
p. 111
Concept
M

Illusions can be produced by
a. cognitive processes only.
b. distortions of physical conditions only.
c. both cognitive processes and distortions of physical conditions.
d. neither cognitive processes nor distortions of physical conditions.

3.128
d
p. 111
Concept
C

One explanation for some illusions is that we interpret parts of what we see as cues that some things in view are farther away than other things. This information then leads us to
a. misinterpret what is figure and what is ground.
b. fail to apply the basic principles of size constancy.
c. group the wrong objects together.
d. adjust our perception of how large the things are.

3.129
a
p. 111
Concept
C

The illusion in which two equal lines appear to be of different lengths if they have different arrows attached to their ends is called the _____ illusion.
a. Muller-Lyer
b. Ponzo
c. railroad
d. Poggendorf

3.130
c
p. 111
Concept
M

One recent theory on the causes of illusions such as the Muller-Lyer and the Poggendorf illusions is that they are created by
a. differences in how the lines are imaged on the retina.
b. complex processes in the receptive fields of the cortex.
c. the observer's expectations and perceptual constancies.
d. training in the use of illusions from early childhood.

3.131
b
p. 112
Applied
M

The moon illusion, in which the moon appears much larger when near the horizon, is due to being led astray by
a. the law of closure.
b. size constancy.
c. interposition cues.
d. linear perspective.

3.132
d
p. 113
Fact
M
PT/OLSG

Exact representation of stimuli stored in memory are called
a. features.
b. binocular cues.
c. prototypes.
d. templates.

3.133
d
p. 113
Concept
M

When attempting to perceive stimuli (e.g., letters of the alphabet), one theory suggests that we automatically compare each letter to an abstract representation of these stimuli in our memory. This abstract representation is called a
a. jnd.
b. complex category.
c. feature constancy.
d. prototype.

3.134 d p. 113 Concept M

A bottom-up theory of perception would say that the process of reading would proceed in order from _____ to _____.
a. developing an idea; identifying words
b. identifying words; developing an idea
c. understanding sentences; identifying lines and angles
d. identifying lines and angles; identifying words

3.135 b p. 114 Concept M PT/OLSG

Theories that propose that perceptions may be determined by our expectations are
a. prototype theories.
b. top-down theories.
c. bottom-up theories.
d. feature theories.

3.136 b p. 114 Concept M

Which of the following theories emphasizes expectations based on past experiences in explaining perception?
a. bottom-up theory
b. top-down theory
c. template theory
d. prototype-matching theory

3.137 d p. 114 Concept M

Size cues, linear perspective, texture gradient, and overlap are all examples of
a. binocular cues used for perception of movement.
b. binocular cues used for perception of depth.
c. monocular cues used for perception of movement.
d. monocular cues used for perception of depth.

3.138 d p. 114 Concept M

Convergence and retinal disparity are examples of
a. monocular cues used for perception of movement.
b. monocular cues used for perception of depth.
c. binocular cues used for perception of movement.
d. binocular cues used for perception of depth.

3.139 a p. 114 Fact M

Cues to depth perception that require the use of two eyes are called _____ cues, while those that work with only one eye are called _____ cues.
a. binocular; monocular
b. monocular; binocular
c. opponent; constancy
d. constancy; opponent

3.140 d p. 114 Fact M

The binocular cue derived from the inward movement of the eyes as objects come closer is
a. overlap.
b. retinal disparity.
c. parallel perspective.
d. convergence.

3.141 b p. 115 Fact M

Retinal disparity is a depth cue that depends on
a. the scattering of blue light in the atmosphere.
b. the two eyes receiving slightly different images.
c. the shape of the lens changing to focus an image.
d. distant objects seeming to move more slowly.

Chapter 3 - Sensation and Perception: Making Contact with the World around Us

The Plasticity of Perception: To What Extent Is It Innate or Learned?

3.142
a
p. 115
Fact
M

The debate concerning the extent to which various aspects of behavior are determined as a result of learning or as a result of innate factors is an example of the
a. nature-nurture controversy.
b. opponent process controversy.
c. two-factor controversy.
d. psychobiology controversy.

3.143
b
p. 116
Study
M

When shown squares of different colors or of gray, babies less than three days old
a. looked equally at all the squares.
b. looked more at the colored squares.
c. looked more at the gray squares.
d. did not seem to see the squares at all.

3.144
c
p. 116
Study
M
PT/OLSG

Blakemore and Cooper (1970) demonstrated that raising kittens in a restricted visual environment seemed to cause permanent deficits in the kitten's later perceptions. These results support the notion that some aspects of perception are
a. determined by nature.
b. modified by phi stimuli.
c. learned.
d. innate.

3.145
d
p. 116
Study
M

When kittens are raised in an environment where the only things they see are vertical lines, they show a tendency later to
a. be frightened of things that are mostly horizontal.
b. respond aggressively or violently to horizontal things.
c. completely ignore vertical objects.
d. completely ignore horizontal objects.

3.146
d
p. 116
Concept
M

The fact that humans can learn to read a book when wearing goggles that invert their visual field supports the view that some aspects of perception are
a. determined by signal detection.
b. modified by prototypical stimuli.
c. innate.
d. learned.

3.147
c
p. 117
Concept
M

When all the evidence is considered, the most reasonable conclusion about how the nature-nurture issue applies to perception is that
a. most perceptual processes are biologically inherited.
b. most perceptual processes are learned through experience.
c. both nature and nurture have important effects on perception.
d. the results are so confused we can draw no conclusions at all.

3.148
c
p. 117
Concept
M

With respect to perception, the best resolution of the nature-nurture controversy seems to be the conclusion that
a. perception is biologically determined.
b. perception is learned through experience.
c. both nature and nurture strongly affect perception.
d. nature and nurture are really the same concept.

3.149
d
p. 117
Concept
M

When we say that the perceptual system is plastic, we mean that it
a. is controlled by our biological inheritance.
b. is an artificial result of modern human experience.
c. is stiff and hard and cannot be easily changed.
d. can be changed through our experiences.

Extrasensory Perception: Perception without Sensation?

3.150　　　　　Perception without a basis in sensation is called
a
p. 117　　　　a.　extrasensory perception.
Fact　　　　　b.　a mirage.
E　　　　　　c.　prosopagnosia.
　　　　　　　d.　passive perception.

3.151　　　　　Unusual processes of information or energy transfer that are currently unexplained
b　　　　　　in terms of known physical or biological mechanisms are referred to as
p. 115　　　　a.　negative afterimages.
Fact　　　　　b.　psi.
M　　　　　　c.　mirages.
　　　　　　　d.　prosopagnosia.

3.152　　　　　The ability to foretell future events is called
c
p. 117　　　　a.　clairvoyance.
Fact　　　　　b.　telepathy.
M　　　　　　c.　precognition.
　　　　　　　d.　psychokinesis.

3.153　　　　　When she woke up in the morning, Lisa "just knew" that something exciting would
b　　　　　　happen that day. That evening her aunt won a large prize on the lottery. This
p. 117　　　　experience would be an example of which form of psi?
Applied　　　a.　psychokinesis
M　　　　　　b.　precognition
　　　　　　　c.　telepathy
　　　　　　　d.　clairvoyance

3.154　　　　　The ability to perceive objects or events that do not directly stimulate your sensory
d　　　　　　organs is called
p. 117　　　　a.　precognition.
Fact　　　　　b.　telepathy.
M　　　　　　c.　psychokinesis.
　　　　　　　d.　clairvoyance.

3.155　　　　　Even though he lived in another state, Ralph said he "just knew" when his brother
d　　　　　　was in an automobile accident. This experience would be an example of which form
p. 117　　　　of psi?
Applied　　　a.　precognition
M　　　　　　b.　psychokinesis
　　　　　　　c.　telepathy
　　　　　　　d.　clairvoyance

3.156　　　　　The ability to affect the physical world purely by thought is called
a
p. 118　　　　a.　psychokinesis.
Fact　　　　　b.　clairvoyance.
M　　　　　　c.　telepathy.
　　　　　　　d.　precognition.

3.157　　　　　Overt transmission of thoughts from one person to another is
a
p. 118　　　　a.　telepathy.
Fact　　　　　b.　clairvoyance.
M　　　　　　c.　precognition.
PT/OLSG　　　d.　psychokinesis.

Chapter 3 - Sensation and Perception: Making Contact with the World around Us 67

3.158
b
p. 118
Concept
C

The most important reason why psychologists are skeptical about the existence of psychic phenomena is that
a. the only people involved in the research are people who don't believe in psi.
b. certain procedures produce positive results sometimes but not at other times.
c. there is not enough research of all kinds being done on psychic phenomena.
d. the explanations for psi are too closely tied to specific biochemical events in the brain.

3.159
c
p. 118
Concept
M

One main reason why psychologists are skeptical about the reality of psi phenomena is that
a. there is very little research being conducted on parapsychology.
b. none of the people who believe in psychic phenomena are involved in the research.
c. the more carefully controlled the research, the less likely it is to demonstrate psi.
d. the brain mechanisms of psychic phenomena are too limited and specific.

3.160
d
p. 118
Concept
M

Which of the following is a procedure used to study psi phenomena in laboratory studies?
a. systematic desensitization
b. meta-analysis techniques
c. placebo procedure
d. ganzfield procedure

3.161
a
p. 118
Concept
M

In the ganzfield procedure used to measure the action of psi, if the receiver gives higher ratings to "target" stimuli viewed by the senders, it means that
a. the sender may have sent the information mentally.
b. there must have been some way to cheat the procedure.
c. the experiment is flawed by experimenter bias.
d. no scientific conclusions can be drawn.

3.162
c
p. 118
Concept
M

Which of the following best expresses the attitude of most psychologists toward the existence of psi phenomena?
a. They accept the reality of telepathy but not other psi phenomena.
b. They accept the reality of all psi phenomena except telepathy.
c. They are skeptical of all psi phenomena.
d. They reject the idea that psi phenomena could exist.

3.163
b
p. 119
Study
C

One study issued personal stereo headsets to employees who wanted them, and no headsets to other employees, and then asked these employees to engage in complex tasks. The results indicated that
a. as job complexity decreased, performance decreased.
b. as job complexity increased, performance decreased.
c. as the music got softer, the performance decreased.
d. as the music got softer, the performance increased.

3.164
c
p. 120
Concept
M
PT/OLSG

The use of personal stereo headsets at high volume increases the probability of the occurrence of
a. auditory latitude.
b. ocular latitude.
c. tinnitus.
d. nystagmus.

CHAPTER 4

Multiple-Choice Questions

4.1   Consciousness can be defined as
b
p. 125   a. a state of awareness and focus on the environment.
Fact   b. our awareness of ourselves and our environment.
M   c. the thoughts and ideas in our minds at any moment.
          d. our observable, measurable actions and behaviors.

4.2   Strict behaviorists objected to the study of consciousness because consciousness
b
p. 126   a. can be directly observed only in dreams.
Concept   b. cannot be directly observed.
M   c. can be influenced by daily cyclical changes.
          d. cannot be influenced by daily cyclical changes.

Biological Rhythms: Tides of Life - and Conscious Experience

4.3   Regular fluctuations in our bodily processes are called
c
p. 126   a. dissociations.
Fact   b. latent rhythms.
E   c. biological rhythms.
          d. receptive changes.

4.4   Fluctuations in alertness, energy, and moods over the course of a day are examples
b   of
p. 126   a. ultradian rhythms.
Concept   b. circadian rhythms.
M   c. lunar rhythms.
          d. seasonal affective rhythms.

4.5   For which of the following tasks is performance least likely to be correlated with
d   circadian rhythms such as body temperature?
p. 127   a. a tapping task requiring rapid hand movements
Concept   b. visual searching for letters in a word
C   c. simple arithmetic tasks
          d. complex grammatical tasks

4.6   The area of the brain most likely to influence the timing of circadian rhythms is the
c
p. 127   a. cerebellum, a portion of the hindbrain.
Concept   b. lateral geniculate nucleus, a portion of the thalamus.
M   c. suprachiasmatic nucleus, a portion of the hypothalamus.
          d. frontal lobe, a portion of the cerebral cortex.

4.7   A hormone that seems to influence circadian rhythm is
d
p. 127   a. adrenalin.
Fact   b. endorphins.
E   c. testosterone.
PT/OLSG   d. melatonin.

Chapter 4 - States of Consciousness 69

4.8
d
p. 127
Concept
C

Increasing the amount of light an individual experiences is likely to have which of the following effects?
a. increased melatonin and increased tiredness
b. increased melatonin and decreased tiredness
c. decreased melatonin and increased tiredness
d. decreased melatonin and decreased tiredness

4.9
b
p. 127
Fact
M

Which of the following increases suprachiasmatic activity?
a. increased exposure to darkness
b. increased exposure to sunlight
c. increased exposure to indoor dim lighting
d. increased sleep

4.10
c
p. 128
Applied
M

If you were isolated from all cues that you normally use to keep track of time, you would probably adopt a
a. regular 24-hour day.
b. slightly shorter than 24-hour day.
c. slightly longer than 24-hour day.
d. day that has no regular cycles.

4.11
b
p. 128
Applied
M

Lisa recently took a test and found out that she was a "night" person. If you were her academic adviser, what time of day would you advise her to take classes?
a. morning classes
b. afternoon classes
c. all day Saturday classes
d. it really does not matter

4.12
b
p. 128
Applied
M

Ralph was really struggling to increase his grade point average and was looking for any edge that would help him. He went to a psychologist, and after taking some tests, was told that he should probably take classes between 8:00 a.m. and 11:00 a.m. Ralph has a _____ that would classify him as a(n) _____ person.
a. circadian rhythm; evening
b. circadian rhythm; morning
c. biological rhythm; evening
d. biological rhythm; morning

4.13
d
p. 130
Concept
C

Which of the following is the easiest to accomplish when attempting to readjust your biological clock to a new external world clock?
a. an advance in the biological clock
b. activities that increase automatic processing
c. activities that decrease automatic processing
d. a delay in the biological clock

4.14
c
p. 130
Concept
M

Jet lag and changes in work shifts can produce confusion, inefficiency, and mistakes because these changes
a. create psychological depression.
b. reduce our sleep time.
c. disrupt our circadian rhythms.
d. reduce our sense of control.

70   Test Bank - Essentials of Psychology (2nd Edition)

4.15
c
p. 131
Applied
C

Which of the following is likely to lead to an increase in shift workers' productivity and health?
a. standard rotating shift pattern of 7 days followed 2 days later by rotation to earlier shift
b. standard rotating shift pattern of 5 days followed 2 days later by rotation to earlier shift
c. revised rotating shift pattern of several weeks at one shift and then rotated to a later shift for the next several weeks
d. revised shifts that were made randomly by ignoring any patterns in circadian rhythms

4.16
b
p. 131
Concept
M
PT/OLSG

Research on circadian rhythms uses the _____ approach.
a. EEG
b. diary
c. cross-sectional
d. longitudinal

4.17
a
p. 131
Study
M

In one study, the circadian rhythms of nurses were studied using the _____ approach.
a. diary
b. probe
c. experimental
d. labrynth

4.18
b
p. 131
Study
C

One of the findings of the study of circadian rhythms of nurses was that
a. the adverse effects of night shift work dissipated over time.
b. the adverse effects of night shift work cumulated over time.
c. the adverse effects of night shift work did not change over time.
d. the adverse effects of night shift work changed with assigned jobs.

4.19
c
p. 131
Study
C

The common sense approach to swing shift work, that of giving several days of rest between shifts, may _____.
a. be the best solution to counter the adverse effects.
b. be the fairest solution to counter the adverse effects.
c. not be the best solution to counter the adverse effects.
d. not be the honest solution to counter the adverse effects.

Waking States of Consciousness

4.20
b
p. 132
Fact
M

A type of processing whereby you initiate an activity then perform it with relatively little conscious awareness is called
a. controlled processing.
b. automatic processing.
c. latent processing.
d. manifest processing.

4.21
c
p. 132
Applied
M

What type of processing are you demonstrating when you are watching a basketball game on television and listening to your favorite song on your stereo?
a. controlled
b. latent
c. automatic
d. manifest

Chapter 4 - States of Consciousness

4.22　　Which of the following is an example of a task requiring automatic processing?
d
p. 132　　a.　writing a psychology term paper
Applied　b.　listening to a lecture in economics
M　　　　c.　memorizing a list of words for a Spanish class
　　　　　d.　playing a well-rehearsed song on a piano for a music class

4.23　　A type of attention that requires your full attention to the task at hand and allows
b　　　only one task at a time to be performed is called
p. 132　　a.　detection processing.
Fact　　　b.　controlled processing.
M　　　　c.　automatic processing.
　　　　　d.　latent processing.

4.24　　Which of the following is an example of a task most likely to require controlled
c　　　processing?
p. 132　　a.　riding a bicycle
Applied　b.　brushing your teeth
M　　　　c.　reading this question
　　　　　d.　singing your favorite song

4.25　　Which of the following tends to develop with practice as the components of an
d　　　activity become well learned and become associated with specific stimulus conditions?
p. 132　　a.　focused attention
Concept　b.　daydreaming
M　　　　c.　controlled processing
　　　　　d.　automatic processing

4.26　　Research on automatic processing suggests that
d
p. 133　　a.　it requires a lot of attention.
Concept　b.　it is more flexible than controlled processing.
M　　　　c.　it is slower than controlled processing.
PT/OLSG　d.　it requires little conscious awareness.

4.27　　Automatic processing is to controlled processing as
b
p. 133　　a.　conscious is to unconscious.
Concept　b.　unconscious is to conscious.
M　　　　c.　innate is to learned.
　　　　　d.　learned is to innate.

4.28　　Which of the following statements concerning attentional processes is true?
b
p. 133　　a.　Both controlled and automatic processing are equally flexible.
Concept　b.　Controlled processing is more flexible than automatic processing.
M　　　　c.　Automatic processing is more flexible than controlled processing.
　　　　　d.　Neither controlled nor automatic processing is flexible.

4.29　　The effects of practice often lead to a shift from
d
p. 133　　a.　inflexible to flexible processing.
Concept　b.　unconscious to conscious processing.
M　　　　c.　automatic to controlled processing.
　　　　　d.　controlled to automatic processing.

4.30   Those thoughts and images you generate yourself are called _____.
b
p. 133   a.   cognitive dissonance
Concept   b.   daydreams
M   c.   automatic thought processing
          d.   focused attention

4.31   If a daydream becomes so intense that it affects our emotions, it is called _____.
c
p. 133   a.   a supradream
Concept   b.   an affective libation
M   c.   a fantasy
          d.   an emotive release

4.32   One of the most common content areas of daydreams involves
a
p. 133   a.   success or failure.
Concept   b.   marriage.
M   c.   childrearing.
          d.   sports.

4.33   Television may increase children's tendency to _____, and decrease their tendency
b   to use _____.
p. 134   a.   daydream; substantive imagination
Concept   b.   daydream; creative imagination
M   c.   use creative imagination; moderate ideation
          d.   use substantive imagination; conceptual ideation

4.34   A mental image that is sexually arousing or erotic to the individual who has the
c   image is called
p. 134   a.   an erotic fantasy.
Concept   b.   a sexual daydream.
M   c.   a sexual fantasy.
          d.   a consensual daydream.

4.35   Sexual fantasies contain more _____ for men than for women.
b
p. 134   a.   submission content
Concept   b.   explicit visual imagery
E   c.   implicit visual imagery
          d.   affection

4.36   There is a positive correlation between reports of frequent sexual fantasies and
d
p. 134   a.   increased conceptual ideation.
Study   b.   greater implicit visual imagery.
C   c.   increased submission content.
          d.   greater sexual enjoyment.

Sleep: The Pause That Refreshes?

4.37   Most people spend more time _____ than they spend in any other activity.
d
p. 135   a.   problem solving
Fact   b.   daydreaming
E   c.   fantasizing
PT/OLSG   d.   sleeping

Chapter 4 - States of Consciousness

4.38
a
p. 135
Fact
M

Which of the following is used to study sleep because it allows for the recording of the electrical activity of the brain?
a. electroencephalogram
b. electromyogram
c. electroreticular
d. electrocardiogram

4.39
b
p. 135
Fact
M
PT/OLSG

Respiration, muscle tone, heart rate, and blood pressure are behaviors typically used to study
a. aphasia.
b. sleep.
c. controlled processing.
d. automatic processing.

4.40
b
p. 135
Concept
M

Fully awake is to quiet resting as
a. delta is to beta.
b. beta is to alpha.
c. alpha is to delta.
d. beta is to delta.

4.41
c
p. 135
Concept
M

Assuming you are fully awake and alert, your EEG pattern would probably contain many
a. delta waves.
b. alpha waves.
c. beta waves.
d. theta waves.

4.42
b
p. 135
Concept
M

Which of the following statements about sleep is true?
a. Stages of sleep vary greatly from individual to individual.
b. The onset of sleep is quite sudden.
c. Dreaming usually occurs in Stage 1 sleep.
d. Stage 1 sleep is quite restful.

4.43
d
p. 136
Fact
M

Which of the following is characterized by brain waves resembling people who are awake yet paradoxically having bodily muscle characteristics of profound relaxation?
a. stage 2 sleep
b. stage 4 sleep
c. apnea
d. REM sleep

4.44
a
p. 136
Fact
E

When are we most likely to dream?
a. REM periods
b. stage 2 sleep
c. stage 3 sleep
d. stage 4 sleep

4.45
d
p. 136
Concept
M
PT/OLSG

During REM sleep, a person is usually
a. sleeping lightly and very easy to wake up.
b. sleeping deeply and displaying delta waves.
c. displaying sleep spindles and K complexes.
d. experiencing dreams and lack of bodily activity.

74 Test Bank - Essentials of Psychology (2nd Edition)

4.46   Which of the following statements about REM sleep is true?
c
p. 137
Concept
M
a. It occurs once each night, approximately in the middle of your sleep period.
b. It occurs once each night, usually right before you wake up.
c. It alternates throughout the night with other stages of sleep and tends to increase in duration throughout the night.
d. It alternates throughout the night with other stages of sleep and tends to decrease in duration throughout the night.

4.47   After infancy, the total amount of sleep _____ with age, but the proportion of REM sleep _____.
b
p. 137
Concept
C
a. increases, decreases
b. decreases, remains the same
c. remains the same, decreases
d. decreases, increases

4.48   The restorative theory of sleep says that one important function of sleep is to
b
p. 138
Concept
M
a. allow for psychological processing of the day's events.
b. permit the body to recover from wear and tear.
c. keep us quiet and out of danger during the night.
d. help us remember the events that have happened.

4.49   When Randy Gardner stayed awake for eleven days, the most striking result was that
a
p. 138
Applied
M
a. he recovered after sleeping for 14 hours.
b. he had insomnia for weeks afterward.
c. he became unusually depressed and moody.
d. he lost the ability to function coherently.

4.50   When people systematically reduced the amount of sleep they received to about 5 hours per night, the main effect was that the subjects became
d
p. 138
Applied
M
a. extremely nervous and anxious while awake.
b. unable to dream during REM sleep.
c. unable to perform on complex tasks.
d. more efficient in the way they slept.

4.51   Which of the following is not one of the functions that have been identified by psychologists as a possible reason why we sleep?
d
p. 138
Concept
M
a. to allow the body to rest and repair itself
b. to maintain our health by experiencing REM sleep
c. to keep us quiet and safe during the night
d. to protect our sensory organs from overload

4.52   Sleep viewed as merely a neural mechanism that evolved to encourage species to remain inactive during those times of day when they do not engage in activities related to survival emphasizes
d
p. 138
Concept
C
a. the restorative function of sleep.
b. the recuperative function of sleep.
c. the necessity of only critical components of sleep, such as REM.
d. the relationship of sleep to basic circadian rhythms.

4.53   The strongest result of depriving people of REM sleep is that the people begin to show
d
p. 138
Concept
M
PT/OLSG
a. significant memory losses for their daily experiences.
b. major mood changes, including depression.
c. increased risks for infectious diseases.
d. more REM sleep the next few nights.

Chapter 4 - States of Consciousness

4.54
b
p. 139
Fact
M

A disorder involving the inability to fall asleep or maintain sleep once it is attained is called
a. somnambulism.
b. insomnia.
c. narcolepsy.
d. REM deficiency.

4.55
c
p. 139
Concept
M

Which of the following statements is true concerning insomnia?
a. More men than women suffer from insomnia.
b. Sleeping pills are the most effective treatment for insomnia.
c. The disorder seems to increase with age.
d. If not treated, insomnia may lead to somnambulism.

4.56
d
p. 139
Concept
M

Which of the following statements is true concerning insomnia?
a. Sleeping pills are the most effective treatment for insomnia.
b. The disorder is most frequent during adolescence.
c. If not treated, insomnia may lead to somnambulism.
d. More women than men suffer from insomnia.

4.57
b
p. 139
Applied
M
PT/OLSG

Reading something pleasant or taking a warm bath before going to bed and establishing a regular sleep routine are recommended for treating
a. night terrors.
b. insomnia.
c. somnambulism.
d. narcolepsy.

4.58
c
p. 139
Concept
E

The sleep disorder characterized by walking in one's sleep is called
a. apnea.
b. narcolepsy.
c. somnambulism.
d. paradoxical sleep.

4.59
d
p. 140
Applied
M

The sound of a vacuum cleaner, a hair dryer, or other white noise helps a baby sleep by producing a
a. carotid effect.
b. paradoxical effect.
c. somnambulism effect.
d. masking effect.

4.60
a
p. 141
Applied
M

A six-year-old who awakens from Stage 4 sleep with signs of intense arousal, for example, a racing pulse, rapid respiration, and powerful feelings of fear, and claims not to have been dreaming, has probably experienced
a. night terrors.
b. nightmares.
c. apnea.
d. somnambulism.

4.61
c
p. 141
Concept
M

Both somnambulism and night terrors seem to be related to disturbance in the functioning of the
a. cerebellum.
b. thalamus.
c. autonomic nervous system.
d. somatic nervous system.

4.62 A disturbance that involves stopping of breathing while sleeping is
b
p. 141 a. hypersomnia.
Concept b. apnea.   *Extra credit*
E c. night terrors.
PT/OLSG d. somnambulism.

4.63 A hypersomniac
b
p. 141 a. sleeps too little.
Fact b. sleeps too much.
E c. stops breathing when asleep.
 d. has night terrors throughout the night.

4.64 In the middle of a conversation your roommate suddenly falls deeply asleep when
c learning that she has just won $1000. When she awakens she informs you that this
p. 141 has happened on several occasions when she becomes excited. She probably has a
Applied disorder known as
M a. diurnal myoclonus.
 b. sleep apnea.
 c. narcolepsy.
 d. somnambulism.

4.65 Research indicates that sleep disorders may be related to disturbance of areas
a of the brain that regulate
p. 141 a. body temperature.
Concept b. automatic processing.
M c. public self-consciousness.
 d. hypnotic states.

4.66 Brain mechanisms thought to be involved in sleep disturbances include
b a. the somatic nervous system.
p. 141 b. the suprachiasmatic nucleus of the hypothalamus.
Concept c. the cerebellum.
C d. the reticular activating system.

4.67 Which of the following statements about dreams is true?
b a. Most people do not dream every night.
p. 142 b. Judgement of time during dreams is about the same as judgement during
Fact waking periods.
M c. External events happening at the time of sleep cannot be incorporated into dreams.
 d. Sexual content of a dream can be reliably predicted by male erection or female
 vaginal secretions.

4.68 During which stage of sleep do dreams usually occur?
a a. During REM sleep
p. 142 b. During Stage 1 sleep
Fact c. During Stage 2 sleep
M d. During Stage 3 sleep
PT/OLSG

4.69 A stimulus such as a sound or touch while someone is dreaming that does not wake
b the person up will often
p. 142 a. terminate the dream and put the person in NREM sleep.
Fact b. become incorporated into the events of the dream.
M c. make the dreamer feel threatened or frightened.
 d. be reflected in abnormal brain wave patterns.

Chapter 4 - States of Consciousness 77

4.70   If a therapist uses your dreams to probe your unconscious, the therapist probably
b   believes in which of the following views of dreams?
p. 142   a.   cognitive view
Applied   b.   psychodynamic view
M   c.   physiological view
            d.   neodissociation view

4.71   Freud stated that dreams were
c   a.   representations of behaviors acquired from controlled processing.
p. 142   b.   symbolic of universal myths.
Fact   c.   reflections of hidden wishes or impulses.
M   d.   results of random neural activity of the brain.

4.72   Dreams result from random neural activity of the brain according to which of the
d   following views?
p. 143   a.   psychodynamic
Concept   b.   cognitive
M   c.   behavioral
            d.   physiological

4.73   The notion that dreams are produced by active cortical structures that regulate
b   thought and perception, and have minimal sensory input during REM is most
p. 143   compatible with the
Concept   a.   psychodynamic view.
M   b.   cognitive view.
            c.   physiological view.
            d.   behavioral view.

4.74   The belief that dreams reflect aspects of our memories and waking experiences
c   is most compatible with which of the following views of dreaming?
p. 143   a.   physiological view
Concept   b.   behavioral view
M   c.   cognitive view
            d.   psychodynamic view

4.75   Dreams of absent-minded transgression (DAMIT dreams) support the belief that
d   dreams
p. 143   a.   are totally random, unpredictable events.
Concept   b.   are symbolic and represent universal cultural myths.
C   c.   are representations of external stimuli, for example, noises that occur
               during sleep.
            d.   are related to important events in our lives.

4.76   If you wake up disturbed from a dream where you were engaging in a bad habit
b   that you are trying to change, e.g, biting your nails, you probably experienced
p. 143   a.   automatic processing.
Applied   b.   dreams of absent-minded transgression (DAMIT dreams).
M   c.   neodissociation dreams.
PT/OLSG   d.   narcoleptic fantasies.

Hypnosis: Altered State of Consciousness ... or Social Role Playing?

4.77
b
p. 145
Fact
M

The brain waves of someone in a hypnotic trance most closely resemble those of which state of consciousness?
a. sleeping
b. waking
c. alcohol induced stupor
d. sedative induced stupor

4.78
c
p. 145
Fact
M

Which of the following characteristics is associated with high hypnotic susceptibility?
a. not prone to vivid fantasies
b. a disbelief in hypnotism
c. high dependency on others
d. low incidence of imaginative experiences

4.79
b
p. 145
Concept
M

One likely reason why people who daydream a lot are more susceptible to hypnosis is that these people
a. are better actors and can pretend to be hypnotized.
b. clearly imagine the effects suggested by the hypnotist.
c. are lower in intelligence and more easily fooled.
d. decide voluntarily to obey the hypnotist's suggestions.

4.80
a
p. 146
Concept
C
PT/OLSG

Which of the following emphasizes the relationship between the hypnotist and the hypnotized person, where the hypnotized person engages in activities believed to happen in the context of hypnotism?
a. social-cognitive
b. neodissociation
c. automatic processing
d. social-dissociative

4.81
b
p. 146
Concept
M

Hypnotism can be viewed as
a. losing voluntary control.
b. playing a social role.
c. acting out REM sleep.
d. a state of total unconsciousness.

4.82
a
p. 146
Applied
M

A stage hypnotist puts Lisa in a trance and suggests that she has become a dog, and Lisa begins crawling around and barking. According to the social-cognitive view of hypnotism, Lisa is doing this behavior because
a. she believes she has no choice but to obey.
b. her behavior is separated from her own control.
c. she is pretending to be hypnotized to get attention.
d. her "hidden observer" thinks it is amusing.

4.83
c
p. 146
Concept
M

According to Hilgard's neodissociation theory, the hidden observer
a. should be involved in hypnosis procedures to verify that the hypnotist acts ethically toward the subject.
b. is the part of the hypnotized individual that is willing to accept the hypnotic suggestion.
c. is the part of the mind that observes the hypnosis without participating in the process.
d. is the method by which the hypnotist decides which subjects can best be hypnotized.

Chapter 4 - States of Consciousness

4.84 c p. 146 Concept M

When there is a piece of the consciousness of a hypnotized person that watches what is going on but does not participate in it, this part of consciousness is called
a. a split personality.
b. the social role.
c. the hidden observer.
d. a post-hypnotic suggestion.

4.85 c p. 146 Concept M

If the social-cognitive view of hypnotism is correct, then a person who has never heard of hypnosis should be
a. highly susceptible to the hypnotist's suggestions.
b. made very anxious or depressed by the procedure.
c. practically impossible to hypnotize.
d. easier to hypnotize but harder to wake up again.

4.86 a p. 147 Study C

Research by Spanos and his colleagues (1992) support the idea that a hypnotized subject does not experience a change in perception, but is responding to
a. demand characteristics provided by the hypnotist.
b. perceptual characteristics provided by the hypnotist.
c. emotional changes provided by the hypnotist.
d. instructional nuances provided by the hypnotist.

4.87 c p. 148 Concept C PT/OLSG

Research examining the effects of hypnotism on sensation and perception indicates that hypnotism
a. can completely block our sensory systems.
b. can mimic the effects of most hallucinogens.
c. alters the subject's report of the sensory experience and not the actual experience.
d. selectively inhibits the neural sensory systems of the brain but not the cognitive cortical areas.

4.88 b p. 148 Study C

In one study, individuals were hypnotized, told they had undergone a sex change, and then had this information later challenged. The results of this study indicated that
a. individuals low in hypnotic susceptibility maintained their belief that they had actually had a sex change when challenged by a physician.
b. individuals high in hypnotic susceptibility maintained their belief that they had actually had a sex change when challenged by a physician.
c. individuals low in hypnotic susceptibility changed their names to match the sex change.
d. individuals high in hypnotic susceptibility did not change their names to match the sex change.

4.89 c p. 148 Concept M

If hypnotic effects exist, they appear to
a. occur in many different people.
b. occur in selected classes of people.
c. occur in some people only.
d. occur in females only.

Conscious-Altering Drugs: What They Are and What They Do

4.90 a p. 149 Fact E

A drug that changes a person's mood or perceptions of the world is called a(n)
a. consciousness-altering drug.
b. abusive drug.
c. barbiturate.
d. opiate.

4.91 d p. 151 Concept M

The term "drug abuse" is used when drugs are taken
a. to treat a medical condition, but the treatment is unnecessary.
b. because someone else wants to control the person's behavior.
c. simply by habit, without any effect on the person taking them.
d. purely to change mood, and it causes the person problems.

4.92 b p. 151 Concept M

If someone takes a drug for the purpose of changing his or her mood, and the drug causes social or family problems, this situation is called
a. neodissociation.
b. drug abuse.
c. psychological dependence.
d. physiological dependence.

4.93 d p. 151 Concept M

A dependence on drugs can be defined
a. only as a psychological dependence.
b. only as a physiological dependence.
c. neither a psychological nor a physiological dependence.
d. both as a psychological and a physiological dependence.

4.94 c p. 151 Fact M

The term "physiological dependence" is used when someone needs a drug
a. just out of habit, without any strong desire.
b. to fill a psychological fear of going without it.
c. because of physical changes in the body.
d. to cure a dangerous medical condition.

4.95 b p. 151 Fact M

The term "psychological dependence" is used when someone needs a drug
a. just out of habit, without any strong desire.
b. because of their desire for the drug.
c. because of physical changes in the body.
d. to cure a dangerous medical condition.

4.96 b p. 151 Fact M PT/OLSG

If someone takes a drug out of a strong desire to feel its effects and a fear of facing life without it, the person has developed
a. a physiological dependence on the drug.
b. a psychological dependence on the drug.
c. a medical condition for which the drug is the treatment.
d. a hallucinogenic factor in the use of the drug.

4.97 a p. 151 Fact E

A physiological reaction in which the body requires larger and larger doses in order to experience the same effects is called
a. drug tolerance.
b. psychological drug dependence.
c. the hidden observer effect.
d. the placebo effect.

4.98 c p. 151 Fact M

The view that people take drugs because the drugs make them feel good is based on which of the following perspectives?
a. psychodynamic
b. cognitive
c. learning
d. social

Chapter 4 - States of Consciousness

4.99 Which statement best reflects the learning perspective of drug use?
d
p. 151 a. People take drugs as a result of peer pressure.
Concept b. People take drugs to hide feelings of inner turmoil.
M c. People take drugs as an automatic reaction to internal, unconscious motivations.
  d. People take drugs because the drugs make them feel good.

4.100 Which statement best reflects the psychodynamic perspective of drug use?
c
p. 152 a. People use drugs as rewards for "good" behavior.
Concept b. People take drugs to fit in with a social group.
M c. People use drugs to avoid unconscious anxiety.
  d. People take drugs as an automatic behavior.

4.101 People take drugs to reduce anxiety generated by unconscious conflicts according to
a which of the following perspectives?
p. 152 a. psychodynamic
Concept b. cognitive
M c. learning
PT/OLSG d. social

4.102 Research by Sharp and Getz (1996) found that some people do use alcohol as a tactic of
c
p. 152 a. coherence management.
Study b. empathy enhancement.
C c. impression management.
  d. sympathetic enhancement.

4.103 Which statement best reflects the social perspective of drug use?
b
p. 152 a. People use drugs as rewards for "good" behavior.
Concept b. People take drugs to fit in with a social group.
M c. People use drugs to avoid unconscious anxiety.
  d. People take drugs as an automatic behavior.

4.104 Which statement best reflects the cognitive perspective of drug use?
d
p. 152 a. People use drugs as rewards for "good" behavior.
Concept b. People take drugs to fit in with a social group.
M c. People use drugs to avoid unconscious anxiety.
  d. People take drugs as an automatic behavior.

4.105 The view where drug use is thought to be due to a kind of automatic processing
c where people automatically respond to internal and external cues associated with
p. 152 drug use is referred to as the
Concept a. psychodynamic view.
M b. social view.
  c. cognitive view.
  d. learning view.

4.106 Drugs that reduce both behavioral output and activity in the central nervous system
b are classified as
p. 152 a. narcotics.
Concept b. depressants.
E c. opiates.
PT/OLSG d. psychedelics.

4.107 Alcohol is classified as
a
p. 152   a.   a depressant.
Concept   b.   a stimulant.
M   c.   an opiate.
           d.   a hallucinogen.

4.108 A major psychological effect of alcohol is that it acts as a
a
p. 152   a.   depressant, and reduces our inhibitions.
Concept   b.   stimulant, and makes us overactive.
M   c.   tranquilizer, and makes us less fearful.
           d.   aggressor, and makes us more violent.

4.109 As alcohol levels in the bloodstream increase, a person's behavior will become
d
p. 153   a.   more agitated and hyperactive.
Concept   b.   increasingly tolerant to alcohol.
M   c.   more and more restrictive.
           d.   slower and less coordinated.

4.110 In its effect on the nervous system, alcohol is most like
d
p. 153   a.   LSD.
Fact   b.   cocaine.
M   c.   marijuana.
           d.   barbiturates.

4.111 Which of the following depress activity in the nervous system causing a reduction
d   in mental alertness and also produce feelings of relaxation and euphoria?
p. 153   a.   amphetamines
Concept   b.   nicotine
M   c.   LSD
PT/OLSG   d.   barbiturates

4.112 A problem associated with using barbiturates for sleep disorders is that they tend to
a
p. 154   a.   decrease REM sleep.
Fact   b.   increase REM sleep.
M   c.   increase the likelihood of apnea.
           d.   decrease the likelihood of somnambulism.

4.113 The major psychoactive effect of barbiturates is to
c
p. 154   a.   stimulate the sleep centers in the brain.
Concept   b.   stimulate the sensory and motor areas of the brain.
M   c.   decrease activity throughout the nervous system.
           d.   increase activity in the peripheral nervous system.

4.114 A study by Lindman and Lang (1994) investigated the impact of culture on the
a   relationship of alcohol and aggression. The results indicated that
p. 155   a.   students in the United States and Panama believed there was a link between
Study   consuming alcohol and behaving aggressively.
C   b.   students in Spain and Poland believed there was no link between consuming
                alcohol and behaving aggressively.
           c.   students in France and Italy believed there was a link between consuming
                alcohol and behaving aggressively.
           d.   students in Belgium and Poland believed there was no link between consuming
                alcohol and behaving aggressively.

Chapter 4 - States of Consciousness

4.115   The study by Lindman and Lang (1994) indicated that
b
p. 155   a. cultural factors do not play a role in the relationship between alcohol and aggression.
Study   b. cultural factors do play a role in the relationship between alcohol and aggression.
C   c. cultural factors do play a role in the relationship between alcohol and aggression, but their impact depends upon the age of the participants.
   d. cultural factors do not play a role in the relationship between alcohol and aggression because of the difficulty in measuring the perceptions of various cultures.

4.116   Both cocaine and amphetamines act on the nervous system by
d
p. 155   a. decreasing the activity in the pain and sleep centers.
Concept   b. calming the central nervous system and stimulating the brain.
C   c. reducing the activity in the sympathetic nervous system.
   d. increasing the activity in the sympathetic nervous system.

4.117   Amphetamines and cocaine are classified as
b
p. 155   a. hallucinogens.
Fact   b. stimulants.
E   c. opiates.
   d. psychedelics.

4.118   Barbiturate is to cocaine as
c
p. 155   a. opiate is to hallucinogen.
Concept   b. hallucinogen is to opiate.
C   c. depressant is to stimulant.
   d. stimulant is to depressant.

4.119   Which of the following, if ingested, is likely to result in increased blood pressure, heart rate, and respiration?
d
p. 155   a. only cocaine
Fact   b. only amphetamines
E   c. only caffeine
PT/OLSG   d. cocaine, amphetamines, and caffeine

4.120   Amphetamines and cocaine inhibit the reuptake of
a
p. 155   a. norepinephrine and dopamine.
Fact   b. acetylcholine and endorphins.
C   c. heroin and opium.
   d. testosterone and estrogen.

4.121   Which of the following is not a correct statement about stimulants?
d
p. 155   a. They increase arousal.
Fact   b. Cocaine is a stimulant.
E   c. They inhibit the reuptake of transmitter substances.
   d. Alcohol is a stimulant.

4.122   Cocaine is to crack as
b
p. 155   a. smoking is to snorting.
Fact   b. snorting is to smoking.
M   c. swallowing is to injection.
   d. injection is to swallowing.

4.123   Nicotine, found in tobacco, is considered to be
b
p. 155   a. a depressant.
Concept   b. a stimulant.
M   c. an opiate.
   d. a psychedelic.

4.124 Many experts view nicotine as
c　　　a. not at all addictive.
p. 155　b. addictive, but only in younger individuals.
Concept c. highly addictive.
M　　　d. addictive, especially when mixed with alcohol.

4.125 Morphine and heroin are classified as
d　　　a. hallucinogens.
p. 155　b. psychedelics.
Fact　　c. stimulants.
E　　　d. opiates.

4.126 Which of the following produce lethargy and a pronounced slowing of almost all
a　　　bodily functions often accompanied with dream-like states and intense pleasurable
p. 155　sensations?
Fact　　a. opiates
M　　　b. cocaine
　　　　c. psychedelics
　　　　d. marijuana

4.127 Opiates are most similar in chemical structure to
b　　　a. noradrenalin.
p. 156　b. endorphins.
Fact　　c. dopamine.
M　　　d. acetylcholine.

4.128 The drugs that may stop the brain from producing endorphins are
a　　　a. opiates.
p. 156　b. amphetamines.
Fact　　c. hallucinogens.
M　　　d. barbiturates.

4.129 Which of the following is not a correct statement about opiates?
d　　　a. Heroin is an opiate.
p. 156　b. The pain reducing ability of the user may be reduced.
Concept c. Their use produces dramatic slowing of bodily functions.
M　　　d. They may cause an increase in endorphins.
PT/OLSG

4.130 Drugs that generate sensory perceptions for which there are no external stimuli are
c　　　a. stimulants.
p. 156　b. depressants.
Concept c. hallucinogens.
M　　　d. endorphins.

4.131 Psychedelic is to hallucinogen as
c　　　a. cocaine is to alcohol.
p. 156　b. alcohol is to cocaine.
Concept c. marijuana is to LSD.
C　　　d. LSD is to marijuana.

4.132 Marijuana is the most widely used _____ drug.
d　　　a. opiate
p. 156　b. sedative
Concept c. stimulant
M　　　d. psychedelic

Chapter 4 - States of Consciousness

4.133
a
p. 156
Concept
M

Among the negative effects of marijuana are
a. perceptual distortions and possible change in personality.
b. nervousness, anxiety, and fear.
c. extreme lethargy and sleepiness.
d. clumsiness and lack of coordination.

4.134
d
p. 156
Concept
M

The strange blending of sensory experiences such as sounds producing visual sensations, may be produced as a result of taking
a. marijuana.
b. crack.
c. opium.
d. LSD.

4.135
c
p. 157
Fact
M

The effects of LSD are always
a. highly negative.
b. highly exciting.
c. highly unpredictable.
d. highly predictable.

4.136
b
p. 158
Fact
M
PT/OLSG

A technique performed to produce altered states of consciousness in which awareness of and contact with the external world is reduced is called
a. yoga analysis.
b. meditation.
c. synesthesia.
d. regression.

4.137
a
p. 158
Fact
M

Effective meditation generally results in
a. reduced awareness of the external world.
b. increased awareness of the external world.
c. synesthesia and fantasies.
d. cross-tolerance of consciousness and unconsciousness.

4.138
c
p. 158
Applied
M

By repeating the word "shalom," Lisa is able to focus her attention entirely on this word and reduce her awareness of things happening around her. This situation is an example of using a
a. daydream.
b. latent phrase.
c. mantra.
d. delta chant.

CHAPTER 5

Multiple-Choice Questions

5.1
a
p.164
Fact
M
A relatively permanent change in behavior, or behavior potential, due to experience, is called
a. learning.
b. pseudoconditioning.
c. response substitution.
d. behavioral potentiation.

5.2
c
p. 164
Fact
M
A relatively permanent change in behavior, or behavior potential, produced by experience, is called
a. reinforcement.
b. vicarious maturation.
c. learning.
d. implosive modification.

5.3
d
p. 164
Applied
M
Because a moth will approach a light the first time it is encountered, such a response would not be considered learned because it
a. is not relatively permanent.
b. can be influenced by fatigue.
c. is based on vicarious experience.
d. is not a result of experience.

5.4
a
p. 164
Concept
M
Which of the following is considered a form of learning?
a. classical conditioning
b. maturation
c. sensitization
d. classical conditioning, maturation, and sensitization are all forms of learning

5.5
b
p. 164
Concept
M
Learned behavior is to unlearned behavior as
a. maturation is to experience.
b. experience is to maturation.
c. operant conditioning is to vicarious learning.
d. vicarious learning is to operant conditioning.

5.6
c
p. 164
Concept
M
Operant and classical conditioning are forms of
a. vicarious learning.
b. maturational changes.
c. learning.
d. sensitization.

5.7
d
p. 164
Applied
M
PT/OLSG
Learning how to throw a basketball as a result of watching games on television is an example of
a. pseudolearning.
b. classical conditioning.
c. operant conditioning.
d. observational learning.

5.8
b
p. 164
Fact
E
Which of the following is NOT a form of learning?
a. observational learning
b. maturational learning
c. classical conditioning
d. operant conditioning

Chapter 5 - Learning: How We're Changed by Experience

Classical Conditioning: Learning That Some Stimuli Signal Others

5.9
a
p. 164
Applied
M

Whenever you would spill soda on the living room rug your parents would yell loudly. Now, even though you live in your own apartment, whenever you spill a soda you feel anxious. This anxiety can be explained on the basis of
a. classical conditioning.
b. operant conditioning.
c. maturational sensitization.
d. observational learning.

5.10
b
p. 165
Fact
M

A stimulus that comes to elicit a response as a result of repeated pairings with a stimulus that can reliably elicit a response does so because of
a. operant conditioning.
b. classical conditioning.
c. observational learning.
d. classical, operant and observational learning.

5.11
c
p. 165
Fact
M

Ivan Pavlov, a Nobel Prize winning physiologist from Russia, is considered to have "discovered"
a. operant conditioning.
b. conditioned taste aversion.
c. classical conditioning.
d. systematic desensitization.

5.12
d
p. 165
Fact
M

Ivan Pavlov is an important figure in the psychology of learning because he first studied
a. motivational conditioning.
b. respondent conditioning.
c. operant conditioning.
d. classical conditioning.

5.13
c
p. 165
Fact
M

In classical conditioning, a stimulus that _____ becomes one that _____.
a. is a reinforcer; is a punisher
b. is a punisher; is a reinforcer
c. produces no response; produces a response
d. produces a response; produces no response

5.14
b
p. 165
Fact
E

A physical event to which we may or may not respond is called a(n)
a. operant.
b. stimulus.
c. reflex.
d. ratio.

5.15
c
p. 166
Concept
M

When studying classical conditioning, subjects would often salivate at the sight of the pan where food was kept. In this case, the sight of the pan is an example of
a. an unconditioned stimulus.
b. an unconditioned response.
c. a conditioned stimulus.
d. a conditioned response.

5.16
a
p. 166
Concept
M

When studying classical conditioning, subjects would often salivate at the sight of the pan where food was kept. In this case, the food is an example of
a. an unconditioned stimulus.
b. an unconditioned response.
c. a conditioned stimulus.
d. a conditioned response.

5.17 b
p. 166
Concept
M
PT/OLSG

When studying classical conditioning, subjects would often salivate at the sight of the pan where food was kept. In this case, salivating to the food is an example of
a. an unconditioned stimulus.
b. an unconditioned response.
c. a conditioned stimulus.
d. a conditioned response.

5.18 d
p. 166
Concept
M

When studying classical conditioning, subjects would often salivate at the sight of the pan where food was kept. In this case, salivating at the sight of the pan is an example of
a. an unconditioned stimulus.
b. an unconditioned response.
c. a conditioned stimulus.
d. a conditioned response.

5.19 d
p. 166
Concept
M

In classical conditioning, the stimulus that elicits a response the first time it is presented is called the
a. generalized stimulus.
b. neutral stimulus.
c. conditioned stimulus.
d. unconditioned stimulus.

5.20 c
p. 166
Concept
M

In classical conditioning, the stimulus that comes to elicit a response as a result of pairing with another stimulus is called the
a. generalized stimulus.
b. neutral stimulus.
c. conditioned stimulus.
d. unconditioned stimulus.

5.21 b
p. 166
Concept
M

In classical conditioning, the response to a stimulus presented for the first time is called the
a. conditioned response.
b. unconditioned response.
c. extinguished response.
d. helpless response.

5.22 c
p. 166
Concept
M

The response that is learned as a result of classical conditioning is called the
a. operant response.
b. instrumental response.
c. conditioned response.
d. unconditioned response.

5.23 b
p. 166
Applied
M

After repeatedly watching a video of a really scary movie put out by a small independent company, Lisa found that just seeing the company's logo made her heart start to pound. This is an example of what type of learning?
a. operant conditioning
b. classical conditioning
c. observational learning
d. maturational learning

5.24 a
p. 167
Concept
C
PT/OLSG

Simultaneous, trace, delayed, and backward conditioning are produced as a result of manipulating
a. temporal arrangements between the CS and US.
b. temporal arrangements between the CR and US.
c. intensity of the US.
d. intensity of the CS.

Chapter 5 - Learning: How We're Changed by Experience

5.25
b
p. 167
Applied
C

Young children are often frightened by loud noises. This may explain why we fear a flash of lightning that is followed a few seconds later by the sound of thunder. The type of conditioning that best explains this learned fear is
a. backward.
b. trace.
c. delayed.
d. simultaneous.

5.26
c
p. 167
Applied
C

As a result of a painful bee sting, you now get very upset at just the sight of a bee. Assuming you saw the bee land on your hand but could not brush it off before it stung you, the type of conditioning that occurred is
a. backward.
b. trace.
c. delayed.
d. simultaneous.

5.27
d
p. 167
Applied
C

As a result of getting sick two hours after eating pizza, you now feel nauseous when you see a pizza. You have acquired this aversion as a result of
a. simultaneous conditioning.
b. delayed conditioning.
c. backward conditioning.
d. trace conditioning.

5.28
a
p. 168
Concept
M

Most research indicates that the optimal CS-US interval, when all other variables are held constant, is
a. between .2 and 2.0 seconds.
b. less than .2 seconds.
c. between 2.0 and 10.0 seconds.
d. cannot be determined.

5.29
a
p. 168
Concept
M

One factor that will influence whether or not a response will be classically conditioned is the _____ of the pairings of the conditioned and unconditioned stimuli.
a. predictability
b. generalizability
c. adaptability
d. sensitivity

5.30
c
p. 168
Applied
C

According to the principles of classical conditioning, if you want to teach a child to like impressionist art, you should
a. give the child money for hanging impressionist art in his or her bedroom.
b. make sure the child sees that you enjoy impressionist art.
c. have impressionist art nearby while the child is doing something he or she enjoys.
d. do nothing; classical conditioning cannot affect someone's likes and dislikes.

5.31
b
p. 168
Applied
C

Although you have occasionally burned your mouth by eating a hot piece of food, you probably do not fear the sight of cooked food. This can best be explained on the basis of
a. temporal CS-US pairing.
b. stimulus familiarity.
c. CS-US interval limitations.
d. backward conditioning.

5.32 Which of the following is not a factor that influences the acquisition of classical conditioning?
d
p. 168 a. timing
Fact b. familiarity
M c. intensity
PT/OLSG d. implosion

5.33 Due to classical conditioning, your dog salivates every time he hears the special
b electric can opener you use to open his dog food. You switch to dry dog food. You
p. 169 continue to use the can opener, but not for dog food. After repeatedly hearing the
Applied can opener but not getting fed, your dog's salivation to the sound of the can
M opener should
 a. decrease because of spontaneous recovery.
 b. decrease because of extinction.
 c. increase because of blocking.
 d. increase because of instinctive drift.

5.34 The eventual decline and disappearance of a conditioned response in the absence of
d an unconditioned stimulus is known as
p. 169 a. instinctive drift.
Fact b. spontaneous recovery.
M c. acquisition.
 d. extinction.

5.35 Extinction requires which of the following?
c a. delayed CS-US presentations
p. 169 b. US only presentations
Concept c. CS only presentations
M d. blocking

5.36 When the unconditioned stimulus no longer follows the conditioned stimulus, _____ occurs.
b a. spontaneous recovery
p. 169 b. extinction
Fact c. classical conditioning
M d. operant conditioning
PT/OLSG

5.37 Following extinction, an experimental subject is reintroduced to the pairing of a
c flashing light with a very loud noise. Within one or two pairings, the subject again
p. 169 shows a fear response to the flashing light. This procedure is referred to as
Applied a. blocking.
C b. spontaneous recovery.
 c. reconditioning.
 d. instinctive drift.

5.38 If a conditioned stimulus is presented again at a later time after extinction, it may
d evoke a weakened conditioned response even though it is not paired again with the
p. 169 unconditioned stimulus. This phenomenon is referred to as
Concept a. stimulus discrimination.
M b. stimulus generalization.
 c. latent reconditioning.
 d. spontaneous recovery.

Chapter 5 - Learning: How We're Changed by Experience

5.39
a
p. 169
Concept
M

Spontaneous recovery is to extinction as
a. response occurrence is to response nonoccurrence.
b. response nonoccurrence is to response occurrence.
c. reconditioning is to instinctive drift.
d. instinctive drift is to reconditioning.

5.40
b
p. 169
Applied
M

After living in an old house for several months, Lisa finally stopped jumping in fear at every loud creaking noise. Then she went away for a week of vacation. According to the idea of spontaneous recovery, what should happen when she gets back from vacation?
a. She should jump even more than before.
b. She should jump but not as much as before.
c. She should be jumping more and more each day.
d. She should not jump ever again.

5.41
c
p. 169
Applied
M

Following a severe scratching by a Siamese cat, Ralph becomes very anxious whenever he sees any kind of cat. His reaction can best be explained on the basis of
a. instinctive drift.
b. response substitution.
c. stimulus generalization.
d. biological constraints.

5.42
d
p. 169
Fact
M

The tendency of stimuli similar to a conditioned stimulus to evoke a conditioned response is called
a. stimulus blocking.
b. spontaneous recovery.
c. stimulus discrimination.
d. stimulus generalization.

5.43
c
p. 169
Concept
C
PT/OLSG

Stimulus generalization
a. is the tendency of stimuli dissimilar to the conditioned stimulus to produce conditioned responses.
b. is identical to stimulus discrimination.
c. is the tendency of stimuli similar to the conditioned stimulus to produce conditioned responses.
d. occurs when the US and CS are no longer paired.

5.44
b
p. 169
Applied
C

Lisa's first car was so old and unsafe she always felt afraid of driving it and even of looking at it. When her husband got a new car, she was at first afraid of it also. This is _____. After several months of safely driving her husband's car, she was no longer afraid of it, but was still frightened of her own car. This is _____.
a. stimulus discrimination; stimulus generalization
b. stimulus generalization; stimulus discrimination
c. spontaneous recovery; response discrimination
d. response discrimination; spontaneous recovery

5.45
c
p. 169
Fact
M

The process by which organisms learn to respond to certain stimuli and not to respond to others is called
a. stimulus generalization.
b. response generalization.
c. stimulus discrimination.
d. response discrimination.

92 Test Bank - Essentials of Psychology (2nd Edition)

5.46
b
p. 169
Fact
M

In classical conditioning, the phenomenon of stimulus discrimination occurs whenever the learner responds to a stimulus similar to the conditioned stimulus by
a. giving the same conditioned response.
b. giving some different response.
c. showing confusion and anxiety.
d. giving two or more different responses.

5.47
c
p. 169
Concept
C

A person who responds to a stimulus similar to the conditioned stimulus with a similar response is demonstrating _____. while someone who gives a different response is demonstrating _____.
a. response discrimination; response generalization
b. response generalization; response discrimination
c. stimulus generalization; stimulus discrimination
d. stimulus discrimination; stimulus generalization

5.48
d
p. 169
Applied
C

Because Lisa enjoyed playing with her dog, she tried at first to play with a neighbor's dog. This demonstrates _____. After the neighbor's dog scratched her she began avoiding it, though she still enjoyed her own dog. This demonstrates _____.
a. extinction; spontaneous recovery
b. spontaneous recovery; extinction
c. stimulus discrimination; stimulus generalization
d. stimulus generalization; stimulus discrimination

5.49
c
p. 170
Concept
M

Recent evidence seems to indicate that neural activity in the _____ plays a significant role in classical conditioning.
a. reticular activating system
b. hypothalamus
c. cerebellum
d. cerebral cortex

5.50
b
p. 170
Concept
M

After severe damage to the _____, it is extremely difficult to establish classically conditioned responses in these individuals.
a. cerebral cortex
b. cerebellum
c. hypothalamus
d. reticular activating system

5.51
c
p. 171
Concept
M

The ability to acquire conditioned eye-blink responses fades with age. This condition has been related to the number and efficiency of cells in the _____.
a. hypothalamus
b. visual cortex
c. cerebellum
d. pineal gland

5.52
c
p. 171
Study
C

Based on the work of Garcia and Koelling dealing with conditioned taste aversion, which of the following groups of rats would show the strongest conditioning?
a. a water-CS and a footshock-US
b. a water-CS and an X-Ray-US
c. a light-CS and an X-Ray-US
d. a noise-CS and a footshock-US

5.53
a
p. 172
Concept
M

Garcia and Koelling's work on conditioned taste aversion supports the notion that
a. the time interval between the CS and US does not need to be short.
b. conditioning requires at least two CS-US pairings.
c. any neutral stimulus can serve as a CS if it is paired with a poison as the US.
d. physiological responses can not be classically conditioned.

Chapter 5 - Learning: How We're Changed by Experience

5.54
b
p. 172
Concept
E

The fact that types of conditioning readily accomplished by some species are only slowly acquired by other species is usually explained in the context of
a. instinctive drift.
b. biological constraints on learning.
c. stimulus generalization.
d. the Premack principle.

5.55
c
p. 172
Concept
C

The phrase "biological constraints on learning" relates most clearly to which situation?
a. Conditioning works best when the CS and the US are presented close together in time.
b. Stimulus generalization happens automatically, but stimulus discrimination has to be learned.
c. Rats most easily learn to avoid food because of its taste, while pigeons depend more on its appearance.
d. Extinguishing a response does not get rid of it entirely, since it can spontaneously recover.

5.56
b
p. 173
Concept
C
PT/OLSG

Which of the following is false?
a. Conditioning improves as the intensity of either the CS or US increases.
b. All responses or associations are learned with equal ease.
c. Taste aversion research shows that classical conditioning can occur with a relatively long interval between the CS and the US.
d. Chaining usually begins by shaping the final response in a sequence of behaviors.

5.57
c
p. 173
Concept
M
PT/OLSG

Conditioned taste aversions
a. are easy to extinguish.
b. require many CS-US pairings.
c. are difficult to extinguish.
d. occur with animals, but not with people.

5.58
d
p. 173
Applied
M

Garcia and Koelling's work on conditioned taste aversion explains
a. the predator-prey relationship in carnivores.
b. the phenomenon of stimulus generalization.
c. why sugars are added to processed foods.
d. weight loss following chemotherapy.

5.59
c
p. 173
Applied
M

Which of the following is an area in which knowledge of conditioned taste aversions can improve people's lives?
a. Training animals to perform tricks in circuses.
b. Controlling excess digestive system activity.
c. Improving the appetites of chemotherapy patients.
d. Teaching sheep to avoid wolves and other predators.

5.60
c
p. 173
Applied
M

To reduce their chances of developing conditioned taste aversions, cancer chemotherapy patients should
a. try to eat as shortly before treatment as possible.
b. eat only new, unusual foods before treatment.
c. choose foods that are bland, not strong-tasting.
d. eat food with spices other than salt.

5.61
a
p. 173
Concept
M

Pavlov's perspective is to the cognitive perspective as
a. association is to expectation.
b. expectation is to association.
c. trace conditioning is to delayed conditioning.
d. delayed conditioning is to trace conditioning.

5.62 c p. 173 Concept M

Which of the following perspectives suggests that expectations are formed as a result of CS-US pairings?
a. Pavlov's principles of associationism
b. the biological constraint notion of conditioning
c. the cognitive view of conditioning
d. Premack's principles of associationism

5.63 b p. 173 Concept C

According to the cognitive perspective, what exactly is learned during classical conditioning?
a. An automatic conditioned response to the conditioned stimulus.
b. An expectation that the unconditioned stimulus will follow the conditioned stimulus.
c. A decision to produce the desired behavior in order to gain a reward.
d. A social pattern of observed behavior that will fit into society.

5.64 b p. 174 Concept M

Which of the following phenomena is most likely to be used to support a cognitive view of learning?
a. conditioned taste aversion
b. blocking
c. extinction
d. spontaneous recovery

5.65 a p. 174 Concept M

After a conditioned response has been learned, a new neutral stimulus could be combined with the US. This stimulus will probably not become conditioned, because of the phenomenon of
a. blocking.
b. spontaneous recovery.
c. stimulus generalization.
d. flooding.

5.66 d p. 174 Concept M PT/OLSG

Preventing conditioning to a neutral stimulus as a result of presenting this new neutral stimulus along with a previous unconditioned stimulus is called
a. omission training.
b. conditioning constraints.
c. flooding.
d. blocking.

5.67 a p. 174 Concept M

The view that conditioning is a complex process where representations of relationships among a variety of factors are compared, including the context in which the CS and US are paired, is best described as
a. a cognitive view.
b. the Premack principle.
c. Pavlov's principle of associationism
d. a Skinnerian view.

5.68 b p. 174 Applied M

The classical study by Watson and Raynor in which their subject, Albert, was conditioned using a white rat and a loud noise demonstrated that conditioning produced
a. biological constraints.
b. phobias.
c. flooding.
d. blocking.

Chapter 5 - Learning: How We're Changed by Experience 95

5.69
c
p. 175
Applied
M

In order to eliminate a fear of insects, your therapist has you come to her office and touch plastic models of dragonflies. Eventually the fears are reduced because the therapist takes steps to guarantee that nothing bad happens as a result of exposure to these models. The therapist's procedure is called
a. blocking.
b. biofeedback.
c. flooding.
d. omission training.

5.70
d
p. 175
Concept
M

A progressive technique in therapy designed to replace anxiety with a relaxation response is called
a. defusing.
b. flooding.
c. learned decisiveness.
d. systematic desensitization.

5.71
b
p. 176
Applied
C

The psychotherapist, Joyce Ashley, has her clients remember an anxiety producing event, asks them to remember a person who had humiliated them, and then has them reconstruct the event from the perspective of these two individuals. She has been effective in using this technique to reduce _____ in her clients.
a. stimulus generalization
b. stage fright
c. learned indecisiveness
d. blocking

5.72
c
p. 176
Applied
C

The technique used by psychotherapist Joyce Ashley to reduce stage fright in her clients depends, in large part, on _____ and _____, established principles of classical conditioning.
a. pairing; reinforcement
b. blocking; flooding
c. systematic desensitization; flooding
d. systematic desensitization; blocking

5.73
a
p. 177
Applied
M

Research indicates that classical conditioning can have an effect on the level of antibodies in an animal's
a. immune system.
b. central nervous system.
c. peripheral nervous system.
d. reticular activating system.

5.74
b
p. 177
Applied
C
PT/OLSG

Pairing saccharin-flavored water with injection of a substance known to raise the level of antibodies in rats' bodies later resulted in _____ after being again exposed to saccharin-flavored water.
a. decreases in antibodies
b. increases in antibodies
c. increased liking for saccharin-flavored water
d. aversion to saccharin-flavored water

Operant Conditioning: Learning Based on Consequences

5.75
d
p. 178
Concept
M

The principle that behaviors change consistent with the nature of the consequences they produce is the foundation of
a. taste aversion.
b. forward conditioning.
c. classical conditioning.
d. operant conditioning.

5.76
b
p. 178
Concept
C

Reinforcement is to punishment as
a. suppression is to strengthen.
b. strengthen is to suppression.
c. extinction is to spontaneous recovery.
d. spontaneous recovery is to extinction.

5.77
c
p. 178
Concept
E

Stimulus events or consequences that strengthen responses that precede them are called
a. operant stimuli.
b. unconditioned stimuli.
c. positive reinforcers.
d. omission stimuli.

5.78
d
p. 178
Concept
M

Using dog biscuits to teach your dog to sit is an example of using
a. conditioned reinforcers.
b. secondary reinforcers.
c. biological constraints.
d. primary reinforcers.

5.79
a
p. 178
Concept
M

Some reinforcers seem to exert their effects because they are related to basic biological needs. They are called
a. primary reinforcers.
b. need reinforcers.
c. biological reinforcers.
d. conditioned reinforcers.

5.80
a
p. 178
Concept
M

In positive reinforcement, some event or stimulus is _____ after a behavior, and the behavior is _____ as a result.
a. produced; strengthened
b. produced; weakened
c. removed; weakened
d. removed strengthened

5.81
b
p. 178
Concept
M

The fact that preferred activities can serve as reinforcers is referred to as
a. contractual conditioning.
b. the Premack Principle.
c. the Garcia Principle.
d. blocking conditioning.

5.82
a
p. 179
Fact
M
PT/OLSG

Stimuli that strengthen responses related to their escape or avoidance are
a. negative reinforcers.
b. positive reinforcers.
c. primary reinforcers.
d. secondary reinforcers.

Chapter 5 - Learning: How We're Changed by Experience 97

5.83 Which of the following is an example of a negative reinforcer?
d   a. Getting a low grade on an exam because you did not study.
p. 179   b. Losing car privileges because you broke curfew.
Applied   c. Paying $15 to see a movie you did not like.
M   d. Cleaning your room to avoid your roommate's nagging.

5.84 Negative reinforcement is to punishment as
b   a. response decrease is to response increase.
p. 179   b. response increase is to response decrease.
Concept   c. response decrease is to response decrease.
C   d. response increase is to response increase.
PT/OLSG

5.85 In negative reinforcement, some event or stimulus is _____ after a behavior, and the
d behavior is _____ as a result.
p. 179   a. produced; weakened
Concept   b. produced; strengthened
M   c. removed; weakened
        d. removed; strengthened

5.86 Getting a ticket after speeding is an example of
b   a. positive reinforcement.
p. 179   b. negative reinforcement.
Applied   c. positive punishment.
M   d. negative punishement.

5.87 As a child, Ralph would sometimes hit his sister. His parents would then give him "time out" by making
b him stay in a corner for a specified time. This procedure is an example of
p. 180   a. positive punishment.
Applied   b. negative punishment.
M   c. negative reinforcement.
        d. positive reinforcement.

5.88 In classical conditioning, the responses of the organism are _____, while in operant
b conditioning they are _____.
p. 181   a. emitted by the organism; elicited by a stimulus
Concept   b. elicited by a stimulus; emitted by the organism
M   c. conditioned; unconditioned
        d. unconditioned; conditioned

5.89 When an organism emits a behavior in order to receive a reward, it is _____
a conditioning; when the behavior is elicited rather automatically by some stimulus
p. 181 event, it is _____ conditioning.
Concept   a. operant; classical
C   b. classical; operant
        c. experimental; perceptual
        d. perceptual; experimental

5.90 Voluntary is to involuntary as
d   a. blocking is to flooding.
p. 181   b. flooding is to blocking.
Concept   c. classical conditioning is to operant conditioning.
M   d. operant conditioning is to classical conditioning.

5.91 a
p. 181
Concept
M

Learning an association between particular behaviors and their consequences occurs in
a. operant conditioning.
b. classical conditioning.
c. conditioned taste aversion.
d. blocking.

5.92 a
p. 181
Concept
M

In operant conditioning, the term "shaping" refers to
a. reinforcing each small step toward a desired behavior.
b. removing privileges when an undesired behavior occurs.
c. using secondary, rather than primary, reinforcers.
d. creating a sequence of responses leading to a reward.

5.93 d
p. 181
Concept
E

A procedure whereby subjects are given reinforcers for performing behaviors that get closer and closer to some target behavior is called
a. flooding.
b. tracing.
c. chaining.
d. shaping.

5.94 d
p. 181
Concept
M

In operant conditioning, the term "chaining" refers to
a. reinforcing each small step toward a desired behavior.
b. removing privileges when an undesired behavior occurs.
c. using secondary, rather than primary, reinforcers.
d. creating a sequence of responses leading to a reward.

5.95 b
p. 181
Applied
M

A procedure whereby an instructor first rewards the final response in a sequence of to-be-learned responses and then moves backward in training the entire sequence of responses is called
a. shaping.
b. chaining.
c. flooding.
d. backward conditioning.

5.96 b
p. 182
Applied
M
PT/OLSG

Animals that have been shaped to do unusual behavior may return to more natural behavior. This is called
a. extinction.
b. instinctive drift.
c. acquisition.
d. shaping.

5.97 a
p. 182
Applied
M

Even though a person may know that the chances of getting lung cancer may increase as a result of smoking, learning principles may explain why he or she smokes. Of the following, which can best explain such behavior?
a. reward delay
b. reward magnitude
c. instinctive drive
d. spontaneous recovery

5.98 b
p. 182
Applied
M

When given a choice of one cookie now or three cookies later, most children will choose one cookie now. This illustrates which principle of operant conditioning?
a. Larger rewards work better than small ones.
b. Rewards work best if they are immediate.
c. Partial reinforcement produces strong conditioning.
d. The CS should come before the US.

Chapter 5 - Learning: How We're Changed by Experience 99

5.99 Smokers choose immediate pleasure over later potentially negative consequences, a tendency referred to as
c
p. 182   a. pleasurableness.
Applied   b. contrariness.
M   c. impulsiveness.
        d. cohesiveness.

5.100 Mazur (1996) found that when pigeons could choose between an easy, immediate task or a more difficult,
b later task, the pigeons tended to
p. 183   a. seek immediate pleasure.
Study   b. procrastinate.
C   c. behave impulsively.
        d. behave erratically.

5.101 Rules that describe the occurrence or nonoccurrence of reinforcement are referred
b to as
p. 183   a. constraints.
Concept   b. schedules.
M   c. magnitude effects.
        d. observational rules.

5.102 A ratio schedule of reinforcement identifies a response to be reinforced based on
c _____, while an interval schedule identifies the response based on _____.
p. 183   a. principles of operant conditioning; principles of classical conditioning
Concept   b. principles of classical conditioning; principles of operant conditioning
M   c. the number of responses since the last reinforcement; the amount of time since the last reinforcement
        d. the amount of time since the last reinforcement; the number of responses since the last reinforcement

5.103 Which of the following is most likely to be used when helping your child learn
c a new behavior?
p. 183   a. variable ratio schedule
Concept   b. variable interval schedule
M   c. continuous reinforcement schedule
        d. fixed variable schedule

5.104 A cat is trained to press a lever after 40 seconds lapse in order to obtain a piece
b of food. The cat then has to wait another 40 seconds before the lever-press produces
p. 183 another piece of food. Which of the following schedules has been used to train this
Applied cat?
C   a. variable ratio
        b. fixed interval
        c. variable interval
        d. fixed ratio

5.105 The schedule of reinforcement that leads to low rates of responding immediately after
b the presentation of a reward, but a high rate of responding when the time for reward
p. 183 is near is called
Concept   a. fixed ratio.
C   b. fixed interval.
PT/OLSG   c. variable ratio.
        d. variable interval.

5.106 The schedule that tends to produce a steady rate of responding without pauses is a
a
p. 183 a. variable interval schedule.
Concept b. fixed ratio schedule.
M c. variable ratio schedule.
d. fixed interval schedule.

5.107 Fishing, by casting your line and reeling it in after different intervals of time, is an
b example of a
p. 183 a. fixed interval schedule.
Applied b. variable interval schedule.
M c. fixed ratio schedule.
d. variable ratio schedule.

5.108 The schedule where reinforcement occurs only after a constant number of responses
c is called
p. 184 a. fixed interval schedule.
Fact b. fixed contingency schedule.
M c. fixed ratio schedule.
d. fixed blocking schedule.

5.109 If a cash bonus is given to a salesperson for every 10th car sold, the schedule of
b reinforcement in operation is called a
p. 184 a. fixed interval schedule.
Applied b. fixed ratio schedule.
M c. variable ratio schedule.
d. variable interval schedule.

5.110 Given the likelihood of winning a state lottery, the reward schedule in effect
c is best described as a
p. 184 a. variable interval schedule.
Applied b. fixed interval schedule.
M c. variable ratio schedule.
d. fixed ratio schedule.

5.111 Subjects who are required on average to respond six times to obtain a reward are
b more resistant to extinction than subjects who receive a reward for every response.
p. 184 This phenomenon is referred to as the
Concept a. blocking effect.
M b. partial reinforcement effect.
c. flooding effect.
d. spontaneous recovery effect.

5.112 Behaviors acquired by the _____ schedule are the most resistant to extinction.
d a. fixed interval
p. 184 b. fixed ratio
Concept c. variable interval
M d. variable ratio
PT/OLSG

5.113 A _____ is available when two or more different reinforcement schedules are simultaneously available.
c a. continuous schedule of reinforcement
p. 185 b. intermittent schedule of reinforcement
Concept c. concurrent schedule of reinforcement
M d. matching schedule of reinforcement

Chapter 5 - Learning: How We're Changed by Experience

5.114
b
p. 185
Applied
C

If an animal distributes its behavior between alternative schedules of reinforcement in order to get the largest reinforcement possible, it is following the _____.
a. variable/fixed interval schedule rule.
b. matching law.
c. fixed/variable ratio schedule rule.
d. stimulus control law.

5.115
c
p. 186
Applied
C

Lisa was cleaning her room on a Saturday night, even though she had been asked out by a male student. Which of the following learning phenomena best explains her behavior?
a. stimulus control
b. discriminative stimulus
c. matching law
d. behavioral constraints

5.116
c
p. 186
Concept
M

Stimuli that signal the availability of a reinforcer are called
a. unconditioned stimuli.
b. constraining stimuli.
c. discriminative stimuli.
d. omission stimuli.

5.117
d
p. 186
Applied
C

Your niece will "cuss up a storm" when she is alone with you, but she is the perfect child around her parents. A learning phenomenon that can best explain her behavior is
a. partial reinforcement effect.
b. resistance to extinction.
c. spontaneous recovery.
d. stimulus control.

5.118
a
p. 186
Applied
C
PT/OLSG

Which of the following situations illustrates the function of stimulus control?
a. Using proper table manners when eating with your family, but not when eating alone.
b. Finding that one subject, French for example, is easier for you than Math.
c. Working harder for partial rewards, such as paychecks, than for continuous rewards.
d. Choosing a smaller reward that is immediately available over a larger one that is delayed.

5.119
c
p. 186
Applied
E

Mr. Yuk stickers are good examples of
a. partial reinforcement effect.
b. impulsiveness in behavior.
c. stimulus control of behavior.
d. resistance to extinction.

5.120
b
p. 187
Concept
M

When a response has no effect in either producing reinforcement or providing escape from negative events, organisms give up even when taken to a situation where responding can have an effect. This phenomenon is known as
a. blocking.
b. learned helplessness.
c. cognitive frustration.
d. flooding.

5.121
c
p. 187
Applied
C

An abused child is often hit for no apparent reason. Frequently, the child has no control over when the abuse is delivered. Attempts at stopping the abuse frequently fail, and the child often just puts up with the abuse. This situation can be explained on the basis of
a. biological constraints.
b. conditioned phobias.
c. learned helplessness.
d. omission training.

5.122
a
p. 188
Study
C

The results of research on the relationship between neophobia and learned helplessness indicated that in the group that received an intermediate number of shocks,
a. learned helplessness was more likely to occur among neophobic rats.
b. learned helplessness was less likely to occur among neophobic rats.
c. learned helplessness was unrelated to neophobia.
d. learned helplessness was highly related to neophobia, but only in those rats receiving "inescapable" shocks.

5.123
d
p. 188
Concept
M

Research with humans indicates that beliefs about schedules of reinforcement may have
a. no effect on behavior.
b. effects identical to the schedules themselves.
c. less effects than the schedules themselves.
d. greater effects than the schedules themselves.

5.124
a
p. 188
Concept
M
PT/OLSG

A positive contrast effect occurs when subjects are shifted from a _____ to a _____ reward.
a. small; large
b. large; small
c. positive; negative
d. negative; positive

5.125
b
p. 189
Concept
M

A negative contrast effect occurs when subjects are shifted from a _____ to a _____ reward.
a. small; large
b. large; small
c. positive; negative
d. negative; positive

5.126
b
p. 189
Applied
M

Two students take the same Psychology test after studying in their usual way, and both get a B. One student has previously gotten only Cs, while the other has previously gotten only As. The contrast effect would predict that
a. the student who got As before will study harder this week.
b. the student who got Cs before will study harder this week.
c. both students will study much harder this week.
d. their previous experience will have no effect on their future behavior.

5.127
b
p. 190
Concept
M

Tolman theorized that all organisms form a mental representation of their environment. For example, rats form a mental representation of a maze simply by walking through the maze whether or not they receive a reinforcer. This representation is referred to as
a. an excitatory association.
b. a cognitive map.
c. a sensory label.
d. a motor route.

Chapter 5 - Learning: How We're Changed by Experience

5.128
d
p. 190
Concept
M
The term "cognitive map" refers to an organism's
a. beliefs about their schedule of reinforcement.
b. expectations that the US will follow the CS.
c. discriminative control over a stimulus.
d. mental representation of its environment.

5.129
d
p. 190
Concept
M
An internal mental representation of locations in space that can be used to navigate from point to point in a space is called a
a. response locator.
b. routing sequence.
c. behavioral guide.
d. cognitive map.

5.130
b
p. 190
Applied
C
The work of Capaldi and his colleagues indicate that rewards that animals receive provide a basis for reward memories, which may function as _____ for subsequent behavior.
a. reinforcing stimuli.
b. discriminative stimuli.
c. chaining stimuli.
d. conditioned stimuli.

5.131
b
p. 190
Concept
M
The branch of psychology called "applied behavior analysis" was directed primarily toward
a. investigating psychotic behavior.
b. solving problems of everyday life.
c. developing principles of psychoanalysis.
d. investigating problems of learning principles.

5.132
c
p. 190
Concept
M
"DO IT" stands for
a. determine, operate, intervene, terminate.
b. determine, organize, investigate, test.
c. define, observe, intervene, test.
d. define, organize, investigate, terminate.

5.133
c
p. 190
Concept
M
In the "intervene" stage of "DO IT," a researcher develops a technique to
a. change the impact of a response in a targeted situation.
b. intervene in the target behavior of two individuals.
c. change a target behavior in a desired direction.
d. modify the stimulus of the target behavior.

5.134
a
p. 191
Applied
M
The results of the research study on graffiti (Watson, 1996) in your textbook indicated that the
a. posters reduced the amount of graffiti on the bathroom walls.
b. posters increased the amount of graffiti on the bathroom walls.
c. posters were removed from the bathroom walls and had no effect on graffiti.
d. posters were covered with graffiti when the researcher returned.

5.135
c
p. 192
Applied
C
PT/OLSG
The procedure of placing posters in three bathrooms sequentially in order to see the effect of these posters on graffiti is called
a. sequential behavior design.
b. random behavioral technique.
c. multiple-baseline design.
d. sequential baseline technique.

104 Test Bank - Essentials of Psychology (2nd Edition)

5.136 One of the most important functions of computer-assisted instruction (CAI) is that
a it provides
p. 192 a. immediate reinforcement of correct responses.
Concept b. more difficult problems for students to work on.
M c. less work for overburdened teachers to do.
  d. identical experiences for all students.

5.137 Lisa has a headache, but is able to monitor her muscle tension by a light that
b increases or decreases in intensity depending upon the muscle tension. She is able
p. 192 to reduce her headache by reducing the intensity of the light. This technique is
Applied called
M a. muscle monitoring.
  b. biofeedback.
  c. tension reduction.
  d. muscle relaxation.

5.138 By using _____, Petty and his colleagues found that an employee incentive plan
c resulted in increased productivity and increased the perception of employee teamwork
p. 194 and participative decision making.
Applied a. applied industrial/organizational principles
C b. applied operant conditioning
  c. applied behavior analysis
  d. applied production analysis

Observational Learning: Learning from the Behavior and Outcomes of Others

5.139 Lisa constantly watches professional basketball games. Whenever she sees a new
c shot performed, she goes to the court and tries it out. Her change in behavior due
p. 194 to watching the games can best be explained on the basis of
Applied a. instrumental learning.
M b. classical conditioning.
  c. observational learning.
  d. operant conditioning.

5.140 Daytime television is full of programs in which the hosts cook meals, make decorations,
d and paint pictures on camera. The usefulness of these programs depends on the
p. 194 functioning of
Applied a. classical conditioning.
M b. schedules of reinforcement.
  c. chaining.
  d. observational learning.

5.141 Children who watched an adult attack a doll were more likely to later attack the doll.
d This is evidence for the importance of
p. 195 a. classical conditioning.
Applied b. maturational development.
M c. stimulus generalization.
  d. observational learning.

5.142 Albert Bandura analyzed the process of observational learning and concluded that
c four factors were important. These factors are
p. 195 a. the CS, the US, the CR, and the UR.
Applied b. stimulus generalization, discrimination, control, and reinforcement.
C c. attention, retention, production process, and motivation.
PT/OLSG d. classical, operant, motivational, and sensory conditioning.

Chapter 5 - Learning: How We're Changed by Experience

5.143
d
p. 195
Concept
E

Which of the following influences observational learning?
a. flooding
b. biofeedback
c. desensitization
d. motivation

5.144
a
p. 195
Concept
M

Bandura refers to an individual's capacity to monitor performance while adjusting it until it matches that of the model and the individual's physical ability to perform the observed behavior as
a. production processes.
b. learned helplessness.
c. motivational factors.
d. attention factors.

5.145
d
p. 195
Concept
M

Which of the following factors is not necessary for observational learning to occur?
a. attending to appropriate models
b. remembering what the models did
c. motivation to perform the observed behavior
d. being sensitive to the appropriate behavior

5.146
a
p. 196
Concept
M

If you are concerned that television viewers may acquire new ways to express aggression, then as a learning theorist you are most likely to be concerned with
a. observational learning.
b. blocking phenomenon.
c. systematic desensitization.
d. reinforcement schedules.

5.147
b
p. 196
Concept
C

Which of the following has not been shown to be related to television violence?
a. aggressive behavior
b. improved work performance
c. lessened emotional reactions to violence
d. acceptance of violence

5.148
a
p. 196
Concept
M

People who watch violent TV programs will witness new ways of committing violence, which they may then
a. put into practice when they get angry or frustrated.
b. reinforce when they see them in others.
c. classically condition to a conditioned stimulus.
d. put under the control of a discriminative stimulus.

5.149
c
p. 197
Applied
C

Which of the following eighth graders is more likely to start smoking?
a. an "outsider" student whose enemy does not smoke
b. an "outsider" student whose best friend does not smoke
c. an "outsider" student whose best friend started smoking in the seventh grade
d. an "outsider" student whose parents smoke

5.150
a
p. 198
Applied
C

The study that indicated that mildly retarded children learned various behaviors through watching non-handicapped peers model the appropriate behavior supports the idea
a. that observational learning is very efficient, since the retarded students watched the other students for five minutes per day.
b. that observational learning is not efficient because the retarded students had to watch the other students very carefully for 5 minutes per day.
c. that observational learning is not efficient since the behaviors were trivial and not of any lasting importance.
d. that observational learning is important, since without it, we would not have BoBo dolls.

106 Test Bank - Essentials of Psychology (2nd Edition)

5.151
b
p. 151
Concept
M

One major reason for the difficulties that sometimes occur between people of different cultures is that
a. people from different parts of the world have different feelings.
b. some cultures encourage behaviors that other cultures call offensive.
c. most people are intentionally rude to people from other cultures.
d. there is very little that people from different cultures have in common.

5.152
d
p. 198
Concept
C

Early cross-cultural training programs used which technique to teach employees better ways to interact with people from other cultures?
a. classical conditioning
b. operant conditioning
c. observational learning
d. presenting factual information about other cultures

5.153
a
p. 198
Concept
C

Most modern cross-cultural training programs use which technique to teach employees better ways to interact with people from other cultures?
a. information and practice of appropriate social behavior
b. stimulus generalization and stimulus discrimination
c. classical conditioning
d. operant conditioning

5.154
b
p. 199
Concept
M

Research suggests that learning culturally appropriate behaviors can best be accomplished with
a. cognitive training through provision of culture-relevant information.
b. both the provision of culture-relevant information and behavioral modeling through films.
c. behavioral modeling through films.
d. classical conditioning and operant methods of reinforcement.

5.155
a
p. 199
Concept
M

Research findings on reducing cross-cultural difficulties indicate that
a. just as observational learning teaches us our own culture, it can help us learn another culture.
b. we learn our own culture through classical conditioning, but we learn another culture through operant conditioning.
c. culture, either our own or another, is not something that can be learned or taught.
d. everyone learns about culture in a unique, individual way.

5.156
c
p. 199
Applied
M
PT/OLSG

If you were starting a weight loss program, which of the following principles of learning would be of most importance to you?
a. spontaneous recovery
b. blocking
c. shaping
d. extinction

5.157
b
p. 199
Applied
M

If you were going to use the principle of stimulus control in your weight loss plan, how would you use it?
a. only pay attention to stimuli that were relevant to your weight loss goals
b. stay out of places that would tempt you to consume unhealthy foods
c. stay out of places that encourage you to eat healthy foods
d. only pay attention to stimuli that are positive food stimuli

Chapter 6 - Memory: Of Things Remembered ... and Forgotten

CHAPTER 6

Multiple-Choice Questions

6.1 Our cognitive system for storing and retrieving information is called
a
p. 206   a. memory.
Concept   b. sensation.
M   c. perception.
   d. schemata.

6.2 Some of the earliest systematic research in the field of human memory was conducted
b over 100 years ago by
p. 206   a. Pavlov.
Fact   b. Ebbinghaus.
E   c. Thorndike.
   d. Watson.

Human Memory: The Information-Processing Approach

6.3 Human memory is especially superior to a computer in its ability to
a
p. 207   a. locate and retrieve material using only partial cues.
Concept   b. store and retain lots of information in a complete unchanged form.
M   c. quickly encode multiple calculations.
   d. do repetitive memory actions for a long period of time.

6.4 Memory is generally characterized on the basis of
c
p. 207   a. exposure, attention, and retention.
Concept   b. acquisition, extinction, and spontaneous recovery.
M   c. encoding, storage, and retrieval.
   d. reminiscence, attention, and interpretation.

6.5 The way information is entered into memory is called
b
p. 207   a. retrieval.
Concept   b. encoding.
M   c. storage.
   d. programming.

6.6 Retaining information in a memory system over varying periods of time is referred
b to as
p. 207   a. encoding.
Concept   b. storage.
M   c. retrieval.
   d. chunking.

6.7 Locating and accessing specific information from memory when it is needed at later
c times is referred to as
p. 207   a. encoding.
Concept   b. storage.
M   c. retrieval.
PT/OLSG   d. consolidation.

6.8 The trail of light left behind by waving a flashlight in a dark room is an example of
b
p. 207   a. short-term memory.
Concept b. sensory memory.
M   c. working memory.
         d. immediate memory.

6.9 The memory system that holds very briefly all the information available to your senses is called
c
p. 207   a. short-term memory.
Concept b. episodic memory.
M   c. sensory memory.
         d. flashbulb memory.

6.10 Having been introduced to a new person at a party and then forgetting her name a few
a   minutes later is an example of losing information from
p. 207   a. short-term memory.
Applied b. sensory memory.
M   c. meta-memory.
         d. long-term memory.

6.11 Memory that holds small amounts of information for about 30 seconds or less is called
d
p. 207   a. quick memory.
Concept b. sensory memory.
M   c. immediate memory.
         d. short-term memory.

6.12 Memory that holds vast amounts of information for very long periods of time is called
b
p. 208   a. sensory memory.
Concept b. long-term memory.
M   c. prospective memory.
         d. perceptual memory.

6.13 According to the information-processing model of memory, attention and
b   elaborative rehearsal are examples of
p. 208   a. maintenance processes.
Concept b. control processes.
M   c. prospective memory.
         d. chunking.

6.14 According to the information-processing approach, information in short-term
a   memory enters into long-term memory largely as a result of
p. 209   a. elaborative rehearsal.
Concept b. storage rehearsal.
M   c. sensory imaging.
         d. confabulation.

6.15 The control process that is most involved in determining which material moves from
c   sensory memory to the short-term memory is
p. 209   a. elaborative rehearsal.
Concept b. maintenance rehearsal.
M   c. selective attention.
         d. chunking.

Chapter 6 - Memory: Of Things Remembered ... and Forgotten

6.16
a
p. 209
Concept
M

In one model of memory, selective attention is the control process that moves information from _____ to _____.
a. sensory memory; short-term memory
b. short-term memory; long-term memory
c. long-term memory; episodic memory
d. episodic memory; semantic memory

6.17
b
p. 209
Concept
M

Knowing how to drive is an example of _____ memory; remembering when you learned to drive is an example of _____ memory.
a. semantic; procedural
b. procedural; episodic
c. procedural; semantic
d. episodic; procedural

6.18
c
p. 209
Concept
M
PT/OLSG

Memory that involves the total of each person's general, abstract knowledge about the world is called
a. episodic memory.
b. procedural memory.
c. semantic memory.
d. context-dependent memory.

6.19
a
p. 209
Concept
E

Memory that involves specific events personally experienced is called
a. episodic memory.
b. procedural memory.
c. semantic memory.
d. historical memory.

6.20
b
p. 209
Applied
M

Your ability to remember who attended your last party requires you to use
a. procedural memory.
b. episodic memory.
c. semantic memory.
d. elaborative memory.

6.21
c
p. 209
Concept
M

Memory that is the result of basic learning processes and contains information relating to the performance of various tasks is called
a. episodic memory.
b. semantic memory.
c. procedural memory.
d. declarative memory.

6.22
d
p. 209
Concept
M

Performance is to verbal description as
a. episodic memory is to semantic memory.
b. semantic memory is to episodic memory.
c. semantic memory is to procedural memory.
d. procedural memory is to semantic memory.

Sensory Memory, Short-Term Memory, and Long-Term Memory: Our Basic Memory Systems

6.23
b
p. 211
Applied
C

Roger Sperling's research demonstrated that sensory memory
a. holds only a small amount of information.
b. holds an extremely large amount of information.
c. allows for elaborative rehearsal.
d. may last for several minutes.

6.24
c
p. 211
Applied
M

Research by Sperling indicates that an extremely large amount of information is held for a very short time, one second or less, in
a. short-term memory.
b. context-dependent memory.
c. sensory memory.
d. declarative memory.

6.25
d
p. 211
Concept
M

A memory system referred to as the workbench for consciousness that is used for temporarily holding information currently being processed is called
a. sensory memory.
b. episodic memory.
c. procedural memory.
d. short-term memory.

6.26
a
p. 212
Applied
M

According to the serial position curve, if given the list: reptile, monkey, house, computer, report, disk, system, paper, dream, you would most easily remember the word
a. reptile.
b. disk.
c. computer.
d. report.

6.27
c
p. 212
Concept
E

Words at the end of a list are more easily remembered because they may be in
a. sensory memory.
b. long-term memory.
c. short-term memory.
d. procedural memory.

6.28
b
p. 213
Applied
M
PT/OLSG

The finding that memory span for immediate recall of lists of short words is greater than for lists of longer words is known as the
a. word similarity effect.
b. word length effect.
c. word processing effect.
d. word scanning effect.

6.29
c
p. 213
Concept
M

The word similarity effect indicates that memory span for immediate recall is greater for _____ words than for _____ words.
a. similar; dissimilar
b. longer; shorter
c. dissimilar; similar
d. shorter; longer

6.30
d
p. 213
Concept
M

Research dealing with short-term memory suggests that most verbal input is stored
a. visually.
b. episodically.
c. semantically.
d. phonologically.

6.31
b
p. 213
Concept
C

Sound is to meaning as
a. long-term memory is to short-term memory.
b. short-term memory is to long-term memory.
c. context-dependent memory is to procedural memory.
d. procedural memory is to context-dependent memory.

Chapter 6 - Memory: Of Things Remembered ... and Forgotten 111

6.32
a
p. 213
Concept
C

Research examining short-term memory suggests that if given a list of letters to memorize you are most likely to confuse which of the following?
a. T for D
b. O for D
c. S for U
d. Q for P

6.33
a
p. 213
Concept
C

If Lisa is asked to memorize a list of words and recite them days later, which of these pairs of words is she least likely to get mixed up in her memory?
a. Dad and Father
b. Dad and Bad
c. Cup and Cap
d. Book and Look

6.34
c
p. 213
Concept
M

The capacity of short-term memory is
a. only one idea at any one time.
b. essentially unlimited.
c. around seven chunks.
d. impossible to measure.

6.35
d
p. 213
Concept
M

What would make it easier to hold the string "GOF ORT HEG OLD" in your memory for short time?
a. Improving the efficiency of your selective attention process.
b. Removing all proactive and retroactive inhibition processes.
c. Applying the letters to the serial position curve.
d. Reorganizing the letters into meaningful chunks: "GO FOR THE GOLD."

6.36
b
p. 213
Concept
M

The process of combining separate pieces of information into units in short-term memory is called
a. acoustical storage.
b. chunking.
c. reminiscence.
d. paired-associate learning.

6.37
d
p. 215
Concept
M
PT/OLSG

Which of the following is used to keep information active in the short-term memory system?
a. chunking
b. semantic storage
c. acoustical storage
d. rehearsal

6.38
a
p. 215
Concept
M

As long as information is rehearsed, it can remain in short-term memory
a. indefinitely.
b. about 25 seconds.
c. seven (plus or minus two) minutes.
d. no longer than 15 minutes.

6.39
d
p. 215
Applied
C

PET scans have been used to determine the presence of short-term memory. In one study, these scans indicated that the _____ is crucial for the storage of information in short-term memory.
a. reticular activation system
b. anterior occipital system
c. temporal lobe
d. posterior parietal cortex

112 Test Bank - Essentials of Psychology (2nd Edition)

6.40 a
p. 215
Concept
M

The amount of information held in long-term memory is _____, and it lasts a(n) _____ amount of time.
a. effectively infinite; indefinite
b. very large; very short
c. quite small; extremely long
d. limited to important facts; variable

6.41 b
p. 215
Concept
M

The situation where we often feel that a fact, name, or event we want is somewhere in our memory, but is just beyond our reach is called the
a. reminiscence effect.
b. tip-of-the-tongue phenomenon.
c. phi phenomenon.
d. hypermnesia effect.

6.42 a
p. 215
Concept
M
PT/OLSG

The tip-of-the-tongue phenomenon occurs when we are trying to remember a fact, but instead we
a. remember other information related to the fact.
b. can't remember ever having known about it.
c. remember the fact incorrectly.
d. avoid the memory because it is too traumatic.

6.43 c
p. 216
Concept
M

The process of repeating information over and over to hold it in short-term memory is called _____, while the process of associating it with other information and analyzing its meaning is called _____.
a. consolidation; metamemory
b. metamemory; consolidation
c. maintenance rehearsal; elaborative rehearsal
d. elaborative rehearsal; maintenance rehearsal

6.44 c
p. 216
Concept
E

Considering the meaning of new information and relating it to other knowledge already present in memory is referred to as
a. maintenance rehearsal.
b. reminiscence.
c. elaborative rehearsal.
d. chunking.

6.45 a
p. 216
Applied
C

Research results obtained by Birnbaum and Parker (1977) indicate that alcohol
a. interferes with long-term memory performance by interfering with elaborative rehearsal.
b. facilitates long-term memory performance by improving elaborative rehearsal.
c. interferes with long-term memory performance by distorting short-term memory.
d. has no effect on long-term memory.

6.46 b
p. 216
Concept
M

A model of memory in which emphasis is placed on processes that contribute to remembering rather than on different memory systems is called
a. modal model.
b. levels of processing model.
c. parallel distributed processing model.
d. consolidation model.

6.47 c
p. 216
Concept
M

Repetition is to meaning as
a. semantic memory is to episodic memory.
b. episodic memory is to semantic memory.
c. shallow processing is to deep processing.
d. deep processing is to shallow processing.

Chapter 6 - Memory: Of Things Remembered ... and Forgotten

6.48
d
p. 216
Concept
M

Which of the following involves shallow processing of information?
a. determining if two words are synonyms
b. deciding if a word fits in a sentence
c. thinking of antonyms of a specific word
d. counting the number of letters in a word

6.49
b
p. 216
Applied
M
PT/OLSG

Which of the following requires the deepest level of processing when learning a list of words?
a. repeating the information
b. elaborative rehearsal
c. determining whether two words rhyme
d. judgements as to whether two words look alike

6.50
a
p. 216
Applied
M

Which of these questions would lead to the deepest sort of processing?
a. Does the word rhyme with BALL?
b. Is the word pleasant or unpleasant?
c. How many letters are in the word?
d. Is the word printed in red ink?

6.51
c
p. 217
Concept
M

Being able to locate information that has previously been stored in memory refers to
a. encoding specificity.
b. elaborative rehearsal.
c. retrieval.
d. consolidation.

6.52
d
p. 217
Concept
M

Information that was studied for a test, but that you have not been able to remember in answering questions relevant to the learned information, represents a problem with
a. storage.
b. episodic memory.
c. procedural memory.
d. retrieval.

6.53
c
p. 217
Concept
M

One key to effective retrieval of information from long-term memory is _____.
a. persistence
b. rehearsal
c. organization
d. consolidation

6.54
b
p. 217
Applied
M

Ralph is taking a test in physiological psychology and needs to remember the organization of the nervous system and spinal cord. One way for him to increase the probability of remembering the organization of these systems is to construct a
a. scatter plot.
b. hierarchical classification scheme.
c. top-down processing system.
d. coordinated listing program.

6.55
a
p. 218
Concept
E
PT/OLSG

Stimuli that are associated with information stored in memory that help to evoke the memory when it cannot be recalled spontaneously are called
a. retrieval cues.
b. storage cues.
c. shallow cues.
d. deep cues.

6.56 b
p. 218
Fact
M

The fact that material learned in one environment is more difficult to remember in an environment very different than the original one is called
a. episodic retention.
b. context-dependent memory.
c. tip-of-the-tongue phenomenon.
d. Korsakoff's syndrome.

6.57 c
p. 218
Applied
M

If you believe that studying in the classroom where you take your tests will help you do well on the tests, you are attempting to facilitate retention on the basis of
a. flashbulb memory.
b. state-dependent memory.
c. context-dependent memory.
d. phonological memory.

6.58 d
p. 218
Concept
M

The principle of state-dependent retrieval states that information will be remembered better when the learner is
a. in an altered state of consciousness (e.g., drunk).
b. highly motivated to remember the information.
c. trained in certain specific mnemonic techniques.
d. in the same physiological state as when the information was learned.

6.59 d
p. 219
Concept
M

The phenomenon indicating that what you remember in a specific mood may be determined by what you had learned previously in that mood is called
a. mood congruence effect.
b. mood processing effect.
c. mood consolidation memory.
d. mood dependent memory.

6.60 a
p. 219
Concept
C

The mood in which we learned information is to the affective nature of the material as
a. mood dependent memory is to mood congruence effect.
b. mood congruence effect is to mood dependent memory.
c. mood consolidation memory is to mood dependent memory.
d. mood congruence effect is to mood consolidation effect.

6.61 b
p. 220
Applied
C

One of the difficulties with the research indicating that food related odors stimulate sexual arousal in males is that
a. food related aromas do not constitute a legitimate area of research.
b. research participants may have been able to detect the experimenters' expectancies.
c. measuring sexual arousal in males does not constitute an ethical procedure.
d. the subjects were coerced into participation because of being clients.

Forgetting from Long-Term Memory

6.62 c
p. 221
Concept
M
PT/OLSG

Ebbinghaus' early research indicated that forgetting is rapid at first and then slows down with the passage of time. This occurs most often when
a. recognizing faces.
b. retaining motor skills.
c. remembering nonsense syllables.
d. recalling life events.

Chapter 6 - Memory: Of Things Remembered ... and Forgotten

6.63 Which of the following concepts have been put forth to explain forgetting from long-term
d memory?
p. 222   a. episodic and semantic memory
Concept   b. interference and hypermnesia
M   c. decay and phonological loops
    d. decay and interference

6.64 Skills requiring associations between specific stimuli and specific responses are subject to a high degree of
a forgetting in long-term memory. These skills are labeled
p. 222   a. discrete skills.
Concept   b. decay skills.
M   c. association skills.
    d. response skills.

6.65 Most modern research on decay theory as an explanation for why we forget information
b supports the conclusion that decay theory
p. 222   a. explains most forgetting from long-term memory.
Concept   b. explains very little of why forgetting occurs.
M   c. explains why we forget pictures but not words.
    d. explains why we forget skills but not images.

6.66 What is the present status of the trace decay hypothesis?
a   a. It is not widely accepted.
p. 222   b. It is used to explain forgetting in long-term memory, but not short-term memory.
Concept   c. It is used to explain forgetting in procedural memory.
E   d. It is fairly widely accepted by clinicians.

6.67 A few weeks after Lisa had her phone number changed she had difficulty remembering
c her former phone number. The most likely explanation for failing to remember the
p. 223 old number is
Concept   a. prospective memory.
M   b. repression.
    c. retroactive interference.
    d. proactive interference.

6.68 When new items interfere with those learned earlier, the interference is called
b   a. reactive.
p. 223   b. retroactive.
Concept   c. proactive.
M   d. anticipatory.

6.69 Interference that occurs when information previously entered into memory interferes
b with the learning or storage of current information is called
p. 223   a. retroactive interference.
Concept   b. proactive interference.
C   c. prospective interference.
PT/OLSG   d. elaborative interference.

6.70 The most important factor in forgetting appears to be
c   a. attention.
p. 223   b. emotion.
Concept   c. interference.
M   d. decay.

6.71 d p. 223 Applied M

Last year Ralph took Spanish; this year he is taking French. If learning French makes him forget the Spanish he once knew, it is called _____ interference. If the Spanish he learned before makes it harder to learn the French, it is called _____ interference.
a. elaborative; selective
b. selective; elaborative
c. proactive; retroactive
d. retroactive; proactive

6.72 b p. 224 Concept M PT/OLSG

People who challenge the accuracy of recovered memories of childhood abuse will often argue that
a. there are too few of these cases to draw any conclusions.
b. misguided therapists often push these ideas on their clients.
c. people are faking these claims in an attempt to get money.
d. people do not ever forget anything that happens to them.

6.73 d p. 224 Concept M

Which of the following is not true concerning repression?
a. Little, if any research evidence has been obtained supporting its existence.
b. Reading about repression may influence an individual into believing that traumatic events must have taken place to explain current psychological problems.
c. Therapists can create demand characteristics that can produce reports of access to repressed memories.
d. There is considerable support from memory researchers concerning the existence of repression.

6.74 d p. 225 Concept M

When people forget material because they want to forget, consciously or unconsciously, it is called
a. retroactive interference.
b. proactive interference.
c. state-dependent learning.
d. intentional forgetting.

6.75 b p. 225 Applied M

The "lost car" effect is an example of failure of
a. proactive forgetting
b. intentional forgetting.
c. retroactive forgetting.
d. consistency forgetting.

6.76 c p. 225 Concept C

One explanation for the success of intentional forgetting is that we tend
a. rehearse the information so that it is easy to eliminate.
b. retrieve the information with special cues.
c. encode the information so that it is easy to eliminate.
d. store the information so that it is easy to eliminate.

Memory in Natural Contexts

6.77 d p. 226 Fact E

Memory for events of our lives is called _____ memory.
a. semantic
b. procedural
c. personal
d. autobiographical

6.78 b p. 226 Applied M PT/OLSG

Questioning 60-year-old subjects about their college years by asking them the names of their teachers, courses they took, dorms they lived in, etc., is investigating
a. prospective memory.
b. autobiographical memory.
c. phonological loop.
d. method of loci.

Chapter 6 - Memory: Of Things Remembered ... and Forgotten

6.79
c
p. 226
Study
M

Willem Wagenaar (1986) investigated his autobiographical memory by using the
a. episodic recall approach.
b. personal questionnaire approach.
c. diary study approach.
d. method of loci.

6.80
a
p. 226
Concept
M

The inability to recall events that happened to us during the first two or three years of life is known as
a. infantile amnesia.
b. toddler repression.
c. neonatal interference.
d. childhood suppression.

6.81
d
p. 226
Concept
M

Which of the following is an illustration of infantile amnesia?
a. Lisa has forgotten the French her first nanny taught her.
b. "I know my sister got married, and I know I got a new car, but I cannot remember which came first."
c. "I remember I moved in 1988, because my son started kindergarten right after that, when he was five."
d. "I remember starting my new job, but I cannot remember where I lived as a baby, or whether my daughter was born there."

6.82
c
p. 227
Applied
M
PT/OLSG

According to Howe and Courage, the most likely explanation currently held for the inability to remember what happened during the first two or three years of life is
a. insufficient brain mechanisms.
b. the lack of language during this time period.
c. the lack of self-concept during this time period.
d. immaturity of the autonomic nervous system.

6.83
a
p. 227
Concept
M

Infantile amnesia appears to be due to children not having well-developed
a. self-concepts.
b. memory systems.
c. language systems.
d. semantic memory systems.

6.84
c
p. 227
Concept
M

The component whose development finally gives us the ability to remember the events in our lives is
a. the ability to use language to express ideas.
b. hemispheric connections through the corpus callosum.
c. the concept of ourselves as individuals.
d. a functioning long-term memory system.

6.85
b
p. 227
Concept
M

Which of these questions is most likely to elicit a flashbulb memory?
a. Who was the best student in your high school graduating class?
b. Where were you when you heard about the LA earthquake?
c. How many states of the United States can you name in 10 minutes?
d. What did you have for breakfast yesterday?

6.86
c
p. 227
Concept
M
PT/OLSG

Compared with other memories, flashbulb memories are generally
a. more semantic and less episodic.
b. of events that happened long ago.
c. not particularly accurate.
d. extremely accurate.

6.87   c   p. 227   Concept   M

A vivid image of what we were doing at the time we learned of some dramatic event such as the space shuttle disaster is called
a. tip-of-the-tongue phenomenon.
b. confabulation.
c. flashbulb memory.
d. prospective memory.

6.88   b   p. 227   Concept   M

Flashbulb memories
a. are perceived as extremely accurate and when checked turn out to be very accurate.
b. are perceived as extremely accurate by the individual, but often involve errors.
c. are vague yet highly accurate.
d. are more accurate as we age.

Memory Distortion and Memory Construction

6.89   c   p. 228   Concept   M

With respect to memory errors, alteration is to addition as
a. procedural memory is to declarative memory.
b. declarative memory is to procedural memory.
c. distortion is to construction.
d. construction is to distortion.

6.90   d   p. 228   Concept   M

Memory errors involving alteration in what is remembered and reported are called _____ errors.
a. schema
b. phonological
c. construction
d. distortion

6.91   a   p. 228   Concept   M

Memory errors involving addition of information that was not originally present, or in some cases, creation of memories that never took place, are called _____ errors.
a. construction
b. distortion
c. omission
d. phonological

6.92   b   p. 228   Concept   M   PT/OLSG

Cognitive structures representing individuals' knowledge and assumptions about the world are called
a. phonological loops.
b. schemas.
c. flashbulb memories.
d. distortions.

6.93   c   p. 229   Concept   M

Recognizing inconsistent information is to recognizing consistent information as
a. procedure memory is to episodic memory.
b. semantic memory is to declarative memory.
c. new schema is to established schema.
d. proactive interference is to retroactive interference.

6.94   c   p. 229   Concept   M   PT/OLSG

Information that is _____ with well-developed schemas is encoded more readily than information that is _____ with our schemas.
a. inconsistent; consistent
b. not parallel; parallel
c. consistent; inconsistent
d. parallel; not parallel

Chapter 6 - Memory: Of Things Remembered ... and Forgotten

6.95
a
p. 229
Study
M

McDonald and Hirt (1997) found that students who liked a stranger distorted their memories to place this individual in a more favorable light, indicating that _____ plays a role in memory.
a. motivation
b. distortion
c. enhancement
d. elaboration

6.96
a
p. 230
Applied
C

There is a growing body of evidence that indicates that among children, false memories may
a. be more persistent than real memories.
b. be more varied than real memories.
c. be less persistent than real memories.
d. be less persistent than real memories.

6.97
b
p. 230
Study
C

Brainerd and his colleagues (1995), in testing children's recall for words, found that for older children
a. accuracy was greater for animate than inanimate categories.
b. errors were more persistent than accurate memories.
c. accurate memories were more persistent than errors.
d. errors only occurred for specific words.

6.98
d
p. 231
Study
M

Research dealing with simulations of eyewitness testimony completed by Loftus and her colleagues suggests that eyewitness testimony
a. is very resistant to retroactive interference.
b. can be easily explained on the basis of encoding specificity.
c. is rather accurate and not easily influenced by other factors.
d. can be influenced by leading questions.

6.99
b
p. 231
Concept
M

A growing body of evidence seems to indicate that if events that really didn't happen are _____ they will have a greater likelihood of being accepted as part of someone's memory.
a. exciting
b. plausible
c. consistent
d. memorable

6.100
a
p. 232
Concept
M

Which of the following is a recommendation for improving the accuracy of eyewitness memory?
a. Have subjects recall the events they have seen in a variety of different orders or sequences.
b. Have subjects describe the crime in their own words and then ask specific questions about the events.
c. Tell subjects to focus only on the specifics of the crime they supposedly saw.
d. Tell subjects to isolate memories of the crime from the context in which it occurred.

6.101
b
p. 232
Applied
M

One ineffective technique for increasing the accuracy of eyewitness testimony is to
a. ask the eyewitness to report everything that can be remembered.
b. ask the eyewitness to recall over and over what was seen.
c. ask the eyewitness to imagine being back at the scene and reconstruct the as many details as possible.
d. ask the eyewitness to describe the event from as many perspectives as possible.

6.102
c
p. 232
Applied
M

Most of the research indicates that hypnotizing an eyewitness will
a. probably increase the accuracy of the report.
b. probably decrease the accuracy of the report.
c. probably not increase the accuracy of the report.
d. probably raise different issues concerning the report.

120   Test Bank - Essentials of Psychology (2nd Edition)

6.103   Children from traditional societies many times perform more poorly on standardized
b   memory tests than children from industrial societies. This finding emphasizes the fact that
p. 234   a. memory is not culturally contained.
Concept   b. memory occurs against a cultural background.
M   c. memory is culturally contained.
PT/OLSG   d. memory occurs independent of cultural background.

The Biological Bases of Memory: How the Brain Stores Knowledge

6.104   Impairment of memory for events that occur prior to severe head injury is called
b   a. anterograde amnesia.
p. 235   b. retrograde amnesia.
Applied   c. hypermnesia.
M   d. selective forgetting.

6.105   Impairment of memory for events that occur after a serious operation is called
c   a. hypermnesia.
p. 235   b. distortion.
Applied   c. anterograde amnesia.
M   d. retrograde amnesia.

6.106   Lisa cannot remember events that occurred immediately before her accident. She is
a   suffering from
p. 235   a. retrograde amnesia.
Applied   b. anterograde amnesia.
M   c. proactive interference.
PT/OLSG   d. retroactive interference.

6.107   The severe anterograde amnesia experienced by H.M., whose medial temporal lobes
c   had been removed, was apparently due to an inability to
p. 236   a. hold information in short-term memory.
Applied   b. hold information in long-term memory.
C   c. move information from short-term memory to long-term memory.
           d. move information from long-term memory to short-term memory.

6.108   The process through which information entered into long-term memory becomes
d   stable and durable is
p. 236   a. chunking.
Concept   b. parallel distributed processing.
E   c. schematization.
           d. consolidation.

6.109   An area of the brain assumed to be important in shifting new information from
a   short-term memory to long-term memory is the
p. 236   a. hippocampus.
Concept   b. pineal gland.
M   c. putamen.
           d. occipital lobe.

6.110   Verbal is to nonverbal as
c   a. episodic memory is to semantic memory.
p. 236   b. semantic memory is to episodic memory.
Concept   c. explicit memory is to implicit memory.
M   d. implicit memory is to explicit memory.
PT/OLSG

Chapter 6 - Memory: Of Things Remembered ... and Forgotten

6.111　　　　The hippocampus seems to be important for
c
p. 236　　　　a.　procedural memory.
Concept　　　b.　implicit memory.
　　　　　　　c.　explicit memory.
M　　　　　　d.　semantic memory.

6.112　　　　If the hippocampus is damaged, patients would have the most difficulty with
a
p. 236　　　　a.　explicit memories.
Applied　　　b.　implicit memories.
　　　　　　　c.　procedural memories.
M　　　　　　d.　nonverbal memories.

6.113　　　　If the occipital lobe is damaged, patients would have the most difficulty with
b
p. 236　　　　a.　explicit memory.
Applied　　　b.　implicit memory.
　　　　　　　c.　procedural memory
M　　　　　　d.　nonverbal memory.

6.114　　　　Korsakoff's syndrome is an illness that generally results from
a
p. 237　　　　a.　severe, long-term alcohol abuse.
Concept　　　b.　damage to the hippocampus.
　　　　　　　c.　a viral infection of the liver.
M　　　　　　d.　overuse of amphetamines.

6.115　　　　Which portions of the brain are damaged in patients with Korsakoff's syndrome?
a
p. 237　　　　a.　The thalamus and hypothalamus
Concept　　　b.　The campus and hippocampus
　　　　　　　c.　The cerebrum and cerebellum
C　　　　　　d.　The pons and medulla

6.116　　　　Korsakoff's syndrome is accompanied by
c
p. 237　　　　a.　retrograde amnesia only.
Concept　　　b.　anterograde amnesia only.
　　　　　　　c.　both retrograde and anterograde amnesia.
M　　　　　　d.　neither retrograde nor anterograde amnesia.

6.117　　　　N.A., the Air Force soldier who had a portion of his brain damaged, provides evidence that the _____ is
a　　　　　　involved in long-term memory.
p. 237　　　　a.　thalamus
Applied　　　b.　medulla
　　　　　　　c.　hippocampus
C　　　　　　d.　pituitary gland

6.118　　　　Which of the following is a symptom of Alzheimer's disease?
a
p. 237　　　　a.　almost total loss of memory
Concept　　　b.　hypermnesia
　　　　　　　c.　reminiscence
E　　　　　　d.　flashbulb memory

6.119　　　　A decrease in acetylcholine and increases in bundles of amyloid beta protein that
c　　　　　　may damage projections from nuclei in the basal forebrain to the hippocampus and
p. 237　　　　cerebral cortex appears to be associated with
Concept　　　a.　flashbulb memories.
C　　　　　　b.　Korsakoff's syndrome.
PT/OLSG　　c.　Alzheimer's disorder.
　　　　　　　d.　schizophrenia.

6.120 The results of research examining Alzheimer's patients suggests that _____ plays a
b   role in memory.
p. 237   a. thyroxin
Concept b. acetylcholine
M   c. adrenalin
         d. endorphins

6.121 A modern view of memories suggests that they are represented
a   a. in multiple locations in the brain.
p. 238   b. only in the hippocampus.
Concept c. in the left hemisphere.
M   d. linearly in the thalamus and hypothalamus.

6.122 When the brain changes so that information can move more easily between certain
a   nerve cells, this creates a(n)
p. 239   a. localized neural circuit.
Concept b. neurological cluster.
C   c. localized memory dysfunction.
         d. greater mental health.

6.123 Possible mechanisms for storing memories in the brain include changes in
c   a. the rate of production of specific neurotransmitter only.
p. 239   b. the structure of the neurons only.
Concept c. both the rate of production of specific neurotransmitters and the structure
C   of the neurons.
PT/OLSG d. neither the rate of production of specific neurotransmitter nor the structure
             of the neurons.

6.124 One very practical suggestion for improving memory is to
b   a. maximize similarity.
p. 240   b. minimize interference.
Applied c. maximize practice.
M   d. minimize mnemonics.

6.125 Using state-dependent retrieval is a way to
a   a. increase retrieval cues.
p. 240   b. decrease retrieval cues.
Applied c. increase coherence.
E   d. decrease coherence.

6.126 Remembering the order of the nine planets by using the sentence "My Very Earnest
c   Mother Just Served Us Purple Nectarines" is an example of memory improvement using
p. 240   a. elaborative rehearsal.
Applied b. method of loci.
M   c. first-letter technique.
         d. confabulation.

Chapter 7 - Cognition and Intelligence

CHAPTER 7

Multiple-Choice Questions

7.1 A general term used to describe various aspects of higher mental processes is
a
p. 246
Fact
E
a. cognition.
b. algorithms.
c. grammar.
d. linguistics.

Thinking: Forming Concepts and Reasoning to Conclusions

7.2 The mental process whereby we transform available information in order to reach
c conclusions is called
p. 246
Concept
M
a. heuristics.
b. algorithms.
c. reasoning.
d. thinking.

7.3 Mental frameworks for categorizing diverse items as belonging together are
d
p. 247
Concept
M
PT/OLSG
a. hypotheses.
b. ideas.
c. prototypes.
d. concepts.

7.4 Which of the following is an example of a concept?
c
p. 247
Applied
M
a. your pet dog
b. the letter z
c. vegetables
d. syllogisms

7.5 Concepts that can be clearly defined by a set of rules or properties are called
d
p. 247
Concept
M
a. propositions.
b. realistic concepts.
c. natural concepts.
d. artificial concepts.

7.6 Concepts such as circle, mammal, and subtraction are examples of
b
p. 247
Applied
C
a. natural concepts.
b. artificial concepts.
c. morphological concepts.
d. available concepts.

7.7 Concepts that have no fixed and readily specified set of defining features are called
c
p. 247
Concept
M
a. expected utilities.
b. availability heuristics.
c. natural concepts.
d. artificial concepts.

7.8 Concepts such as sport, automobile, and scientist are best described as
d
p. 247
Applied
M
a. illogical concepts.
b. logical concepts.
c. artificial concepts.
d. natural concepts.

7.9 A prototype of a concept is a member of the concept that
b
p. 247   a. specifies exactly what members must be like.
Concept   b. is one of the best examples of the concept.
M   c. gives correct and incorrect properties of the concept.
     d. applies to artificial concepts, but not fuzzy concepts.

7.10 The best and clearest example of a natural concept is called a
a
p. 247   a. prototype.
Concept   b. syllogism.
E   c. neural network.
     d. available heuristic.

7.11 Which of the following is a prototype of vehicles?
c
p. 247   a. elevator
Applied   b. motorized skateboard
M   c. automobile
     d. jet backpack

7.12 Concepts can be represented as
d
p. 248   a. images.
Concept   b. features.
M   c. schemas.
PT/OLSG   d. images, features, or schemas.

7.13 Cognitive frameworks that represent our knowledge of and assumptions about the world are called
c
p. 248   a. visual images.
Concept   b. sensory memories.
M   c. schemas.
     d. concepts.

7.14 Schemas differ from concepts in that schemas are
d
p. 248   a. based only on intuition.
Concept   b. acquired through experience.
M   c. more efficient than concepts.
     d. more complex than concepts.

7.15 Specific is to general as
a
p. 248   a. concept is to schema.
Concept   b. schema is to concept.
M   c. artificial intelligence is to availability heuristic.
     d. availability heuristic is to artificial intelligence.

7.16 Which of the following may contain many different concepts?
b
p. 248   a. phonemes
Concept   b. schemas
M   c. morphemes
     d. prototypes

7.17 When asked to explain the route you take to work, you probably rely on _____ to give an answer.
b
p. 248   a. heuristics
Applied   b. visual images
M   c. syllogisms
     d. artificial concepts

Chapter 7 - Cognition and Intelligence

7.18 One technique for studying cognitive processes consists of having individuals "think aloud"
c and then their responses are evaluated. This technique is called
p. 248   a. introspection.
Applied   b. verbal report system.
C   c. verbal protocol analysis.
    d. retrospection.

7.19 One of the problems with verbal protocol analysis is that
a   a. verbalizing thoughts may alter the mental processes of interest.
p. 249   b. talking aloud interferes with thought processes of others.
Applied   c. the content of talking aloud is not measurable.
C   d. verbalized thoughts are not coherent.

7.20 Research by Blessing and Ross (1996) found that experts tended to use _____ to solve problems.
b   a. surface content
p. 249   b. deep structure
Study   c. surface structure
C   d. deep content

7.21 Lisa noticed her teacher plugging in a projector and pulling down a projection screen,
b so she concluded that they were going to see a film in class. This is an example of
p. 249 which cognitive activity?
Applied   a. problem solving
M   b. reasoning
    c. mental set
    d. concept formation

7.22 Cognitive activity that transforms information in order to reach specific conclusions
b is called
p. 249   a. semantic development.
Concept   b. reasoning.
M   c. artificial intelligence.
    d. syntax.

7.23 Explicit is to implicit as
d   a. phoneme is to morpheme.
p. 249   b. morpheme is to phoneme.
Concept   c. everyday reasoning is to formal reasoning.
M   d. formal reasoning is to everyday reasoning.

7.24 Reasoning in which two premises are used as the basis for deriving logical conclusions
b is an example of
p. 249   a. everyday reasoning.
Concept   b. formal reasoning.
M   c. artificial intelligence.
    d. natural intelligence.

7.25 The main advantage of everyday reasoning, compared with formal reasoning, is that
a it can handle situations in which
p. 249   a. there is not enough information.
Concept   b. the two propositions are reversed.
M   c. it is guaranteed to give a correct answer.
PT/OLSG   d. it is not influenced by cultural factors.

7.26 Research indicates that
b   a. reasoning is not altered by emotions.
p. 250   b. emotions may alter reasoning.
Concept   c. emotions and reasoning are independent cognitive activities.
M   d. reasoning and emotions are two forms of artificial concepts.

126   Test Bank - Essentials of Psychology (2nd Edition)

7.27 Oaksford and his colleagues (1996), in their study of mood and problem solving, found that participants
d   who were in a
p. 250   a. positive mood required significantly fewer trials to solve the problem.
Study   b. negative mood required significantly more trials to solve the problem.
C   c. neutral mood required significantly more trials to solve the problem.
         d. positive mood required significantly more trials to solve the problem.

7.28 Our tendency to gather evidence that will confirm rather than refute a hypothesis we
b   believe is called
p. 250   a. functional bias.
Concept b. confirmation bias.
M   c. oversight bias.
         d. artificial intelligence.

7.29 The confirmation bias results when we
d   a. test conclusions by examining serially evidence related to our initial views.
p. 250   b. test conclusions by examining simultaneously evidence related to our initial views.
Concept c. test conclusions by examining primarily evidence that refutes our initial views.
C   d. test conclusions by examining primarily evidence that supports our initial views.

7.30 Ralph always wears his lucky socks whenever he plays baseball. He usually has a good
c   game, probably because he is a good player. He never tests this belief in his lucky
p. 250 socks by wearing a different pair of socks. Ralph's superstition is an example of
Applied a. emotional bias.
M   b. hindsight effect.
         c. confirmation bias.
         d. means-ends analysis.

7.31 People who tell you after-the-fact that they "knew" you would win an athletic competition,
b   for example, a bicycle race, demonstrate a reasoning bias known as the
p. 251   a. means-ends analysis.
Applied b. hindsight bias.
M   c. confirmation bias.
         d. motivation bias.

7.32 Which of the following can reduce the tendency for the hindsight effect?
b   a. eliminate the element of surprise in discussing the event
p. 251   b. have people discuss reasons for the obtained outcome and other possible outcomes
Concept c. reassure people that they have no emotional and no cultural biases
M   d. have people write down their interpretations

Making Decisions: Choosing among Alternatives

7.33 The process of choosing among various courses of action or alternatives is
a   a. decision making.
p. 251   b. escalation of commitment.
Fact   c. confirmation bias.
E   d. hindsight effect.

7.34 When making a decision based on the value of each of all possible outcomes and the
b   likelihood of each outcome, you are making decisions on the basis of
p. 251   a. syllogisms.
Concept b. rationality.
M   c. means-ends analysis.
         d. comprehensive analogs.

Chapter 7 - Cognition and Intelligence

7.35
b
p. 251
Concept
M

Rational decisions are based on two factors, which are
a. intuition and heuristics.
b. expected utility and the probability of outcomes.
c. confirmation bias and hindsight effect.
d. biases and algorithms.

7.36
c
p. 251
Concept
M

Rules of thumb that allow for rapid and efficient decision making are called
a. syllogisms.
b. expected utilities.
c. heuristics.
d. fast mappings.

7.37
d
p. 252
Concept
M

The tendency to make judgments about the frequency of various events or objects in terms of how readily you can bring examples of them to mind is called
a. propositional rules.
b. representativeness heuristic.
c. fast mappings.
d. availability heuristic.

7.38
a
p. 252
Concept
M
PT/OLSG

According to the availability heuristic, the more easily we think of something, the more
a. frequent we judge it to be.
b. we like it.
c. we dislike it.
d. we understand it.

7.39
b
p. 252
Concept
M

After watching television shows of crime in a large U. S. city, many individuals overestimate the likelihood of becoming a crime victim. This can be explained on the basis of
a. hindsight effect.
b. availability heuristic.
c. confirmation bias.
d. representative heuristic.

7.40
d
p. 252
Study
C

The Tversky and Kahneman (1973) study mentioned in the book, in which people judged men or women to be more common on a list of names based on whether the men or women were more famous, shows that
a. we are not very good at knowing who is or is not famous.
b. we are good at remembering how often something happens.
c. most people overestimate the number of men on any list.
d. our familiarity with things affects how likely we think they are.

7.41
d
p. 253
Concept
M

Judging the likelihood of events in terms of how typical they seem of prototypes is based on the principle of
a. natural heuristics.
b. availability heuristics.
c. functional heuristics.
d. representativeness heuristics.

7.42
b
p. 253
Concept
M

The representative heuristic can lead us to ignore information about _____, the relative frequency of different objects or events in the world around us.
a. parameters
b. base rates
c. prototypes
d. exemplars

7.43 Reaching decisions by making adjustments in information that is already available is called the
c
p. 253 a. representativeness heuristic.
Concept b. availability heuristic.
M c. anchoring-and-adjustment heuristic.
d. categorical heuristic.

7.44 As a movie critic for a local newspaper, you have to rate five movies. The first four are
d rather boring and the fifth is better but not exceptional. The tendency to rate the fifth
p. 253 movie as better than it actually is can be explained on the basis of
Applied a. confirmation effect.
C b. hindsight effect.
c. availability heuristic.
d. anchoring-and-adjustment.

7.45 When purchasing an old sofa at a flea market, you ask the seller what it is worth. With
a regard to decision making, you have allowed the seller to
p. 253 a. establish the reference point.
Applied b. determine the heuristic.
M c. define the base rate.
d. choose the utility function.

7.46 The anchoring-and-adjustment heuristic is strongly influenced by
c a. expected utility.
p. 253 b. base rates.
Concept c. a reference point.
M d. ambiguous information.
PT/OLSG

7.47 Presentation of information about potential outcomes in terms of gains or losses is called
c a. hindsight effect.
p. 254 b. base rate judgments.
Concept c. framing.
M d. heuristics.

7.48 When alternatives are presented in terms of the losses that might result, most people are
d a. risk neutral.
p. 254 b. risk avoidant.
Concept c. risk averse.
M d. risk prone.

7.49 With respect to framing, gain is to loss as
a a. risk averse is to risk prone.
p. 254 b. risk prone is to risk averse.
Applied c. heuristic is to algorithm.
M d. algorithm is to heuristic.

7.50 In decision making, when the emphasis is on potential gains, people are _____, and
b when the emphasis is on potential losses, people are _____.
p. 254 a. risk averse; gain averse
Concept b. risk averse; risk prone
M c. gain prone; gain averse
d. risk prone; risk averse

7.51 Jou and colleagues (1996), in a study examining the effect of rational on framing effects, found that
b a. when given a rationale for a choice between lives lost and lives saved, framing effects were enhanced.
p. 254 b. when given a rationale for a choice between lives lost and lives saved, framing effects were diminished.
Study c. when given a rationale for a choice between lives lost and lives saved, framing effects were not
C   affected.
d. when given a rationale for a choice between lives lost and lives saved, framing effects were neutral.

Chapter 7 - Cognition and Intelligence

7.52   The tendency to become trapped in bad decisions is known as
d
p. 254   a. framing.
Concept   b. confirmation bias.
M   c. overconfidence.
    d. escalation of commitment.

7.53   The tendency to keep trying harder to make an idea work when it doesn't seem to
c   be working out, thereby "throwing good money after bad," is known as
p. 254   a. divergent thinking.
Concept   b. convergent thinking.
M   c. escalation of commitment.
    d. the hindsight effect.

7.54   The decision to stay married to someone you no longer love can be explained on the basis of
a
p. 254   a. escalation of commitment.
Applied   b. confirmation bias.
M   c. framing.
    d. divergent thinking.

7.55   Which of the following may explain escalation of commitment?
b   a. means-ends analysis.
p. 255   b. self-justification.
Concept   c. deep structure.
M   d. convergent thinking.

7.56   Which of the following can lead to a decrease in escalation of commitment?
c   a. no lack of resources
p. 255   b. uncertainty of future failure
Concept   c. diffusion of responsibility
C   d. divergent interpretation of conclusions

7.57   Which of these factors would tend to make it more likely that someone will escalate a
a   commitment that has already been made?
p. 255   a. A need to justify one's decision.
Concept   b. A limit on the resources that are available.
C   c. A diffusion of personal responsibility.
    d. Overwhelming evidence of failure.

Problem Solving: Finding Paths to Desired Goals

7.58   Attempting to reach a goal for which there is no simple or direct way is called
a
p. 256   a. problem solving.
Concept   b. belief perseverance.
E   c. syllogisms.
    d. expected utility.

7.59   Trying different responses with the hope that one will be a solution to the problem at hand
c   is an example of which type of problem-solving technique?
p. 256   a. heuristics
Concept   b. algorithm
M   c. trial and error
    d. means-ends analysis

7.60   Which is the least efficient problem-solving strategy?
a   a. trial and error
p. 256   b. heuristic
Concept   c. algorithm
M   d. means-ends analysis

7.61 b
p. 256
Concept
M

Rules for a particular kind of problem, that if followed will yield a solution, refers to
a. heuristics.
b. algorithms.
c. escalation of commitments.
d. confirmation biases.

7.62 d
p. 256
Concept
M

A disadvantage associated with using algorithms to solve problems is that algorithms often
a. are too difficult to understand.
b. produce contradictory solutions.
c. are written for experts.
d. are very inefficient.

7.63 a
p. 256
Concept
M

Which of the following is generally the most efficient technique for solving problems?
a. heuristics
b. algorithms
c. trial and error
d. syllogisms

7.64 a
p. 256
Concept
M
PT/OLSG

Dividing a problem into a series of sub-problems is the technique of
a. means-ends analysis.
b. analogies.
c. anchoring-and-adjustment.
d. schematizing.

7.65 c
p. 257
Concept
M

Using solutions to solve new problems similar to those experienced in the past is an example of using
a. algorithms.
b. means-ends analysis.
c. analogies.
d. trial and error.

7.66 a
p. 257
Concept
C

Talking through a problem and emphasizing the process of solving the problem is called
a. metacognitive processing.
b. verbalization processing.
c. talking therapy.
d. retrospection processing.

7.67 b
p. 257
Applied
C

Metacognitive processing can be a useful tool in problem solving, especially when there is
a. a focus on the actual problem.
b. a focus on the problem-solving process.
c. a focus on the results of problem-solving.
d. a focus on the difficulty of the problem.

7.68 d
p. 258
Concept
M

A strong tendency to think of using objects only in ways they have been used before is called
a. entrapment.
b. escalation of commitment.
c. confirmation bias.
d. functional fixedness.

7.69 b
p. 258
Applied
M

Failing to realize that the metal portion of a glass-handled screwdriver can be used to complete an electrical circuit is an example of
a. unexpected utility.
b. functional fixedness.
c. confirmation bias.
d. anchoring-and-adjustment heuristic.

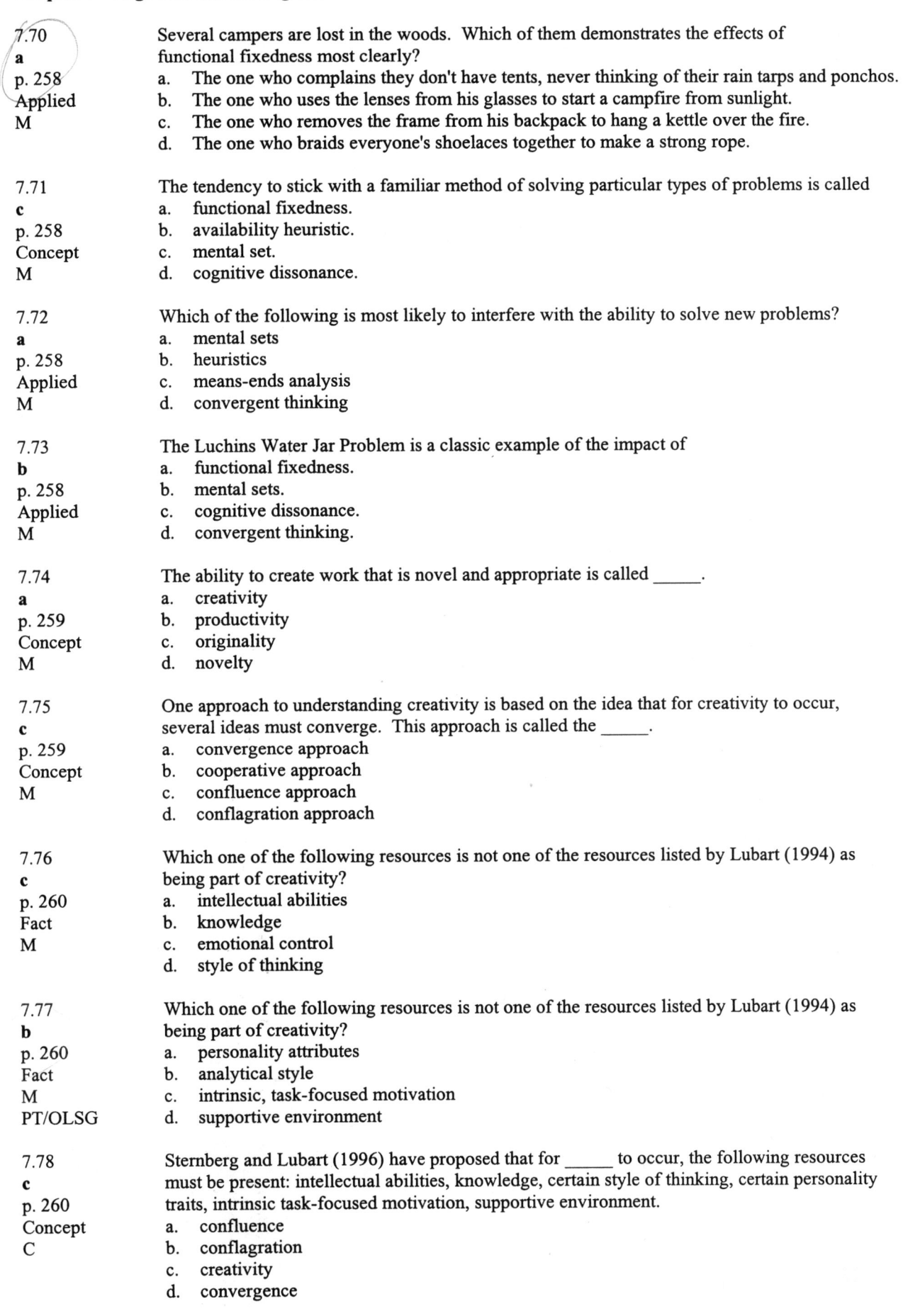

Chapter 7 - Cognition and Intelligence

7.70
a
p. 258
Applied
M

Several campers are lost in the woods. Which of them demonstrates the effects of functional fixedness most clearly?
a. The one who complains they don't have tents, never thinking of their rain tarps and ponchos.
b. The one who uses the lenses from his glasses to start a campfire from sunlight.
c. The one who removes the frame from his backpack to hang a kettle over the fire.
d. The one who braids everyone's shoelaces together to make a strong rope.

7.71
c
p. 258
Concept
M

The tendency to stick with a familiar method of solving particular types of problems is called
a. functional fixedness.
b. availability heuristic.
c. mental set.
d. cognitive dissonance.

7.72
a
p. 258
Applied
M

Which of the following is most likely to interfere with the ability to solve new problems?
a. mental sets
b. heuristics
c. means-ends analysis
d. convergent thinking

7.73
b
p. 258
Applied
M

The Luchins Water Jar Problem is a classic example of the impact of
a. functional fixedness.
b. mental sets.
c. cognitive dissonance.
d. convergent thinking.

7.74
a
p. 259
Concept
M

The ability to create work that is novel and appropriate is called _____.
a. creativity
b. productivity
c. originality
d. novelty

7.75
c
p. 259
Concept
M

One approach to understanding creativity is based on the idea that for creativity to occur, several ideas must converge. This approach is called the _____.
a. convergence approach
b. cooperative approach
c. confluence approach
d. conflagration approach

7.76
c
p. 260
Fact
M

Which one of the following resources is not one of the resources listed by Lubart (1994) as being part of creativity?
a. intellectual abilities
b. knowledge
c. emotional control
d. style of thinking

7.77
b
p. 260
Fact
M
PT/OLSG

Which one of the following resources is not one of the resources listed by Lubart (1994) as being part of creativity?
a. personality attributes
b. analytical style
c. intrinsic, task-focused motivation
d. supportive environment

7.78
c
p. 260
Concept
C

Sternberg and Lubart (1996) have proposed that for _____ to occur, the following resources must be present: intellectual abilities, knowledge, certain style of thinking, certain personality traits, intrinsic task-focused motivation, supportive environment.
a. confluence
b. conflagration
c. creativity
d. convergence

Language: The Communication of Information

7.79   Communication involving the use of symbols and the rules for combining them is called
d
p. 261
Concept
E
a. intelligence.
b. heuristics.
c. reasoning.
d. language.

7.80   Three criteria that must be met if sounds and symbols are considered to be a language are
c
p. 261
Concept
C
a. phonemes, morphemes, and analogies.
b. prototypes, algorithms, and heuristics.
c. meaning, infinite combinations, and conveying meaning independent of specific situations.
d. propositional reasoning, infinite combinations of concepts, and comprehension.

7.81   When three-year-old Lisa tells her mother, "I goed to the store and I buyed a toy," her mother corrects her words, telling her, "No, Lisa, you WENT to the store and you BOUGHT a toy." This exchange would best fit which theory of language development?
a
p. 262
Applied
M
a. social learning view
b. innate mechanism view
c. cognitive view
d. grammatical view

7.82   Chomsky (1968) hypothesized that human beings have a _____ that provides them with an intuitive grasp of language.
c
p. 262
Concept
C
a. linguistic relativity concept
b. conative language operator
c. language acquisition device
d. functional linguistic principle

7.83   The rule, "Pay attention to the ends of words" is an example of
d
p. 262
Applied
C
a. a functional linguistic principle in the development of language.
b. a conative language operator in the development of language.
c. a language acquisition device in the development of language.
d. an operating principle in the development of language.

7.84   Hypothesized information-processing abilities or strategies used by children in acquiring language are called
b
p. 262
Concept
M
a. neural networks.
b. operating principles.
c. grammatical rules.
d. deep structures.

7.85   What are the three basic milestones of language development?
b
p. 263
Concept
M
a. overextension, underextension, operating principles
b. phonological, semantic, grammatical
c. intuitive, semantic, phonological
d. deep structure, surface structure, fast mapping

7.86   The development of the ability to pronounce the sounds and words of one or more languages is called
c
p. 263
Concept
M
a. babbling.
b. semantic development.
c. phonological development.
d. grammar.

Chapter 7 - Cognition and Intelligence

7.87　　　　　The type of knowledge that involves understanding of the meaning of words is known as
a
p. 263　　　　a.　semantic development.
Concept　　　b.　phonological development.
E　　　　　　c.　syntactical development.
PT/OLSG　　　d.　morphological development.

7.88　　　　　Learning to understand the meaning of words is to learning to understand the rules by
d　　　　　　which words are arranged into sentences as
p. 263　　　　a.　phonological development is to babbling.
Concept　　　b.　babbling is to phonological development.
M　　　　　　c.　grammar is to semantic development.
　　　　　　　d.　semantic development is to grammar.

7.89　　　　　Babbling is initially
a
p. 263　　　　a.　every sound used in all human speech.
Concept　　　b.　sounds typical of the child's native culture.
M　　　　　　c.　sounds typical of the parent's native culture.
　　　　　　　d.　composed only of morphemes.

7.90　　　　　Young children use single word utterances that convey much meaning. These utterances are
c
p. 263　　　　a.　morphemes.
Fact　　　　　b.　phonemes.
E　　　　　　c.　holophrases.
　　　　　　　d.　syntax.

7.91　　　　　Your nephew does not use the word apple for green apples because he thinks apples are
b　　　　　　always red. In language development this is an example of
p. 264　　　　a.　overextension.
Applied　　　b.　underextension.
M　　　　　　c.　relative linguistics.
　　　　　　　d.　holophrastic grammar.

7.92　　　　　The use of two words to express complex meaning by young children is referred to as
a
p. 264　　　　a.　telegraphic speech.
Concept　　　b.　cognitive syntax.
M　　　　　　c.　holophrastic grammar.
　　　　　　　d.　heuristic syntax.

7.93　　　　　The phrase, "Mommy work," may be used by a child about two years of age instead of,
d　　　　　　"Mommy is going to work." This is an example of
p. 264　　　　a.　holophrastic grammar.
Concept　　　b.　underextension.
M　　　　　　c.　relative linguistics.
　　　　　　　d.　telegraphic speech.

7.94　　　　　Which of the following views suggests that people who speak different languages may
b　　　　　　perceive the world in different ways because their thinking is influenced by the words
p. 264　　　　available to them?
Concept　　　a.　Noam Chomsky's view
M　　　　　　b.　linguistic relativity view
　　　　　　　c.　availability heuristic view
　　　　　　　d.　social learning view

134 Test Bank - Essentials of Psychology (2nd Edition)

7.95
b
p. 264
Applied
C

According to the linguistic relativity hypothesis, we would have less racial prejudice in our society if
a. everyone had the same skin color.
b. English had fewer words for racial differences.
c. everyone's vision actually were color blind.
d. we worked harder to maintain our cultural heritages.

7.96
d
p. 264
Applied
C

If people are able to have ideas that they can't put into words, this contradicts which theory of language?
a. Chomsky's innate mechanism view
b. the availability heuristic
c. surface versus deep structure
d. the linguistic relativity hypothesis

7.97
c
p. 264
Concept
C

Research on the linguistic relativity hypothesis generally supports the position that
a. the language we speak controls how we think.
b. the linguistic relativity hypothesis is true.
c. the language we speak reflects how we think.
d. there is no relationship between thought and language.

7.98
d
p. 264
Concept
M

The Dani language has only two different words for colors, and yet they perceive as many different colors as English speakers. This is evidence for the belief that
a. the linguistic relativity hypothesis is true.
b. our perceptions are controlled by our language.
c. children learn language the same way all over the world.
d. language does not control our experience of the world.

7.99
c
p. 265
Concept
M

Early attempts to teach chimpanzees were complete failures, primarily because
a. the researchers didn't use scientific conditioning methods.
b. the chimpanzees used were not of the proper species.
c. chimpanzees lack the physical ability to produce speech.
d. the researchers did not understand the language being taught.

7.100
a
p. 265
Concept
M

Washoe the chimpanzee learned to communicate with the Gardners using
a. American Sign Language.
b. computer symbols.
c. phonetic spelling.
d. flash cards.

7.101
b
p. 265
Concept
M

Researchers investigating language in nonhuman species have had the most difficulty in clearly demonstrating that nonhuman species
a. can learn to use symbols.
b. grasp generativity.
c. can learn sign language.
d. understand syntax.

7.102
a
p. 265
Study
C

Kanzi, a chimpanzee, learned grammatical concepts through a process of
a. combining spoken language and corresponding symbols.
b. repeating the names of objects many times in a single session.
c. pointing at abstract visual symbols.
d. combining spoken language and actual objects.

7.103
d
p. 265
Concept
C

One complaint about early research on the language abilities of animals is that
a. the animals were not actually taught to speak.
b. the research only used gorillas, not other animals.
c. the animals showed no signs of creativity.
d. the researchers may have been giving cues to the animals.

Chapter 7 - Cognition and Intelligence

7.104
a
p. p. 266
Concept
M

When dolphin Ake is given requests that don't fit the grammar she has been taught, she responds by
a. completing the request correctly.
b. ignoring the grammatical errors.
c. obeying the closest grammatical command.
d. performing random actions that sometimes match.

7.105
c
p. 266
Concept
M

The current view of language based on research on the linguistic abilities of animals is that
a. some features of language are impossible for animals.
b. with proper training, animals can learn human language.
c. language is a range of skills different animals may have to some degree.
d. language means different things to different species, and each animal has its own language.

7.106
c
p. 267
Concept
M
PT/OLSG

Artificial intelligence primarily involves the study of
a. all animal communication.
b. all primate communication.
c. computer capabilities.
d. analogies and algorithms.

7.107
c
p. 267
Concept
M

The study of how computers perform actions that in humans require cognitive abilities is called
a. computer psychology.
b. electronic cognition.
c. artificial intelligence.
d. mechanical thought.

7.108
a
p. 267
Concept
M

One cognitive function that is simple for humans but which turns out to be very difficult for computers is
a. using language.
b. solving problems.
c. arithmetic calculations.
d. playing chess.

7.109
a
p. 268
Applied
M

In your textbook, the chess master Kasparov, defeated "Deep Blue" by using what tactic?
a. Pitting overall strategy against computing power.
b. Playing randomly.
c. Playing so that the computer would have to advance one move at a time.
d. Reconstructing board configurations and then playing away from those configurations.

Intelligence: Contrasting Views of Its Nature

7.110
c
p. 269
Concept
M

Intelligence can be defined as
a. knowledge of a great many facts.
b. the ability to get good grades in school.
c. the ability to think abstractly and learn from experience.
d. all the factors that make one person different from another.

7.111
a
p. 269
Fact
M

Individual differences in intelligence are important primarily because they allow us to predict
a. how quickly someone will learn a new skill.
b. how many friends someone is likely to have.
c. how likely someone is to become mentally ill.
d. how happy someone is likely to be in life.

7.112
d
p. 269
Fact
C

Most people believe that high intelligence goes with better grades, quicker learning in new situations, and more success in life. In general, research in this area has shown that
a. intelligence is related to grades but not life success.
b. quicker learning is not related to intelligence.
c. lower intelligence usually leads to greater success.
d. these ideas are mostly true.

136 Test Bank - Essentials of Psychology (2nd Edition)

7.113
d
p. 270
Concept
M

According to Spearman, our ability to perform any and all cognitive tasks is most dependent on
a. crystallized intelligence.
b. fluid intelligence.
c. s factor.
d. g factor.

7.114
a
p. 270
Fact
M
PT/OLSG

Spearman felt that intelligence consisted of
a. a single primary factor.
b. multiple types of intelligence.
c. a composite of seven primary mental abilities.
d. culturally determined skills.

7.115
c
p. 270
Applied
E

If you had to select a person who was the most likely to be successful in life, you should probably choose the person with
a. moderate intelligence.
b. the lowest intelligence.
c. the highest intelligence.
d. any intelligence; it would make no difference.

7.116
d
p. 270
Fact
E

Which of the following individuals viewed intelligence as composed of many separate mental abilities that operate more or less independently?
a. Cattell
b. Spearman
c. Skinner
d. Thurstone

7.117
d
p. 270
Fact
M

Spearman is to Thurstone as
a. crystallized is to fluid.
b. fluid is to crystallized.
c. multifaceted is to unified.
d. unified is to multifaceted.

7.118
b
p. 270
Fact
C

Thurstone believed that intelligence was multifaceted and comprised of seven distinct primary abilities. Which of the following are included as part of those seven abilities?
a. cognitive, word recognition, number
b. number, space, verbal meaning
c. people recognition, place recognition, thing recognition
d. number manipulation, people recognition, cognition reconstruction

7.119
b
p. 270
Fact
M

Gardner argued that conventional views of intelligence were limiting, and should include the idea that there are _____ intelligences.
a. single
b. multiple
c. general
d. functional

7.120
c
p. 270
Fact
M

Which of the following is not one of the intelligences considered by Gardner?
a. musical intelligence
b. interpersonal intelligence
c. localized intelligence
d. bodily-kinesthetic intelligence

Chapter 7 - Cognition and Intelligence

7.121
b
p. 270
Concept
C

In Sternberg's triarchic theory of intelligence, the ability to use one's capability in a specific situation is _____ intelligence, while the ability to apply information one has learned from the world is _____ intelligence.
a. componential; experiential
b. experiential; contextual
c. contextual; experiential
d. experiential; componential

7.122
d
p. 270
Fact
M

In Sternberg's triarchic theory, the type of intelligence that involves the ability to think critically and analytically is called
a. experiential intelligence.
b. crystallized intelligence.
c. contextual intelligence.
d. componential intelligence.

7.123
b
p. 270
Fact
M

Which theory analyzes intelligence into contextual, experiential, and componential dimensions?
a. Thurstone's factor approach
b. Sternberg's triarchic theory
c. Gardner's multiple intelligences theory
d. Guilford's structure of intellect model

7.124
b
p. 270
Fact
M
PT/OLSG

In Sternberg's triarchic theory, the ability to formulate new ideas or to combine seemingly unrelated facts is referred to as
a. componential intelligence.
b. experiential intelligence.
c. contextual intelligence.
d. crystallized intelligence.

7.125
b
p. 271
Fact
M

In Sternberg's triarchic theory, the type of intelligence that involves the ability to quickly recognize what factors influence success on various tasks and is adept at both adapting to and shaping the environment is called
a. componential intelligence.
b. contextual intelligence.
c. fluid intelligence.
d. experiential intelligence.

7.126
c
p. 271
Fact
M
PT/OLSG

According to Sternberg's triarchic theory, people who have practical sense have _____ intelligence.
a. componential
b. experiential
c. contextual
d. intuitive

7.127
a
p. 271
Applied
C

Ralph is very good at organizing a lot of information to make it easier to find what he needs. This ability helps him run his small business, lead Boy Scouts on camping trips, and win sailboat races. According to Sternberg's triarchic theory of intelligence, Ralph would have a high level of _____ intelligence.
a. contextual — practical
b. experiential
c. componential
d. referential

7.128
b
p. 271
Fact
M

In order to achieve the kind of intelligence that Sternberg believes is important, people must learn
a. more specific skills for more specific situations.
b. practical skills to help them solve real-world problems.
c. to increase their general intellectual ability.
d. more automatic, highly-practiced skills, such as reading.

138 Test Bank - Essentials of Psychology (2nd Edition)

7.129   Knowledge that is action-oriented, practically useful, and usually unspoken is called
c
p. 271   a. real-world knowledge.
Fact   b. adaptive knowledge.
M   c. tacit knowledge.
           d. functional knowledge.

7.130   Research investigating practical intelligence has found that _____ is a good predictor of
b   salary level and number of promotions.
p. 271   a. response knowledge
Fact   b. tacit knowledge
M   c. experiential knowledge
           d. conceptual knowledge

Measuring Human Intelligence: From Tests to Underlying Psychological Processes ... and Beyond

7.131   The purpose of the first intelligence tests, developed around the beginning of this century
d   by Alfred Binet, was to
p. 271   a. gain a better theoretical understanding of intelligence.
Concept   b. help employees determine who to hire for a job.
M   c. screen Army recruits for officer's school.
           d. identify school children who were mentally retarded.

7.132   For what purpose was the original device for measuring human intelligence developed by
c   Binet and Simon?
p. 271   a. to develop a unified measure of intelligence
Concept   b. to identify children who should acquire a post-secondary education
M   c. to identify children who were mentally retarded and would not benefit from regular education
           d. to develop a measure of academic intelligence

7.133   Probably the most traditional, widely used intelligence test in recent decades has been the
a
p. 272   a. Stanford-Binet intelligence test.
Fact   b. Wechsler Adult Intelligence Scale.
M   c. Kaufmann Assessment Battery.
           d. Minnesota Multiphasic Measurement Scale.

7.134   Originally, IQ scores were obtained by dividing _____ by _____ and multiplying by 100.
c
p. 273   a. functional age; actual age
Fact   b. actual age; functional age
M   c. mental age; chronological age
           d. chronological age; mental age

7.135   When the original method of calculating IQ is used, a score of 100 means that one's mental
a   age is
p. 273   a. equal to chronological age.
Fact   b. slightly greater than chronological age.
E   c. much greater than chronological age.
           d. slightly less than chronological age.

7.136   Lisa is 10 years old. A standardized IQ measured Lisa's mental age as 7. This means that
d   Lisa's IQ score would be
p. 273   a. 80th percentile.
Applied   b. 70.
M   c. 95.
           d. 110.

Chapter 7 - Cognition and Intelligence

7.137
a
p. 273
Concept
C

When IQ scores are determined in the traditional manner using chronological and mental age, IQ shows a steady decline that begins in the early teenage years. Today IQ scores are now
a. based on the relative standing of one's scores among same-aged persons.
b. based on a proportion of mental age to chronological age.
c. determined by one's score at age 16.
d. adjusted by adding points to correct for age effects.

7.138
d
p. 273
Concept
M
PT/OLSG

A major problem with intelligence tests developed and adapted by Binet and Terman was that they paid relatively little attention to
a. verbal abilities.
b. memory abilities.
c. age-related changes in intelligence.
d. nonverbal abilities.

7.139
b
p. 273
Fact
M

The two major scales of the Wechsler tests measure
a. verbal reasoning and arithmetic reasoning.
b. performance and verbal ability.
c. mathematical and verbal ability.
d. cognitive skills and vocabulary.

7.140
b
p. 273
Applied
C

Children who have patterns of scores on the WISC that include high scores on Picture Completion and Object Assembly, but low scores on Arithmetic, Information, and Vocabulary are more likely to have
a. gifted abilities.
b. intellectual dysfunction.
c. cognitive aberrations.
d. learning disabilities.

7.141
c
p. 273
Concept
M

Practical uses of intelligence tests include identification
a. only of those who gain from special training for mental retardation.
b. only of those who would gain from special education because they are intellectually gifted.
c. of mental retardation and intellectually gifted.
d. of neither mental retardation nor intellectually gifted.

7.142
b
p. 273
Fact
C

The four broad categories of retardation are
a. mild, slight, serious, and extreme.
b. mild, moderate, severe, and profound.
c. slight, moderate, serious, and severe.
d. slight, serious, severe, and extreme.

7.143
a
p. 273
Fact
C

A retarded person is someone who demonstrates
a. intellectual abilities substantially below average and difficulty with everyday life.
b. intellectual abilities slightly below average and difficulties with everyday life.
c. difficulty with everyday life, regardless of intellectual abilities.
d. intellectual abilities slightly below average, regardless of difficulties with everyday life.

7.144
c
p. 274
Applied
M

Tasks, such as picture arrangement, are examples of _____ tasks on the Wechsler Intelligence Test. Tasks, such as vocabulary and information, are examples of _____ tasks.
a. abstract; concrete
b. quantitative; qualitative
c. performance; verbal
d. complex; simple

7.145
a
p. 274
Fact
M

When searching for the causes of retardation, the most common result is
a. specific causes cannot be determined.
b. Down's Syndrome.
c. lack of oxygen before or during birth.
d. lead poisoning.

7.146 d
p. 274
Fact
M

A person whose intelligence test scores indicate a very high level of intellectual functioning is called
a. mentally anteceded.
b. intelligently motivated.
c. moderately advanced.
d. intellectually gifted.

7.147 b
p. 274
Fact
M

In Terman's long-term study of intellectually gifted students, the social and emotional adjustment of people with IQs over 130 was
a. worse than that of most people.
b. better than that of most people.
c. no different from that of most people.
d. worse for men but better for women.

7.148 d
p. 275
Fact
M

Group is to individual as
a. Wechsler is to Stanford-Binet.
b. Simon-Binet is to Wechsler.
c. Army Alpha is to Army Beta.
d. Army Alpha is to Wechsler.

7.149 b
p. 275
Fact
M
PT/OLSG

One major problem with the use of group tests of intelligence is that they may be
a. too difficult.
b. culturally biased.
c. too easy.
d. not influenced by training.

7.150 b
p. 276
Concept
C

Research by Fry and Hale (1996) on the reason that fluid intelligence increases with age finds that with age, _____ increases, which leads to increases in _____, which leads to increases in fluid intelligence.
a. functional memory; general intelligence
b. processing speed; working memory
c. working memory; processing speed
d. general intelligence; functional memory

7.151 b
p. 276
Concept
C

Research on the neurological basis of intelligence finds that the higher the _____, the _____ the measured intelligence.
a. action potential; lower
b. nerve conduction velocity; higher
c. dendritic firing; lower
d. galvanic skin response; higher

7.152 c
p. 276
Study
C

PET scans indicate that the brains of individuals with higher intelligence
a. are more active in the temporal lobe when working on various tasks.
b. expend more energy on various tasks.
c. expend less energy on various tasks.
d. are less active in the temporal lobe when working on various tasks.

Reliability and Validity: Basic Requirements for all Psychological Tests

7.153 b
p. 277
Concept
M

Which of the following is a measure of the consistency of a test?
a. validity
b. reliability
c. standardization
d. objectivity

Chapter 7 - Cognition and Intelligence

7.154
c
p. 277
Applied
M

On two separate occasions, Ralph took a test to measure his ability to solve mathematical problems. He earned the same score each time he took the test. This suggests that the test is
a. valid.
b. standardized.
c. reliable.
d. normal.

7.155
d
p. 277
Fact
M

Dividing a test into two halves in order to determine whether individuals attained equivalent scores on the two halves is called
a. test-retest reliability.
b. concurrent validity.
c. predictive reliability.
d. split-half reliability.

7.156
b
p. 277
Applied
M

After Professor Stearns gave a 100-questions final exam, she separated the odd-numbered questions from the even-numbered questions and compared each student's scores on both sets. Professor Stearns was probably trying to find out
a. whether the test was a valid one.
b. the split-half reliability of the test.
c. if the test needed to be curved.
d. whether any of the students cheated.

7.157
b
p. 277
Fact
M

The statistical formula for assessing internal consistency, called coefficient alpha, is used to determine whether a psychological test is
a. valid.
b. reliable.
c. standardized.
d. objective.

7.158
b
p. 277
Fact
M
PT/OLSG

Assessment of similarity of scores over time is
a. split-half reliability.
b. test-retest reliability.
c. split-half validity.
d. test-retest validity.

7.159
c
p. 277
Applied
M

On two separate occasions, Lisa took a test measuring an aspect of her personality and obtained very similar scores. In other words, the test has been shown to have
a. concurrent validity.
b. predictive validity.
c. test-retest reliability.
d. split-half reliability.

7.160
c
p. 277
Fact
M

Practice effects are most likely to be a problem when determining
a. split-half reliability.
b. content validity.
c. test-retest reliability.
d. objectivity.

7.161
b
p. 277
Fact
M

Giving someone two different versions of the same test on two different occasions and comparing the scores is a measure of _____ reliability.
a. content
b. alternate forms
c. split-half
d. test-retest

141

7.162 The ability of a test to measure what it is supposed to measure is its
d
p. 278   a. predictive power.
Fact   b. internal consistency.
E   c. reliability.
PT/OLSG d. validity.

7.163 If you develop a test to measure good study skills and when evaluated, it is determined
a   that it actually measures good study skills, the test is said to be
p. 278   a. valid.
Applied b. standardized.
M   c. reliable.
         d. objective.

7.164 The extent to which the items on a test sample the behaviors that are related to the
b   characteristic in question refers to the test's
p. 278   a. construct validity.
Fact   b. content validity.
C   c. predictive validity.
         d. objective validity.

7.165 Tests determining whether a person should become a licensed psychologist need to contain
c   questions related to skills used by competent psychologists. Tests that accomplish this
p. 278 are said to have good
Applied a. test-retest reliability.
M   b. concurrent validity.
         c. content validity.
         d. split-half reliability.

7.166 Suppose someone designed a test that could accurately predict how successful someone
c   would be at police work by measuring how quickly they answered a lot of questions about
p. 278 math. If it worked, this test would have high _____, but low _____.
Applied a. reliability; validity
C   b. test-retest reliability; split-half reliability
         c. predictive validity; content validity
         d. construct validity; criterion-related validity

7.167 To determine whether a test has criterion-related validity, an investigator needs to
d   a. administer the test to the same persons on at least two occasions.
p. 278   b. examine many test scores and derive test norms.
Concept c. compare the test to concepts derived from theories.
M   d. measure a behavior that should be related to the test.

7.168 Tests such as the Scholastic Aptitude Test are used to predict later performance in college.
a   Tests that accurately predict such future performance are said to possess
p. 278   a. predictive validity.
Applied b. content validity.
C   c. concurrent validity.
         d. criterion-referenced validity.

7.169 The type of validity in which test scores are related to present behavior is
c   a. content.
p. 278   b. predictive.
Fact   c. concurrent.
E   d. construct.
PT/OLSG

Chapter 7 - Cognition and Intelligence

7.170 If items on a test of intelligence require specific cultural experience or knowledge, that test is said to be
c
p. 278   a. cognitively biased.
Fact   b. socially enhanced.
M   c. culturally biased.
             d. intellectually biased.

7.171 Many tests of intelligence implicitly accept European standards and values. This approach
b   is described as the
p. 280   a. European intelligence model.
Concept   b. Eurocentric perspective.
C   c. European-centered approach.
             d. Eurocentered bias.

7.172 Which of the following is considered to be a culture-fair test of intelligence?
d   a. the Army Alpha test
p. 280   b. the Stanford-Binet
Fact   c. the Wechsler Adult Intelligence Scale
M   d. the Raven Progressive Matrices test

7.173 The Raven Progressive Matrices test focuses primarily on _____.
b   a. crystallized intelligence
p. 280   b. fluid intelligence
Fact   c. tacit intelligence
M   d. conjoint intelligence

Human Intelligence: The Role of Heredity and the Role of Environment

7.174 The more closely two people are related, the _____ their IQs.
c   a. lower
p. 281   b. higher
Fact   c. more similar
M   d. more different
PT/OLSG

7.175 A primary method for assessing the importance of genetic factors in intelligence is to compare
b   a. the average IQ scores of people of different racial groups.
p. 281   b. the similarity of IQ scores of biological and adopted families.
Fact   c. the intelligence levels of people from different countries.
M   d. the scores people get on different intelligence tests.

7.176 Some researchers have estimated that the heritability of intelligence to be as much as
d   a. 10% in adulthood.
p. 282   b. 25% in adulthood.
Study   c. 50% in adulthood.
C   d. 75% in adulthood.

7.177 What has happened to IQ scores worldwide during recent decades?
c   a. They have decreased significantly.
p. 283   b. They have not changed significantly.
Fact   c. They have increased significantly.
M   d. They initially increased and are now decreasing significantly.

7.178 Which of the following supports the notion that the environment influences intelligence?
a   a. changes in IQ scores over the past few decades
p. 283   b. high correlations between adopted children and their biological parents
Concept   c. the lack of effects of environmental deprivation
M   d. the similarity of twins reared together

7.179 a p. 283 Fact M PT/OLSG

It seems likely that the worldwide increase in IQ scores is due to
a. environmental factors.
b. genetic factors.
c. actual increase in intelligence.
d. the ozone layer.

7.180 b p. 283 Study C

In the same family, a first-born child will tend to have a slightly higher IQ score than a second-born child, who will have a slightly higher IQ than a third-born child, etc. The theory that addresses this finding is called
a. birth order theory.
b. confluence theory.
c. social contagion theory.
d. social influence theory.

7.181 a p. 283 Concept M

Evidence for the role of environmental factors in intelligence comes from studies investigating
a. environmental deprivation.
b. environmental confluence.
c. social mitigation.
d. social facilitation.

7.182 d p. 284 Concept M

The major controversy over the influence that environmental and genetic factors have on intelligence is
a. whether there is any genetic influence.
b. whether there is any environmental influence.
c. whether both factors have any influence.
d. the relative importance of both factors.

7.183 b p. 284 Concept M

One reason some people dislike the idea that genetics has a strong influence on intelligence is that it seems to mean that
a. genetics restricts how we can react to our environments.
b. we can do nothing to improve people's intelligence.
c. different people's brains function differently.
d. anyone is capable of doing anything at all.

7.184 c p. 284 Fact M

Although it is not clear how much influence genetic and environmental factors have on intelligence, there is some evidence to suggest that
a. neither genetic nor environmental factors have any influence.
b. environmental factors have stronger influence.
c. genetic factors have stronger influence.
d. there is no evidence to support one factor over the other.

7.185 b p. 285 Concept C

If genetic factors have a stronger influence on intelligence than environmental factors, the best response would be to
a. abandon any useless efforts to change someone's intelligence.
b. modify the environment so each person reaches his or her maximum potential.
c. create separate environments for people of different levels of intelligence.
d. encourage research into how to biologically improve people's intelligence level.

7.186 d p. 285 Fact M

In *The Bell Curve*, it is argued that the effect of affirmative action programs and educational opportunity programs will be
a. to raise the IQ scores of the underclass.
b. to change the genetic heritage of Americans.
c. to help people overcome an inherently low IQ score.
d. nothing; these programs have little effect.

Chapter 7 - Cognition and Intelligence

7.187
b
p. 285
Fact
C

One of the claims of *The Bell Curve* that is not scientifically justified is that
a. a person's IQ score predicts his or her success in life.
b. differences in IQ scores between groups are determined by genetic inheritance.
c. crime and poverty are associated with low IQ scores.
d. different racial groups have different average IQ scores.

7.188
c
p. 285
Applied
C

The harshest criticism of the *The Bell Curve* centered on the book's contention that because _____ differences in intelligence are strongly influenced by genetic factors, so were _____ differences in intelligence.
a. age, gender
b. group, individual
c. individual, group
d. gender, age

7.189
d
p. 286
Fact
M

Your author's reaction to The Bell Curve can be best summarized by saying that
a. it has interesting ideas that should be tested further.
b. the authors had great moral courage in writing the book.
c. the ideas are not new, but they put them together well.
d. their conclusions are based on incomplete scientific knowledge.

Emotional Intelligence: The Feeling Side of Intelligence

7.190
c
p. 286
Concept
M

The type of intelligence that is concerned with the ability to recognize and manage emotions, restrain impulses, and handle interpersonal relationships effectively is called
a. impulsive intelligence.
b. interpersonal intelligence.
c. emotional intelligence.
d. cognitive intelligence.

7.191
b
p. 287
Concept
M

Individuals who are oblivious to their own feelings are often
a. emotionally barren.
b. low in expressiveness.
c. low in emotionality.
d. low in energy.

7.192
d
p. 287
Concept
M

One of the most important tasks in managing our emotions relates to
a. countering negative cognitions.
b. countering positive emotions.
c. countering positive cognitions.
d. countering negative emotions.

7.193
c
p. 287
Concept
M

In looking at one aspect of emotional intelligence, it has been found that Asian Americans outperform other groups in terms of occupational success, yet their IQ scores are quite close to average. Their success has been attributed to the fact that this group
a. is high in tacit knowledge.
b. is high in organizational knowledge.
c. is high in motivation.
d. is high in cooperation.

7.194
b
p. 287
Concept
M
PT/OLSG

One part of emotional intelligence is being able to read the _____ of other people.
a. cognitive overtones
b. nonverbal cues
c. potential conflicts
d. overt emotions

145

7.195   "Getting along with others" is a phrase that describes
a
p. 287   a. interpersonal intelligence.
Concept   b. social skills.
M   c. cooperative knowledge.
   d. organizational knowledge.

7.196   In interpersonal relationships, _____ have a higher level of emotional intelligence.
b
p. 288   a. males
Fact   b. females
M   c. young people
   d. old people

7.197   In general, _____ as compared to _____ are less skilled in recognizing and expressing emotions.
c
p. 289   a. younger people, older people
Fact   b. older people, younger people
M   c. males, females
   d. females, males

7.198   In general, males tend to be
a
p. 289   a. more sensitive to criticism.
Fact   b. less sensitive to criticism.
M   c. more sensitive in expressing emotions.
   d. less sensitive in expressing thoughts.

7.199   One key aspect of emotional intelligence is the ability to manage
a
p. 289   a. anger.
Fact   b. conflict.
E   c. relationships.
   d. cognition.

7.200   One way to deal with anger is to laugh. It is almost impossible to be angry when you are
c   laughing. This approach is called the
p. 290   a. laugh-cry approach.
Applied   b. humorous response approach.
M   c. incompatible response approach.
   d. emotional dissonance approach.

7.201   According to your author, one of the things you should definitely not do in managing anger
b   is "get it out of your system," or rely on
p. 290   a. attack.
Applied   b. catharsis.
M   c. confluence.
   d. constraints.

Chapter 8 - Human Development

CHAPTER 8

Multiple-Choice Questions

8.1
a
p. 293
Fact
E

The branch of psychology that focuses on changes in one's lifetime is called _____ psychology.
a. developmental
b. aging
c. personality
d. child

8.2
d
p. 294
Concept
M

Three major categories when examining shifts due to age include
a. physical growth, assimilation, and attachment.
b. cognitive development, social and emotional development, and attachment.
c. physical growth, cognitive development, and accommodation.
d. physical growth, cognitive development, and social development.

Physical Growth and Development during Childhood

8.3
c
p. 294
Concept
M

Once a fertilized egg becomes implanted in the uterine wall, it becomes a(n)
a. zygote.
b. fetus.
c. embryo.
d. teratogen.

8.4
d
p. 294
Fact
M
PT/OLSG

The face, arms, and legs are present by the _____ week of prenatal development.
a. third
b. fourth
c. sixth
d. eighth

8.5
c
p. 294
Fact
M

Which of the following places the prenatal stages of physical development into the correct chronological order?
a. embryo, uterine implantation, fetus
b. fetus, uterine implantation, embryo
c. uterine implantation, embryo, fetus
d. embryo, fetus, uterine implantation

8.6
d
p. 295
Concept
M

Factors in the environment that can harm the developing fetus and interfere with normal patterns of growth are called
a. mutations.
b. toxins.
c. analgesics.
d. teratogens.

8.7
a
p. 296
Fact
M

The structure that surrounds, protects, and nourishes the developing fetus is called the
a. placenta.
b. epidermal sac.
c. dura matter.
d. fallopian tube.

8.8
b
p. 296
Concept
M

Rubella (German measles) contracted by the mother has been shown to cause blindness, deafness, or heart disease if contracted
a. during the final month of pregnancy.
b. during the first four weeks of pregnancy.
c. between two and four months of pregnancy.
d. during the middle trimester of pregnancy.

8.9   Disease during pregnancy, over-the-counter drugs, and alcohol are all examples of
c
p. 296   a. pathos substances.
Concept   b. analgesics.
M   c. teratogens.
   d. neural inhibitors.

8.10   The fetal disorder that may involve retarded growth, irritability, and hyperactivity is associated
a   with maternal
p. 296   a. alcohol consumption.
Concept   b. caffeine intake.
M   c. illegal drug use.
PT/OLSG   d. smoking.

8.11   Ralph's characteristics include an abnormally small head, irritability, hyperactivity, retarded
a   motor and mental development, and heart defects. During pregnancy, Ralph's mother
p. 296   probably
Applied   a. drank heavily.
M   b. smoked excessively.
   c. consumed caffeinated beverages.
   d. contracted German measles.

8.12   If a child displays only some of the symptoms produced by heavy use of alcohol by its mother
b   during pregnancy, the child is said to be suffering from
p. 296   a. fetal alcohol syndrome.
Fact   b. fetal alcohol effects.
M   c. drug-induced neurological inhibition.
   d. drug-induced neurological syndrome.

8.13   Babies born to mothers who smoke during pregnancy are more likely to
d   a. engage in criminal behaviors as adults.
p. 296   b. become smokers themselves.
Fact   c. be unusually large at birth.
M   d. be smaller at birth.

8.14   The best advice to give pregnant women would be
d   a. do not smoke cigarettes, but moderate alcohol consumption is not harmful.
p. 296   b. do not drink alcohol, but moderate smoking is not harmful.
Concept   c. do not smoke cigarettes or drink alcohol, but caffeine consumption is not harmful.
M   d. avoid smoking, alcohol, and caffeine during pregnancy.

8.15   Newborns possess a number of simple reflexes at birth, including all except which of the following?
d   a. following a moving light with their eyes
p. 296   b. sucking on a finger or nipple placed in the mouth
Fact   c. turning the head in the direction of a touch on the cheek
M   d. reaching for a visible object placed near the face

8.16   The text summarizes milestones of physical development by presenting an age at which various
a   behaviors are performed. The age presented for each of these milestones is the
p. 297   a. average age at which the behavior develops.
Concept   b. youngest age at which the behavior develops.
E   c. age by which the behavior must appear if a child is to be considered normal.
   d. age at which the behavior invariably develops.

8.17   When comparing the development of a specific child to the motor milestones given in the book,
d   it is important to remember that
p. 297   a. most children will reach each goal before the age is given.
Concept   b. a child who is more than a week or two "late" is unusual.
M   c. not all children will reach the goals in the same order.
   d. small differences from the ages given don't matter.

Chapter 8 - Human Development   149

8.18   Evidence indicates that newborns can show classical conditioning, but primarily with respect to stimuli
b
p. 297   a. that are familiar to the newborn.
Concept b. that have survival value for the newborn.
M   c. that are not familiar to the newborn.
         d. that are noxious to the newborn.

8.19   Research suggests that newborns are capable of
d
p. 297   a. classical conditioning only.
Study   b. operant conditioning only.
M   c. imitation only.
         d. classical conditioning, operant conditioning, and imitation.

8.20   Infants as young as two or three days old will show _____ in response to subtle differences
c   in human speech.
p. 298   a. nervousness
Concept b. an increase in anxiety
M   c. differential attention patterns
         d. similar, but decreased, attention patterns

8.21   Research indicates that infants spend more time looking in the direction of _____ rather than in
b   the direction of other names.
p. 298   a. different speakers
Study   b. their own names
M   c. different sounding names
         d. names that have been repeated several times

8.22   Research by Frantz and others on the visual preferences of infants showed that they prefer to look at
b
p. 298   a. sharp angles.
Study   b. human faces.
M   c. bright colors.
         d. funny pictures.

8.23   The patterns that babies spend the most looking at
c
p. 298   a. are solid, bright colors.
Concept b. have bold black-and-white lines.
M   c. resemble human faces.
         d. contain circles instead of straight lines.

8.24   The visual cliff apparatus is used to study
a
p. 298   a. depth perception.
Fact   b. pattern recognition.
E   c. form perception.
         d. cognitive dissonance.

8.25   An infant being tested on a visual cliff will demonstrate depth perception by
c
p. 298   a. becoming frightened and crying.
Fact   b. refusing to crawl on the "shallow" end.
M   c. refusing to crawl on the "deep" end.
         d. refusing to crawl on either end.

8.26   Research with the visual cliff apparatus suggests that depth perception is developed in humans
b   as early as
p. 299   a. six days.
Study   b. six months when infants start to crawl.
M   c. one year when infants start to walk.
         d. birth.

8.27   Which of the following characterizes longitudinal research?
d
p. 299
Fact
M
a. Separate groups of subjects of various ages are compared.
b. It allows researchers to complete a study quickly.
c. It is difficult to pinpoint developmental factors as actual causes with this method.
d. Repeated access to the same subjects is required at several points in time.

8.28   A research technique in which the same individuals are studied over substantial periods of time is called
c
p. 299
Concept
M
a. cross-sectional method.
b. age-similarity method.
c. longitudinal method.
d. age-transfer method.

8.29   The major disadvantage of longitudinal research is that
b
p. 299
Concept
C
a. the individual differences between people may obscure the changes over time.
b. measuring the same people over and over may affect their performance on the tests.
c. differences between groups may be due to different experiences not related to age.
d. sometimes the type of groups needed for this research is difficult to identify.

8.30   Which of the following techniques is most likely to be affected by subject attrition and practice effects?
b
p. 299
Concept
M
a. cross-sectional method
b. longitudinal method
c. hypothetical-deductive method
d. meta-analysis

8.31   Research methods in which children of different ages are studied at the same point in time are referred to as
b
p. 299
Fact
M
a. longitudinal methods.
b. cross-sectional methods.
c. contextual methods.
d. longitudinal-sequential methods.

8.32   Which of the following methods is most likely to be influenced by cohort effects?
c
p. 299
Fact
M
a. meta-analysis
b. hypothetical-deductive
c. cross-sectional
d. longitudinal

8.33   Differences between persons of different ages stemming from the fact that they experienced contrasting social or cultural conditions are referred to as
d
p. 299
Fact
M
a. longitudinal errors.
b. ethological biases.
c. script effects.
d. cohort effects.

8.34   The major disadvantage of cross-sectional research is that
a
p. 299
Concept
C
a. differences between groups may be due to different experiences not related to age.
b. it is often difficult to contact the same individuals over and over again for a long time.
c. sometimes the type of groups needed for this research is difficult to identify.
d. it is more time-consuming and expensive to conduct than other types of research.

8.35   Methods involving the study of several samples of people of different ages for a number of years are called
a
p. 300
Fact
M
a. longitudinal-sequential designs.
b. cross-sectional designs.
c. longitudinal designs.
d. meta-analysis designs.

Chapter 8 - Human Development 151

8.36 Which of the following designs allows for assessing developmental changes and cohort effects
b by comparing persons born in different years with one another when they have reached the
p. 300 same age?
Concept   a. cross-sectional
C   b. longitudinal-sequential   *Short answer*
    c. longitudinal
    d. post-hoc

8.37 The method of studying development that provides the clearest picture of the course of human
c development is the
p. 300   a. cross-sectional approach.
Concept   b. longitudinal approach.
M   c. longitudinal-sequential approach.
PT/OLSG   d. experimental design.

Cognitive Development During Childhood

8.38 Jean Piaget believed that children
c   a. think as adults do.
p. 301   b. have innate cognitive capacities for mathematics and reasoning.
Fact   c. acquire cognitive capacities in an orderly sequence.
M   d. can not acquire cognitive capacities until language has developed.

8.39 Which theory of development proposes that human beings move through an orderly and
d predictable series of changes?
p. 301   a. process
Fact   b. longitudinal
E   c. reactive
    d. stage

8.40 According to Piaget, the process of building mental representations of the world through direct
a interaction with it is
p. 301   a. adaptation.
Fact   b. egocentrism.
M   c. metacognition.
    d. conservation.

8.41 In Piaget's theory of development, the two processes that together control how someone deals
d with new experiences are
p. 301   a. proximal and distal.
Concept   b. biology and experience.
M   c. perception and cognition.
    d. assimilation and accommodation.

8.42 Small babies put everything they grab into their mouths, even toys, books, or car keys. This
b is _____. An older child may learn that food and thumbs go in the mouth, but rattles are for
p. 301 shaking and books are for turning pages. This is _____.
Applied   a. accommodation; assimilation
M   b. assimilation; accommodation
    c. conservation; decentration
    d. decentration; conservation

8.43 Fitting experience into existing schema is known as
d   a. preoperation.
p. 301   b. adaptation.
Concept   c. accommodation.
M   d. assimilation.
PT/OLSG

152 Test Bank - Essentials of Psychology (2nd Edition)

8.44
b
p. 301
Fact
M

According to Piaget, the process of understanding the world in terms of existing concepts, schema, and modes of thought by putting new information into existing mental frameworks is called
a. accommodation.
b. assimilation.
c. conservation.
d. metacognition.

8.45
a
p. 301
Concept
M

The tendency of young children to call all adult females "Mommy" is an example of what Piaget would call
a. assimilation.
b. accommodation.
c. decentration.
d. conservation.

8.46
c
p. 301
Concept
M

According to Piaget, the tendency to alter existing concepts or mental frameworks in response to new information or new recognizable dimensions of the external world is called
a. conservation.
b. assimilation.
c. accommodation.
d. hypothetico-deductive reasoning.

8.47
c
p. 301
Fact
M
PT/OLSG

According to Piaget, cognitive development involves interplay between _____ and _____.
a. sensation and cognition.
b. the id and the ego.
c. assimilation and accommodation.
d. emotion and motivation.

8.48
c
p. 302
Fact
M

In which of the following stages do children learn that there is a relationship between their actions and their external world?
a. preoperational
b. concrete operations
c. sensorimotor
d. formal operations

8.49
b
p. 302
Concept
M

In Piaget's theory of development, object permanence refers to a child's ability to
a. think logically about the events he or she observes.
b. think about objects that are not immediately present.
c. understand things from someone else's point of view.
d. trust that necessary objects will not be removed.

8.50
d
p. 302
Applied
M

The baby is playing intently with Lisa's car keys. She manages to get them away and put them in a drawer. The baby immediately begins playing intently with something else. This shows that the baby has not yet developed
a. stranger anxiety.
b. conservation.
c. postoperational thinking.
d. object permanence.

8.51
d
p. 302
Concept
M

When your nephew's toy rolls out of sight under the bed, he immediately begins to search for it. What Piagetian concept does his behavior illustrate?
a. symbolic thought
b. reversibility
c. sensorimotor action
d. object permanence

Chapter 8 - Human Development

8.52
a
p. 302
Concept
M

Which of the following is not attained during the sensorimotor stage?
a. the principle of conservation
b. the concept of object permanence
c. a basic understanding of cause-and-effect relationships
d. a relationship between one's actions and the external world

8.53
d
p. 302
Concept
M

The preoperational stage of Piaget's theory of cognitive development begins when a child is able to
a. apply specific logical operations to answer questions correctly.
b. tell that two things have the same amount even though they look different.
c. group objects into logical categories taking many factors into account.
d. form mental representations of objects and events.

8.54
a
p. 302
Concept
M

The primary difference between children in the preoperational and sensorimotor stages of cognitive development is that children in the preoperational stage are able to
a. represent the world symbolically.
b. think logically about hypothetical events.
c. understand the concept of conservation.
d. use both assimilation and accommodation.

8.55
d
p. 302
Applied
M

Four-year-old Lisa, when talking on the phone to her aunt, is distressed that the aunt has not commented on the new hat Lisa is wearing. Her belief that the aunt can see the hat illustrates
a. object permanence.
b. conservation.
c. syllogistic reasoning.
d. egocentrism.

8.56
a
p. 302
Fact
E

In Piaget's theory of cognitive development, the term "egocentrism" refers to
a. a child's inability to see the world from someone else's viewpoint.
b. the belief that objects that are out of sight no longer exist.
c. the ability to play other roles in games of make-believe.
d. a selfish disregard for the thoughts and feelings of others.

8.57
c
p. 302
Fact
M

According to Piaget, children's difficulty in understanding that others may perceive the world differently than they do is called
a. conservation deficits.
b. comprehension inhibition.
c. egocentrism.
d. belief perseverance.

8.58
b
p. 302
Applied
C

A mother overheard her little boy, as he was getting milk from the refrigerator, saying to himself, "I like white, this must be my milk." This is an example of
a. assimilation.
b. egocentrism.
c. concrete operations.
d. conservation.

8.59
b
p. 302
Concept
M

The lack of the principle of conservation accompanied with egocentric thought are characteristic of Piaget's
a. formal operations stage.
b. preoperational stage.
c. concrete operations stage.
d. object permanence stage.

8.60
c
p. 302
Applied
M

Ralph is upset because his older sister took two cookies, but he only has one. His sister cuts Ralph's cookie in half, and he is satisfied that they now have the same amount. Ralph would be in which of Piaget's stages of cognitive development?
a. Sensorimotor
b. Concrete operations
c. Preoperational
d. Formal operations

8.61 b p. 302 Fact M

The major difference between children in the concrete operational stage and the preoperational stage of development is that in the concrete operational stage, children
a. develop a sense of object permanence.
b. understand the concept of conservation.
c. are generally more egocentric.
d. can think logically about hypothetical things.

8.62 d p. 302 Concept M

In Piaget's theory, knowledge that certain physical attributes of an object remain unchanged even though the outward appearance of the object is altered is called
a. egocentrism.
b. object permanence.
c. assimilation.
d. conservation.

8.63 a p. 302 Concept E

According to Piaget, mastery of conservation marks the beginning of the
a. concrete operations stage.
b. formal operations stage.
c. sensorimotor stage.
d. preoperational stage.

8.64 c p. 302 Concept M

Conservation and logical thought are characteristics of Piaget's
a. sensorimotor stage.
b. preoperational stage.
c. concrete operations stage.
d. hypothetical-deductive stage.

8.65 d p. 302 Concept M

The stage in which logical thought first occurs is
a. preoperational.
b. sensorimotor.
c. formal operations.
d. concrete operations.

8.66 d p. 303 Fact M

The primary difference between children in the formal operational and the concrete operational stages of development is that in the formal operational stage, children are able to
a. understand that appearance is not the same as reality.
b. think about the world from another person's point of view.
c. think about objects that are not immediately present.
d. think logically about theoretical, abstract ideas.

8.67 a p. 303 Fact M

In Piaget's theory of cognitive development, the idea of propositional reasoning refers to the ability of a child to think logically about
a. possibilities.
b. actual, concrete events.
c. objects hidden from view.
d. the reasons for things.

8.68 c p. 303 Concept M

When children have entered Piaget's stage of formal operations, their thought processes differ from an adult's mainly in that the children
a. cannot apply logical analysis to concrete situations.
b. believe that others will see things from their point of view.
c. don't have as much information or experience as adults.
d. don't understand how to apply logic to possibilities.

8.69 d p. 303 Concept M

Real examples are to imaginary abstract examples as
a. sensorimotor is to preoperational.
b. preoperational is to sensorimotor.
c. formal operations is to concrete operations.
d. concrete operations is to formal operations.

Chapter 8 - Human Development

8.70 Hypothetico-deductive reasoning and propositional reasoning are characteristic of Piaget's
a
p. 303
Concept
M
a. formal operations stage.
b. concrete operations stage.
c. sensorimotor stage.
d. preoperational stage.

8.71 Which list places Piaget's stages in the correct chronological order?
c
p. 303
Fact
E
a. concrete operations, formal operations, sensorimotor, preoperational
b. preoperational, sensorimotor, formal operations, concrete operations
c. sensorimotor, preoperational, concrete operations, formal operations
d. sensorimotor, concrete operations, formal operations, preoperational

8.72 When it comes to evaluating the concrete abilities of infants and young children, Jean Piaget
d
p. 303
Concept
M
a. was highly inaccurate.
b. was highly accurate.
c. tended to overestimate their abilities.
d. tended to underestimate their abilities.

8.73 Research with children on the development of cognitive abilities has found that Piaget
b
p. 303
Concept
M
PT/OLSG
a. was essentially correct.
b. underestimated cognitive abilities.
c. overestimated cognitive abilities.
d. overemphasized the role of sensory processes.

8.74 Piaget proposed that cognitive development passes through discrete stages, and these stages are _____, meaning that a child must complete one stage before entering another stage.
b
p. 303
Concept
M
a. egocentric
b. discontinuous
c. static
d. contextual

8.75 An important criticism of Piaget's theory of cognitive development is that
d
p. 303
Concept
C
a. young children can't do what Piaget claims they can.
b. it puts too much emphasis on linguistic interactions.
c. progression through stages is really more discrete.
d. progression through stages is really more gradual.

8.76 As an alternative to Piaget, the theories that focus on a child's capacity to process, store, retrieve, and actually manipulate information as a function of age are called
c
p. 304
Concept
C
a. Vygotsky's theories.
b. process theories.
c. information-processing theories.
d. artificial intelligence theories.

8.77 The information processing perspective of cognitive development
b
p. 304
Concept
M
PT/OLSG
a. seeks to map out the stages of development.
b. seeks to understand how, and in what ways, children's capacity to process, store, retrieve, and actively manipulate information changes with age.
c. proposes that private speech is egocentric.
d. proposes that private speech represents attempts in social communication.

8.78 The information processing perspective on development focuses on how children's _____ changes with age.
c
p. 304
Fact
M
a. ability to use language to communicate with others
b. distribution of functions within the brain
c. capacities to process, store, and use information
d. mathematical and arithmetical capabilities

156 Test Bank - Essentials of Psychology (2nd Edition)

8.79
d
p. 304
Concept
M
PT/OLSG

The proposal that changes in the ability of children to perform cognitive tasks results from changes in their ability to block out distractors and focus attention is most consistent with _____ view of development.
a. Piaget's
b. Vygotsky's
c. the psychodynamic
d. the information processing

8.80
b
p. 304
Concept
C

One reason why the information processing perspective on development is an important one today is that it
a. emphasizes the importance of classical conditioning.
b. is supported by a growing body of scientific evidence.
c. is quite different from other modern theories.
d. makes specific predictions about brain processes.

8.81
a
p. 304
Fact
M

Research on attention and aging indicates that
a. we move from unfocused scanning to focused planfulness as we age.
b. we move from focused scanning to unfocused planfulness as we age.
c. all ages show comparable amounts of unfocused scanning and focused planfulness.
d. unfocused scanning increases with age.

8.82
a
p. 304
Concept
M

A key characteristic of attention-deficit hyperactivity disorder is that children with this problem
a. are unable to focus their attention on a task for long.
b. have lower intelligence and reading ability than others.
c. process verbal and auditory but not visual information.
d. have uncontrollable aggressive impulses toward others.

8.83
d
p. 304
Concept
C

Adoptive children whose biological parent has ADHD (attention deficit hyperactivity disorder) are more likely to develop this problem than adoptive children without such a biological parent. This indicates that
a. ADHD cannot be helped with behavioral treatments.
b. ADHD is an inherited condition, like color blindness.
c. ADHD is caused by being rejected by one's parents.
d. heredity plays a role in the development of ADHD.

8.84
a
p. 305
Applied
M

A memory strategy that appears in children as young as three years who are trying to remember a group of toys is to
a. spend more time naming them than playing with them.
b. organize them into meaningful groups or chunks.
c. rehearse the list of toys over and over in order.
d. incorporate the toys into a complex toy schema.

8.85
c
p. 305
Concept
M

Generally, the use of rehearsal
a. in short-term memory decreases as children get older.
b. in long-term memory decreases as children get older.
c. in short-term memory increases as children get older.
d. in long-term memory increases as children get older.

8.86
d
p. 305
Study
C

Butler and colleagues (1995), in a study investigating the effect of drawing as an aid to memory, found that
a. younger children recalled more information after not drawing a picture of an event.
b. older children recalled more information after not drawing a picture of an event.
c. younger children recalled more information after drawing a picture of an event.
d. older children recalled more information after drawing a picture of an event.

8.87
a
p. 306
Fact
C

The term "metacognition" refers to our awareness of
a. our own cognitive processes.
b. the typical sequence of events in some situation.
c. what is morally right and wrong in certain situations.
d. the emotional relationships we have with others.

Chapter 8 - Human Development

8.88 a p. 306 Applied M
A student who simply reads a textbook chapter from beginning to end and then doesn't understand why he or she gets low test scores has a problem with
a. metacognition.
b. moral development.
c. formal reasoning.
d. short-term memory.

8.89 c p. 306 Fact E
Awareness and understanding of our own cognitive processes is called
a. auto-awareness.
b. episodic memory.
c. metacognition.
d. cognitive dissonance.

8.90 d p. 306 Applied M
Noting things to yourself such as "I need to study more for the next exam if I want to do well," is an example of
a. episodic memory.
b. domain-specific knowledge.
c. egocentric thought.
d. metacognition.

8.91 b p. 306 Study C
Miller and his colleagues (1995) found that, overall, Chinese children outperformed American students on counting tasks, but not on counting tasks with numbers between
a. eleven and twenty.
b. one and ten.
c. twelve and fifteen.
d. twenty and thirty.

8.92 c p. 306 Concept M
In counting tasks, Chinese children have an advantage over American children because of their _____.
a. age
b. training
c. language
d. gender

Moral Development: Reasoning about "Right" and "Wrong"

8.93 c p. 307 Fact C
In research dealing with imaginary moral dilemmas, which involve competing courses of action, Kohlberg assessed level of moral development on the basis of
a. subjects' selected course of action only.
b. subjects' selected course of action and explanations for their selected course of action.
c. subjects' explanation for their selected course of action only.
d. neither subjects' course of action nor explanation for their selected course of action.

8.94 c p. 307 Fact C
At Kohlberg's preconventional level of moral understanding, what determines whether a particular action is viewed to be moral?
a. whether or not the actions help the individual to satisfy personal needs.
b. whether or not the actions uphold self-chosen ethical standards.
c. whether or not the actions result in punishment.
d. whether or not the individual's actions adhere to social norms.

8.95 a p. 308 Fact M
According to Kohlberg, at what level of moral development do children tend to judge behaviors in terms of the consequences they produce?
a. preconventional
b. conventional
c. postconventional
d. eclectic

158 Test Bank - Essentials of Psychology (2nd Edition)

8.96
c
p. 308
Applied
M

Ralph took money from his dad's wallet to pay off a bully who was threatening his little sister. Was this right or wrong? A child at the preconventional level of morality would most likely say that
a. it was wrong, because the bully will just do it again next time.
b. it was right, because Ralph should protect his little sister.
c. it was wrong, because his dad will punish him if he finds out.
d. it was right, because Ralph's sister will know he loves her.

8.97
b
p. 308
Applied
M

Suppose in an imaginary moral dilemma a parent steals food for hungry children. If a subject states that the parent was wrong for stealing the food because, if caught, the parent will be sent to prison, the subject is showing moral judgement at the
a. conventional level.
b. preconventional level.
c. postconventional level.
d. social contract level.

8.98
d
p. 308
Fact
M

In Kohlberg's theory of moral development, children at the conventional level of morality will base their moral decisions on
a. whether a behavior will be rewarded or punished.
b. their own personal moral beliefs and principles.
c. maintaining the welfare of the whole of society.
d. whether other people will approve or disapprove.

8.99
a
p. 308
Applied
M

Ralph took money from his dad's wallet to pay off a bully who was threatening his little sister. Was this right or wrong? A child at the conventional level of morality would most likely say that
a. it was wrong, because the teacher would not approve.
b. it was right, because his sister will be extra nice to him.
c. it was wrong, because his dad will punish him if he finds out.
d. it was right, because we have a commitment to our family.

8.100
b
p. 308
Concept
M
PT/OLSG

At the _____ level of moral development, we tend to judge morality in terms of what supports and preserves the social order.
a. preconventional
b. conventional
c. postconventional
d. abstract

8.101
a
p. 308
Concept
M

At Kohlberg's conventional level of moral judgment, the morality of a particular action is determined by whether or not the
a. individual's actions support the laws of the society.
b. individual's actions result in punishment.
c. actions help the individual to satisfy personal needs.
d. individual's actions uphold self-chosen ethical standards.

8.102
d
p. 308
Applied
C

Ralph took money from his dad's wallet to pay off a bully who was threatening his little sister. Was this right or wrong? An individual at the postconventional level of morality would most likely say that
a. it was right, because his sister will be extra nice to him.
b. it was wrong, because his dad will punish him if he finds out.
c. it was right, because it will make his sister happy.
d. it was wrong, because it encourages bullying and aggression.

8.103
c
p. 308
Concept
C

Consider the moral dilemma faced by the husband who is trying to decide to steal a drug he cannot afford, but which will save his wife's life. The person who reasons that it would be all right to steal the drug because the right to life is more important than property rights has reached the _____ stage of moral development.
a. preconventional
b. conventional
c. postconventional
d. humanistic

Chapter 8 - Human Development   159

8.104   Morality judged in terms of abstract principles and values, rather than in terms of existing
d   laws or rules of society, is characteristic of Kohlberg's _____ stage of moral development.
p. 308   a. religious
Concept   b. preconventional
M   c. conventional
            d. postconventional

8.105   The idea that drug use can be reduced in the United States by appealing to the conscience of
b   drug users and to their concern for the welfare of the society implies that drug users operate
p. 308   at Kohlberg's _____ level of morality.
Applied   a. unconventional
M   b. postconventional
            c. conventional
            d. preconventional

8.106   When men and women are asked to describe moral conflicts they have personally experienced,
d   modern research shows that
p. 309   a. women describe these conflicts in terms of personal relationships.
Fact   b. men describe these conflicts in terms of impersonal rights.
M   c. women describe these conflicts in terms of caring for others.
            d. men and women do not differ in how they describe these conflicts.

8.107   Early research on how Kohlberg's theory of moral development applies to males and females
c   indicated that
p. 309   a. females progress to higher stages than males do.
Fact   b. males progress to higher stages than females do.
M   c. males and females progress through the stages equally.
            d. the theory has never been tested with females.

8.108   Recent research, using both Kohlberg's dilemmas and real-life dilemmas, found that
b   the majority of college age students
p. 309   a. made judgments in one particular stage.
Study   b. made judgments ranging across three different stages.
C   c. made consistent judgments for real-life dilemmas.
            d. made consistent judgments for Kohlberg's dilemmas.

8.109   Kohlberg's work has been criticized on the grounds that it is _____, in that it may be biased
b   against groups different from the populations with which he worked.
p. 309   a. culture-free
Concept   b. culture-bound
C   c. culture-sensitive
            d. culture-consistent

Social and Emotional Development during Childhood

8.110   Which of the following correctly describes children's emotional development?
b   a. Emotional and cognitive development occur independently.
p. 309   b. Emotional and cognitive development occur simultaneously.
Fact   c. Ability to express all emotions appear at about the same age in each child.
M   d. Social referencing as a means of expressing emotions occurs as soon as they are born.

8.111   Infant emotional development is measured by
a   a. facial expressions.
p. 309   b. EEG recordings.
Fact   c. body gestures.
M   d. neurological calculations.

8.112
b
p. 309
Fact
M

Social smiling to a human face occurs around
a. four months.
b. two months.
c. one day.
d. one week.

8.113
c
p. 309
Fact
M

Using others' reactions to appraise an uncertain situation is called
a. good boy --- good girl orientation.
b. cognitive temperament.
c. social referencing.
d. social facilitation.

8.114
d
p. 310
Concept
M

Social referencing occurs whenever someone
a. judges the friendliness or attractiveness of another person.
b. is discriminated against on the basis of physical appearance.
c. acts in a certain way in order to please other members of a social group.
d. decides how to respond to a situation on the basis of how others are responding.

8.115
a
p. 310
Concept
E

Stable individual differences in the quality and intensity of emotional reactions refers to
a. temperament.
b. euphemism.
c. motivation.
d. drives.

8.116
b
p. 310
Fact
M

The term "temperament" refers to
a. the quality of a relationship between a child and its mother and father.
b. stable individual differences in mood, activity, and emotional reactivity.
c. the level of moral development a person is able to achieve.
d. consistent patterns of behavior, thought, and feelings in different situations.

8.117
b
p. 310
Fact
M

Research examining temperament in infants indicates that the most common type of temperament is the category
a. difficult children.
b. easy children.
c. slow-to-warm-up children.
d. unclassifiable children.

8.118
c
p. 310
Fact
M

Psychologists classify a baby as a "difficult child" when the child shows a pattern of responding including
a. quickly establishing a firm routine.
b. a relatively apathetic response to events.
c. irregularity in their daily routines.
d. mildly negative responses to new experiences.

8.119
d
p. 310
Fact
M

In classifying temperament, children who are irregular in daily routines, slow to accept new situations or experiences, and show many negative reactions such as frequent crying, are referred to as
a. unclassifiable children.
b. attention-deficit children.
c. slow-to-warm-up children.
d. difficult children.

8.120
d
p. 310
Applied
M

When two-month-old Lisa was given a large stuffed elephant for her birthday, she began to cry loudly, wave her arms, and kick her feet. Lisa would probably be classified as
a. slow-to-warm-up.
b. easy.
c. neutral.
d. difficult.

Chapter 8 - Human Development

8.121
c
p. 310
Fact
M

In classifying temperament, children who are relatively inactive and apathetic and show mild negative reactions to many new situations or experiences are referred to as
a. difficult children.
b. aggressive children.
c. slow-to-warm-up children.
d. unclassifiable children.

8.122
c
p. 311
Fact
M

In comparing difficult children with easy children, it was found that
a. a lower proportion of difficult children experience behavioral difficulties later in life.
b. a higher proportion of easy children experience behavioral difficulties later in life.
c. a higher proportion of difficult children experience behavioral difficulties later in life.
d. there was no difference in the proportion of these two classes of children in terms of behavioral difficulties later in life.

8.123
a
p. 311
Fact
M

The term attachment refers to
a. the strong affectional tie between a child and its caregiver.
b. an innate connection between an infant and its biological parents.
c. the bonding a biological parent feels toward its child.
d. the emotional connection between siblings.

8.124
d
p. 311
Fact
E
PT/OLSG

What are psychologists measuring when they use the strange situation test?
a. cognitive development
b. conservation
c. the appearance-reality distinction
d. attachment to the mother

8.125
d
p. 311
Concept
M

The nature of the bond between child and caregiver is tested with an arrangement called the
a. visual cliff.
b. caregiver separation test.
c. appearance-reality distinction.
d. strange situation test.

8.126
a
p. 312
Concept
M

When studying attachment, research results indicate that the vast majority of American middle-class infants show
a. secure attachment.
b. avoidant attachment.
c. resistant attachment.
d. ambivalent attachment.

8.127
b
p. 312
Concept
C

With respect to the strange situation test, active contact is to anger as
a. avoidant attachment is to resistant attachment.
b. secure attachment is to resistant attachment.
c. resistant attachment is to difficult child.
d. difficult child is to slow-to-warm-up child.

8.128
c
p. 312
Concept
M

In the strange situation test, children who prior to the separation seek contact with their mother, and then after separation and return, are angry and push her away are classified as
a. slow-to-warm-up children.
b. avoidant attachment children.
c. resistant attachment children.
d. difficult children.

8.129 d p. 312 Concept M

Children who look away from the mother while being held by her or approach her with a lack of emotion and often show a dazed facial expression when returned to the mother after separation during the strange situation test are referred to as showing
a. avoidant attachment.
b. resistant attachment.
c. stranger attachment.
d. disorganized attachment.

8.130 c p. 312 Fact M

According to most psychologists, which has the more important role in controlling their interactions, the parent or the baby?
a. The parent initiates and directs the interactions.
b. The baby triggers and maintains the interactions.
c. They both affect the responses of the other.
d. The interactions are controlled by factors outside of them both.

8.131 b p. 313 Study M

In his studies of monkeys raised with artificial mothers, Harlow found that monkeys demonstrated an attachment to
a. only the artificial mother that had supplied them with milk.
b. only the cloth mother that provided contact comfort.
c. only the wire mother with the realistic monkey face.
d. only the cloth mother with the realistic monkey face.

8.132 c p. 313 Concept M PT/OLSG

Harlow's research with monkeys showed that
a. baby monkeys' attachments to their cloth mother could be reversed by rejection.
b. the satisfaction provided by feeding is sufficient for attachment.
c. the satisfaction provided by feeding is not sufficient for attachment.
d. attachment in human infants is not the same as attachment in monkeys.

8.133 a p. 313 Concept M

Contact comfort is a factor that seems to influence
a. attachment.
b. temperament.
c. egocentrism.
d. heuristics.

8.134 c p. 313 Concept M

Research on contact comfort in humans has shown that when two- and three-year-old children are left alone to play in a strange room, they will play longer without distress if
a. the toys present in the room are novel.
b. they know that they are being observed.
c. they have a security blanket with them.
d. they have never had a security blanket.

Gender: Gender Identity and Gender Differences

8.135 a p. 314 Concept M PT/OLSG

Different patterns of behavior that are expected of people because they are male or female are called
a. gender roles.
b. sexism.
c. sexual harassment.
d. feminism.

8.136 c p. 314 Fact M

All societies have fairly clear definitions of _____, or how each gender is expected to behave.
a. gender differences
b. gender identies
c. gender roles
d. gender stereotypes

Chapter 8 - Human Development

8.137 When a child understands that he or she is a boy or a girl the child has acquired
a
p. 314   a. gender identity.
Fact   b. sex-typing.
E   c. sex roles.
         d. androgyny.

8.138 Gender constancy is usually established about the age of
b
p. 315   a. two years.
Fact   b. four years.
M   c. six years.
         d. seven years.

8.139 Social learning theorists suggest that gender identity is acquired on the basis of
d
p. 315   a. underlying cognitive mechanisms.
Fact   b. classical conditioning and gender schema.
M   c. societal pressures and classical conditioning.
         d. operant conditioning and observational learning.

8.140 In explaining the acquisition of gender identity, which of the following focuses primarily on
a   the cognitive mechanisms reflecting children's experiences with their society's beliefs about the
p. 315 attributes of males and females?
Fact   a. gender schema theory
E   b. operant conditioning theory
         c. social learning theory
         d. psychoanalytic theory

8.141 A gender schema is
a   a. a set of beliefs about how males and females are expected to behave.
p. 315   b. a set of moral judgments about the proper behavior of males and females.
Concept   c. an expectation that one will be rewarded for certain types of behaviors.
M   d. an understanding that one's sex will not change easily over time.

8.142 Research results suggest that gender identity is established on the basis of principles described
b   a. only in gender schema theory.
p. 315   b. both in gender schema theory and social learning theory.
Fact   c. only in social learning theory.
M   d. neither gender schema theory nor social learning theory.

8.143 The results of psychological research on gender stereotypes are not simple, but essentially
b   boils down to
p. 315   a. the fact that there are significant differences between males and females.
Fact   b. the fact that the differences among genders are greater than the differences between genders.
C   c. the fact that males have significantly more socially acceptable behaviors than females.
         d. the fact that females have significantly more socially acceptable behaviors than males.

8.144 In terms of differences regarding emotional expression, _____ tend to be more adept at reading
b   nonverbal cues from others.
p. 316   a. males
Fact   b. females
E   c. older people
         d. younger people

8.145 In terms of differences regarding aggression,
b   a. females tend to be more likely to engage in direct aggression.
p. 316   b. females tend to be more likely to engage in indirect aggression.
Fact   c. males tend to be more likely to engage in indirect aggression.
M   d. there are no gender differences in indirect aggression.

8.146 Recent research indicates that there appears to be
a
p. 316 a. no real difference between males and females with respect to cognitive abilities.
Concept b. a difference between males and females with respect to spatial abilities.
C c. a difference between males and females with respect to susceptibility to influence.
  d. no real difference between males and females on indirect aggression.

8.147 Recent research indicates that
b
p. 316 a. males score slightly higher on verbal ability tests than females.
Concept b. females are more likely to experience depression than males.
C c. males are more likely to be leaders than females.
  d. females are more likely to report friendships based on shared interests than males.

Adolescence: Between Child and Adult

8.148 The years between puberty and adulthood are called
b
p. 317 a. adult transition.
Concept b. adolescence.
E c. gender transition.
  d. primary aging.

8.149 Characteristics of adolescence, such as its length or whether it even exists as a distinct
d period of development, are most influenced by
p. 317 a. maturation.
Concept b. hormones.
M c. gender.
  d. culture.

8.150 Adolescence is traditionally viewed as beginning with the
a
p. 317 a. onset of puberty.
Concept b. ending of puberty.
M c. entrance into high school.
  d. establishment of gender identity.

8.151 A sudden spurt in physical growth accompanied by sexual maturity defines
b
p. 317 a. gender identity.
Concept b. puberty.
M c. adolescence.
  d. androgyny.

8.152 In the United States of the last century, the period of adolescence was
c
p. 319 a. even longer than it is now.
Fact b. accompanied by many formal transitions.
M c. not recognized as a distinct phase.
  d. longer for boys than for girls.

8.153 The culture in which a person is growing up will have a large effect on the person's
c experience of
p. 319 a. puberty.
Fact b. sexual maturity.
M c. adolescence.
  d. maturation.

8.154 In the transition from childhood to adulthood, puberty is a _____ transition, and
c adolescence is a _____ transition.
p. 319 a. cognitive; physical
Fact b. physical; cognitive
M c. physical; cultural
  d. cultural; physical

Chapter 8 - Human Development

8.155 The growth spurt occurs
c
p. 319   a. at the same time for males and females.
Fact   b. earlier in males.
M   c. earlier in females.
    d. with such variability that no consistent statement can be made about sex differences.

8.156 The belief that adolescents view themselves as immune from the potential harm of
b high-risk behaviors is called adolescent
p. 319   a. egocentrism.
Fact   b. recklessness.
E   c. immunization.
    d. safety.

8.157 Recent research findings indicate that adolescents' high-risk behaviors are least likely to
c be due to
p. 319   a. social norms.
Concept   b. high reward value of the behaviors.
M   c. perceived invulnerability.
    d. peer pressure.

8.158 Adolescents seek out novel and intense experiences, characteristic of individuals who
a are high on
p. 319   a. sensation seeking.
Concept   b. peer pressure.
M   c. drugs.
PT/OLSG   d. invulnerability.

8.159 Lisa is an adolescent girl who has engaged in unprotected sex. She highly underestimates the probability
c that she will get pregnant. Lisa is engaging in
p. 319   a. cognitive coercion.
Applied   b. emotional blunting.
M   c. egocentric thinking.
    d. sensation seeking.

8.160 Interest in developing friendships and the capacity for intimacy generally heightens during
a   a. adolescence.
p. 320   b. childhood.
Fact   c. adulthood.
E   d. old age.

8.161 An adolescent's friendships help the adolescent develop
a   a. a sense of personal identity.
p. 320   b. primary sexual characteristics.
Fact   c. better relations with parents.
M   d. a sense of integrity.

8.162 Which of the following is not among the social goals desired by adolescents?
d   a. dominance
p. 320   b. nurturance
Fact   c. intimacy
M   d. confidence

8.163 Erikson is to Piaget as
b   a. cognitive development is to stage theory.
p. 320   b. social development is to cognitive development.
Concept   c. intelligence is to emotional development.
C   d. continuity is to education.

166 Test Bank - Essentials of Psychology (2nd Edition)

8.164
a
p. 320
Fact
E

Erikson's theory emphasizes the importance of _____ development across the life span.
a. social
b. cognitive
c. sexual
d. emotional

8.165
d
p. 320
Concept
E

A theory of adult development that emphasizes the resolution of special conflicts that must be faced at each stage is called a(n) _____ theory.
a. generative
b. elaborative
c. life-event
d. crisis

8.166
d
p. 320
Fact
E

Erikson's theory is an example of a _____ approach of adult development.
a. crystallized
b. fluid
c. life-event
d. crisis

8.167
c
p. 321
Concept
M

Erikson's first stage occurs during the first year of life where others must satisfy a baby's needs. This stage centers around
a. autonomy versus shame and doubt.
b. competence versus inferiority.
c. trust versus mistrust.
d. generativity versus stagnation.

8.168
d
p. 321
Concept
M

Erikson's second stage occurs during the second year of life where toddlers learn to regulate their own bodies and to act in independent ways. This stage centers around
a. initiative versus guilt.
b. trust versus mistrust.
c. industry versus inferiority.
d. autonomy versus shame and doubt.

8.169
a
p. 321
Concept
M

Erikson's third stage occurs during the preschool years, between the ages of three and five, where children acquire new physical and mental skills and the capacity to control their impulses. This stage centers around
a. initiative versus guilt.
b. trust versus mistrust.
c. industry versus inferiority.
d. autonomy versus shame and doubt.

8.170
c
p. 321
Concept
M

Erikson's fourth stage occurs during the early school years, between the ages of six and twelve, where children learn to make things, use tools, and acquire many of the skills necessary for adult life. This stage centers around
a. initiative versus guilt.
b. trust versus mistrust.
c. industry versus inferiority.
d. autonomy versus shame and doubt.

8.171
d
p. 324
Concept
M

According to Erikson's theory of psychosocial development, someone who is struggling with issues of who he or she really is and what role he or she wants to adopt in life is most likely
a. an androgynous person.
b. in the last stages of life.
c. having a midlife crisis.
d. an adolescent.

Chapter 8 - Human Development

8.172
c
p. 321
Concept
M

Erikson's fifth stage occurs during adolescence where adolescents seek to establish an understanding of their own unique traits and what is really of central importance to them. This stage centers around
a. trust versus mistrust.
b. initiative versus guilt.
c. identity versus role confusion.
d. autonomy versus shame and doubt.

8.173
d
p. 321
Concept
M
PT/OLSG

According to Erikson's theory, the most important internal crisis faced by adolescents concerns resolving
a. competence versus inferiority.
b. initiative versus guilt.
c. sexuality versus sexual confusion.
d. identity versus role confusion.

8.174
d
p. 321
Concept
E

According to Erikson, an understanding of an individual's unique traits and what is really of central importance to them is called
a. crystallized intelligence.
b. fluid intelligence.
c. life structure.
d. self-identity.

8.175
a
p. 321
Concept
M

According to Erikson, the central question of adolescence would be
a. "Who am I?"
b. "When should I leave home?"
c. "Who should I marry?"
d. "What will my job be after high school?"

8.176
c
p. 321
Applied
M

Forty-year-old Ralph has no children of his own, but gets satisfaction from his volunteer work as a leader and camping director for the Boy Scouts. According to Erikson's theory of adult development, this would indicate that Ralph has successfully resolved the _____ crisis.
a. integrity versus despair
b. intimacy versus isolation
c. generativity versus self-absorption
d. initiative versus guilt

8.177
a
p. 321
Concept
M

In Erikson's final crisis of adult development, people tend to look back and ask, "Did my life have meaning?" This crisis occurs during the stage that centers around
a. integrity versus despair.
b. generativity versus self-absorption.
c. intimacy versus isolation.
d. competence versus inferiority.

8.178
b
p. 321
Concept
C

Which of the following is a question that typifies Erikson's integrity versus despair?
a. "Who am I?"
b. "Did my being here really matter?"
c. "What can I do now?"
d. "Does anybody really care about me?"

8.179
a
p. 322
Fact
M

Issues associated with growing up in a parent-absent family include
a. increased risk for delinquent behaviors.
b. increased school performance.
c. decreased difficulties in forming meaningful relationships.
d. decreased probability of depression.

8.180 Families that do not meet the needs of their members and may do them serious harm are called
a
p. 322   a. dysfunctional.
Fact   b. fluid.
M   c. crystallized.
         d. debilitating.

8.181 What factor seems to be most important in allowing adolescents raised in high-risk settings
c   to develop into well-adjusted adults?
p. 323   a. a sound education
Fact   b. appropriate use of discipline
M   c. interactions between individuals, families, and communities
         d. the absence of alcohol and other drugs in the immediate family

Adulthood and Aging

8.182 Aging is a continuous process that begins _____ in life. This
b   process proceeds _____ at first.
p. 324   a. late; slowly
Fact   b. early; slowly
M   c. late; rapidly
PT/OLSG d. early; rapidly

8.183 Which of the following is characteristic of physical change during early adulthood?
c   a. considerable weight loss for many men and women
p. 324   b. increased flexibility of the eyes' lenses
Fact   c. slow and minimal change throughout the entire period
M   d. increased flexibility in body joints

8.184 People usually become aware of declines in their physical systems
c   a. in their twenties.
p. 324   b. in their thirties.
Fact   c. in their forties.
M   d. in their fifties.
PT/OLSG

8.185 A period of several years during which the functioning of the reproductive system, and
a   various aspects of sexual activity, change greatly during mid-life aging is called
p. 324   a. climacteric.
Fact   b. mid-life transition.
E   c. mid-life crisis.
         d. self-absorption.

8.186 The climacteric is associated with
a   a. menopause.
p. 324   b. a person's ability to withstand intense heat.
Fact   c. a person's ability to withstand intense cold.
M   d. Erikson's third stage.
PT/OLSG

8.187 Which of the following is most likely to be the best predictor of physical vigor and
b   health as we age?
p. 325   a. biological age
Fact   b. life-style
M   c. family history
         d. career

Chapter 8 - Human Development

8.188
c
p. 325
Fact
M

Compared to younger people, adults between the ages of 60 and 80 are
a. much more likely to suffer from chronic illness.
b. much more likely to be hospitalized.
c. in reasonably good health overall.
d. relatively healthy if they are men, but not women.

8.189
d
p. 325
Fact
E

A chronic illness is one that is
a. caused by changes due to aging.
b. best treated with antibiotics.
c. caused by a poor life style.
d. long-term, progressive, and incurable.

8.190
c
p. 325
Fact
M

With respect to short-term memory, older persons in comparison to young adults have a
a. slightly greater capacity.
b. slightly smaller capacity.
c. similar capacity.
d. extremely smaller capacity.

8.191
b
p. 326
Concept
C

The most important characteristic determining whether an older adult performs comparably to a younger adult on a memory task is whether the task involves
a. short-term memory or long-term memory.
b. low meaningful material or high meaningful material.
c. recall or recognition.
d. visual or auditory information.

8.192
a
p. 326
Fact
M

When compared to young adults, older persons' long-term memory is
a. poorer with respect to recall.
b. better with respect to recall.
c. poorer with respect to recognition.
d. better with respect to recognition.

8.193
a
p. 326
Concept
M

The author suggests that the best way to ensure that your mental abilities will continue to function well as you get older is to
a. use your mental abilities actively throughout your life.
b. eat a healthy diet and get lots of exercise.
c. avoid smoking, drinking, or using drugs.
d. lead a quiet life with very few distractions.

8.194
b
p. 326
Concept
M

Aspects of intelligence that involve drawing on previously learned information to make decisions or solve problems are referred to as
a. fluid intelligence.
b. crystallized intelligence.
c. standardized intelligence.
d. formal intelligence.

8.195
c
p. 326
Concept
M

Aspects of intelligence that involve the abilities to form concepts, reason, and identify similarities are referred to as
a. formal intelligence.
b. standardized intelligence.
c. fluid intelligence.
d. crystallized intelligence.

8.196
a
p. 326
Fact
M

Which of the following tends to increase across the lifespan?
a. crystallized intelligence
b. fluid intelligence
c. memory recall tests
d. incidental memory

8.197 d
p. 326
Fact
M
PT/OLSG

Fluid intelligence appears to _____ after the early twenties. Crystallized intelligence appears to _____ across the lifespan.
a. increase; remain constant
b. increase; decrease
c. decrease; remain constant
d. decrease; increase

8.198 b
p. 327
Concept
C

According to Levinson, the time where we come to believe that we are reaching a point of no return where if we remain in our present life course we will have too much invested to change is
a. mid-life crisis.
b. age 30 transition.
c. early adulthood, that is, around twenty-two.
d. late adult transition.

8.199 b
p. 327
Fact
M

Levinson's theory of adult development describes adulthood as a series of
a. dilemmas that must be resolved.
b. eras and transitions.
c. personality shifts.
d. new skills that must be mastered.

8.200 b
p. 328
Fact
C

When interpreting Levinson's theory of adult development as discussed in your textbook, it should be noted that his hypothesis is based on data collected
a. with the experimental technique.
b. from a small number of men.
c. from men and women between the ages of 35 to 45.
d. from a small sample of women only.

8.201 a
p. 328
Fact
M

The baby boomer generation is different from other generations because it may be in the unique position of
a. being financially dependent on their parents for a long time, but having to care for these parents.
b. being financially independent at an early age.
c. being emotionally independent at an early age.
d. being responsible for financial decisions before having financial independence.

8.202 c
p. 329
Study
C

In surveys to investigate self-reported happiness, it was found that the majority of people reported having relatively high levels of
a. frustration.
b. satisfaction with job, but not with family.
c. subjective well-being.
d. dissatisfaction with their lives.

8.203 d
p. 329
Concept
C

One possible reason for the relatively high levels of reported subjective well-being is that most people
a. are simply relieved to be surviving.
b. replied to the questionnaire in a socially acceptable way.
c. live lives that are quite higher than the survival level.
d. are in a relatively good mood most of the time.

Aging and Death

8.204 a
p. 330
Concept
M
PT/OLSG

The importance of free radicals in aging is emphasized by which of the following theories of aging?
a. wear-and-tear theory.
b. genetic theory.
c. homeostatic theory.
d. social theory.

Chapter 8 - Human Development 171

8.205
b
p. 330
Fact
M

One theory of aging is that body metabolism produces atoms that react violently with other molecules in cells producing declines in biological functioning associated with aging. This theory is referred to as
a. gene mutation theory.
b. free radical theory.
c. genetic programming theory.
d. homeostatic theory.

8.206
d
p. 330
Applied
M

As a young adult, Ralph was a real "party animal," frequently overindulging in alcohol, smoking, and eating. Although only 50, Ralph acts and looks like a much older person. Aging in this example can be used to support which of the following theories?
a. genetic theory
b. homeostatic theory
c. tertiary theory
d. wear-and-tear theory

8.207
b
p. 330
Fact
M

A wear-and-tear theory of aging emphasizes the importance of
a. an internal biological clock.
b. accumulating damage to parts of our bodies.
c. a genetic program to live for a certain amount of time.
d. social support while one is growing older.

8.208
b
p. 330
Fact
M

Some genetic theories of aging emphasize a biological mechanism that controls
a. the amount of chemical damage done by free radicals.
b. the number of times body cells can reproduce.
c. how strongly an individual wants to continue living.
d. how aggressively cancer cells divide and spread.

8.209
c
p. 330
Fact
M

The theory of aging that suggests there is a biological clock that regulates the aging process is referred to as a
a. wear-and-tear theory.
b. free radical theory.
c. genetic theory.
d. homeostatic theory.

8.210
a
p. 330
Fact
M

Which of these is evidence that supports a genetic theory of aging?
a. Certain cells will only divide a certain number of times before dying.
b. Free radicals produced in the lab will cause cellular damage.
c. Many animals will live for very long times in ideal conditions.
d. The life expectancy of humans has risen dramatically over several decades.

8.211
a
p. 330
Fact
M

The absence of any brain activity is to the absence of cortical activity as
a. brain death is to cerebral death.
b. cerebral death is to brain death.
c. cortical death is to physiological death.
d. biological clock death is to physiological death.

8.212
b
p. 330
Concept
M

Physiological death refers to a time when
a. there is no electrical activity in the brain for ten minutes.
b. all physical activities that sustain life have stopped.
c. there is no electrical activity in the cerebral cortex.
d. people give up their relationships with the dead one.

8.213
a
p. 330
Concept
M

Brain death refers to a time when
a. there is no electrical activity in the brain for ten minutes.
b. all biological activities that sustain life has stopped.
c. there is no electrical activity in the cerebral cortex.
d. people give up their relationships with the dead one.

172 Test Bank - Essentials of Psychology (2nd Edition)

8.214
d
p. 330
Concept
M

Social death refers to a time when
a. there is no electrical activity in the brain for ten minutes.
b. all biological activities that sustain life has stopped.
c. there is no electrical activity in the cerebral cortex.
d. people give up their relationships with the dead one.

8.215
c
p. 330
Concept
M

Cerebral death refers to a time when
a. there is no electrical activity in the brain for ten minutes.
b. all biological activities that sustain life has stopped.
c. there is no electrical activity in the cerebral cortex.
d. people give up their relationships with the dead one.

8.216
b
p. 330
Concept
E

If a person's heart is still beating but there is no activity anywhere in the person's brain, that person is said to have experienced
a. physiological death.
b. brain death.
c. social death.
d. near death.

8.217
d
p. 330
Concept
E

If a person's heart is still beating and there is still activity in the lower areas of the brain, but no signs of activity in the cerebral cortex, the person is said to have experienced
a. brain death.
b. social death.
c. physiological death.
d. cerebral death.

8.218
a
p. 331
Fact
E
PT/OLSG

According to Kubler-Ross, the first stage of the dying process is
a. denial.
b. anger.
c. depression.
d. bargaining.

8.219
c
p. 331
Fact
E

According to Kubler-Ross, the order or sequence that patients face when they are told that they have a terminal illness that eventually results in their death is
a. denial, depression, anger, bargaining, acceptance.
b. depression, denial, anger, bargaining, acceptance.
c. denial, anger, bargaining, depression, acceptance.
d. anger, denial, bargaining, depression, acceptance.

8.220
a
p. 331
Fact
M

According to Kubler-Ross, a patient's refusal to believe that the end is in sight characterizes the
a. first stage referred to as denial.
b. third stage referred to as denial.
c. first stage referred to as anger.
d. third state referred to as anger.

8.221
d
p. 331
Applied
M

Lisa's mother has terminal cancer. She is now promising to change her life and become a model human being and to lead a very religious life if only she can be cured. According to Kubler-Ross, she is in the stage of
a. optimism.
b. denial.
c. recruitment.
d. bargaining.

Chapter 8 - Human Development

8.222
b
p. 331
Fact
C

According to the text, the current evaluation of Kubler-Ross's theory of the stages of dying is that
a. there are clearly distinct stages, but perhaps not in exactly the order claimed.
b. the theory should be treated with caution until it is supported by careful research.
c. most reach a stage of peaceful acceptance, but do not show denial or anger.
d. Kubler-Ross's research was too cold and impersonal to have much value.

8.223
d
p. 331
Concept
M

An important criticism of Kubler-Ross's theory of dying is that
a. her research is too cold and heartless.
b. she did not observe people for a very long time.
c. her ideas do not agree with our understanding of death.
d. her research and results are not very systematic.

8.224
b
p. 332
Concept
M

Research by Friedman and his colleagues (1995) found that the personality factor of _____ was highly related to living longer.
a. assertiveness
b. conscientiousness
c. flexibility
d. persistence

8.225
a
p. 334
Applied
M

In getting children to follow rules of acceptable behavior, parents must learn to avoid common discipline mistakes, such as
a. laxness, overreactivity, and verbosity.
b. overreactivity, sensitivity, and loudness.
c. vigilance, sensitivity, and laxness.
d. vigilance, dominance, and harshness.

CHAPTER 9

Multiple-Choice Questions

9.1 Which of the following refers to processes assumed to guide, activate, and maintain persistence
a of behavior?
p. 340 a. motivation
Fact b. emotion
E c. reflexes
 d. icons

9.2 Motivation is defined as an internal process that
d a. is a relatively stable personality tendency.
p. 340 b. changes behavior as a result of prior experience.
Fact c. reflects physical and behavioral attempts to cope and adapt.
M d. activates, guides and maintains behavior.

9.3 Emotions are complex reactions consisting of
b a. anger, joy, and sadness.
p. 340 b. physiological arousal, subjective states, and expressions.
Fact c. triggers, guides, and maintainers of behavior.
M d. chaotic electrical activity in the brain.

9.4 Complex reactions involving physiological responses, subjective cognitive states, and expressive
a reactions refer to
p. 340 a. emotions.
Fact b. motives.
M c. both emotions and motives.
 d. emotions, motives and innate behaviors.

9.5 In which of these situations would a psychologist apply the concept of motivation?
d a. Why do cats have reflective eyes?
p. 340 b. Why do parents love their children?
Applied c. Why do Pavlov's dogs salivate when the bell rings?
M d. Why do writers spend decades on one book?

Motivation: The Activation and Persistence of Behavior

9.6 Lisa wonders why her brother continues to drive so carelessly when he has wrecked three
c cars and broken six bones, and is now paying triple the normal insurance. Lisa's question
p. 341 is about
Applied a. gender issues.
M b. emotions and cognition.
 c. motivation.
 d. homeostasis.

9.7 Motivational processes are used to explain behavior whenever
b a. there are apparent experiences, for example, prior rewards, that cause the behavior.
p. 341 b. the causes of the behavior are not readily discerned in the immediate surroundings.
Applied c. the behavior is lacking in energy, that is, its intensity is constant.
C d. emotions are influencing the behavior.
PT/OLSG

Chapter 9 - Motivation and Emotion

9.8
c
p. 341
Fact
M

Whenever the causes of a specific form of behavior cannot be readily discerned in the immediate surroundings, psychologists often attribute the behaviors to
a. rewards.
b. past experiences.
c. motives.
d. instincts.

9.9
b
p. 341
Fact
M

An instinct is a pattern of behavior that occurs in response to
a. a conditioned stimulus.
b. a specific stimulus or condition.
c. a reinforcing event.
d. a biological need.

9.10
d
p. 341
Concept
M

To qualify as an instinct, a pattern of behavior must be _____ in a species, _____ of experience, and a response to _____.
a. fairly rare; the result; conditioning
b. universal; the result; conditioning
c. fairly rare; independent; specific stimuli
d. universal; independent; specific stimuli

9.11
a
p. 341
Fact
M

Which of the following is characteristic of instincts?
a. independent of experience
b. independent of specific external stimuli
c. unique to each member of a species
d. occurs quite rarely in a species

9.12
a
p. 342
Concept
C

Which of these is reasoning similar to that which has reduced support for instinct theory?
a. Sexual behavior is caused by a sexual instinct, which we know exists because there is so much sexual behavior.
b. All male fish of a species attack other males of the species in breeding season, even when raised alone.
c. People often engage in risky or dangerous behaviors, even when there are no rewards for doing so.
d. No true instincts have ever been observed, in humans or in other animals.

9.13
b
p. 342
Concept
M

Which of the following is a major problem with the instinct theory of motivation?
a. It has no empirical support.
b. Much of it is based on circular reasoning.
c. It cannot account for consistency of behavior among all members of a species.
d. It is dependent on acceptance of evolutionary theory.

9.14
c
p. 342
Concept
M
PT/OLSG

One major problem with instinct theory of motivation is that the existence of the instinct is inferred from
a. physiological measures.
b. observations.
c. the behavior it was designed to explain.
d. experimental analyses.

9.15
c
p. 342
Concept
M

The view that biological needs arise within our bodies, which create unpleasant states of arousal that push us into action is called
a. arousal theory.
b. expectancy theory.
c. drive theory.
d. genetic theory.

9.16
d
p. 342
Fact
M

The body's normal state of physiological balance is referred to as
a. arousal theory.
b. instinct theory.
c. homogeneity.
d. homeostasis.

176 Test Bank - Essentials of Psychology (2nd Edition)

9.17   A state of physiological balance, when all biological systems are functioning optimally, is called
d
p. 342
    a. arousal.
Fact
    b. motivation.
    c. achievement.
M
    d. homeostasis.

9.18   Which of the following theories suggests that motivation is basically a process in which various
a
biological needs push us to actions designed to satisfy these biological needs?
p. 342
    a. drive theory
Concept
    b. instinct theory
E
    c. expectancy theory
    d. intrinsic motivation theory

9.19   According to drive theory, behaviors will be repeated if they tend to
c
    a. increase drives.
p. 342
    b. have no effect on drives.
Fact
    c. decrease drives.
M
    d. initiate drives.
PT/OLSG

9.20   Seeking an increase in stimulation, for example, riding a roller coaster, is most likely to be
d
used as evidence to discredit which of the following theories?
p. 342
    a. power theory
Applied
    b. arousal theory
M
    c. achievement
    d. drive theory

9.21   Behaviors that return a person to homeostasis are likely to be repeated according to which
b
of the following theories?
p. 342
    a. expectancy
Concept
    b. drive
M
    c. innate
    d. power

9.22   Which of the following examples cannot be explained by drive theory?
b
    a. After playing basketball, Ralph always has at least a quart of his favorite fruit juice.
p. 342
    b. Your 10-year-old nephew reads scary stories before going to bed and then has trouble falling asleep.
Applied
    c. A cat learns to hide in a group of flowers near a bird feeder.
M
    d. A dog waits for the dog food can to be opened.

9.23   Arousal theories of motivation focus on an organism's efforts to
c
    a. maintain their basic biological systems so they can survive.
p. 343
    b. reach a goal it believes to be reasonable and important.
Fact
    c. achieve an optimum level of nervous system activation.
M
    d. establish a sense of self-worth and personal growth.

9.24   The theory that suggests that we seek an optimal level of activation, which is reflected in
d
physiological measures is _____ theory.
p. 343
    a. drive
Fact
    b. achievement
E
    c. instinct
    d. arousal

9.25   According to the Yerkes-Dodson law, a person will demonstrate the best performance at many
b
tasks when the level of arousal is
p. 343
    a. very low.
Fact
    b. moderate.
M
    c. very high.
    d. changing rapidly.

Chapter 9 - Motivation and Emotion

9.26
d
p. 343
Applied
M

Ralph performs best at his soccer matches when he is not too bored and not too nervous. This illustrates the
a. need-drive connection.
b. expectancy hypothesis.
c. Cannon-Bard theory.
d. Yerkes-Dodson law.

9.27
a
p. 343
Fact
M
PT/OLSG

When studying behavior, Lisa likes to listen to classical music whereas her roommate insists that it be totally silent. The theory of motivation that can best explain these differences is
a. arousal theory.
b. drive theory.
c. achievement theory.
d. expectancy theory.

9.28
b
p. 343
Fact
M

According to arousal theory, people seek _____ arousal.
a. minimized
b. optimal
c. increased
d. decreased

9.29
c
p. 343
Applied
M

An Olympic skater who felt she was not "up" enough for her competition did a series of sprints up and down the halls before she went on the ice. This behavior would be best explained by which theory?
a. Instinct theory
b. Drive theory
c. Arousal theory
d. Activation theory

9.30
b
p. 343
Fact
M

An important problem with arousal theory of motivation is that
a. there is no evidence that arousal has any effect on one's actual performance on some task.
b. it is difficult to tell in advance what level of arousal will be optimal for a particular behavior.
c. the optimum arousal for going to sleep is different from that for running a race.
d. our arousal level is controlled primarily by the autonomic nervous system.

9.31
c
p. 344
Fact
E

The view that behaviors are determined by your beliefs that your present actions will yield various outcomes in the future is called
a. arousal theory.
b. futures theory.
c. expectancy theory.
d. drive theory.

9.32
d
p. 344
Applied
M

Attending college in order to later pursue a career can best be explained on the basis of
a. arousal theory.
b. drive theory.
c. optimal theory.
d. expectancy theory.

9.33
d
p. 344
Concept
M

Drives are to expectancies as
a. achievements are to aroused states.
b. ghost stories are to textbooks.
c. incentives are to grades.
d. foods are to beliefs.

9.34
a
p. 344
Concept
M

According to expectancy theory, behavior is most strongly influenced by
a. incentives.
b. physiological needs.
c. optimal arousal.
d. culture.

178 Test Bank - Essentials of Psychology (2nd Edition)

9.35
a
p. 344
Concept
M
PT/OLSG

Which of the following theories of motivation include the role of incentives in producing motivation?
a. expectancy theory
b. arousal theory
c. drive theory
d. instinct theory

9.36
a
p. 344
Concept
M

In the old carrot-and-stick notion of motivation, carrot is to stick as
a. expectancy is to drive.
b. drive is to expectancy.
c. instinct is to arousal.
d. arousal is to instinct.

9.37
c
p. 344
Concept
M

Drives are to incentives as
a. desirable is to undesirable.
b. pull is to push.
c. internal is to external.
d. pay is to work.

9.38
c
p. 344
Concept
M

Drives are to incentives as
a. desirable is to undesirable.
b. pull is to push.
c. push is to pull.
d. pay is to work.

9.39
c
p. 344
Concept
M

The area of work motivation has been one of the important applications of _____ theory.
a. drive
b. instinct
c. expectancy
d. reinforcement

9.40
b
p. 344
Concept
M
PT/OLSG

In Maslow's hierarchy of needs, deficiency needs are those that
a. involve the respect and approval of others.
b. must be satisfied before other needs emerge.
c. develop in late childhood or adolescence.
d. increase our overall level of arousal.

9.41
d
p. 344
Concept
M

According to Maslow's theory of motivation, people's behavior will largely be focused on
a. their highest level of achievement.
b. basic biological needs most of the time.
c. spiritual improvement and growth.
d. the lowest level need that is unmet.

9.42
a
p. 344
Fact
M

In the hierarchy of needs, physiological, safety, social needs are classified as
a. deficiency needs.
b. esteem needs.
c. self-actualization needs.
d. work needs.

9.43
b
p. 344
Fact
M

In the hierarchy of needs, the needs to develop self-respect, approval of others, and achieve success are examples of
a. deficiency needs.
b. esteem needs.
c. work needs.
d. self-actualization needs.

Chapter 9 - Motivation and Emotion 179

9.44   In the hierarchy of needs, the desire to become all that one is capable of being and to be
c   concerned with issues that affect the well-being of others are examples of
p. 344   a.   deficiency needs.
Fact   b.   esteem needs.
M   c.   self-actualization needs.
             d.   humanitarian needs.

9.45   Which of the following is not a correct statement about Maslow's theory?
c   a.   Motives exist in a hierarchy.
p. 344   b.   Motives at the bottom must be satisfied before those at the top.
Fact   c.   Deficiency needs include esteem needs.
M   d.   Self-actualization is a growth need.
PT/OLSG

9.46   Research examining Maslow's hierarchy of needs generally
d   a.   supports deficiency and esteem needs.
p. 345   b.   supports self-actualization needs but not deficiency needs.
Fact   c.   supports all assumptions of this theory.
C   d.   fails to verify most of the assumptions of this theory.

9.47   The urge to obtain and consume food is known as
c   a.   consumatory motivation.
p. 345   b.   epicurean motivation.
Fact   c.   hunger motivation.
M   d.   caloric motivation.

9.48   Detectors that respond to certain chemicals in the blood and help regulate caloric intake are located in
b   a.   the cerebral cortex.
p. 345   b.   the hypothalamus and liver.
Fact   c.   the taste buds.
C   d.   the basal ganglia.

9.49   A special cell that responds to the level of glucose, protein, or lipids in the blood is called a
b   a.   body-mass indicator.
p. 345   b.   detector.
Fact   c.   caloric regulator.
M   d.   motivator.

9.50   Detectors associated with controlling caloric intake respond to which of the following?
b   a.   antidiuretic hormone
p. 345   b.   glucose
Fact   c.   endorphins
M   d.   baroreceptors

9.51   Eating and hunger are influenced by all of the following except
d   a.   special cells that detect glucose, protein, and lipids.
p. 346   b.   the sight, smell, and taste of food.
Concept   c.   feedback from chewing and swallowing.
M   d.   the cognitive heuristic related to the consumption of food.

9. 52   The sight of certain foods may arouse hunger pangs or feelings of disgust, depending upon your
a   a.   culture.
p. 346   b.   expectancies.
Fact   c.   lipids.
E   d.   dissonance.

9.53
c
p. 347
Applied
C

When Ralph's family goes camping, they always bring popcorn, chips, candy, and lots of other snacks. Ralph craves these treats when camping, though he never thinks of them at other times. This illustrates the influence of _____ on eating.
a. genetics
b. stress
c. classical conditioning
d. operant conditioning

9.54
d
p. 347
Concept
M

The fact that cues associated with eating can acquire the capacity to elicit eating behavior even when we are not hungry is most likely due to
a. low lipids.
b. high glucose.
c. a damaged hypothalamus.
d. classical conditioning.

9.55
a
p. 347
Applied
M
PT/OLSG

The fact that you always get popcorn and a soda when you go to the movies regardless of the time of day can best be explained on the basis of
a. classical conditioning.
b. cognitive expectancies.
c. homeostasis.
d. lipid detectors.

9.56
d
p. 347
Concept
E

Which of the following is a genetic factor thought to be involved in controlling one's weight?
a. classical conditioning
b. baroreceptor
c. biological clock
d. basal metabolic rate

9.57
b
p. 347
Study
C

Research tends to indicate that _____, rather than _____, have difficulty regulating their weight.
a. nontasters, supertasters
b. supertasters, nontasters
c. sensitizers, nonsensitizers
d. nonsensitizers, sensitizers

9.58
d
p. 348
Applied
M

One important difference between obese people and those who easily maintain a normal weight is that obese people
a. are insensitive to the sight and smell of food.
b. have a higher basal metabolic rate.
c. lose their appetite when under stress.
d. respond to stress by eating more than usual.

9.59
d
p. 348
Fact
M

Obese individuals differ from non-obese in that obese individuals are
a. likely to decrease their intake of food during stress.
b. less influenced by external cues related to food.
c. more influenced by internal cues such as hunger pangs.
d. more likely to increase their intake of food during stress.

9.60
b
p. 348
Fact
M

Obese individuals differ from non-obese in that obese individuals are
a. likely to decrease their intake of food during stress.
b. likely to feel hungrier when exposed to food-related cues, for example, smells of food.
c. not influenced by external cues relating to food.
d. characterized as reduced lipid levels.

9.61
c
p. 348
Fact
E

In comparison to non-obese individuals, individuals who suffer from obesity seem to respond more strongly to
a. reduced lipid levels.
b. reduced glucose levels.
c. external food cues.
d. internal hunger pangs.

Chapter 9 - Motivation and Emotion   181

9.62   Research on the psychological causes of obesity indicate that obese people may have trouble
c   controlling their weight in part because they
p. 348   a.   have inherited an abnormally low metabolism so they need less food to live on.
Fact   b.   think of food as comfort and a reward, so they will work harder to get the food.
C   c.   eat when the food is obvious and available, not just when their bodies need it.
             d.   have never learned the psychological skills necessary to control their behavior.

9.63   Purging is to starvation as
a   a.   bulimia is to anorexia nervosa.
p. 348   b.   anorexia nervosa is to bulimia.
Concept   c.   lipid is to glucose.
M   d.   glucose is to lipid.

9.64   Hormones that most directly affect sexual behavior are produced by
d   a.   the pituitary.
p. 348   b.   the adrenaline glands.
Fact   c.   the pheromones.
M   d.   the gonads.

9.65   The effects of hormones that determine the occurrence or nonoccurrence of sexual behavior
a   on the basis of the presence or absence of the hormone are referred to as
p. 348   a.   activation effects.
Fact   b.   organization effects.
M   c.   andrenogenital syndromes.
             d.   androgen insensitivity syndromes.

9.66   In animals other than humans, what influence do sex hormones have on sexual behavior?
a   a.   an activation effect
p. 348   b.   an inhibitory effect
Fact   c.   a maturational effect
M   d.   a cognitive effect

9.67   The total removal of the ovaries and the hormones they secrete eliminates receptivity in most
b   animals except humans. The hormone effect in this example is referred to as
p. 348   a.   apperception effects.
Fact   b.   activation effects.
M   c.   expectancy effects.
             d.   organizational effects.

9.68   Compared with the sexual behavior of lower organisms, the sexual behavior of humans is
c   a.   much more violent and uncontrolled.
p. 350   b.   more controlled by biology.
Fact   c.   less affected by hormone levels.
M   d.   more affected by hormone levels.

9.69   The Kinsey reports found that
b   a.   females were more sexually active than males.
p. 350   b.   there was great individual variation in sexual behavior.
Fact   c.   only a minority of men and women have premarital sex.
M   d.   rates of homosexuality were higher than expected.
PT/OLSG

9.70   Which of the following describes the typical sequence of phases during sexual behavior
b   described by Masters and Johnson?
p. 350   a.   resolution, orgasmic, excitement, plateau
Fact   b.   excitement, plateau, orgasmic, resolution
M   c.   excitement, resolution, plateau, orgasmic
             d.   resolution, excitement, plateau, orgasmic

182 Test Bank - Essentials of Psychology (2nd Edition)

9.71
c
p. 351
Fact
M
According to Masters and Johnson, the greatest differences between males and females in the four phases of sexual behavior is in the
a. orgasmic phase.
b. plateau phase.
c. resolution phase.
d. refractory phase.

9.72
d
p. 351
Fact
M
The stage of sexual response cycle reported by Masters and Johnson in which the body returns to its normal state is called the _____ phase.
a. refractory
b. recovery
c. plateau
d. resolution

9.73
b
p. 351
Fact
M
PT/OLSG
A refractory period is a time during which
a. an orgasm is imminent.
b. men cannot be sexually aroused.
c. women can have multiple orgasms.
d. the genitals become enlarged.

9.74
a
p. 351
Fact
M
Which of the following statements about sexual behavior among people in different cultures is true?
a. All humans show four phases of sexual behavior involving the same physiological responses.
b. The age at which sexual behavior should begin is relatively consistent across cultures.
c. The particular persons who are appropriate sexual partners are similarly defined across cultures.
d. All cultures have the same definition of appropriate sexual behavior.

9.75
c
p. 351
Fact
M
Unlike other species, humans can be sexually motivated by
a. direct physical contact.
b. naturally occurring odors.
c. real or imagined erotic stimuli.
d. changes in hormonal levels.

9.76
c
p. 351
Fact
M
A person who is sexually attracted to people of the same sex has a _____ orientation; someone who is sexually attracted to people of both sexes has a _____ orientation.
a. heterosexual; bisexual
b. homosexual; heterosexual
c. homosexual; bisexual
d. bisexual; homosexual

9.77
d
p. 351
Fact
M
Which of the following is true concerning homosexuality?
a. Male homosexuals have unusually low levels of testosterone.
b. Female homosexuals have unusually high levels of androgens.
c. Male and female homosexual hormone concentrations are typical of members of the opposite sex.
d. Approximately 2 percent of all adults are homosexual in orientation.

9.78
a
p. 352
Fact
M
Pheromones are
a. odorless substances that trigger sexual arousal.
b. sex hormones produced by the gonads.
c. chemicals released in the brain during sexual arousal.
d. produced during the resolution phase.

9.79
b
p. 352
Applied
M
There is speculation that the small mysterious organ inside the nose is sensitive to odorless substances. This organ is called the
a. pherogonadal organ.
b. vomeronasal organ.
c. pheronasal organ.
d. gonadanasal organ.

Chapter 9 - Motivation and Emotion 183

9.80
a
p. 352
Applied
M

Support for the function of the vomeronasal organ as sensing odorless substances is
a. virtually nonexistent.
b. based on cultural definitions.
c. overwhelmingly positive.
d. based on controlled, rigorous investigations.

9.81
c
p. 353
Fact
E

The majority of adults display which of the following patterns of sexual behavior?
a. bisexual
b. homosexual
c. heterosexual
d. androgenital

9.82
a
p. 353
Fact
M

The causes of homosexuality are
a. largely unknown.
b. probably differences in hormone levels.
c. due to one's family background.
d. based on sexual experiences in puberty.

9.83
a
p. 353
Concept
E

The desire to inflict harm on others is called
a. aggression motivation.
b. pathological motivation.
c. expectancy motivation.
d. arousal motivation.

9.84
c
p. 354
Fact
C

One early view of the causes of aggression, believed by Freud and by ethologist Konrad Lorenz, was that aggression was produced by
a. an event that prevents us from reaching a goal.
b. a desire to gain power or control over another.
c. an inborn, biological tendency to hurt others.
d. patterns of behavior learned in childhood.

9.85
a
p. 355
Fact
M
PT/OLSG

At times, people experience a desire to harm others when they have been prevented by these people from obtaining what they want. This is called the _____ hypothesis.
a. frustration-aggression
b. learning-catharsis
c. frustration-catharsis
d. catharsis-frustration

9.86
a
p. 355
Fact
M

Frustration is most likely to lead to aggression when it is viewed as
a. unfair.
b. expected.
c. appropriate.
d. unappreciated.

9.87
c
p. 355
Concept
M

Being treated unfairly is one of the important factors in _____.
a. anger motivation
b. cognitive appraisal
c. workplace violence
d. cathartic violence

9.88
b
p. 355
Concept
M

One social factor that plays an important role in aggression is
a. indirect provocation from another person.
b. direct provocation from another person.
c. direct reciprocity from another person.
d. indirect reciprocity from another person.

9.89 c
p. 355
Applied
M

Ralph found that when he provoked one of his friends who was drunk, this friend behaved in a very
a. irritated manner.
b. sociable manner.
c. aggressive manner.
d. apologetic manner.

9.90 c
p. 355
Applied
M

There is a fairly large body of research that indicates that exposure to violence in the media is related to _____ on the part of the viewers.
a. apathy
b. jealousy
c. aggression
d. contriteness

9.91 a
p. 356
Applied
M

Research indicates that continuous exposure to media violence can lead individuals to become
a. desensitized to the harm produced by violence.
b. sensitized to the harm produced by violence.
c. alarmed at the harm produced by violence.
d. indignant to the harm produced by the violence.

9.92 b
p. 357
Applied
M

Which of these situations would produce the strongest sexual jealousy in men?
a. A mate who cares deeply about another man.
b. A mate who admits to sex with another man.
c. A mate who spends a lot of time with someone else.
d. A mate who seems more interested in someone else.

9.93 a
p. 357
Applied
C

According to evolutionary psychology, the reasons for sexual jealousy have changed for _____, and that is why
a. males; females show more jealousy.
b. females: males show more jealousy.
c. females; females show more jealousy.
d. males; males show more jealousy.

9.94 b
p. 358
Applied
M

Lisa is coming home from work and gets caught in traffic when the temperature is 92 degrees. This situation has the potential to trigger _____, which increases the probability of aggression.
a. shock
b. negative thoughts
c. aggressive thoughts
d. hostile intentions

9.95 c
p. 358
Concept
M

Buss is to Milgram as
a. apathy is to violence.
b. violence is to apathy.
c. aggression is to obedience.
d. obedience is to aggression.

9.96 c
p. 358
Concept
M

The "aggression machine" is
a. an apparatus used by experimenters to instigate aggression.
b. an apparatus used by prisoners to measure their level of aggression.
c. an apparatus used by experimenters to supposedly administer shock to other individuals.
d. an apparatus used by teachers to teach learners to be more aggressive.

9.97 b
p. 359
Study
M

Research by Anderson and Bushman (1997) indicate that results of studies in the laboratory and in the field indicate that
a. being anonymous decreases aggression.
b. being anonymous increases aggression.
c. being verbal increases aggression.
d. being verbal decreases aggression.

Chapter 9 - Motivation and Emotion   185

9.98　　　　　The behavior that is at the heart of aggressive motivation is _____, which can be studied by the aggression
c　　　　　　machine.
p. 359　　　　a.　aggressive desensitization
Concept　　　b.　aggressive enhancement
M　　　　　　c.　aggressive intent
　　　　　　　d.　aggressive consistency

9.99　　　　　The desire to meet standards of excellence - to accomplish difficult tasks - is called
a　　　　　　a.　achievement motivation.
p. 360　　　　b.　power motivation.
Concept　　　c.　excellence motivation.
M　　　　　　d.　thematic motivation.
PT/OLSG

9.100　　　　A psychologist shows Ralph a picture in which it is not clear what the people are doing or
a　　　　　　how they are feeling, and asks him to answer questions about what is going on. This psychologist
p. 360　　　　is most likely
Applied　　　a.　using the Thematic Apperception Test.
M　　　　　　b.　measuring Ralph's developmental level.
　　　　　　　c.　using a Polygraphic Arousal Test.
　　　　　　　d.　applying behavioral therapy techniques.

9.101　　　　Achievement motivation is to power motivation as
b　　　　　　a.　doing is to being.
p. 360　　　　b.　excelling is to influencing.
Concept　　　c.　getting is to giving.
C　　　　　　d.　taking is to receiving.

9.102　　　　Lisa spends many hours practicing the flute because it is very important to her to be the
a　　　　　　best flute player in her city's orchestra. Lisa exhibits a strong
p. 360　　　　a.　need for achievement.
Applied　　　b.　arousal motivation.
M　　　　　　c.　homeostatic drive.
　　　　　　　d.　sense of expectancy.

9.103　　　　Which of the following are most likely to prefer situations involving moderate levels of risk
d　　　　　　or difficulty to ones that are very low or very high risk or difficulty?
p. 360　　　　a.　those with no achievement motives
Concept　　　b.　those with low achievement motives
C　　　　　　c.　those with moderate achievement motives
　　　　　　　d.　those with high achievement motives

9.104　　　　Which of the following is not true of high achievement oriented individuals?
b　　　　　　a.　high grades in school
p. 360　　　　b.　prefer difficult tasks
Concept　　　c.　success in running their own business
C　　　　　　d.　rapid promotions.
PT/OLSG

9.105　　　　Individuals who are _____ in achievement motivation prefer jobs that are _____ to individual performance.
d　　　　　　a.　low, unrelated
p. 361　　　　b.　high, unrelated
Concept　　　c.　low, closely related
M　　　　　　d.　high, closely related

9.106 The research by McClelland (1985) on achievement motivation clearly indicates that
b
p. 361   a. achievement motivation scores are negatively correlated with economic growth.
Study   b. achievement motivation scores are positively correlated with economic growth.
C   c. achievement motivation scores are negatively correlated with population growth.
         d. achievement motivation scores are positively correlated with population growth.

9.107 The greater the emphasis on achievement in children's stories in various nations, the
c
p. 361   a. greater the later aggression in those nations.
Concept b. lower the later economic growth in those nations.
C   c. greater the later economic growth in those nations.
         d. lower the later aggression in those nations.

9.108 Research by Furnham and colleagues (1994) found that the stronger the attitudes toward
a   competitiveness,
p. 361   a. the greater the economic growth.
Concept b. the lower the economic growth.
C   c. the greater the crime rate.
         d. the lower the crime rate.

9.109 Behaviors performed because of the pleasure they yield, not because they lead to other
c   external rewards, are said to be high in
p. 362   a. achievement motivation.
Fact   b. arousal motivation.
M   c. intrinsic motivation.
         d. apperception motivation.

9.110 When Lisa discovered that keeping a journal of reactions to the readings in her psychology
b   course would not be counted toward her grade, she continued keeping it anyway. Lisa is
p. 362   demonstrating
Applied a. lack of motivation.
M   b. intrinsic motivation.
         c. motivational fortitude.
         d. operant conditioning.

9.111 Which of these extrinsic rewards is most likely to reduce a person's intrinsic motivation?
c
p. 362   a. A big smile from a loved one.
Applied b. A word of praise from your boss.
M   c. A small tip for giving good service.
         d. A positive written communication from a teacher.

9.112 Doing something because we are paid or forced to do it is _____ motivation; doing it just
b   because you enjoy it is _____ motivation.
p. 362   a. intrinsic; extrinsic
Concept b. extrinsic; intrinsic
M   c. compliance; extrinsic
         d. compliance; intrinsic

9.113 If we are going to reward people for intrinsically motivated activities, it is best if these rewards
a   a. are a sign of recognition.
p. 362   b. are small.
Concept c. are unsatisfying.
M   d. are external.
PT/OLSG

9.114 Providing a ready excuse for potentially poor performance is called
c   a. lying.
p. 362   b. deception.
Concept c. self-handicapping.
M   d. self-serving.

Chapter 9 - Motivation and Emotion   187

9.115   Lisa has not studied for the upcoming psychology test. Outside the test room, she tells Ralph, "I really
b   don't feel very good today." Lisa is engaging in
p. 362   a. self-enhancement.
Applied   b. self-handicapping.
M   c. self-expressiveness.
                d. self-lying.

Emotions: Their Nature, Expression, and Impact

9.116   The scientific definition of an emotion includes
d   a. only our internal, subjective feelings.
p. 363   b. only our physiological responses.
Concept   c. only our external, observable behaviors.
M   d. physiological changes, subjective cognitive states, expressive behaviors.

9.117   According to the Cannon-Bard theory of emotion, what is the relationship between one's
b   physiological response and one's emotional feeling?
p. 364   a. The emotional feeling triggers the physiological response.
Concept   b. The feeling and the response occur simultaneously.
M   c. The physiological response triggers the emotional feeling.
                d. The physiological response is not part of the emotion at all.

9.118   The theory that holds that emotional stimuli produce both the experience of emotion and
b   accompanying physiological changes is
p. 364   a. James-Lange.
Fact   b. Cannon-Bard.
M   c. Schachter-Singer.
                d. Watson-Levin.

9.119   The Cannon-Bard theory of emotion is based upon arousal that is mediated by the _____, and feelings that
a   are mediated by the _____.
p. 364   a. autonomic nervous system, cerebral cortex
Fact   b. autonomic nervous system, thalamus
C   c. peripheral nervous system, cerebral cortex
                d. peripheral nervous system, thalamus

9.120   According to the James-Lange theory of emotions, what is the sequence of events when
c   someone feels an emotion?
p. 364   a. First they feel the emotion, then the body responds physiologically.
Concept   b. First they interpret the situation, they feel the emotion, then the body responds.
M   c. First the body responds physiologically, then they feel the emotion.
                d. The order varies depending on the person and the emotion being experienced.

9.121   Which theory of emotion suggests that smiling can make people happy?
c   a. Cannon-Bard
p. 365   b. Shoaf-Strouss
Concept   c. James-Lange
M   d. Schachter-Singer

9.122   Which theory of emotion suggests that you become happy as a result of noticing that you
a   are smiling and laughing?
p. 365   a. James-Lange
Concept   b. Cannon-Bard
M   c. Schachter-Singer
                d. Opponent-process

9.123 b
p. 365
Concept
M

The facial feedback hypothesis is most similar to which of the following theories of emotion?
a. Cannon-Bard
b. James-Lange
c. Opponent-process
d. Expectancy

9.124 d
p. 365
Fact
M

Research on emotions comparing Cannon-Bard and James-Lange theories have found support for
a. neither.
b. only Cannon-Bard.
c. only James-Lange.
d. both.

9.125 c
p. 365
Fact
M

According to the Schachter-Singer two-factor theory of emotion, a key factor in determining which emotion we feel is
a. our level of physiological arousal.
b. the direct impression of a situation on our brain.
c. our cognitive interpretation of the situation.
d. our previous experience of the opposite emotion.

9.126 a
p. 365
Fact
M

The most important process in the Schachter-Singer two-factor theory of emotion is
a. an active search of the environment to determine the causes of our arousal.
b. a direct impression of a situation on the sensory portions of our brains.
c. a measurement of the exact nature of our body's physical reaction to the situation.
d. a reaction to a certain strong emotion by producing the opposite emotion.

9.127 a
p. 365
Fact
M

Which theory of emotion states that our emotional feelings depend on how we interpret our body's physiological responses in the context of the situation we are in?
a. Schachter-Singer
b. Cannon-Bard
c. James-Lange
d. Jackson-Stearns

9.128 d
p. 365
Study
M

Which of these college males was most likely to call a female research assistant for a date, as predicted by the Schachter-Singer two-factor theory of emotion?
a. One who was very tired from lack of sleep.
b. One who had drunk alcohol.
c. One who met her standing on solid ground.
d. One who met her on a rope bridge over a gorge.

9.129 d
p. 365
Concept
C
PT/OLSG

What are the two factors that determine a person's emotional experience according to the Schachter-Singer two-factor theory?
a. intensity of affect and behavior being performed
b. intensity of affect and whether the situation is positive or negative
c. body gestures and transfer of excitation
d. internal arousal and choice of label for this arousal based on external stimuli

9.130 d
p. 365
Concept
M

If you believe that subjective emotional states are determined by the labels you attach to your internal feelings of arousal, you are most likely to subscribe to the theory of emotion referred to as
a. Cannon-Bard.
b. James-Lange.
c. Facial-feedback.
d. Schachter-Singer.

Chapter 9 - Motivation and Emotion

9.131
b
p. 365
Concept
C
PT/OLSG

The primary difference between the Schachter-Singer theory and the older theories of emotion is that the Schachter-Singer theory emphasizes
a. overt behaviors.
b. conscious thoughts.
c. physiological changes.
d. subjective feelings.

9.132
c
p. 365
Fact
M

Which of the following theories suggests emotional reactions often occur in action-reaction cycles where the intensity of the action decreases with experience and the intensity of the reaction increases with experience?
a. James-Lange
b. Schachter-Singer
c. Opponent-Process
d. Cannon-Bard

9.133
c
p. 366
Applied
M

In agreement with the predictions of Opponent-process theory, small children who approach their birthdays with enormous excitement will often feel _____ when the birthday is over.
a. relief
b. pleasure
c. depression
d. less excitement

9.134
d
p. 366
Applied
M
PT/OLSG

According to the Opponent-process theory, if taking an exam makes you experience anxiety, when you finish the exam you will experience
a. greater anxiety.
b. depression.
c. anger.
d. relief.

9.135
b
p. 366
Applied
M

According to the Opponent-process theory, the severity of drug withdrawal symptoms will _____ with use and elation will _____ with use.
a. increase; increase
b. increase; decrease
c. decrease; decrease
d. decrease; increase

9.136
b
p. 366
Concept
M

Opponent-process theory assumes that repeated exposure to a stimulus causes the initial reaction to _____ and the opponent process to _____.
a. strengthen; weaken
b. weaken; strengthen
c. weaken; weaken
d. strengthen; strengthen

9.137
b
p. 366
Fact
M

The physiological arousal associated with emotion is regulated largely by the _____ nervous system.
a. medial
b. autonomic
c. somatic
d. lateral

9.138
c
p. 366
Concept
M

With respect to the body's resources, sympathetic is to parasympathetic as
a. voluntary is to involuntary.
b. peripheral is to central.
c. readiness is to restoration.
d. afferent is to efferent.

190 Test Bank - Essentials of Psychology (2nd Edition)

9.139 When careful physiological measurements are made of people experiencing different emotions,
a   research indicates that
p. 366   a. different emotions show slightly different patterns of biological responses.
Fact   b. all emotions show exactly the same patterns of biological responses.
M   c. different emotions have different patterns of responses, but the patterns are different for each person.
          d. different emotions have responses that vary randomly and unpredictably.

9.140 Someone with brain damage in the left cerebral hemisphere is more likely to show what emotional reaction?
c   a. Anger
p. 366   b. Euphoria
Applied   c. Depression
M   d. Lack of emotions

9.141 Someone who spends an evening watching a Marx Brothers movie, a Naked Gun movie,
b   and two hours of stand-up comedy is likely to show more than usual brain activity in
p. 366   a. the right cerebral hemisphere.
Applied   b. the left cerebral hemisphere.
C   c. the brain stem.
PT/OLSG   d. the parasympathetic nervous system.

9.142 Left hemisphere is to right hemisphere as
d   a. sympathetic is to parasympathetic.
p. 366   b. voluntary is to involuntary.
Fact   c. readiness is to restoration.
M   d. positive feeling is to negative feeling.

9.143 A polygraph machine, or lie detector, is based on the theory that
c   a. positive emotions produce more arousal than negative.
p. 367   b. negative emotions produce more arousal than positive.
Fact   c. telling a lie produces more arousal than telling the truth.
M   d. telling a lie produces less arousal than telling the truth.

9.144 The biggest problem with using polygraph machines to detect lying is that
b   a. it is impossible to measure enough different physiological reactions.
p. 367   b. no one knows the exact relationship between arousal and lying.
Concept   c. criminals do not actually feel the same emotions as the rest of us.
C   d. it can't be applied to people with psychological disorders who believe their own lies.

9.145 When people learn to control their emotional responses, they are able to alter
a   a. their basic physiological responses.
p. 367   b. their emotional state, but not their biological responses.
Fact   c. their expressions, but not their biological responses or their emotional states.
M   d. nothing; emotions are something people cannot control.

9.146 The best that can be said about polygraphs is that they measure
a   a. arousal.
p. 367   b. truthfulness.
Fact   c. positive emotions.
E   d. negative emotions.

9.147 In the directed lie technique of a polygraph lie detector test, the examiner will compare the
d   testee's arousal levels when answering the relevant questions with
p. 367   a. arousal levels when sitting quietly and relaxing.
Fact   b. arousal levels before the relevant questions were asked.
M   c. arousal levels of other people not under suspicion.
          d. arousal levels when lying to control questions.

Chapter 9 - Motivation and Emotion

9.148
b
p. 368
Fact
E

Outward signs of others' emotional states, for example, facial expressions, are called
a. unconditioned responses.
b. nonverbal cues.
c. conditioned responses.
d. display rules.

9.149
c
p. 368
Concept
M

Facial expression, eye contact, body movements, posture, and touching are examples of
a. negative emotional responses.
b. positive emotional responses.
c. nonverbal cues.
d. social signifiers.

9.150
d
p. 368
Concept
M

What do the following six emotions have in common: happiness, sadness, surprise, fear, anger, and disgust?
a. They are all learned during adolescence.
b. They are expressed very differently among cultures.
c. They are all composites of pleasure and pain.
d. They are the most basic emotions reflected in facial expressions.

9.151
b
p. 368
Study
C

Recent research by Russell (1995) on emotional expression and interpretation of these expressions has called the idea of _____ of facial expressions into question.
a. consistency
b. universality
c. specificity
d. enhancement

9.152
c
p. 369
Fact
M

A high level of body movement, reflected in such behaviors as fidgeting, scratching, and stroking one's hair, indicates
a. a specific meaning that depends on one's culture.
b. hostility of anger.
c. an emotionally aroused or anxious person.
d. a physiological reaction to lying.

9.153
a
p. 369
Study
C

Aronoff and colleagues (1992) did a study of dancers, their postures, and the emotion supposedly expressed. They found that _____ postures expressed _____, while _____ postures expressed _____.
a. angular, threat; rounded, sympathy
b. angular, sympathy; rounded, threat
c. frontal, threat; lateral, sympathy
d. frontal, sympathy; lateral, threat

9.154
d
p. 369
Fact
E

Body movements that convey a specific meaning to others and that are specific to a given culture are called
a. nonverbal cues.
b. display movements.
c. posturing.
d. gestures.

9.155
b
p. 370
Study
M

Research by Crusco and Wetzel (1984) indicated that when waitresses briefly touched their customers on the hand or on the shoulder
a. their tips were smaller.
b. their tips were larger.
c. their tips were basically the same if they had not touched the customer.
d. their tips were placed in a more conspicuous place than if they had not touched the customer.

9.156 What is the effect of mood on interviewers' ratings of an applicant?
b
p. 370 a. Interviewers in a good mood give more critical ratings.
Fact b. Interviewers in a good mood give more positive ratings.
M c. Interviewers' mood only affects ratings when the mood is negative.
PT/OLSG d. Interviewers' mood is not related to ratings given applicants.

9.157 Which of these events would you be more likely to remember if it happened while you were
b in a bad mood?
p. 370 a. Your little girl giving you a hug.
Applied b. Your boss pointing out a mistake you made.
M c. An especially beautiful sunset.
 d. A stranger giving you a smile as you walked by.

9.158 When we are in a negative mood, we tend to retrieve
b a. positive information.
p. 370 b. negative information.
Concept c. irrelevant information.
M d. relevant information.

9.159 Estrada and colleagues (1995) found that a happy mood
b a. increased moodiness.
p. 371 b. increased creativity.
Study c. decreased creativity.
M d. had no impact on creativity.

9.160 Which of the following theories is most likely to support the notion that cognition influences
c affect?
p. 371 a. Facial-feedback theory
Fact b. Opponent-process theory
M c. Schachter-Singer theory
 d. James-Lange theory

9.161 Stereotypes influencing our current feelings or moods is an example of emotions being
d affected by
p. 372 a. facial-feedback.
Fact b. gestures.
M c. opponent-processes.
 d. schema.

9.162 One way that cognition influences affect involves the impact of _____ on reactions and judgments.
b a. perception
p. 372 b. expectancies
Fact c. contagion
E d. dissonance

9.163 Which of the following has not been shown to increase our emotions?
d a. expectancies
p. 372 b. schema
Fact c. cognitive labels
M d. cognitive consistency

9.164 Fleeting facial expressions that last only a few tenths of a second can be useful in detecting
c lying. These expressions are called
p. 373 a. schemas.
Fact b. channel expressions.
M c. microexpressions.
 d. facial tics.

Chapter 9 - Motivation and Emotion

9.165   Inconsistencies between nonverbal cues and other channels are called
a
p. 373   a. interchannel discrepancies.
Fact   b. complex channel discrepancies.
M   c. intrachannel discrepancies.
          d. nonverbal channel discrepancies.

9.166   Individuals who are lying often tend to
b
p. 373   a. speak more quickly.
Fact   b. speak more slowly.
M   c. speak more distinctively.
          d. speak more softly.

9.167   An individual who is lying may engage in more _____ than usual.
b
p. 373   a. grammatical confabulation
Applied   b. sentence repairs
M   c. cognitive restructuring
          d. emotional restructuring

9.168   Individuals who are lying often _____ more frequently than usual.
c
p. 373   a. show facial tics
Applied   b. show constricted pupils
M   c. blink their eyes
          d. wink

9.169   One indicator of lying may be
a
p. 373   a. exaggerated facial expressions.
Applied   b. subdued facial expressions.
E   c. unusual facial expressions.
          d. unacceptable facial expressions.

9.170   Which of the following behaviors is not an indicator of lying?
c
p. 373   a. The pitch of a person's voice often rises.
Fact   b. The pupils of a person's eyes often become dilated.
M   c. The ears of a person turn red.
PT/OLSG   d. The facial expressions of a person are often exaggerated.

194 Test Bank - Essentials of Psychology (2nd Edition)

CHAPTER 10

Multiple-Choice Questions

Personality: Is It Real?

10.1   Individuals' unique and relatively stable patterns of behaviors, thoughts, and emotions refer to
a
p. 378   a. personality.
Fact   b. humanism.
E   c. ego ideal.
     d. self-awareness.

10.2   The definition of the term personality includes
c
p. 378   a. idiosyncratic characteristics that change over time.
Fact   b. features for which no measurement devices exist.
M   c. unique and relatively stable features.
     d. inconsistent features that change with environmental pressures.

10.3   At present, many psychologists believe that behavior is
a
p. 378   a. often shaped by stable traits or characteristics.
Concept   b. completely shaped by environmental influences.
M   c. only minimally affected by inherited characteristics like emotionality.
     d. driven by variable traits and unstable impulses.

10.4   Recent evidence indicate that genetic factors may account for as much as _____ of individual variability in
d   the tendency to behave aggressively.
p. 379   a. 20%
Fact   b. 30%
M   c. 40%
     d. 50%

10.5   Most psychologists agree that even though individuals may have specific traits that predispose them to
b   behave in particular ways, the actual behavior depends on
p. 379   a. the strength of the trait.
Concept   b. situational factors.
M   c. the depth of the situation.
     d. central configuration.

10.6   "Don't worry about Ralph, he's always late to everything." This statement reflects a belief that
d
p. 379   a. Ralph doesn't have very much personality.
Applied   b. Ralph has too much personality.
M   c. Ralph's personality is quite unstable.
     d. Lateness is a trait of Ralph's personality.

The Psychoanalytic Approach: Messages from the Unconscious

10.7   Freud's initial career plans were to become
d
p. 380   a. a clinical psychologist.
Fact   b. a musician.
M   c. an important politician.
     d. a famous medical researcher.

10.8   Freud developed most of his theory
c
p. 380   a. while teaching at several universities.
Fact   b. while employed in industry.
M   c. during his private practice.
     d. as an undergraduate psychology major.

Chapter 10 - Personality: Uniqueness and Consistency in the Behavior of Individuals

10.9
a
p. 381
Fact
M

Which of the following individuals influenced Freud early in his career?
a. Jean-Martin Charcot and Joseph Breuer.
b. John Watson and Burris Skinner.
c. Carl Rogers and Abraham Maslow.
d. Gordon Allport and Albert Bandura.

10.10
c
p. 381
Applied
C

Until you read this question, you were probably not aware of the name of your state capital, but once it is mentioned you can think of it fairly easily. This would be part of your
a. conscious mind.
b. available mind.
c. preconscious mind.
d. unconscious mind.

10.11
b
p. 381
Concept
M

According to Freud, the bulk of the mind resided in the
a. preconscious.
b. unconscious.
c. conscious.
d. superego.

10.12
c
p. 381
Fact
E
PT/OLSG

The part of the mind that contains the impulses of which we are not aware, according to Freud, is the
a. conscious.
b. preconscious.
c. unconscious.
d. subconscious.

10.13
b
p. 381
Fact
M

According to Freud, most of the things we do, think, and feel are caused by
a. conditioned responses to our surroundings.
b. unconscious forces of which we are not aware.
c. a strong desire to grow and develop.
d. the beliefs and ideas we have about the world.

10.14
a
p. 381
Fact
M

The process by which material is driven from consciousness because it is too anxiety-provoking is called
a. repression.
b. the reality principle.
c. tension reduction.
d. suppression.

10.15
d
p. 381
Concept
M

Tip of the iceberg is to base of an iceberg as
a. preconscious is to conscious.
b. conscience is to ego ideal.
c. unconscious is to preconscious.
d. conscious is to unconscious.

10.16
c
p. 381
Fact
M

The method of treating psychological disorders devised by Freud whereby repressed material is brought back into consciousness is called
a. self-actualization.
b. client-centered.
c. psychoanalysis.
d. humanism.

10.17
b
p. 381
Fact
M

Sigmund Freud developed the theory of
a. self-actualization.
b. psychoanalysis.
c. trait psychology.
d. humanism.

10.18 a
p. 382
Concept
M

Desire is to reason is to conscience as
a. id is to ego is to superego.
b. conscious is to unconscious is to preconscious.
c. superego is to ego is to id.
d. preconscious is to unconscious is to conscious.

10.19 b
p. 382
Fact
E

According to Freud, the part of our mind that includes various bodily needs, sexual desires, and aggressive impulses is the
a. ego.
b. id.
c. superego.
d. conscience.

10.20 c
p. 382
Fact
E

According to Freud, a person who readily displays aggressive and sexual tendencies is likely to have a very strong
a. ego.
b. superego.
c. id.
d. reality principle.

10.21 d
p. 382
Concept
C

According to Freud, the id operates on the basis of the
a. conscience.
b. punishment.
c. reality principle.
d. pleasure principle.

10.22 a
p. 382
Concept
M

Pleasure principle is to reality principle as
a. id is to ego.
b. ego is to id.
c. conscience is to superego.
d. superego is to conscience.

10.23 b
p. 382
Concept
M

Which of the following wants immediate, total gratification and is incapable of considering the potential costs of seeking total gratification?
a. ego
b. id
c. superego
d. libido

10.24 a
p. 382
Applied
M

Imagine that your boss has just reprimanded you for something you did not do. According to Freud, your id will most likely be sending you what message?
a. "Punch the boss!"
b. "Be polite, or you may get fired."
c. "Anger is wrong, be more tolerant."
d. "Take ten deep breaths."

10.25 d
p. 382
Applied
M

Imagine that your boss has just reprimanded you for something you did not do. According to Freud, your ego will most likely be sending you what message?
a. "Punch the boss!"
b. "This is making me feel terrible."
c. "Anger is wrong, be more tolerant."
d. "I'll report this to the office manager, with proof."

10.26 c
p. 382
Applied
M

Imagine that your boss has just reprimanded you for something you did not do. According to Freud, your superego will most likely be sending you what message?
a. "Punch the boss!"
b. "Be polite, or you may get fired."
c. "Anger is wrong, be more tolerant."
d. "Maybe I'll push him down the stairs when no one's looking."

Chapter 10 - Personality: Uniqueness and Consistency in the Behavior of Individuals 197

10.27
c
p. 383
Fact
E

According to Freud, which of the following holds our primitive urges or impulses in check until appropriate conditions exist?
a. id
b. ego ideal
c. ego
d. superego

10.28
b
p. 383
Fact
E
PT/OLSG

According to Freud, the part of our personality that functions on the basis of the reality principle is the
a. id.
b. ego.
c. superego.
d. conscious.

10.29
d
p. 383
Fact
M

Which of the following directs behavior so as to maximize pleasure and minimize pain?
a. id
b. conscience
c. superego
d. ego

10.30
d
p. 383
Fact
E

According to Freud, which of the following is concerned with morality?
a. ego
b. unconscious
c. id
d. superego

10.31
a
p. 383
Fact
E

According to Freud, which of the following represents our internalization of our parents' moral teachings and norms of society?
a. superego
b. id
c. ego
d. morality principle

10.32
b
p. 383
Concept
M

The primary function of the superego is to
a. satisfy the desires of the id as quickly as possible.
b. satisfy the desires of the id in a morally acceptable way.
c. respond on the basis of the pleasure principle.
d. deny and overpower the ego.

10.33
d
p. 383
Concept
M

According to Freud, when our ego senses that unacceptable impulses are expressing themselves we experience
a. the reality principle.
b. the pleasure principle.
c. enlightenment.
d. anxiety.

10.34
a
p. 383
Concept
C

Which of the following Freudian concepts is thought to keep unacceptable impulses from the id out of consciousness and thus prevent these impulses from open expression?
a. defense mechanism
b. reality principle
c. superego
d. anxiety

10.35
d
p. 383
Fact
M
PT/OLSG

A defense mechanism that channels unacceptable impulses into a socially acceptable action is called
a. reaction formation.
b. repression.
c. regression.
d. sublimation.

10.36 In Freud's theory of personality, a defense mechanism is used
b
p. 383   a. by the id to protect itself from the superego's rules.
Applied b. by the ego to protect itself from anxiety.
C   c. by the superego to prevent the id from taking over.
         d. by all aspects of personality to remain strong.

10.37 Channeling aggressive impulses into a strong desire to become a surgeon would be described
c   by Freud as an example of
p. 383   a. reaction formation.
Applied b. differentiation.
C   c. sublimation.
         d. ego alteration.

10.38 The defense mechanism of projection involves
a
p. 384   a. putting your own feelings onto someone else.
Fact   b. finding a socially acceptable outlet for your feelings.
M   c. thinking of a logical, rational excuse for doing what you want.
         d. adopting behaviors that are the opposite of your true feelings.

10.39 The defense mechanism of sublimation involves
b
p. 384   a. putting your own feelings onto someone else.
Fact   b. finding a socially acceptable outlet for your feelings.
M   c. thinking of a logical, rational excuse for doing what you want.
         d. adopting behaviors that are the opposite of your true feelings.

10.40 The defense mechanism of rationalization involves
c
p. 384   a. putting your own feelings onto someone else.
Fact   b. finding a socially acceptable outlet for your feelings.
M   c. thinking of a logical, rational excuse for doing what you want.
         d. adopting behaviors that are the opposite of your true feelings.

10.41 Image that you work for a nasty boss, but have repressed your hostility toward him. If anxiety
d   about this hostility begins to surface, you might go in one day to "straighten up some files
p. 384 for him" and throw out some crucial papers "by accident." This is an example of
Applied a. projection.
C   b. denial.
         c. reaction formation.
         d. rationalization.

10.42 The instinctual life force that energizes the id is the
a
p. 384   a. libido.
Concept b. thanatos.
M   c. reality principle.
         d. pleasure principle.

10.43 According to Freud, too little or too much gratification during the psychosexual stages of
b   development can result in psychic energy being left behind in one of the stages. This
p. 384 process is referred to as
Concept a. repression.
M   b. fixation.
         c. ego transference.
         d. id transference.

10.44 According to Freud, individuals may develop an immature personality and thus be subject
c   to several forms of psychological disorders as a result of
p. 384   a. libido.
Concept b. sublimation.
M   c. fixation
         d. punishment.

Chapter 10 - Personality: Uniqueness and Consistency in the Behavior of Individuals

10.45
c
p. 384
Fact
M

Ralph's parents were extremely strict about toilet training him, and punished him severely every time he made a mistake. According to Freud, Ralph is likely to display a(n)
a. unrealistic self-concept.
b. weak superego.
c. fixation.
d. erogenous zone.

10.46
d
p. 384
Fact
E
PT/OLSG

According to Freud, adult personality is determined by what happens during
a. adulthood.
b. the prenatal period.
c. infancy.
d. the psychosexual stages.

10.47
a
p. 384
Fact
C

Psychosexual stages are structured by the fact that, as we grow, different parts of the body serve as the focus of our constant quest for
a. pleasure.
b. self-actualization.
c. anxiety.
d. attachment.

10.48
d
p. 384
Fact
M

Which of the following lists accurately portrays Freud's stages of psychosexual development in their correct order?
a. anal, phallic, latency, oral, genital
b. oral, genital, anal, phallic, latency
c. anal, oral, genital, latency, phallic
d. oral, anal, phallic, latency, genital

10.49
b
p. 384
Fact
E

One's sense of pleasure is focused on the mouth during Freud's _____ stage of psychosexual development.
a. latency
b. oral
c. frontal
d. Oedipal

10.50
c
p. 384
Applied
M

According to Freud, an adult who smokes, overeats, and has a "biting" sense of humor probably had difficulty during which stage of development?
a. Genital
b. Phallic
c. Oral
d. Latency

10.51
c
p. 385
Fact
E

According to Freud, the process of elimination becomes the primary focus of pleasure during the _____ stage.
a. genital
b. oral
c. anal
d. latency

10.52
d
p. 385
Concept
M
PT/OLSG

Fixation at the _____ stage, stemming from traumatic toilet training experiences, may result in individuals who are excessively orderly.
a. latency
b. genital
c. oral
d. anal

199

10.53
c
p. 385
Fact
M

According to Freud, an adult who hangs all of his shirts in the closet in order by color, keeps all clocks set to within 10 seconds of the correct time, and boils all the dishes to make sure they are really clean probably had difficulty during which stage of development?
a. Genital
b. Phallic
c. Anal
d. Oral

10.54
a
p. 385
Fact
M

According to Freud, a boy will successfully resolve the Oedipus complex by
a. identifying with his father.
b. identifying with his mother.
c. accepting his sexual feelings.
d. strengthening his id.

10.55
c
p. 385
Fact
M

How is the Oedipal complex resolved in both sons and daughters?
a. repression of sexual feelings
b. attachment to the opposite-sex parent
c. identification with the same-sex parent
d. displacement of sexual urges into substitute objects

10.56
b
p. 385
Fact
M

According to Freud, the crisis where children must give up their sexual attractions for their opposite-sex parent is called
a. the phallic trauma.
b. the Oedipus complex.
c. castration anxiety.
d. genital retentiveness.

10.57
c
p. 385
Fact
M

In Freud's theory of psychosexual development, the genital stage is the time in life when people should develop
a. an identification with the same-sex parent.
b. an ego to control the id's impulses.
c. normal adult sexual relationships.
d. a moral sense of right and wrong.

10.58
c
p. 385
Fact
M

During Freud's notion of the phallic stage, male is to female as
a. ego is to superego.
b. preconscious is to conscious.
c. castration anxiety is to loss of love.
d. reaction formation is to sublimation.

10.59
b
p. 385
Fact
M

The period of psychosexual development where sexual urges are largely repressed is called the _____ stage.
a. oral
b. latency
c. anal
d. genital

10.60
b
p. 386
Fact
M

One of the major contributions Freud made to our understanding of people is the concept of
a. a fixed series of psychosexual stages of development.
b. unconscious motives and wishes that affect behavior.
c. fixation at an early stage of development.
d. the conflict between the id, the ego, and the superego.

10.61
b
p. 387
Fact
C

Which of these is not an important criticism of Freud's theory of personality?
a. Very little of the theory can be scientifically tested.
b. It emphasizes the importance of unconscious forces.
c. It was based on a very limited set of observations.
d. It is general enough to explain any sort of behavior.

Chapter 10 - Personality: Uniqueness and Consistency in the Behavior of Individuals

10.62
a
p. 387
Fact
C

No matter how a person might behave, no matter what the person's childhood was like, Freud's theory can explain that person's behavior. This is
a. a major problem with Freud's theory.
b. the reason Freud's theory is so important.
c. because he based the theory on so many observations.
d. a sign that Freud was a genius.

10.63
a
p. 387
Fact
M

Freud based his theory of personality on the study of
a. a small number of cases who were all very similar.
b. a large number of cases who were all very similar.
c. a small number of cases who were all very different.
d. a large number of cases who were all very different.

10.64
b
p. 387
Fact
M

Readings in your text indicate that Freud's ideas have had a _____ effect on twentieth century thinking generally; it is also suggested in your text that Freud's theory of personality is _____.
a. small; accurate
b. large; inaccurate
c. large; accurate
d. small; inaccurate

10.65
c
p. 387
Fact
C

Which of the following statements is not a typical criticism of Freudian theory?
a. The theory is difficult to test.
b. Several of his proposals are inconsistent with research findings.
c. Behavior is not affected by unconscious thoughts.
d. His data collection methods were not appropriate.

10.66
d
p. 387
Concept
C

If so few psychologists believe Freud's theory of personality, why then is it still taught in psychology courses?
a. The teachers want to give the students a good laugh.
b. It can be analyzed as a way of teaching students how NOT to develop scientific theories.
c. It is simply a traditional part of the field of psychology, and no one bothers to remove it.
d. His theory has had a lasting influence on psychology and on society in general.

10.67
b
p. 387
Fact
E

Individuals who were initially strong supporters of Freud, and then broke away from him to develop their own theories and treatments are called
a. protagonists.
b. neo-Freudians.
c. defectors.
d. colleagues.

10.68
c
p. 387
Fact
M

According to Jung, the store of ideas that we inherit from our ancestors that is a part of our biological heritage is the
a. personal unconscious.
b. Oedipal crisis.
c. collective unconscious.
d. psychic memory.

10.69
b
p. 387
Fact
E
PT/OLSG

The neo-Freudian who proposed the existence of the collective unconscious was
a. Adler.
b. Jung.
c. Horney.
d. Fromm.

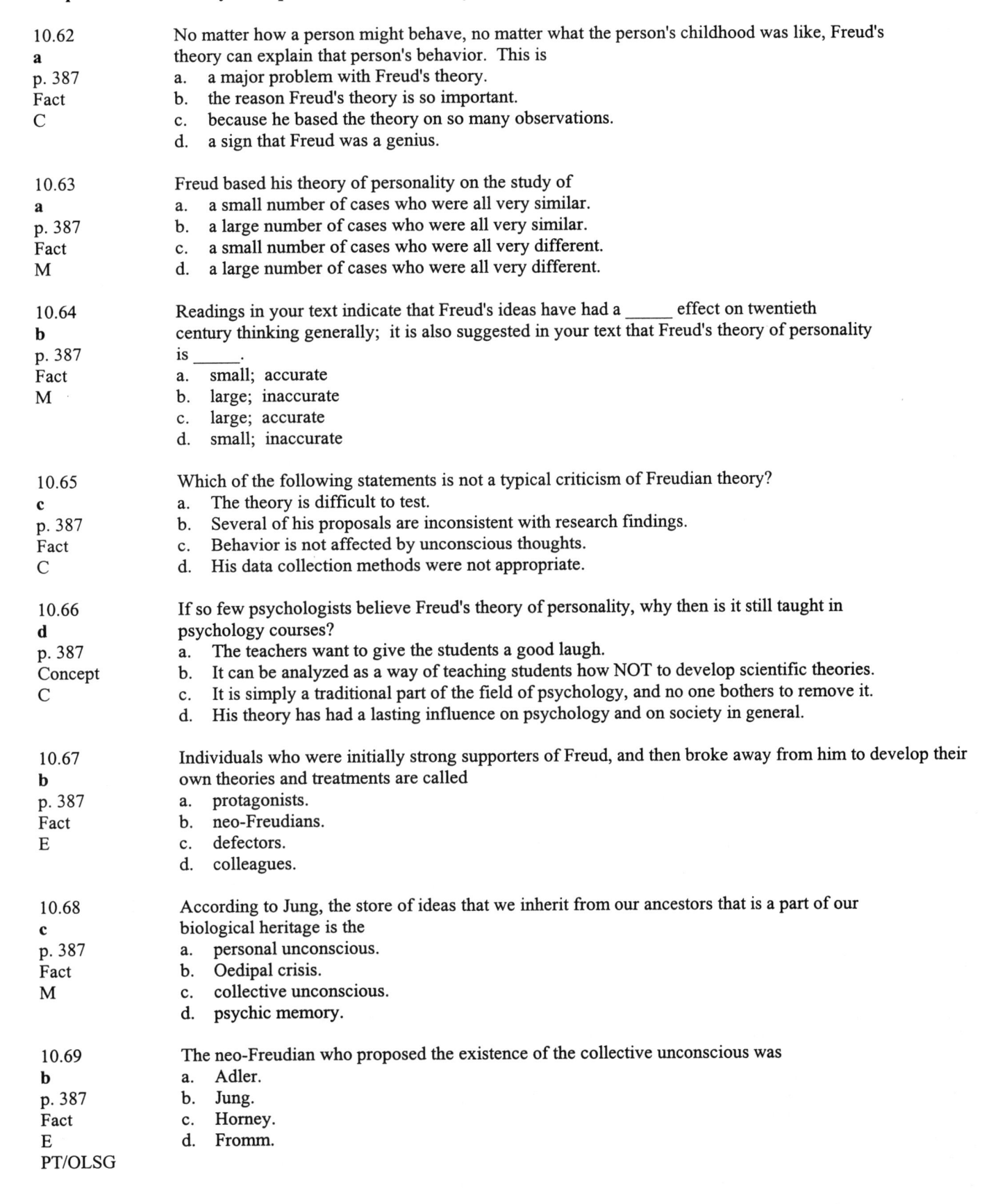

10.70 According to Jung, an archetype is
c
p. 387   a. manifestations of the collective preconscious.
Fact   b. manifestations of the personal preconscious.
M   c. manifestations of the collective unconscious.
          b. manifestations of the personal unconscious.

10.71   According to Jung, when a woman looks for a husband, she will search for someone who
b   projects her own
p. 388   a. anima.
Concept   b. animus.
M   c. sublimations.
          d. introversions.

10.72   Masculine side of females is to feminine side of males as
d   a. introvert is to extrovert.
p. 388   b. inferiority is to superiority.
Concept   c. libido is to thanatos.
M   d. animus is to anima.
PT/OLSG

10.73   Lisa is rather hesitant and cautious and does not make friends easily. Jung would classify
a   Lisa as high in
p. 388   a. introversion.
Applied   b. extroversion.
M   c. penis envy.
          d. libido.

10.74   Ralph is very open and confident. He also makes friends easily and enjoys high levels of
b   stimulation. Based on Jung's theories, Ralph is high in
p. 388   a. introversion.
Applied   b. extroversion.
M   c. castration anxiety.
          d. libido.

10.75   Freud is to _____ as Horney is to _____.
c   a. social factors; personal factors
p. 388   b. childhood experiences; adulthood experiences
Concept   c. personal factors; social factors
C   d. castration anxiety; penis envy

10.76   According to Karen Horney, psychological disorders are the result of
d   a. the collective unconscious
p. 388   b. libidinal conflicts.
Fact   c. the fixation of psychic energy.
C   d. disturbed interpersonal relationships.

10.77   Which of the following viewed feelings of inferiority and a drive for superiority as major
d   factors in determining one's personality?
p. 388   a. Horney
Fact   b. Freud
E   c. Rogers
          d. Adler

10.78   According to Adler, when people feel a sense of inferiority, it will generally result in
a   a. striving to improve, succeed, and achieve superiority.
p. 388   b. strong anxiety that will produce defense mechanisms.
Fact   c. becoming fixated at an early stage of development.
C   d. the development of the superego.

Chapter 10 - Personality: Uniqueness and Consistency in the Behavior of Individuals

10.79 According to Alfred Adler, the major force that drives a person's personality is
a
p. 388　　a.　inferiority.
Fact　　　b.　pleasure.
M　　　　c.　sex.
　　　　　d.　aggression.

10.80　　Alfred Adler, a neo-Freudian theorist, viewed most of our behavior as driven by
b
p. 388　　a.　the aggressive drive.
Fact　　　b.　striving for superiority.
M　　　　c.　the pleasure principle.
　　　　　d.　the superego.

10.81　　Alfred Adler believed that personality development is shaped as a result of
a
p. 389　　a.　birth order.
Fact　　　b.　the collective unconscious.
M　　　　c.　penis envy.
　　　　　d.　disturbed libidinal conflicts.

10.82　　One of the factors Alfred Adler believed to be important in shaping personality is
b
p. 389　　a.　difficulty with toilet training.
Fact　　　b.　birth order within a family.
M　　　　c.　unconditional positive regard.
　　　　　d.　the collective unconscious.

10.83　　Adler believed that important aspects of a person's adult personality are based on
c
p. 389　　a.　sexual anxiety that occurs before age five.
Fact　　　b.　a single overwhelming cardinal trait.
C　　　　c.　family structure, including birth order.
　　　　　d.　classically conditioned emotional responses.

10.84　　According to neo-Freudian Adler, the second-born child in a family is more likely to become
b
p. 389　　a.　depressed.
Fact　　　b.　competitive.
C　　　　c.　fixated.
　　　　　d.　self-actualized.

10.85　　Many neo-Freudians have modified Freud's original theory of personality to give more
b　　　　emphasis to
p. 389　　a.　childhood sexuality.
Fact　　　b.　social factors.
M　　　　c.　differences between the sexes.
　　　　　d.　unconscious forces.

10.86　　The text indicates that one important result of the struggle between the neo-Freudians over
c　　　　Freud's theory was that they
p. 389　　a.　disproved all the important features of Freud's theory.
Concept　b.　demonstrated how useless such theories were.
C　　　　c.　built a bridge from Freud to more modern theories.
PT/OLSG　d.　developed a theory that most people believe today.

Humanistic Theories: Emphasis on Growth

10.87　　A major focus of humanistic psychology stresses the importance of
b
p. 389　　a.　unconscious anxiety.
Concept　b.　personal growth.
M　　　　c.　superiority.
　　　　　d.　reinforcement and punishment.

204 Test Bank - Essentials of Psychology (2nd Edition)

10.88   Primitive motives are to growth and dignity as
c
p. 389   a. Adler is to behavioral psychology.
Concept   b. Rogers is to psychodynamic psychology.
C   c. Freud is to humanistic psychology.
     d. Horney is to learning psychology.

10.89   Which of the following approaches emphasizes personal responsibility, focusing on the present,
b   and the importance of personal growth in personality development?
p. 389   a. Freudian
Concept   b. Humanistic
M   c. Adlerian
     d. Neo-Freudian

10.90   Humanistic theorists generally emphasize
c   a. the struggle to contain unacceptable impulses.
p. 389   b. primitive motives such as pleasure and pain.
Fact   c. present choices and experiences.
M   d. lifelong effects of past experiences.

10.91   The humanistic theorists emphasize
b   a. early development.
p. 389   b. personal responsibility.
Fact   c. the unconscious.
E   d. learning.

10.92   Humanistic theorists generally believe that people constantly struggle to
d   a. achieve sexual gratification.
p. 389   b. gain power over other people.
Fact   c. control their unconscious impulses.
M   d. become the best individuals they can be.

10.93   According to most humanistic theorists, psychological problems are largely due to
b   a. too much or too little pleasure as a child.
p. 389   b. obstacles that prevent personal growth.
Fact   c. unacceptable impulses breaking through.
M   d. unresolved conflicts with one's parents.

10.94   The belief that people are basically good and that they will move toward becoming
c   fully functioning is characteristic of the theory proposed by
p. 390   a. Karen Horney.
Fact   b. Albert Bandura.
M   c. Carl Rogers.
     d. Gordon Allport.

10.95   Rogers postulated that changing our perceptions of reality so that they are consistent with our self-concept is
b   an example of the defense of
p. 390   a. adjustment.
Concept   b. distortion.
M   c. denial.
PT/OLSG   d. contagion.

10. 96   Lisa overheard a conversation between two boys describing her as pushy. She believes that she has been
c   very cooperative when interacting with these two boys. If she acts as if she did not understand what these
p. 390   boys are talking about, she is engaging in the defense of
Applied   a. distortion.
M   b. contagion.
     c. denial.
     d. adjustment.

Chapter 10 - Personality: Uniqueness and Consistency in the Behavior of Individuals 205

10.97　According to humanist Carl Rogers, what is the force that distorts our self-concept and
a　　 makes us anxious?
p. 390　　a.　The belief that others won't approve of certain thoughts and feelings.
Fact　　 b.　The experience of too much or too little pleasure early in childhood.
C　　　 c.　A life-long experience in a family full of unconditional positive regard.
　　　　 d.　Nothing; the self-concept is not an important part of Rogers's theory.

10.98　According to Rogers, distortions in one's self-concept, that is, a gap between an individual's
c　　　 self-concept and reality, is brought about by
p. 391　　a.　fixation in one of the early stages of personality development.
Concept　b.　unsuccessful resolution of the Oedipus complex.
C　　　 c.　parents' use of conditional positive regard.
　　　　 d.　overcompensation for feelings of inferiority.

10.99　According to Rogers, a setting in which we realize that we will be accepted by others, no
b　　　 matter what we say or do is referred to as
p. 391　　a.　conditional positive regard.
Fact　　 b.　unconditional positive regard.
M　　　 c.　self-actualization.
　　　　 d.　self-monitoring.

10.100　According to Rogers, healthy development of the self-concept requires
d　　　 a.　conditional regard.
p. 391　　b.　environmental blocking.
Fact　　 c.　control of emotions.
M　　　 d.　unconditional positive regard.
PT/OLSG

10.101　A form of therapy developed by Carl Rogers is
d　　　 a.　psychoanalysis.
p. 391　　b.　systematic desensitization.
Concept　c.　rational-emotive therapy.
M　　　 d.　client-centered therapy.

10.102　In his theory of personality development, Maslow emphasized
c　　　 a.　unconscious conflicts.
p. 391　　b.　feelings of inferiority.
Fact　　 c.　self-actualization.
M　　　 d.　unconditional positive regard.

10.103　In Maslow's theory of personality, a self-actualized person is one who
c　　　 a.　has a very low self-concept.
p. 391　　b.　has a very high self-concept.
Fact　　 c.　has reached his or her full potential.
M　　　 d.　experiences conditional positive regard.

10.104　Lisa wants to express her full potential and be the best person she possibly can be while
d　　　 maintaining childhood wonder and amazement of the world. Maslow would probably
p. 391　　characterize this as
Applied　a.　conditional positive regard.
M　　　 b.　self-monitoring.
　　　　 c.　compensation.
　　　　 d.　self-actualization.

10.105 a p. 391 Fact M

Maslow described self-actualized individuals as occasionally experiencing powerful feelings of unity with the universe and tremendous waves of power and wonder. The experiences are referred to as
a. peak experiences.
b. hallucinations.
c. esteem fulfillment events.
d. synesthesia.

10.106 a p. 391 Fact M

In Maslow's theory of personality, a peak experience generally includes feelings of
a. power, wonder, and unity with the universe.
b. anxiety as id impulses threaten to break free.
c. separation between the aspects of personality.
d. power and control over other people.

10.107 b p. 392 Concept M

Among the lasting benefits of the humanistic approach to personality is an emphasis on
a. unconscious drives and motivations.
b. the importance of the concept of the self.
c. careful testable definitions of key terms.
d. the lasting effects of childhood experiences.

10.108 c p. 393 Fact M

The humanistic emphasis on personal responsibility is in conflict with which belief of modern scientific psychology?
a. The concept of free will.
b. The notion of objectivism.
c. The idea of determinism.
d. The belief in communication.

10.109 d p. 393 Fact M

The belief that a person's behavior is determined by various factors and can be predicted from them is in conflict with which basic belief of most humanistic theories of personality?
a. Personal growth as a motive for behavior.
b. The use of self-disclosure to improve adjustment.
c. Self-actualization.
d. Personal responsibility.

10.110 b p. 393 Fact M

One criticism of many of the key concepts of humanistic theories, such as self-actualization, is that they are
a. much too optimistic to be realistic.
b. not defined clearly enough to be tested.
c. too deterministic to allow for free will.
d. common to all other personality theories as well.

10.111 a p. 393 Concept C

An important difference between humanistic psychology and psychology in general is that humanists believe strongly in
a. responsibility and free will.
b. biological determinism.
c. control by environmental forces.
d. unconscious sexual drives.

10.112 c p. 393 Fact E

Humanistic theories are criticized for
a. specific definitions of concepts.
b. being overly pessimistic.
c. overemphasizing free will.
d. emphasizing learning principles.

10.113 a p. 393 Fact E

Humanistic theories are criticized for
a. loose definitions of concepts.
b. being overly pessimistic.
c. underemphasizing free will.
d. emphasizing learning principles.

Chapter 10 - Personality: Uniqueness and Consistency in the Behavior of Individuals   207

Trait Theories: Seeking the Key Dimensions of Personality

10.114
b
p. 393
Fact
E

Stable dimensions of personality along which people can vary are called
a. motives.
b. traits.
c. unconscious drives.
d. peak experiences.

10.115
c
p. 393
Applied
M

When Ralph describes his friend as warm and friendly with a good sense of humor, he is supporting the ideas about personality proposed by _____ theorists.
a. psychodynamic
b. behavioral
c. trait
d. neo-Freudian

10.116
a
p. 393
Concept
M

One way of dealing with the multitude of traits is to search for traits that go together, or
a. clusters of traits.
b. factors of traits.
c. dimensions of traits.
d. contagion of traits.

10.117
b
p. 394
Fact
M

Single trait is to several (five to ten) traits as
a. central trait is to cardinal traits.
b. cardinal trait is to central traits.
c. secondary trait is to cardinal traits.
d. central trait is to secondary traits.

10.118
d
p. 394
Fact
M

According to Allport, a core of about five to ten traits can account for the uniqueness of most individuals' personality. These traits are called _____ traits.
a. secondary
b. primary
c. cardinal
d. central

10.119
a
p. 394
Concept
C
PT/OLSG

Allport's concept in which patterns of behavior initially acquired under one set of circumstances to satisfy one set of motives are later performed for very different reasons or motives is called
a. functional autonomy.
b. self-actualization.
c. unconditional positive regard.
d. ideal self.

10.120
c
p. 394
Applied
M

What concept best describes this example? A child first learned to play the piano because his parents made him do so but later plays because he enjoys it.
a. sublimation
b. reaction formation
c. functional autonomy
d. self-efficacy

10.121
c
p. 394
Fact
C
PT/OLSG

Cattell used factor analysis techniques to identify _____ basic personality dimensions.
a. 4
b. 8
c. 16
d. 32

10.122 d
p. 394
Fact
M

Cattell hypothesized that the personality of an individual reflects the individual's cluster of _____ traits.
a. core
b. primary
c. cardinal
d. source

10.123 c
p. 394
Study
M

Cattell hypothesized that _____ traits were made up of many other less important _____ traits.
a. source, cardinal
b. cardinal, source
c. source, surface
d. surface, source

10.124 b
p. 395
Concept
M

One of the five robust factors of personality is defined as a dimension ranging from sociable, talkative, fun-loving, affectionate, and adventurous at one end to retiring, sober, reserved, silent and cautious at the other. This factor is called
a. agreeableness.
b. extraversion.
c. conscientiousness.
d. openness to experience.

10.125 c
p. 395
Concept
M

One of the five robust factors of personality is defined along a dimension ranging from well-organized, careful, self-disciplined, responsible, and scrupulous at one end through disorganized, careless, weak-willed, and unscrupulous at the other. This factor is called
a. extraversion.
b. agreeableness.
c. conscientiousness.
d. emotional stability.

10.126 c
p. 395
Concept
M
PT/OLSG

Which of the following is not one of the five key dimensions of personality identified by recent research?
a. extraversion
b. agreeableness
c. intelligence
d. conscientiousness

10.127 b
p. 395
Study
C

Recent research has found that ratings of an individual by strangers and by family members on the Big Five dimensions indicated
a. a high degree of dissimilarity.
b. a high degree of similarity.
c. a high degree of idiosyncratic responses.
d. a high degree of combinations.

10.128 c
p. 395
Applied
M

Carl Rogers, known for his gentle, caring, trusting way with people, would probably score high on which of the five central personality dimensions?
a. Conscientiousness
b. Emotional stability
c. Agreeableness
d. Openness to experience

10.129 a
p. 395
Applied
M

A school child who rarely remembers to bring home assignments, never turns work in on time, and fails to complete long-term projects, would probably score low on which of the five central personality dimensions?
a. Conscientiousness
b. Agreeableness
c. Openness to experience
d. Extraversion

Chapter 10 - Personality: Uniqueness and Consistency in the Behavior of Individuals

10.130
c
p. 395
Applied
M

Someone who remains calm and composed almost all the time even when the car breaks down and the kids are screaming, would probably score high on which of the five central personality dimensions?
a. Agreeableness
b. Extraversion
c. Emotional stability
d. Openness to experience

10.131
b
p. 395
Applied
M

When the clerk at the store overcharged Lisa, she yelled at the clerk and complained to the manager; when the same thing happened to Ralph, he accepted the correction with a smile. These people differ most strongly on which of these Big Five personality dimensions?
a. Openness to experience
b. Agreeableness
c. Extraversion
d. Conscientiousness

10.132
a
p. 395
Fact
M

Most recent research on personality reflects the approach of
a. trait theorists.
b. humanistic theorists.
c. neo-Freudian theorists.
d. self-actualization theorists.

10.133
c
p. 395
Fact
M

Most research in personality today is aimed at
a. measuring the exact functions of the id.
b. determining what leads people to self-actualization.
c. understanding specific personality traits.
d. contrasting the stages of personality development.

10.134
b
p. 395
Study
M

A large-scale study by Barrick and Mount (1993) found that a good predictor of success in many types of jobs was how high a person scored on the Big Five trait of
a. Extraversion.
b. Conscientiousness.
c. Emotional Stability.
d. Agreeableness.

10.135
a
p. 396
Study
M

The study by Barrick and Mount (1993) found that success in managerial positions was related to high scores on the Big Five trait of
a. Extraversion.
b. Conscientiousness.
c. Emotional Stability.
d. Agreeableness.

10.136
a
p. 396
Fact
M
PT/OLSG

One important criticism of the trait approach to personality is that it does not
a. explain how traits influence behavior.
b. predict how a specific person will behave.
c. define what a personality trait is.
d. show how to measure the basic traits.

10.137
b
p. 396
Fact
M

Which of the following characterizes trait theory?
a. It is very theoretical and abstract.
b. It is largely descriptive in nature.
c. It involves poorly defined concepts.
d. It emphasizes the principles of learning.

10.138 Trait theories of personality are described as largely
c
p. 396
Fact
E
a. affective.
b. cognitive.
c. descriptive.
d. predictive.

10.139 One important criticism of the trait approach to personality is that it does not
d
p. 396
Concept
C
a. explain why people act consistently in different situations.
b. allow us to predict how a specific person will behave.
c. show how the various aspects of the personality interact.
d. describe how various personality traits develop.

10.140 Which of the following theories has been criticized for failing to provide an account of personality development?
a
p. 396
Fact
E
a. trait
b. psychoanalytic
c. humanistic
d. behavioral

10.141 One important criticism of the trait approach to personality is that
d
p. 396
Concept
C
a. it tries to explain all of personality with a few basic traits.
b. there is not enough emphasis on sexual desires.
c. there is very little scientific research done on the traits.
d. no one agrees on just which traits are most important.

10.142 According to the text, which of these approaches to personality are considered most useful to the majority of psychologists today?
b
p. 396
Concept
M
a. The Freudian approach
b. The trait approach
c. The humanistic approach
d. The psychodynamic approach

10.143 Ms. McColm is the lady who was a "professional litigant." In analyzing her behavior, we could speculate that she was _____ on the Big Five traits of agreeableness and emotional stability.
a
p. 398
Applied
E
a. low
b. high
c. moderate
d. extremely high

10.144 Your textbook speculates that the unique combination of high _____ combined with low _____ set the stage for Ms. McColm's lawsuits.
b
p. 398
Applied
C
PT/OLSG
a. extraversion and intelligence, conscientiousness and openness to experience
b. intelligence and acting skill, agreeableness and emotional stability
c. agreeableness and emotional stability, intelligence and acting skill
d. conscientiousness and openness to experience, extraversion and intelligence

Learning Approaches to Personality

10.145 Which of the following emphasizes external factors in shaping one's personality?
d
p. 399
Concept
M
a. humanistic theorists
b. psychoanalytic theorists
c. neo-Freudian theorists
d. learning theorists

Chapter 10 - Personality: Uniqueness and Consistency in the Behavior of Individuals

10.146 Learning approaches to personality account for the uniqueness of personality by observing that
b
p. 399　　a. we are all born with a unique genetic heritage.
Fact　　　b. everyone has a unique set of life experiences.
M　　　　c. innate life forces operate differently in each of us.
　　　　　d. there is actually no real uniqueness in personality.

10.147 In the learning approach to personality, the fact that each person has a different set of life experiences
c
p. 399　　a. is a problem that no one has yet to overcome.
Fact　　　b. accounts for our consistency of personality.
M　　　　c. accounts for our uniqueness of personality.
　　　　　d. is what makes it different from Freud's theory.

10.148 In the learning approach to personality, the fact that learned responses tend to persist
d
p. 399　　a. is what makes each person different from everyone else.
Fact　　　b. is a problem that behaviorists have not overcome.
M　　　　c. has nothing to do with their theory of personality.
　　　　　d. accounts for our consistency of personality.

10.149 Early learning theories of personality were characterized by
a
p. 399　　a. a denial that there were any important internal factors.
Fact　　　b. a blend of learning and Freudian theories.
M　　　　c. a blend of learning and humanistic theories.
　　　　　d. a larger emphasis on social and cognitive factors.

10.150 Modern learning theories differ from the earliest learning theories in that the modern theories
b
p. 399　　a. deny that internal factors have any importance.
Fact　　　b. put more emphasis on internal factors.
C　　　　c. emphasize classical rather than operant conditioning.
　　　　　d. are moving away from social learning theory.

10.151 A learning approach to personality would claim that a girl who is outgoing and talkative is that way because she
c
p. 399　　a. has become fixated at the oral stage of development.
Applied　b. is becoming a self-actualized personality.
C　　　　c. has been reinforced for that behavior in the past.
　　　　　d. is compensating for her feelings of inferiority.

10.152 In his social cognitive theory of personality, Albert Bandura emphasizes the importance of
b
p. 399　　a. inborn personality traits.
Concept　b. observational learning.
M　　　　c. classical conditioning.
　　　　　d. operant conditioning.

10.153 Ralph has been watching his father change a tire on the family car. Later in the evening, while Ralph is riding with his friend, the friend has a flat tire. Ralph has the knowledge to change the tire because of
c
p. 399　　a. self-reinforcement learning.
Applied　b. operant conditioning.
M　　　　c. observational learning.
　　　　　d. contagion learning.

10.154 In Bandura's social cognitive theory of personality, self-reinforcement occurs when we
a
p. 400　　a. provide our own rewards for our own behavior.
Fact　　　b. strengthen the control of our superego over our id.
M　　　　c. shift from classical to operant conditioning.
　　　　　d. shift from operant to classical conditioning.

10.155
a
p. 400
Concept
C

According to Bandura, although humans respond to external factors, such as positive reinforcement and punishment, they may choose to ignore them and operate in terms of internal standards and values through a process he called
a. self-regulation.
b. self-actualization.
c. self-disclosure.
d. self-monitoring.

10.156
b
p. 400
Concept
M
PT/OLSG

In Bandura's theory, our perceived ability to carry out a desired action is called
a. self-reinforcement.
b. self-efficacy.
c. self-regulation.
d. self-esteem.

10.157
d
p. 400
Fact
M

A person's belief about whether he or she can successfully engage in and complete a specific behavior is called
a. locus of control.
b. self-actualization.
c. superiority.
d. self-efficacy.

10.158
d
p. 400
Fact
M

Bandura's social cognitive theory of personality differs from strictly behavioristic views because Bandura emphasized the importance of
a. classical conditioning.
b. operant conditioning.
c. inborn genetic factors.
d. self-determined goals.

2.159
b
p. 400
Fact
M

Which of the following theorists emphasized concepts such as self-reinforcement and self-efficacy in explaining human behavior?
a. Carl Rogers
b. Albert Bandura
c. Gordon Allport
d. Abraham Maslow

10.160
b
p. 400
Fact
M

Which theory emphasizes the importance of generalized expectancies concerning internal or external control of outcomes?
a. Cattell's Source Trait Theory
b. Rotter's Social Learning Theory
c. Rogers' Self-theory
d. Maslow's Need Theory

10.161
b
p. 400
Applied
M

Which of these statements most clearly reflects what Rotter would term an internal expectancy?
a. "Teachers give good grades to students they like."
b. "I can take night courses to get myself a better job."
c. "I don't wear a seatbelt, because if it's my time, God will take me anyway."
d. "Someday I'll get lucky and find a relationship that will last a long time."

10.162
c
p. 400
Concept
C

Based on the theory of Julian Rotter, control is to helplessness as
a. reaction formation is to functional autonomy.
b. penis envy is to womb envy.
c. internal is to external.
d. extrovert is to introvert.

Chapter 10 - Personality: Uniqueness and Consistency in the Behavior of Individuals

10.163
d
p. 400
Concept
M

Which of the following theories is most likely to involve testable predictions about personality and human behavior?
a. psychoanalytic
b. humanistic
c. neo-Freudian
d. learning

10.164
c
p. 401
Study
C

Eden and Aviram (1993) found that showing unemployed individuals films of appropriate job-hunting skills led to increased _____, and _____ employment.
a. self-efficacy; decreased
b. self-esteem; decreased
c. self-efficacy; increased
d. self-esteem; increased

10.165
c
p. 401
Fact
M
PT/OLSG

One key strength of the learning approach to personality is that it agrees with which of these basic principles of psychology?
a. All human beings are basically evil.
b. All human beings are basically good.
c. Behaviors are acquired through learning.
d. There are a few basic traits of personality.

10.166
d
p. 402
Fact
M

One key strength of the learning approach to personality is that it agrees with the basic principles of psychology that behavior is strongly affected by
a. unconscious drives.
b. instincts.
c. personal growth.
d. cognitive factors.

10.167
a
p. 402
Fact
M

One key strength of learning approaches to personality is that they rest on basic principles that
a. have been extensively and scientifically tested.
b. relate to our inborn genetic inheritance.
c. treat human beings as basically evil.
d. treat human beings as basically good.

10.168
c
p. 402
Concept
M

Which of the following theories is based on widely-accepted principles for which there is an impressive amount of empirical evidence?
a. humanistic
b. psychoanalytic
c. learning
d. neo-Freudian

10.169
d
p. 402
Fact
C

The major criticisms of learning approaches to personality center on
a. their emphasis on internal, innate factors.
b. the fact that these theories can't be tested.
c. whether humans are basically good or evil.
d. the older, more behavioristic theories.

Measuring Personality

10.170
b
p. 402
Fact
M

The process of using tests, interviews, and observations to study personality scientifically is called
a. personality.
b. measurement.
c. psychoanalysis.
d. apperception.

10.171 A measurement of personality that consists of a set of statements to which the person must
c respond with one of a short set of specific answers (similar to this multiple choice question)
p. 403 is called a(n)
Fact   a. projective test.
M   b. subjective test.
    c. objective test.
    d. oblique test.

10.172 When a test is made up of items that seem to be related to the trait being measured, this test is said to have
d   a. predictive validity.
p. 403   b. concept validity.
Fact   c. content validity.
M   d. face validity.

10.173 Some of the items on the MMPI do not seem to be related to the characteristic being measured. The process
a used to develop the MMPI is called
p. 403   a. empirical keying.
Applied   b. factor analysis.
C   c. cluster analysis.
    d. trait analysis.

10.174 The most widely used personality test, which allows therapists to measure various aspects
c of psychological disturbance, is the
p. 403   a. Thematic Apperception Test (TAT).
Fact   b. Rorschach Ink Blot Test.
M   c. Minnesota Multiphasic Personality Inventory (MMPI).
    d. 16 Personality Factor Questionnaire (16PF).

10.175 A test with clinical scales that include hypochondriasis, paranoia, hypomania, and
d psychasthenia is the
p. 403   a. Rorschach Ink Blot Test.
Fact   b. 16 Personality Factor Questionnaire (16PF).
C   c. California Personality Inventory (CPI).
    d. Minnesota Multiphasic Personality Inventory (MMPI).

10.176 One of the major advantages of the MCMI when compared to other personality inventories
a is that it allows the tester to
p. 404   a. screen people for specific psychological disorders.
Concept   b. determine who will work best at a given job.
C   c. predict which therapy will work best for a patient.
PT/OLSG   d. exercise considerable judgment in scoring the results.

10.177 The MCMI is different from the MMPI in that items on the MCMI
b   a. were constructed by having individuals with disorders answer the questions first.
p. 404   b. correspond more closely to psychological disorders used by psychologists.
Concept   c. are more difficult.
C   d. are stated in more abstract form.

10.178 The NEO-PI is different from the MMPI and the MCMI in that it is a personality test
c that is designed to measure
p. 404   a. aspects of personality that are multiaxial in development.
Concept   b. aspects of personality that are in the early stages of formation.
C   c. aspects of personality that are not related to psychological disorders.
    d. aspects of personality that are gender specific.

Chapter 10 - Personality: Uniqueness and Consistency in the Behavior of Individuals

10.179 The NEO-PI is a test designed to measure an individual's standing on the
a
p. 404   a. Big Five dimensions of personality.
Concept b. cardinal traits of personality.
C   c. source traits of personality.
         d. clinical scales of personality.

10.180 Personality inventories are _____ tests, while projective personality tests are _____ tests.
d
p. 404   a. cognitive; behavioral
Concept b. behavioral; cognitive
M   c. subjective; objective
         d. objective; subjective

10.181 A test in which the examinee is shown an ambiguous stimulus (one with many possible
a   meanings) and must describe his or her reactions to it is called a(n)
p. 404   a. projective test.
Fact   b. personality test.
M   c. intellectual assessment.
         d. psychoanalytic device.

10.182 The main idea behind the projective tests of personality is that
b
p. 405   a. our personality traits are fixed before birth by the genetic heritage we inherit from our parents.
Concept b. our reactions to ambiguous stimuli reflect various facets of our personality.
C   c. personality develops from environmental reinforcement and can be changed in the same way.
         d. tests cannot be valid unless they are normed on a large, representative sample of subjects.

10.183 Select an example of a projective test of personality.
c
p. 405   a. Minnesota Multiphasic Personality Inventory (MMPI)
Fact   b. 16 Personality Factor Questionnaire (16PF)
M   c. Rorschach Ink Blot Test
         d. California Personality Inventory (CPI)

10.184 The Rorschach test has been criticized for its
b
p. 405   a. standardized scoring.
Concept b. questionable validity.
M   c. ambiguous stimuli.
         d. consistent administration.

10. 185 Selecting a good measure of personality depends upon whether the test meets the criteria of
d
p. 405   a. administration and scoring.
Concept b. consistency and fairness.
M   c. bias and comprehensiveness.
         d. reliability and validity.

10.186 The main criticism of projective tests of personality is that they
a
p. 405   a. are too subjective and unreliable.
Concept b. are too sterile and structured.
M   c. cannot be applied to groups of people.
         d. take too long to administer.

Key Aspects of Personality: A Sample of Recent Research

10.187 The extent to which our self-evaluations are favorable or unfavorable refers to
c
p. 406   a. self-actualization.
Fact   b. self-disclosure.
M   c. self-esteem.
         d. self-reinforcement.

216 Test Bank - Essentials of Psychology (2nd Edition)

10.188 In comparison to people with low self-esteem, those with high self-esteem
b
p. 406   a. express more negative emotions.
Fact   b. experience fewer negative health effects.
M   c. are more susceptible to influence by others.
         d. are less inclined to take risks.

10.189 One biological effect of low self-esteem seems to be that it can
a
p. 406   a. reduce the efficiency of the immune system.
Fact   b. increase activity in cortical regions of the brain.
C   c. activate the somatic nervous system.
         d. nothing; self-esteem has no biological effects.

10.190 The personality trait that relates primarily to the ability to adapt one's behavior to the demands
c   of a current social situation refers to
p. 407   a. potentiality.
Fact   b. assertiveness.
M   c. self-monitoring.
         d. self-regulation.

10.191 The term "self-monitoring" refers to the tendency to
b
p. 407   a. work toward goals we have set for ourselves.
Fact   b. vary our behavior according to the situation.
M   c. be highly consistent in different situations.
         d. repress our more unacceptable desires.

10.192 Consistency is to variety as
a
p. 407   a. low self-monitoring is to high self-monitoring.
Concept b. high self-monitoring is to low self-monitoring.
C   c. unconscious motivation is to preconscious motivation.
         d. preconscious motivation is to unconscious motivation.

10.193 On which of these skills do high self-monitors perform better than other people?
b
p. 407   a. Maintaining consistent behavior across situations.
Fact   b. Judging how others will react to their actions.
M   c. Setting their own goals and rewarding their own behavior.
PT/OLSG d. Expressing their true attitudes in every situation.

10.194 Someone who strongly desires new, exciting experiences that usually involve danger is
d   considered
p. 407   a. self-actualized.
Fact   b. orally fixated.
M   c. highly extraverted.
         d. sensation seeking.

10.195 Which of the following is not a characteristic of high sensation seekers?
c
p. 407   a. more likely to engage in high risk sports
Fact   b. more likely to engage in substance abuse
M   c. less likely to withstand stress
PT/OLSG d. operate best at high level of stress

10.196 There is considerable evidence that the tendency toward sensation seeking is related to
b
p. 408   a. traumatic toilet training.
Fact   b. biological processes.
M   c. low self-esteem.
         d. conditional positive regard.

Chapter 10 - Personality: Uniqueness and Consistency in the Behavior of Individuals

10.197
c
p. 408
Fact
M

Someone who is high in sensation seeking is probably someone whose nervous system
a. was exposed to dangerous drugs before birth.
b. is particularly unable to deal well with stress.
c. operates best at a high level of arousal.
d. is no different from anyone else's nervous system.

10.198
c
p. 408
Fact
M

Compared with low sensation-seekers, high sensation-seekers are better able to
a. stay out of trouble with the law and other authorities.
b. control their behavior to avoid dangerous situations.
c. select and concentrate on important stimuli.
d. control pain through internal biological processes.

10.199
c
p. 408
Concept
C

In looking at the impact of culture on personality, it has been found that individuals from Western nations tend to have a/an _____ orientation, while individuals from Asian and African nations tend to have a/an _____ orientation.
a. collectivistic; individualistic
b. collectivistic; collegial
c. individualistic; collectivistic
d. individualistic; collegial

CHAPTER 11

Multiple-Choice Questions

Health Psychology: An Overview

11.1
a
p. 416
Fact
E
The branch of psychology that studies the relation between psychological variables and health is called
a. health psychology.
b. lifestyles psychology.
c. physiological psychology.
d. stress psychology.

11.2
a
p. 416
Concept
M
Health psychology is the subfield of psychology that focuses on
a. the application of psychological variables to issues of health.
b. the appropriate psychological training for medical doctors.
c. understanding unconscious motivations that make people ill.
d. developing better organizational structures for hospitals.

11.3
b
p. 416
Fact
M
PT/OLSG
The field that combines behavioral and biomedical knowledge for the prevention and treatment of medical disorders is
a. physiological psychology.
b. behavioral medicine.
c. bio-behaviorism.
d. neuroscience.

11.4
b
p. 416
Fact
M
A related field of health psychology that emphasizes the application of behavioral science to medical knowledge and treatments is called
a. genetic engineering.
b. behavioral medicine.
c. medical conditioning.
d. internal medicine.

11.5
d
p. 417
Fact
M
In the early 1900s the leading causes of death were
a. lifestyles.
b. genetic defects.
c. cancers.
d. infectious diseases.

11.6
c
p. 417
Fact
M
The leading causes of death today can be traced to
a. AIDS.
b. infectious diseases.
c. lifestyles.
d. genetic defects.

11.7
b
p. 417
Fact
M
During the 1980s, major declines occurred in the death rates associated with all of the following except
a. alcohol consumption.
b. smoking.
c. lack of exercise.
d. inappropriate eating habits.

11.8
b
p. 417
Concept
M
Which of the following is most likely to have contributed to recent changes in the leading causes of death?
a. decreased smoking
b. lifestyles
c. increased alcohol consumption
d. genetic defects

Chapter 11 - Health, Stress, and Coping

1.9
c
p. 417
Fact
M

A person's lifestyle is that person's
a. profile of temperament or personality traits.
b. cultural heritage or ethnic background.
c. decisions and behaviors that affect health.
d. genetic predispositions toward certain illnesses.

11.10
c
p. 418
Concept
M

Large-scale studies that have been conducted to determine risk factors for the development of certain diseases are called
a. risk-disease studies.
b. environmental cohort studies.
c. epidemiological studies.
d. attendant health studies.

11.11
b
p. 418
Concept
M
PT/OLSG

The Alameda County, California study in which the relationship between healthy lifestyles and incidence of death was investigated is one of the best examples of a/an
a. longitudinal study.
b. epidemiological study.
c. cross-sectional study.
d. lifestyle study.

Stress: Its Causes, Effects, and Control

11.12
d
p. 418
Concept
E

The response to events that disrupt or threaten to disrupt our physical or psychological functioning is called
a. aversiveness.
b. cognitive stressor.
c. a negative emotion.
d. stress.

11.13
c
p. 419
Fact
M

Stress is a complex process that occurs in reaction to events or situations in our environment called
a. interactions.
b. contagions.
c. stressors.
d. appraisers.

11.14
b
p. 419
Concept
M

A major feature of stress is that
a. events that cause stress in one individual will consistently cause stress in other individuals.
b. there is large variability in how individuals interpret events as stressful.
c. it always disrupts behavior.
d. it causes few if any psychological changes.

11.15
a
p. 419
Concept
M

Which of the following leads to a decrease in perceived stress?
a. predictability
b. unpredictability
c. increases in evoking incompatible tendencies
d. future positive events, such as a new job promotion

11.16
d
p. 419
Concept
C
PT/OLSG

Which of the following is not typical of stressful events?
a. a state of overload, feeling that you can not adapt to the stress
b. evoking of incompatible tendencies
c. the belief that the stress is beyond our limits of control
d. a predictable situation for most individuals

11.17
a
p. 419
Concept
M

Evidence indicates that whenever a person can _____ an aversive event, they perceive it to be less stressful.
a. predict, control, or terminate
b. predict, escape, or challenge
c. control, manipulate, or determine
d. terminate, evaluate, or manipulate

11.18
c
p. 419
Fact
M

If we feel we have control over something that happens, in general that makes it
a. our responsibility so it is more stressful.
b. less interesting and challenging to us.
c. more predictable and less stressful.
d. harder to ignore and harder to deal with.

11.19
a
p. 419
Fact
M

A sequence of responses activated in order to adapt to a chronic source of stress is referred to as the
a. general adaptation syndrome.
b. emotional overload reaction.
c. autonomic adaptation reactance.
d. response activation syndrome.

11.20
b
p. 419
Fact
M

The alarm, resistance, and exhaustion stages in reaction to stress make up what is called the
a. autonomic overload disorder.
b. general adaptation syndrome.
c. free-floating anxiety disorder.
d. response activation syndrome.

11.21
c
p. 419
Fact
E

Arousal level is highest during which of the following stages of Hans Selye's general adaptation syndrome?
a. exhaustion
b. resistance
c. alarm
d. recovery

11.22
d
p. 419
Applied
M

As a result of continued stress, you seem to catch every flu bug that comes around. Which stage of the general adaptation syndrome are you most likely to be experiencing?
a. weakness
b. alarm
c. resistance
d. exhaustion

11.23
b
p. 419
Fact
M
PT/OLSG

The stage of the GAS when arousal is lowered as the body copes with the stressor is the
a. coping stage.
b. resistance stage.
c. alarm stage.
d. exhaustion stage.

11.24
a
p. 419
Fact
C

During the resistance stage of the general adaptation syndrome, people will exhibit
a. moderate, sustained levels of arousal.
b. low levels of arousal.
c. high levels of arousal.
d. rapidly fluctuating levels of arousal.

11.25
a
p. 420
Fact
M

A person's active evaluation of a situation and his or her own ability to deal effectively with it is called
a. cognitive appraisal.
b. physiological arousal.
c. stress.
d. anxiety.

Chapter 11 - Health, Stress, and Coping 221

11.26 Cognitive appraisal is a process by which people
d
p. 420 a. develop emotional reactions to environmental events.
Fact   b. assess how successful they have been in the past.
M   c. try out various stress-reduction strategies.
       d. evaluate a situation and their ability to deal with it.

11.27 According to the cognitive appraisal perspective, stress occurs when people
d
p. 420 a. are in the coping stage.
Fact   b. are goal oriented.
M   c. are in the resistance stage.
PT/OLSG d. feel unable to cope with demands.

11.28 With regard to cognitive appraisals of stress, threats to important goals are to perceived inabilities to cope as
b
p. 420 a. secondary appraisals are to primary appraisals.
Concept b. primary appraisals are to secondary appraisals.
M   c. alarm is to exhaustion.
       d. exhaustion is to alarm.

11.29 At times, individuals experience stress because they perceive the situation as threatening
b   to important goals. This is termed
p. 420 a. secondary appraisal.
Fact   b. primary appraisal.
M   c. the general adaptation syndrome.
       d. post-traumatic stress syndrome.

11.30 Threat is to coping as
c
p. 420 a. exhaustion is to alarm.
Concept b. alarm is to exhaustion.
M   c. primary appraisal is to secondary appraisal.
       d. secondary appraisal is to primary appraisal.

11.31 Tomaka and his colleagues (1993), in a study investigating cognitive appraisal, found that individuals in the
d   "challenge group" had _____ and the individuals in the "threat group" had _____.
p. 420 a. feelings of weaker stress, greater physiological arousal
Study   b. weaker physiological arousal, feelings of greater stress
C   c. feelings of greater stress, feelings of weaker stress
       d. greater physiological arousal, feelings of greater stress

11.32 According to the ratings completed by Holmes and Rahe, the most stressful life event is
a
p. 422 a. death of a spouse.
Fact   b. a job promotion.
M   c. getting married.
       d. getting a divorce.

11.33 Which of the following life events would probably be the most stressful?
c
p. 422 a. having trouble with your boss.
Fact   b. moving to a new residence.
M   c. getting married.
       d. going on vacation.

11.34 The more stressful life events we experience, the more likely we are to
b
p. 423 a. change jobs.
Fact   b. experience health problems.
M   c. commit a crime.
       d. have problems with a spouse.

11.35 a p. 423 Concept M

According to research on stressful life events, it appears that people who have experienced a large number of serious events in a prior 12-months period will show
a. a high incidence of illness.
b. a high level of stress resistance.
c. hardiness.
d. strong alarm reactions.

11.36 c p. 423 Fact M

After losing his job, getting a divorce, and moving out of town, Ralph is most likely to
a. have fewer physical problems as a result of facing the past stressors.
b. have about the same physical problems as anyone else.
c. have more physical problems as a result of these past stressors.
d. initially experience very good health followed by a short period of minor illnesses.

11.37 d p. 423 Concept C

An important criticism of the Holmes-Rahe Social Readjustment Rating Scale is that it
a. makes no distinction between positive and negative stress.
b. puts too much emphasis on social and family events.
c. does not include events that primarily affect women.
d. ignores many factors affecting how people respond to stress.

11.38 b p. 423 Fact M

Individuals who remain healthy after prolonged exposure to stressful events are characterized as being
a. resilient.
b. hardy.
c. avoidant.
d. functional.

11.39 a p. 423 Fact E PT/OLSG

In general, the greater the number of stressful life events for an individual, the greater the likelihood that the person's _____ will be negatively affected.
a. health
b. emotions
c. cognitions
d. dissonance

11.40 d p. 424 Fact E

The term that refers to the frequently occurring, repetitive sources of stress that happen to us on an almost daily basis is
a. stressors.
b. overload.
c. annoyers.
d. hassles.

11.41 a p. 424 Fact M

In the psychology of stress, which of these would be termed a "hassle?"
a. Not being able to find your car keys.
b. Living in constant fear of violence.
c. Death of a close family member.
d. A big promotion at work.

11.42 b p. 424 Concept M

Which of the following are negatively correlated with good health?
a. number of life changes only
b. both number of life changes and number of hassles
c. number of hassles only
d. neither number of hassles nor number of life changes

11.43 c p. 424 Concept M

Recent evidence indicates that major life events may exert their harmful effects by
a. damaging an individual's cognitive structure.
b. overwhelming the individual's resources.
c. creating a ripple effect of minor problems.
d. damaging an individual's emotional structure.

Chapter 11 - Health, Stress, and Coping

11.44
c
p. 424
Study
C

In an investigation of the relationship between traumatic events and hassles, research by Pillow and colleagues (1996) found that participants reported
a. more hassles before a traumatic life event.
b. fewer hassles after a traumatic life event.
c. more hassles after a traumatic life event.
d. fewer hassles before a traumatic life event.

11.45
c
p. 424
Applied
M

After two years as an over-the-road truck driver, Bret is starting to make errors and take chances, and is becoming convinced that he cannot accomplish what is asked of him. Bret is probably suffering from
a. an approach-avoidance conflict.
b. a panic attack.
c. overload.
d. boredom.

11.46
b
p. 424
Fact
M

Which of the following work-related experiences is often a factor in producing stress?
a. extreme overload only
b. extreme overload and underload
c. neither extreme overload nor underload
d. underload only

11.47
b
p. 424
Fact
E
PT/OLSG

Being asked to do too many things in a short period of time is called work
a. conflict.
b. overload.
c. underload.
d. incompatibility.

11.48
c
p. 424
Fact
M

The plight of first-time managers caused by the demands of subordinates and the demands of managers' bosses is referred to as
a. underload.
b. hassles.
c. role conflict.
d. manager syndrome.

11.49
a
p. 424
Applied
M

Lisa's immediate supervisor at the advertising firm expects her to be creative, imaginative, and somewhat flamboyant, but the unit manager expects her to be punctual, conservative, and reliable. Lisa is probably experiencing
a. role conflict.
b. daily hassles.
c. major life stressors.
d. posttraumatic stress disorder.

11.50
d
p. 425
Fact
M

Which of the following has not been listed as something that can produce stress in a work environment?
a. work underload
b. role conflict
c. arbitrary performance appraisals
d. intermittent training regimen

11.51
c
p. 425
Fact
M

One thing employers can do to make performance appraisals less stressful is to
a. conduct them less often.
b. conduct them more often.
c. make sure they are seen as fair.
d. base them on more personal information.

11.52
a
p. 425
Concept
C

Which of the following can be done to reduce the stress of the work environment and possibly reduce related health problems?
a. the practice of person-environment fit
b. the use of arbitrary performance appraisals
c. reinforce individuality
d. assign tasks randomly

11.53
b
p. 425
Applied
M

Lisa is working for a company that tries to match her characteristics to the work she will be doing. This company is considering the
a. production-environment relationship.
b. person-environment fit.
c. personnel-evaluation interaction.
d. performance-environment interaction.

11.54
c
p. 426
Concept
M

Increased susceptibility to heart disease, high blood pressure, and ulcers may result from
a. inhibition of aggression.
b. person-environment fit.
c. prolonged stress.
d. cognitive reactance.

11.55
d
p. 426
Fact
M
PT/OLSG

The negative effects of stress on health appears to result from its interference in the _____ system.
a. nervous
b. endocrine
c. cardiovascular
d. immune

11.56
b
p. 426
Fact
M

In terms of our general health, the system thought to be disrupted by stress is the
a. nervous system.
b. immune system.
c. temperature regulation system.
d. gastro-intestinal system.

11.57
d
p. 426
Fact
M

Foreign substances, called _____ enter our body and are attacked by the immune system.
a. antimedians
b. collagens
c. contagens
d. antigens

11.58
c
p. 426
Fact
E

Our immune system is most disrupted by
a. task complexity.
b. behavioral contrasts.
c. prolonged stress.
d. centenarian clusters.

11.59
c
p. 426
Fact
M

The condition that is frequently involved in the health consequences of stress is
a. muscular dysfunction.
b. a hormone imbalance.
c. a weakened immune system.
d. disturbed patterns of eating and sleeping.

11.60
d
p. 426
Concept
M

Which of the following is most likely to provide a buffer against chronic stress?
a. immune system suppression
b. daily hassles
c. decreased affiliative behaviors
d. social support

Chapter 11 - Health, Stress, and Coping

11.61 Which of the following tasks will be most disrupted by moderate stress?
a
p. 427 a. complex
Concept b. medium difficulty
M c. easy
  d. physical tasks

11.62 Research indicates that the _____ the complexity of a task, the _____ the level of arousal at which a
b downturn in performance occurs.
p. 427 a. greater, higher
Concept b. greater, lower
M c. more ambiguous, higher
  d. less ambiguous, lower

11.63 One of the reasons that even mild stress could interfere with task performance is that
b a. such stress could present a cognitive task to accomplish.
p. 427 b. such stress could prove to be distracting, and take attention from the task at hand.
Concept c. such stress could provide an explanation for poor performance.
C d. such stress could prevent the adoption of an already used problem solving strategy.

11.64 Your author points out that generalizations about the impact on work effectiveness should be made with
d a. great clarity.
p. 427 b. great contagion.
Fact c. great confidence.
E d. great caution.

11.65 If you have a job involving prolonged exposure to stress and start to feel tired, useless,
b and unappreciated, then you may be suffering from
p. 427 a. post-traumatic stress syndrome.
Applied b. burnout.
M c. role conflict.
  d. behavioral contrast.

11.66 A type of attitudinal exhaustion, known as depersonalization, characterized by a cynical
c view of others and a tendency to derogate oneself, one's job and life in general can be produced
p. 427 as a result of
Concept a. post-traumatic stress syndrome.
M b. cognitive restructuring.
  c. burnout.
  d. carcinogens.

11.67 Which of the following factors is not one of those likely to be a cause of burnout?
b a. being unappreciated
p. 427 b. feelings of control
Fact c. inflexible rules
M d. poor opportunities for promotion

11.68 Victims of burnout frequently
a a. change jobs or withdraw psychologically by simply passing time until retirement.
p. 428 b. remain helpless and suffer several bouts of depression.
Fact c. initiate the resistance stage of the stress reactions.
M d. seek out social support.
PT/OLSG

11.69 People who have general expectancies for poor outcomes in challenging situations are said to be
c a. unrealistic.
p. 429 b. delusional
Fact c. pessimists.
M d. exhausted.

11.70 Optimists tend to be more stress-resistant than pessimists. This may be due to
a optimists using _____ coping.
p. 429 a. problem-focused
Fact b. emotion-focused
E c. denial
PT/OLSG d. psychological modification

11.71 Stress resistance is to stress susceptibility as
d a. work underload is to work overload.
p. 429 b. work overload is to work underload.
Fact c. pessimism is to optimism.
M d. optimism is to pessimism.

11.72 In comparison to pessimists, optimists tend to cope with stress by
a a. seeking social support.
p. 429 b. reporting more physical illness when stressed.
Concept c. denying the existence of stress.
M d. adopting a strategy to deal with the stress that involved goal modification.

11.73 Problem-focused coping is to giving up a goal as
b a. pessimist is to optimist.
p. 429 b. optimist is to pessimist.
Concept c. hardiness is to cognitive restructuring.
M d. cognitive restructuring is to hardiness.

11.74 Problem-focused coping is associated with more positive outcomes when the source of stress is _____.
c a. limited
p. 429 b. flexible
Fact c. controllable
M d. disjunctive

11.75 It has been found that _____ coping is associated with _____ outcomes when the stress is controllable.
d a. emotion-focused, negative
p. 429 b. emotion-focused, positive
Concept c. problem-focused, negative
M d. problem-focused, positive

11.76 Some studies report that males tend to use _____ coping, and females tend to use _____ coping.
b a. primary-focused, secondary-focused
p. 429 b. problem-focused, emotion-focused
Study c. emotion-focused, problem-focused
M d. secondary-focused, primary-focused

11.77 Recent research indicates that men and women do not differ in the _____ of stress they
b report, but do differ in the _____ of their problems.
p. 429 a. category; interpretation
Study b. amount; content
C c. content: amount
d. interpretation; category

11.78 An optimistic attitude can help reduce our experience of stress, probably because optimism leads to
a a. engaging in behaviors that will improve the situation.
p. 429 b. acceptance of the situation staying the way it is.
Fact c. an increased level of nervous system reactance.
C d. an ability to avoid thinking too much about the stressor.

Chapter 11 - Health, Stress, and Coping

11.79
b
p. 429
Applied
M

When Ralph got a bad grade on his first History exam, he immediately went to see the teacher to see what he could do to improve his grade, and made plans with another student in the class to meet often to study. Ralph's response could best be labeled
a. pessimistic.
b. optimistic.
c. a cognitive appraisal.
d. a stressor.

11.80
b
p. 430
Fact
M

In relation to stress, a cluster of traits that include high levels of commitment, viewing change as a chance for growth and development, and strong sense of control over events and outcomes of one's life is referred to as being
a. optimistic.
b. hardy.
c. gregarious.
d. cope adaptive.

11.81
c
p. 430
Fact
M

People who are considered hardy with respect to stress have
a. a low sense of control over events in their lives.
b. a dislike for change in their lives.
c. a deeper involvement in whatever they do.
d. a tendency to show more stress-related illnesses.

11.82
b
p. 430
Fact
M
PT/OLSG

Which is true of hardy individuals? They
a. are not stress resistant.
b. see change as a challenge.
c. do not have a sense of control.
d. have a low level of commitment.

Understanding and Communicating Our Health Needs

11.83
c
p. 430
Concept
M

Which of the following is false?
a. People are generally aware of lifestyle habits that influence health.
b. People generally know which lifestyle habits to change in order to improve their health.
c. People will usually change their lifestyle habits to improve personal health.
d. People usually do not have sufficient motivation to change their lifestyle habits.

11.84
d
p. 431
Concept
M

Physical symptoms associated with illness are most likely to be perceived by people who
a. lead interesting and enjoyable lives.
b. are generally in good moods and upbeat in their thinking.
c. have challenging and rewarding careers.
d. tend to focus on themselves.

11.85
d
p. 431
Fact
M

Which of the following have not been found to be related to perception of physical symptoms?
a. differences in attention to our bodies
b. past experiences
c. expectations
d. social relevance

11.86
a
p. 431
Fact
E

People who are in a good mood rate themselves
a. healthier than other people.
b. less healthy than other people.
c. more concerned about health than other people.
d. generally the same as others with respect to health.

11.87 Our past experiences with certain physical symptoms generally lead us to
c
p. 431　a. treat them as more serious than they really are.
Fact　b. treat them as less serious than they really are.
M　c. compare current symptoms with past experience.
　d. forget that these symptoms have appeared before.

11.88 We generally interpret the symptoms that we recognize
d
p. 431　a. as more serious than they really are.
Fact　b. as less serious than they really are.
M　c. based on our doctor's diagnosis.
　d. in light of our previous experience.

11.89 Which of these illustrates the effects of expectations on symptom interpretation?
b
p. 431　a. A mother who keeps a child home from school who has been running a low-grade fever for two days.
Applied
C　b. A medical student who diagnoses someone with a runny nose as having the rare disease she just learned about.
　c. A busy executive planning a long-awaited family vacation who doesn't notice a slight cough every morning.
　d. An elderly man who is so afraid of doctors that he never reports the constant pain he feels in his legs.

11.90 The health belief model was developed to explain why people
a
p. 432　a. do not use medical screening devices.
Fact　b. have preferences for the age of their physician.
M　c. have preferences for the sex of their physician.
　d. do not trust folk-medicine.

11.91 Our decision to practice a particular health-related behavior depends, among other things, on our belief that
a
p. 432　a. there is a real threat to our health if we do not.
Fact　b. the health threat does not actually apply to us.
M　c. the behavior will make no difference to our health.
　d. others will join us in this new behavior.

11.92 According to the health belief model, our willingness to seek medical help depends on the
b
p. 432　a. amount of role conflict in our lives.
Fact　b. extent to which we perceive a threat to our health.
M　c. stage of the general adaptation syndrome.
　d. level of education earned.

11.93 If you have a family history of cancer and you believe you cannot do anything to lessen your chances of cancer, you may continue to smoke. Such behavior can be explained on the basis of
c
p. 432
Applied　a. the general adaptation syndrome.
M　b. the person-environment fit hypothesis.
　c. the health belief model.
　d. the cognitive appraisal model.

11.94 The health belief model asserts that the two factors that affect our decision to change a health-related behavior are
d
p. 432
Applied　a. self-confidence and the fear of doctors.
M　b. optimism and pessimism.
　c. living an exciting life with other people, and living a boring life alone.
　d. belief that there is a threat, and belief that the behavior will make a difference.

Chapter 11 - Health, Stress, and Coping

11.95
a
p. 432
Applied
M

According to the health belief model, which of these beliefs would make it less likely for a woman to take part in a screening for breast cancer?
a. Cancer treatments are unpleasant and unsuccessful.
b. My family history puts me at high risk for breast cancer.
c. Detecting cancer early would improve my chances.
d. Breast cancer is an extremely dangerous disease.

11.96
d
p. 432
Applied
M

According to the health belief model, which of these beliefs would make it more likely for a man to take part in a screening for high cholesterol?
a. Low cholesterol diets are boring and tasteless.
b. The man has no relatives who have had heart attacks.
c. The body makes cholesterol no matter what you eat.
d. Reducing cholesterol could help the man live longer.

11.97
d
p. 432
Concept
M

Which of the following is least likely to be communicated between a doctor and a patient?
a. telling the patient how to take a prescription medicine
b. telling the patient the purpose of a specific test being given
c. explaining how the illness will be treated
d. asking the patient what he knows about the illness

11.98
c
p. 432
Fact
M

When communications between doctors and patients were studied, the doctors proved to be worse at communications involving
a. the mechanics of the examination process.
b. the basic facts about a patient's illness.
c. the patient's thoughts and feelings about illness.
d. the nature of the prescribed medications.

11.99
c
p. 433
Study
C
PT/OLSG

Ford and colleagues (1996), in a study on communication between physicians and new cancer patients, found that the interactions tended to be _____ rather than _____.
a. cooperative, directive
b. psychological-focused, medical-focused
c. clinician-dominated, patient-centered
d. patient-centered, clinician-dominated

11.100
d
p. 433
Study
C

Recent research by Wechsler and his colleagues (1996) indicates that in 1981, the focus of doctor-patient interactions was on _____, and in 1994, the focus of doctor-patient interactions was on _____.
a. social issues, psychological issues
b. medical issues, psychological issues
c. psychological issues, social issues
d. psychological issues, medical issues

Behavioral and Psychological Correlates of Illness: The Effects of Actions and Thoughts on Health

11.101
a
p. 434
Fact
E
PT/OLSG

Lifestyle features that affect our chances of becoming ill are termed _____ factors.
a. risk
b. carcinogen
c. punishment
d. individual

11.102
b
p. 434
Fact
M

Aspects of our lifestyles that affect our chances of developing a particular disease within the limits established by our genes are called
a. carcinogens.
b. risk factors.
c. alarm reactions.
d. stressors.

229

11.103 Someone who inherits a genetic tendency toward cancer
c
p. 434 a. will develop the disease no matter what.
Fact   b. should consider not having children and passing it on.
M   c. might develop cancer in response to certain risk factors.
        d. must take care to consume enough carcinogens.

11.104 Carcinogens are
c
p. 434 a. the body's immune cells.
Fact   b. support cells of the nervous system.
M   c. cancer-producing agents in the environment.
        d. toxins that initiate the general adaptation syndrome.

11.105 Which of these is established as a risk factor for cancer?
a
p. 434 a. A determination to have a great tan all summer.
Fact   b. Eating a diet containing high levels of fiber.
M   c. A personality style including determination and hostility.
        d. A genetic pattern of increased cancer risk.

11.106 A study by Gibbons and colleagues (1997), which measured perceptions of health risks before and after
b   quitting smoking found that
p. 435 a. smokers who did not smoke perceived smoking as being less risky.
Study   b. smokers who resumed smoking perceived smoking as being less risky.
C   c. smokers who resumed smoking perceived smoking as being more risky.
        d. there was no relationship between resuming smoking and perception of risk of smoking.

11.107 The fact that some smokers may hold the false belief that they will be exempt from the harmful
a   consequences of cigarette smoking is an example of a
p. 435 a. cognitive factor.
Concept b. psychosocial factor.
M   c. psychophysiological factor.
        d. stress factor.

11.108 Nicotine is not one of the following.
d
p. 435 a. addictive
Fact   b. alters the availability of a neurotransmitter
M   c. may affect some smokers because of genetic predisposition
        d. a derivative from cocaine

11.109 One piece of evidence to support a biological reason for smoking is
d
p. 435 a. more men than women smoke.
Fact   b. more people smoke as they get older.
M   c. smoking tends to run in families.
        d. some people are not affected by nicotine.

11.110 Which of the following is not likely to influence your decision to smoke?
b
p. 435 a. biological factors
Fact   b. racial factors
M   c. psychological factors
        d. cognitive factors

11.111 The role of parents and peers in influencing an adolescent's tendency to smoke is an example of a
b
p. 435 a. cognitive factor.
Concept b. psychosocial factor.
M   c. psychophysiological factor.
        d. repressed factor.

Chapter 11 - Health, Stress, and Coping

11.112   Which of the following is false?
d
p. 435
Fact
M
PT/OLSG
- a. Individuals who have experienced stressful life events tend to have a high incidence of illness.
- b. Optimists are more resistant to stress than pessimists.
- c. Persons who have few distractions in their lives are more likely to notice symptoms than those who have many distractions.
- d. Smoking does not appear to be influenced by psychosocial factors.

11.113   Developing the smoking habit seems to be related to all but which of the following factors?
b
p. 435
Concept
M
- a. biological susceptibility to nicotine
- b. type A behavior
- c. peer pressure
- d. role models who smoke

11.114   Passive smoke refers to
c
p. 436
Fact
E
- a. smog from automobiles and factories.
- b. smoke absorbed through the skin in the fingertips.
- c. second-hand smoke.
- d. smoke that accumulates close to the floor.

11.115   When a nonsmoker breathes cigarette smoke that comes from another person's cigarette, it is referred to as
b
p. 436
Fact
M
- a. social smoking.
- b. passive smoking.
- c. diluted smoking.
- d. conditional smoking.

11.116   What factor has been shown to increase a nonsmoking woman's chance of developing lung cancer?
d
p. 436
Fact
M
PT/OLSG
- a. Moderate drinking
- b. Eating a high-fat diet
- c. Sun exposure
- d. Passive smoking

11.117   Increases in the incidence of respiratory and cardiovascular disease are correlated with
a
p. 436
Fact
M
- a. both actual smoking behavior and passive smoke.
- b. only with actual smoking behavior.
- c. only with passive smoking.
- d. neither actual nor passive smoke.

11.118   Emmons and colleagues (1994) found that individuals can drastically reduce the harmful effects of passive smoking by
b
p. 436
Study
M
- a. taking steps to eliminate smoking in the workplace.
- b. taking steps to eliminate smoking at home.
- c. taking steps to eliminate smoking in the automobile.
- d. taking steps to exchange the air in a room more often.

11.119   Which of the following have been found to be related to a reduced risk of colon and rectal cancer?
c
p. 437
Fact
M
- a. foods containing proteins
- b. daily exposure to sunshine and fresh air
- c. consumption of broccoli
- d. foods low in sugars

11.120   A term used to describe all diseases of the heart and blood vessels is
a
p. 437
Fact
M
- a. cardiovascular disease.
- b. arteriosclerosis.
- c. coronary heart disease.
- d. stroke.

11.121 Cardiovascular disease is a group of illnesses that affect
a
p. 437   a. the heart and blood vessels.
Fact   b. the brain and nervous system.
M   c. the body's immune system.
          d. the throat and lungs.

11.122 Cardiovascular disease includes
d
p. 437   a. cancer of the heart.
Fact   b. cancer of the lungs.
M   c. immune system diseases.
          d. arteriosclerosis

11.123 Serum cholesterol is
b
          a. negatively correlated with cardiovascular disease.
p. 437   b. positively correlated with cardiovascular disease.
Fact   c. not correlated with cardiovascular disease.
M   d. another term for coronary heart disease.

11.124 Diets high in fiber, fruits, and vegetables are
c
          a. not related to levels of serum cholesterol.
p. 437   b. related to high levels of serum cholesterol.
Fact   c. related to low levels of serum cholesterol.
M   d. related to high risks of cardiovascular diseases.

11.125 Evidence indicates that although most interventions designed to help people lose weight work _____, the
a   weight loss typically _____.
p. 437   a. initially, does not last
Fact   b. initially, does last for an extended period
E   c. after a period of time, does not initially work
          d. after a period of time, does work initially

11.126 In the area of weight loss, self determination theory predicts that _____ weight loss
b   will be maintained over time, whereas weight loss by _____ is not maintained.
p. 438   a. cognitively motivated; emotional motivation
Concept   b. autonomously motivated; controlled motivation
C   c. control motivated; autonomous motivation
          d. emotionally motivated; cognitive motivation

11.127 Williams and his colleagues (1996), in a study of self-determination theory over time, found that those
d   individuals joining a weight loss program for _____ lost more weight, attended more regularly, and
p. 438   maintained the weight loss longer than individuals joining the program for _____.
Study   a. congruence motivation reasons, incongruence motivation reasons
C   b. cognitive motivation reasons, emotional motivation reasons
          c. controlled motivation reasons, autonomous motivation reasons
          d. autonomous motivation reasons, controlled motivation reasons

11.128 Cancer, impaired sexual function and cognitive impairment have been found to be related to
c
p. 438   a. smoking.
Fact   b. caffeine.
M   c. alcohol.
          d. sugar.

11.129 A study by Heien (1996) found that _____ tended to have higher earnings.
b
p. 438   a. compulsive drinkers
Study   b. moderate drinkers
E   c. abstainers
          d. abusive drinkers

Chapter 11 - Health, Stress, and Coping

11.130
d
p. 438
Fact
M

Alcohol consumption is related to all of the following except
a. development of colon and rectal cancer.
b. retardation in children whose mothers drank during pregnancy.
c. impaired sexual functioning.
d. development of cancer of cardiovascular system.

11.131
a
p. 438
Fact
M

A condition of retardation and physical abnormalities that occurs in children of mothers who drink heavily while pregnant is called
a. matriarchal alcohol syndrome.
b. fetal alcohol syndrome.
c. early development alcoholism.
d. hypoglycemia.

11.132
a
p. 438
Fact
M

Heavy drinking has been shown to be related to all of these except
a. high serum cholesterol.
b. fetal alcohol syndrome.
c. stomach and intestinal diseases.
d. reduced cognitive functioning.

11.133
b
p. 438
Fact
C
PT/OLSG

A smoker who also drinks alcohol regularly is likely to show
a. a reduced risk of cancer.
b. an increased risk of cancer.
c. little or no cognitive impairment.
d. extreme risks of birth defects.

11.134
b
p. 439
Fact
M

Suppressed immune systems, greater recurrence of cancer, and higher mortality rates are typical of people who
a. demonstrate positive affect.
b. keep their negative emotions to themselves.
c. express their negative emotions openly.
d. are characterized as combative individuals.

11.135
c
p. 439
Fact
C

Which of the following categories of individuals is least likely to recover from a serious illness such as cancer?
a. People who demonstrate positive affect.
b. Individuals who express their negative emotions openly.
c. People who keep their negative emotions to themselves.
d. Combative individuals, for example, those who express anger about their illness toward their family members.

11.136
d
p. 439
Fact
M

Hypertension refers to
a. having excessive stress in one's life.
b. excess strain on the muscle system.
c. extensive damage to the cardiovascular system.
d. prolonged high blood pressure.

11.137
a
p. 439
Concept
C

Which of the following is associated with an increase in blood pressure and is boosted by emotions such as hostility and anxiety?
a. catecholamine.
b. endorphins.
c. carcinogens.
d. nicotine.

11.138   Individuals who tend to be competitive, aggressive, hostile, and impatient display a pattern
b   of behaviors termed
p. 439   a.   Type B.
Fact   b.   Type A.
M   c.   general adaptation syndrome.
          d.   catecholaminergic activity.

11.139   Which of the following is most likely to result in heart disease?
d   a.   Type B personalities
p. 439   b.   competitiveness
Fact   c.   hard work
C   d.   cynical hostility

11.140   The characteristic of the Type A pattern that is most associated with increased risk of heart disease is
a   a.   cynical hostility.
p. 439   b.   competitiveness.
Concept   c.   perfectionism.
M   d.   impatience.

11.141   Matthews and her colleagues (1996) found that _____ were predictive of hostility measures taken years
d   later.
p. 440   a.   low frequencies of positive behaviors between mothers and sons
Study   b.   high frequencies of positive behaviors between fathers and sons
C   c.   high frequencies of positive behaviors between both parents and sons
          d.   low frequencies of positive behaviors between fathers and sons

11.142   Gidron and Davidson (1996), in a project designed to investigate effectiveness of interventions for cynical
b   hostility, found that
p. 440   a.   individuals participating in the intervention showed no change in the level of cynical hostility.
Study   b.   individuals participating in the intervention showed lower levels of cynical hostility.
M   c.   individuals who did not participate in the intervention showed increased levels of cynical hostility.
          d.   there was no change in the level of cynical hostility for either group.

11.143   The reduction of the immune system's ability to defend itself against the introduction of
a   any foreign matter is called
p. 440   a.   acquired immune deficiency syndrome.
Fact   b.   HIV.
M   c.   stress exhaustion.
PT/OLSG   d.   antibody deficiencies.

11.144   The cause of AIDS is
b   a.   unusual sexual behavior.
p. 440   b.   human immunodeficiency virus.
Fact   c.   IV drug use.
M   d.   physical contact.

11.145   A serious, incurable condition that causes death because the body's immune system can
d   no longer fight off infection is
p. 440   a.   central neurological dysfunction (CND).
Fact   b.   cardiovascular deficiency disease (CVDD).
M   c.   derived immune deficiency illness (DIDI).
          d.   acquired immune deficiency syndrome (AIDS).

11.146   People who have AIDS eventually die from
a   a.   infections their bodies can no longer fight off.
p. 440   b.   an attack on their brains by the HIV virus.
Fact   c.   paralysis caused by muscular weakening.
M   d.   growths of HIV in their lungs that prevent breathing.

Chapter 11 - Health, Stress, and Coping 235

11.147 Individuals who are HIV infected can spread the disease to others without knowing it because
d the incubation period for AIDS may be
p. 440   a.   1 year.
Fact   b.   2 years.
M   c.   5 years.
     d.   10 years.

11.148 A new class of drugs, called _____, in combination with an older set of medicines, can significantly
b reduce the level of HIV in the blood.
p. 441   a.   blood-barrier interacters
Fact   b.   protease inhibitors
C   c.   collagen reactors
     d.   antigen delimiters

11.149 The human immunodeficiency virus is spread primarily through
c   a.   unprotected sexual intercourse only.
p. 441   b.   infected blood or blood products only.
Fact   c.   unprotected sexual intercourse and infected blood or blood products.
M   d.   unprotected sexual intercourse, infected blood or blood products, and hugging and holding hands.

11.150 At present, the best ways to deal with the epidemic of AIDS are through
c   a.   avoiding homosexuals and homosexual behavior.
p. 442   b.   the use of AZT and many other related drugs.
Concept   c.   changing lifestyles to avoid risky behaviors.
M   d.   a vaccination to prevent HIV infection.

11.151 The IMB model for developing interventions that accommodate both individual and group
c differences involves
p. 442   a.   insistence-moderation-belief.
Concept   b.   incarceration-medication-biotechnology.
C   c.   information-motivation-behavioral skills.
     d.   inculturation-mediation-between individuals.

11.152 Research that attempts to measure a group's current knowledge of AIDS and the strategies
b they currently use to avoid it is called
p. 442   a.   educational research.
Fact   b.   elicitation research.
C   c.   evaluative research.
     d.   prevention research.

11.153 Growing evidence suggests that in order to be effective in reducing the spread of AIDS,
d educational programs must provide not only information but also
p. 442   a.   condoms.
Fact   b.   medical care.
M   c.   HIV testing.
     d.   motivation to avoid AIDS.

11.154 Growing evidence suggests that in order to be effective in reducing the spread of AIDS,
b educational programs must provide not only information but also
p. 442   a.   sterile needles.
Fact   b.   behavioral skills.
M   c.   HIV immunizations.
     d.   moral counseling.

236 Test Bank - Baron (4th Edition)

11.155   The chances of _____ transmission of HIV are much greater than _____ transmission.
c
p. 443   a. different ethnic, same ethnic
Fact   b. different culture, same culture
C   c. male-to-female, female-to-male
PT/OLSG   d. female-to-male, male-to-female

11.156   Adherence to the _____ may increase the probability that a woman will engage in unprotected sex.
c
p. 443   a. coherent gender role
Fact   b. non-traditional gender role
M   c. traditional gender role
          d. contagion gender role

Promoting Wellness: Developing a Healthier Lifestyle

11.157   The most important factor contributing to longevity and good health seems to be
b
p. 444   a. lack of alcohol consumption.
Concept   b. regular exercise.
M   c. high protein diets.
          d. relatively high caloric intake.

11.158   All of the following affect longevity, except
b
p. 444   a. remaining sexually active.
Fact   b. competitive personality.
M   c. continued involvement in family and community.
          d. regular exercise.

11.159   Perhaps the most important factor contributing to the ability of some people to live very long lives is
a
p. 444   a. getting enough vigorous physical activity.
Fact   b. avoiding diets with too much grains.
M   c. eating enough meat and animal protein.
          d. cutting back on sexual activity in old age.

11.160   Promoting healthy behavior is to early detection of disease as
d
p. 444   a. lifestyle is to meditation.
Concept   b. meditation is to lifestyle.
M   c. secondary prevention strategy is to primary prevention strategy.
          d. primary prevention strategy is to secondary prevention strategy.

11.161   Attending a workshop to decrease smoking is an example of
a
p. 444   a. primary prevention strategy.
Concept   b. secondary prevention strategy.
M   c. tertiary prevention strategy.
          d. general prevention strategy.

11.162   Which of the following would be an example of a primary prevention strategy?
b
p. 444   a. Having a suspicious mole checked.
Fact   b. Avoiding exposure to cigarette smoke.
M   c. Conducting breast self-examinations.
          d. Going for regular medical exams.

11.163   Which of the following would be an example of a secondary prevention strategy?
c
p. 444   a. Eating more fruits, vegetables, and grains.
Fact   b. Becoming more physically active.
M   c. Conducting testicular self-examinations.
          d. Cutting down on your alcohol consumption.

Chapter 11 - Health, Stress, and Coping

11.164　　One explanation for the reason that people continue to get suntans and increase the risk for cancer is
b
p. 445　　a.　ignorance bias.
Concept　b.　optimistic bias.
M　　　　c.　representative bias.
　　　　　d.　heuristic bias.

11.165　　One possible explanation for why young people continue to stay out in the sun and increase their
c　　　risk for skin cancer is
p. 445　　a.　the recognition that the sun is healthy.
Fact　　　b.　the feeling that sunscreens really don't work anyway.
C　　　　c.　the time frame for getting skin cancer exceeds their comprehension.
　　　　　d.　the belief that most of the issues surrounding skin cancer is media hype.

11.166　　Most research examining the role of television in promoting healthy lifestyles indicates that
b
p. 446　　a.　the dominant message is on primary prevention strategies.
Fact　　　b.　the majority of commercials encourage unhealthy habits.
C　　　　c.　there is an adequate balance of ads that promote healthy and unhealthy habits.
　　　　　d.　there is an equal balance of ads emphasizing primary and secondary prevention strategies.

11.167　　Results of the Stanford Heart Disease Prevention Project indicate that successful promotion
c　　　of good habits to fight heart disease requires
p. 447　　a.　simply an effective media campaign.
Fact　　　b.　a solid personal instruction program.
M　　　　c.　both an effective media campaign and personal instruction program.
　　　　　d.　neither an effective media campaign nor a personal instruction program since people
　　　　　　　will not change their behavior until it is too late.

11.168　　Which of the following are most likely to accept an advertisement's intended message
d　　　dealing with primary prevention strategies about AIDS?
p. 447　　a.　people who are certain they are in a monogamous relationship.
Concept　b.　people who believe their daily intake of massive vitamins and rigorous exercise can
M　　　　　　protect them from just about any disease.
　　　　　c.　an adolescent who is sexually inactive.
　　　　　d.　a college student uncertain about the risk of AIDS.

11.169　　Recent research examining exercise in the U.S. indicates that the number of individuals
b　　　exercising regularly and intensely enough to reduce the risk for chronic disease and
p. 447　　premature death is about
Fact　　　a.　one in ten.
M　　　　b.　one in five.
　　　　　c.　five in ten.
　　　　　d.　four in five.

11.170　　Exercise has been found to
c　　　a.　reduce coronary heart disease only.
p. 447　　b.　alleviate feelings of depression only.
Fact　　　c.　improve self-concept, reduce coronary heart disease, and alleviate feelings of depression.
M　　　　d.　reduce coronary heart disease and alleviate feelings of depression only.

11.171　　As mentioned in your textbook, improvements in self-concept and some alleviation of feelings
c　　　of depression can result from
p. 447　　a.　a diet high in fats.
Fact　　　b.　a high protein diet.
M　　　　c.　an program of regular exercise.
　　　　　d.　a routine including all of the other alternatives combined.

11.172 Which of the following can increase adherence to an exercise program?
a
p. 448
Fact
M
PT/OLSG
a. arranging cues to signal exercise, for example, working out in the same location
b. arranging cues that allow you to be alone and away from a social support network
c. minimizing consequences that can lead to rewards
d. recognizing the importance of exercise.

11.173 Prevention strategies that are designed to increase early detection are called
d
p. 448
Fact
E
PT/OLSG
a. preliminary.
b. tertiary.
c. primary.
d. secondary.

11.174 The most significant factor predicting the use of early screening for disease is
b
p. 449
Fact
M
a. physician reminder systems.
b. beliefs about vulnerability to disease.
c. local advertising campaigns.
d. knowledge about specific diseases.

11.175 One key thing men can do to protect themselves from testicular cancer is
c
p. 449
Fact
M
a. avoid foods high in animal fat.
b. quit smoking.
c. use testicular self-examination.
d. avoid stressful situations.

11.176 When Lisa gets up in the morning, she goes through a routine of stretching and relaxing her arms, her neck, etc. until she finally gets to her toes. This procedure is called
a
p. 451
Applied
E
a. progressive relaxation.
b. structured relaxation.
c. coherent relaxation.
d. restructuring relaxation.

11.177 One way of regaining cognitive control over the stressors in our lives is to use the technique of _____, which means replacing negative appraisals of stressors with positive appraisals of the stressors.
b
p. 451
Fact
C
a. progressive relaxation
b. cognitive restructuring
c. successive approximation
d. partial denial

CHAPTER 12

Multiple-Choice Questions

Changing Conceptions of Psychological Disorders

12.1 The percent of all humans who will have a psychological disorder at some point during their lives is
c
p. 458   a. 10%.
Fact   b. 15%.
M   c. 50%.
        d. 25%.

12.2   "Maladaptive patterns of behavior and thought that cause persons experiencing them
a   considerable distress," is a brief definition of
p. 458   a. psychological disorders.
Fact   b. iatrogenic disorders.
E   c. teratogenic disorders.
        d. psychotic disorders.

12.3   A part of the definition of abnormality is that a behavior
a   a. is different from the behavior of most other people in the same situation.
p. 458   b. poses the danger of physical harm to the individual and to others nearby.
Fact   c. does not seem strange, threatening, or unusual to the person involved.
M   d. meets the diagnostic categories of established mental illnesses.

12.4   A behavior is maladaptive if it
a   a. causes problems with daily life.
p. 458   b. is extremely unusual.
Fact   c. is viewed by society as unacceptable.
M   d. causes harm to others.

12.5   A young woman who displayed her ankles in public was once considered wanton and
b   sexually promiscuous. The fact that this is no longer true in the U.S. demonstrates that
p. 458   a. distressing behavior is not always abnormal.
Applied b. social definitions of abnormality change over time.
M   c. society no longer labels certain actions as unacceptable.
PT/OLSG d. people are more sexually active than they once were.

12.6   One hundred fifty years ago, many American slaves were diagnosed as suffering from
b   "drapetomania," a disorder characterized by an inability to accept the natural state of
p. 458   slavery and a tendency to run away. At the time, this behavior met one of the criteria
Applied for abnormality, in that it was
M   a. maladaptive.
        b. socially unacceptable.
        c. distressing.
        d. resulting from faulty cognitions.

12.7   "Patterns of behavior and thought that are atypical, viewed as undesirable or unacceptable
b   by a given culture, are maladaptive, and that usually (although not always) cause the
p. 459   persons who experience them considerable distress" defines the concept of
Fact   a. psychogenic disorders.
M   b. psychological disorders.
        c. psychotic disorders.
        d. teratogenic disorders.

2.8 Which of the following is not part of the agreed-upon definition of the common features
c of psychological disorders?
p. 459 a. They are atypical patterns of behavior.
Fact b. They are atypical patterns of thought.
M c. They are always distressing to the individual.
d. They are viewed as undesirable by a given culture.

Changing Conceptions of Psychological Disorders

12.9 The earliest written description of psychological disorders puts the cause of the maladies on
b a. biological causes.
p. 459 b. supernatural causes.
Fact c. childhood trauma.
E d. diseases.

12.10 Early explanations for abnormal behavior were based on
b a. too much pressure inside the skull.
p. 459 b. possession by spirits or demons.
Fact c. abnormalities inherited from parents.
M d. chemical imbalances in the body.

12.11 The earliest known society to explain psychological disorders on the basis of entirely natural
d causes such as heredity, brain damage, and chemical imbalances were the
p. 459 a. prehistoric peoples of Africa.
Fact b. people of the European Renaissance.
M c. empires of ancient Babylon.
d. scientists of ancient Greece.

12.12 The term "lunatic" was once used to describe bizarre behavior because it was believed that such behavior
a was the result of influence from
p. 460 a. natural forces such as the moon.
Fact b. unnatural forces such as evil spirits.
E c. physical forces such as tics, etc.
d. social forces such as groups.

12.13 Some of the earliest proponents of the medical perspective of mental illness that proposed
d humane treatments, such as kindness, exercise, and good diet, for those afflicted were
p. 460 a. Freud and Horney.
Fact b. Mesmer and Charcot.
M c. Skinner and Watson.
d. Pussin and Pinel.

12.14 The beginnings of the medical view of psychological disorders in France had the immediate effect of
d a. removing the mentally ill from society in a form of guarantee.
p. 460 b. blaming psychological disorders on the actions of spirits or demons.
Fact c. developing highly effective treatments using common herbal remedies.
M d. drastically improving the living conditions in mental institutions.

12.15 The belief that psychological disorders are a form of illness is a characteristic of the _____ perspective.
a a. medical
p. 460 b. humanistic
Fact c. cognitive
E d. psycho-social

Chapter 12 - Psychological Disorders: Their Nature and Causes   241

12.16   Which of the following is most likely to take a medical perspective to psychological disorders?
b   a.   behaviorists
p. 460   b.   psychiatrists
Concept   c.   humanists
M   d.   phenomenologists

12.17   Which of Freud's views is most instrumental today in understanding abnormal behavior?
d   a.   his suggestion that the ego demands immediate gratification
p. 461   b.   his suggestion that mental patients should be treated humanely
Fact   c.   his suggestion that psychological disorders are types of mental illnesses
M   d.   his suggestion that unconscious thoughts or impulses play a role in abnormal behavior
PT/OLSG

12.18   In Freud's theory, maladaptive behavior can result from
c   a.   inappropriate learning experiences in the past.
p. 461   b.   abnormal chemistry in the brain.
Fact   c.   the defense mechanisms used to reduce anxiety.
M   d.   overreliance on peak experiences.

12.19   In the psychodynamic perspective, a defense mechanism can serve the positive function
b   of _____ and the negative function of _____.
p. 461   a.   producing feelings of success; producing depression
Fact   b.   reducing ego anxiety; producing maladaptive behavior
M   c.   releasing physical tension; upsetting brain chemistry
             d.   bringing us closer to others; driving us away from others.

12.20   Which of the following perspectives suggests that abnormal behavior is best understood
a   through studying processes such as learning, cognition, and perception?
p. 461   a.   the psychological perspective
Fact   b.   the biological/medical perspective
M   c.   the psychodynamic perspective
             d.   the descriptive perspective

12.21   Labeling a person "mentally ill" implies that this person can be cured by
c   a.   using appropriate physical intervention.
p. 461   b.   using appropriate cognitive treatment.
Concept   c.   using appropriate medical treatment.
M   d.   using appropriate physiological intervention.

12.22   Current evidence suggests that a disorder such as depression is the result of
a   a.   several factors, including psychological, physiological, cognitive, and social.
p. 461   b.   usually one major factor, such as psychological influence.
Concept   c.   a limited number of factors, usually just two or three.
E   d.   an unknown number of factors.

12.23   Which of the following is most likely to view a psychological disorder as a complex interplay
b   between biological, psychological, and sociocultural factors?
p. 461   a.   psychiatrist
Fact   b.   psychologist
M   c.   physician
             d.   neo-Freudian

12.24   Disorders such as eating disorders have a strong _____ influence.
c   a.   genetic
p. 462   b.   conative
Fact   c.   cultural
M   d.   biological

Identifying Psychological Disorders: The DSM-IV

12.25
b
p. 463
Fact
E

The most widely accepted system of identifying psychological disorders is known by the acronym
a. MMPI.
b. DSM-IV.
c. WISC-R.
d. K-ABC.

12.26
b
p. 463
Fact
M

In the DSM-IV, symptoms that must be present before an individual is diagnosed as suffering from a particular problem are called
a. associated features.
b. diagnostic features.
c. associated disorders.
d. physical examination signs.

12.27
a
p. 463
Fact
M
PT/OLSG

Which of the following statements does not accurately describe the use of the DSM-IV?
a. It provides a useful tool for explaining abnormal behavior.
b. It provides a useful tool for describing abnormal behavior.
c. It classifies disorders along five axes.
d. Its use may be subject to bias in making clinical judgments about the severity or presence of psychological disorders.

12.28
d
p. 463
Fact
C

Evaluation criteria arranged on the basis of (a) major disorders, (b) personality disorders, (c) medical conditions relevant to each disorder, (d) psychosocial and environmental problems that may affect diagnosis and treatment, and (e) global assessment of current functioning, are referred to as
a. diagnostic features.
b. associated features.
c. dimensions.
d. axes.

12.29
a
p. 464
Fact
M

When working with the DSM-IV, a psychologist will use the first axis to describe the person's
a. major psychological disorder.
b. current physical condition.
c. social and environmental situation.
d. overall level of functioning.

12.30
b
p. 464
Fact
M

When working with the DSM-IV, a psychologist will use the fourth axis to describe the person's
a. current physical condition.
b. psychosocial and environmental situation.
c. overall level of functioning.
d. major psychological disorder.

12.31
d
p. 464
Concept
M

Which of the following is not one of the goals of the DSM-IV?
a. organize disorders into categories on the basis of etiological evidence.
b. improve the reliability of diagnosis.
c. introduce a common terminology into the mental health field.
d. describe preventative measures.

12.32
b
p. 464
Fact
M

The DSM-IV contains a new section for each disorder called "culturally related features" that describes
a. specific medications to be used or avoided in different cultures.
b. differences in how the disorder is accepted by different cultures.
c. which symptoms must be present for a disorder to be classified.
d. how seriously the disorder affects the lives of the patient and others.

Chapter 12 - Psychological Disorders: Their Nature and Causes   243

12.33   One of the assessment tools that a psychologist might use to acquire information about a person is the
a   a. assessment interview.
p. 464   b. diagnostic evaluation.
Fact   c. conative factor analysis.
M   d. dissonance checksheet.

12.34   One measure of brain functioning that a psychologist might use is the
c   a. Allport Functional Autonomy Evaluation.
p. 465   b. Bandura Neurological Allocation Survey.
Applied   c. Halstead-Reitan Neuropsychological Battery.
M   d. Wechsler Scale for Psychophysical Functioning.

12.35   Using a behavioral assessment technique may involve gathering information about
b   a. lasting factors related to the target behaviors
p.465   b. antecedents and consequences of behavior.
Fact   c. specific traits of the behavior.
M   d. cardinal traits related to the specific behavior.

Mood Disorders: The Downs and Ups of Life

12.36   There are two major categories of mood disorders. They are _____ and _____ disorders.
d   a. bipolar; euphoric
p. 466   b. euphoric; dysphoric
Fact   c. bipolar; unipolar
M   d. depressive; bipolar
PT/OLSG

12.37   Bipolar disorder and depressive disorders are considered to be _____ disorders.
d   a. personality
p. 466   b. anxiety
Fact   c. dissociative
M   d. mood

12.38   Which of the following is not a criterion of major depression?
d   a. physical symptoms, such as sleeplessness
p. 466   b. lack of interest in activities, such as eating and sex
Fact   c. inability to concentrate or remember
M   d. euphoric, compulsive actions

12.39   Which of these is a list of symptoms associated with major depressive disorder?   *Short answer*
b   a. tension, panic attacks, withdrawal, and avoidance
p. 466   b. sadness, loss of appetite, insomnia, and guilt
Fact   c. delusions, hallucinations, catatonia, and tension
C   d. excessive emotion and attention-getting behavior
PT/OLSG

12.40   Someone who shows five or more of the symptoms of depression is classified by the
b   DSM-IV as showing a(n)
p. 466   a. obsessive-compulsive disorder.
Fact   b. major depressive episode.
M   c. personality disorder.
            d. depressive psychosis.

12.41   Which of these people is most likely to be suffering from clinical depression?
c   a. A four-year-old girl crying because her favorite doll has been lost.
p. 466   b. A twenty-four year old woman crying over her recent breakup with a long-time boyfriend.
Applied   c. A thirty-year-old woman who is often unable to make herself get out of bed in the morning.
M   d. A fifty-year-old woman who always cries at the slightest excuse in movies and weddings.

12.42　　　　　　For several weeks, Lisa has been extremely unhappy. She has difficulty getting out of bed
a　　　　　　　and feels worthless. She is most likely suffering from
p. 466　　　　　a.　major depression.
Applied　　　　b.　a personality disorder.
M　　　　　　　c.　bipolar mood disorder.
PT/OLSG　　　d.　agoraphobia.

12.43　　　　　　When people are seriously depressed, what effect does this usually have on their thought processes?
b　　　　　　　a.　They have fearful thoughts they can't get out of their minds.
p. 466　　　　　b.　They have difficulty thinking, remembering, and concentrating.
Fact　　　　　　c.　They deliberately think pleasant thoughts to try to cheer themselves up.
C　　　　　　　d.　Nothing; depression is a disorder of mood and feelings, not thoughts.

12.44　　　　　　The most frequent type of psychological disorder is
b　　　　　　　a.　schizophrenia.
p. 466　　　　　b.　depression.
Fact　　　　　　c.　obsessive-compulsive.
M　　　　　　　d.　antisocial personality.

12.45　　　　　　According to the text, depression is much more common in
a　　　　　　　a.　women.
p. 466　　　　　b.　men.
Fact　　　　　　c.　older people.
M　　　　　　　d.　younger people.

12.46　　　　　　Varying between deep depression and mania is most characteristic of
c　　　　　　　a.　conversion disorder.
p. 466　　　　　b.　schizophrenia.
Fact　　　　　　c.　bipolar disorder.
E　　　　　　　d.　anxiety disorder.

12.47　　　　　　Ralph acts all-powerful, and believes he is invulnerable to harm. He is extremely elated
d　　　　　　　and energetic. His mood is labeled as
p. 466　　　　　a.　hysteria.
Applied　　　　b.　schizophrenia.
M　　　　　　　c.　obsession.
　　　　　　　　d.　mania.

12.48　　　　　　A disorder that involves extreme changes in mood from depression to mania is called
a　　　　　　　a.　bipolar disorder.
p. 466　　　　　b.　obsessive-compulsive disorder.
Fact　　　　　　c.　somatoform disorder.
M　　　　　　　d.　personality disorder.

12.49　　　　　　Which of these statements is most likely to be made by someone having a manic episode?
b　　　　　　　a.　"I have no energy. I can't make myself get out of bed today."
p. 466　　　　　b.　"I'm going to rip out the back wall and build a new kitchen this afternoon."
Applied　　　　c.　"I can't stop thinking I forgot to lock the door. I'd better check one more time."
M　　　　　　　d.　"If I don't wrap my head in aluminum foil, the Martians will take over my brain."

12.50　　　　　　Which of the following will generally increase your chance of experiencing depression?
d　　　　　　　a.　being on a drug that increases concentrations of acetylcholine
p. 468　　　　　b.　believing that your behavior influences the outcomes of your life
Concept　　　　c.　blaming negative occurrences in your life on prior mistakes that you now know how
M　　　　　　　　　to prevent
　　　　　　　　d.　having a genetically close relative who is depressed

Chapter 12 - Psychological Disorders: Their Nature and Causes   245

12.51   Twin studies and studies of the children of depressed patients suggest what about the causes of depression?
b   a. Genetic factors play no important role in depression.
p. 468   b. Genetic factors play a substantial role in depression.
Fact   c. Genetic factors are important for women but not for men.
M   d. Genetic factors are important for men but not for women.

12.52   Which of the following has not been found to be a potential cause for depression?
c   a. genetic inheritance
p. 468   b. helplessness
Fact   c. high levels of neurotransmitters
M   d. faulty cognitive sets

12.53   The neurotransmitters associated with depression and mania include
b   a. norepinephrine and dopamine.
p. 468   b. norepinephrine and serotonin.
Fact   c. serotonin and acetylcholine.
M   d. dopamine and acetylcholine.

12.54   Depression is to mania as
c   a. low dopamine and acetylcholine is to high dopamine and acetylcholine.
p. 468   b. high dopamine and acetylcholine is to low dopamine and acetylcholine.
Concept   c. low norepinephrine and serotonin is to high norepinephrine and serotonin.
C   d. high norepinephrine and serotonin is to low norepinephrine and serotonin.

12.55   Which of the following is a hypothesis involving a psychological mechanism as a cause of depression?
a   a. learned helplessness
p. 468   b. delusions of grandeur
Concept   c. psychodynamic perspective
M   d. histrionics

12.56   Which of the following views of depression includes individuals' attributions about the
a   causes behind their lack of control over events in their life?
p. 468   a. learned helplessness
Concept   b. learned hopelessness
M   c. modeling
            d. paraphilia

12.57   When asked to describe themselves, depressed people are more likely to
a   a. give negative ratings to themselves.
p. 468   b. give negative ratings to others.
Fact   c. give neutral ratings to themselves.
M   d. give positive ratings to themselves.
PT/OLSG

12.58   A tendency to view events in a distorted way that puts blame on one's self for everything
b   that happens and makes one feel worthless is a common symptom of a(n)
p. 468   a. anxiety disorder.
Fact   b. depressive disorder.
M   c. dissociative disorder.
            d. sexual disorder.

12.59   When a negative event has happened in the life of a depressed person, the likely result is
d   a. the person will avoid thinking about it.
p. 468   b. the person will blame it on someone else.
Fact   c. the person will develop a good excuse.
M   d. the person will amplify its importance.

12.60 d p. 468 Concept M

According to one view of depression, which of these errors in judgment is a depressed person most likely to make?
a. Expecting that they will succeed at everything.
b. Thinking that whatever one does is "good enough."
c. Exaggerating the positive events in their lives.
d. Exaggerating the negative events in their lives.

12.61 b p. 468 Fact M

In comparison to non-depressed individuals, depressed individuals tend not to
a. have more negative self-schema.
b. have more positive evaluations about events.
c. hold more negative views about others.
d. have better memory for failures and other unpleasant events.

12.62 c p. 469 Study M

Research by Watkins and colleagues (1996) on the unconscious thoughts of depressed and nondepressed individuals found that
a. depressed individuals remembered more positive words.
b. nondepressed individuals remembered more negative words.
c. depressed individuals remembered more negative words.
d. nondepressed individuals remembered more neutral words.

12.63 b p. 470 Study M

The research by Terry and colleagues (1996) on postpartum depression found that for new mothers,
a. the more experience they had, the more severe the depression.
b. the more support they had, the less depression they experienced.
c. the less support they had, the less depression they experienced.
d. the less experience they had, the less severe the depression.

12.64 a p. 471 Fact E

The risk of suicide is greatest for individuals with the psychological disorder of
a. depression.
b. hypochondriasis.
c. agoraphobia.
d. dissociative disorders.

12.65 b p. 471 Fact M PT/OLSG

Suicide is more often attempted by _____. Ending of one's life through suicide is more often completed by _____.
a. men; men
b. women; men
c. women; women
d. men; women

12.66 d p. 471 Fact M

The main reason why men are more often successful at taking their own lives than women is that
a. women are naturally hardier and more likely to survive.
b. women have more friends who talk them out of it.
c. men attempt suicide when they are older than women.
d. men use more lethal methods, such as handguns.

12.67 b p. 471 Fact M

Among Americans between the ages of 15 and 24, the second most common cause of death is
a. accidents.
b. suicide.
c. AIDS.
d. homicide.

12.68 a p. 471 Fact M

Which of these suicide techniques is more commonly used by women?
a. Overdosing on sleeping pills.
b. Jumping from a high building.
c. Shooting with a gun.
d. Hanging from an exposed beam.

Chapter 12 - Psychological Disorders: Their Nature and Causes

12.69 One of the major reasons for suicides is
b
p. 471   a. lack of confidence.
Fact   b. problems with a relationship.
M   c. role conflict.
         d. confusion about the unknown.

12.70 Which of these people is most likely to commit suicide in the immediate future?
d
p. 471   a. Someone deeply depressed and unhappy.
Fact   b. Someone in the midst of a manic episode.
M   c. Someone who is afraid of many things.
         d. Someone who was agitated but is now calm.

12.71 Research shows that people are most likely to commit suicide when they are
b
p. 471   a. suffering a deep depressive episode.
Fact   b. beginning to recover from depression.
M   c. very young, barely out of their teens.
         d. experiencing highly manic episodes.

12.72 Suicide is most likely to occur
c
p. 471   a. when an individual is in the depths of his or her deepest despair.
Fact   b. when the person shows considerable agitation.
M   c. when some improvement from depression occurs, and the person seems relatively calm.
         d. when the person is exceedingly afraid.

12.73 People who are contemplating suicide report being most afraid of which aspect of death?
d
p. 471   a. Being forgotten by friends and loved ones.
Fact   b. Its consequences for their families.
C   c. Not knowing what comes after death.
         d. Nothing; suicides fear all aspects of death equally.

Anxiety Disorders: When Dread Debilitates

12.74 Increased arousal accompanied by generalized feelings of fear or apprehension is called
b
p. 472   a. dysthymia.
Fact   b. anxiety.
E   c. mania.
         d. depression.

12.75 Which of these is not a common symptom of a panic attack?
a
p. 472   a. Specific fear of a particular object
Fact   b. Pounding heart and chest pains
M   c. Fear of losing control or going crazy
         d. Chills, trembling, dizziness, and numbness

12.76 Without any specific warning sign, Ralph experiences intense fear of losing control and a
d variety of physiological reactions such as a pounding heart, chest pains, nausea, feeling
p. 472 dizzy, and fear of going crazy. Ralph is most likely experiencing a
Applied   a. delusion.
M   b. hallucination.
         c. somatoform disorder.
         d. panic attack.

12.77 Intense fear of specific situations in which individuals fear that they will not receive help for an
a embarrassing event is referred to as
p. 472   a. agoraphobia.
Fact   b. somatoform disorder.
M   c. subliminal phobia.
         d. conversion disorder.

12.78 b p. 472 Concept M
Fear of being in a crowd, standing in a line, being on a bridge, traveling in a bus, train, or crowd, or merely leaving home are common patterns of
a. somatoform disorder.
b. agoraphobia.
c. antisocial personality disorder.
d. conversion disorder.

12.79 a p. 472 Concept M
Agoraphobia involves the strong fear and avoidance of
a. being alone or in public places that are hard to get out of.
b. any specific object or situation that is not really dangerous.
c. interacting with or being observed by other individuals.
d. any small, confined space with no obvious way out.

12.80 c p. 472 Fact M
Current research indicates that panic attacks are caused
a. only by biological factors.
b. only by psychological factors, such as conditioning.
c. by biological factors and cognitive factors.
d. by inherited genetic disorders.

12.81 b p. 473 Concept M
Thoughts about impending disaster that may result in a full-blown panic attack are called
a. disaster thinking.
b. catastrophic thinking.
c. fuzzy thinking.
d. calamity thinking.

12.82 d p. 473 Fact M PT/OLSG
Disorders in which an individual experiences intense anxiety toward specific objects or situations are called
a. personality fears.
b. antisocial personality disorders.
c. fugue.
d. phobias.

12.83 c p. 473 Fact M
When a person experiences intense anxiety, considerably greater than justified by reality, triggered by the presence of some particular object, the person is suffering from a
a. multiple personality.
b. somatoform disorder.
c. phobia.
d. delusion.

12.84 d p. 473 Applied C
Ralph's father would drag Ralph out of the park in a panic whenever a dog appeared. The classical conditioning perspective on phobias would suggest that after a few instances of this, the dog would become a(n)
a. unconditioned response.
b. conditioned response.
c. unconditioned stimulus.
d. conditioned stimulus.

12.85 a p. 473 Concept M
Which of the following is one explanation of the occurrence of phobias?
a. classical conditioning
b. id impulses
c. unconscious motives
d. negative self-concept

12.86 d p. 473 Fact M
Many psychologists think that social phobias are caused by
a. childhood fears and thoughts over being abandoned.
b. a high level of autonomic nervous system arousal.
c. a genetically controlled program in brain chemistry.
d. traumatic experiences in crowded or public places.

Chapter 12 - Psychological Disorders: Their Nature and Causes 249

12.87
a
p. 473
Fact
M

Someone with a social phobia exhibits extreme fear and avoidance of
a. situations that involve being observed by other individuals.
b. being alone or in public places that are hard to exit.
c. any small, confined space with no obvious way out.
d. any specific object or situation that is not really dangerous.

12.88
c
p. 473
Applied
C

Ralph refuses to eat, speak, drive, or even ride his bike in a situation where someone else might pay attention to him and judge how well he is doing. Ralph most likely suffers from
a. generalized anxiety disorder.
b. dissociative identity disorder.
c. a social phobia.
d. panic attacks.

12.89
b
p. 473
Study
C

Research indicates that individuals who were shy as children and had also had an early traumatic experience were much more likely to experience _____ than individuals for whom neither of these experiences occurred.
a. depressive attacks
b. social phobias
c. manic attacks
d. panic attacks

12.90
d
p. 474
Concept
M

Thought is to behavior as
a. hallucination is to delusion.
b. panic attack is to anxiety disorder.
c. neurotic is to psychotic.
d. obsession is to compulsion.

12.91
a
p. 475
Fact
M

Compulsions serve to
a. reduce anxiety.
b. increase obsessions.
c. reduce norepinephrine.
d. decrease phobia.

12.92
b
p. 475
Fact
M

Anxiety disorders in which individuals are unable to stop thinking the same thought or performing the same ritualistic behaviors are called
a. paraphilia disorders.
b. obsessive-compulsive disorders.
c. somatoform disorders.
d. agoraphobia.

12.93
a
p. 475
Fact
E
PT/OLSG

The disorder that involves anxieties that involve repetitive behaviors is called
a. obsessive-compulsive.
b. phobia.
c. panic.
d. generalized anxiety.

12.94
c
p. 475
Applied
M

Lisa adopts ritualistic behaviors to help reduce anxiety that occurs when unwanted thoughts intrude into awareness. This is an example of
a. a dissociative disorder.
b. a conversion disorder.
c. an obsessive-compulsive disorder.
d. a histrionic personality.

12.95
d
p. 475
Fact
M

Compulsions are attempts to
a. bring attention to oneself.
b. protect one's self-concept by repressing painful memories.
c. eliminate physiological symptoms that accompany hallucinations.
d. neutralize threatening thoughts by engaging in actions that ensure one's safety.

12.96   The excessive concern with cleanliness in Japan emphasizes the point that
b
p. 475
Applied
M
     a. compulsive behaviors are more prominent in traditional cultures.
     b. what is normal or abnormal is partly defined by the culture.
     c. obsessive-compulsive disorders are easy to acquire.
     d. psychological disorders are not respective of any culture.

12.97   A disorder in which an individual exposed to a traumatic event reexperiences the event persistently in thought or dreams, persistently avoids stimuli linked with the trauma, and experiences persistent symptoms of increased arousal is called
a
p. 476
Fact
M
     a. post-traumatic stress disorder.
     b. somatoform disorder.
     c. dissociative disorder.
     d. schizophrenia.

12.98   Which of these is not a common symptom of posttraumatic stress disorder?
d
p. 476
Fact
M
     a. Persistent thoughts or dreams about an experience.
     b. Persistent avoidance of things related to the experience.
     c. Persistent problems with sleep or concentration.
     d. Persistent clinging and a need to be taken care of.

12.99   Which of these is a common symptom of posttraumatic stress disorder?
c
p. 476
Fact
M
     a. Repeating an action over and over to avoid anxiety.
     b. Feeling unrealistic elation and excessive energy.
     c. Re-experiencing the traumatic event over and over.
     d. Paralysis that has no physical cause.

12.100   Vernberg and his colleagues (1996) found that three factors played a role in whether experiencing Hurricane Andrew led to a posttraumatic stress disorder. These factors are
a
p. 476
Study
C
     a. social support, actual exposure to the hurricane, and coping strategies.
     b. social support, physiological structure, and visual interpretation.
     c. coping strategies, cognitive sophistication, and contagion activities.
     d. actual exposure to the hurricane, contagion activities, and previous experience.

12.101   Recent evidence indicates that _____ may be especially important in posttraumatic stress dosorder.
b
p. 477
Fact
M
     a. social factors
     b. cognitive factors
     c. philosophical factors
     d. conative factors

Somatoform Disorders: Physical Symptoms without Physical Causes

12.102   Disorders in which psychological conflicts or other problems take on a physical form are called
d
p. 477
Fact
M
     a. dissociative disorders.
     b. obsessive-compulsive disorders.
     c. schizophrenic disorders.
     d. somatoform disorders.

12.103   A somatoform disorder involves
b
p. 477
Fact
M
     a. persistent, irrational thoughts and uncontrollable actions.
     b. real physical symptoms with no apparent physical cause.
     c. persistent fear and avoidance of specific objects or events.
     d. a lack of concern over the rights and feelings of others.

Chapter 12 - Psychological Disorders: Their Nature and Causes

12.104
d
p. 477
Fact
E
PT/OLSG

People who exhibit physical symptoms that have no underlying physical cause have _____ disorders.
a. anxiety
b. organic
c. dissociative
d. somatoform

12.105
d
p. 477
Applied
C

Lisa has been sickly for years, with frequent blackouts, double vision, weakness, and nausea, though several doctors have failed to find any cause for these problems. Lisa most likely suffers from
a. dissociative identity disorder.
b. dependent personality disorder.
c. bipolar disorder.
d. somatization disorder.

12.106
c
p. 478
Fact
M

Preoccupation with fears of having a serious disease best describes
a. somatization disorder.
b. conversion disorder.
c. hypochondriasis.
d. fugue.

12.107
d
p. 478
Fact
M

Individuals suffering from disorders such as blindness or deafness for which there is no underlying medical condition are showing behaviors characteristic of
a. hypochondriasis.
b. paranoid personality disorder.
c. dissociative disorder.
d. conversion disorder.

12.108
c
p. 478
Applied
M

When the demands of taking care of her ailing parents became intolerable, Lisa woke one morning to find herself blind and unable to walk, though doctors could find nothing wrong with her. Lisa most likely suffers from
a. panic attacks.
b. bipolar disorder.
c. conversion disorder.
d. schizophrenic disorder.

12.109
d
p. 478
Study
M

Recent research indicates that individuals suffering from _____ have more health-related goals than most people.
a. conversion reaction
b. panic attacks
c. bipolar disorder
d. hypochondria

Dissociative Disorders: When Memory Fails

12.110
d
p. 478
Fact
M

Disorders characterized by relatively profound and lengthy losses of identity or memory are called
a. somatoform disorders.
b. schizophrenic disorders.
c. antisocial personality disorders.
d. dissociative disorders.

12.111
c
p. 478
Fact
E
PT/OLSG

Lengthy losses of memory are known as _____ disorders.
a. anxiety
b. personality
c. dissociative
d. cognitive

12.112 a p. 478 Fact E

Dissociative amnesia is classified as a _____ disorder.
a. dissociative
b. schizophrenic
c. somatoform
d. personality

12.113 d p. 478 Fact M

A disorder involving the sudden inability to remember large amounts of personally important information, usually triggered by a traumatic experience is
a. hypochondriasis.
b. somatization disorder.
c. catatonic schizophrenic.
d. dissociative amnesia.

12.114 b p. 479 Applied M

Patient Ralph cannot remember any event that occurred during his junior and senior years of college. Ralph's type of amnesia is
a. generalized amnesia.
b. localized amnesia.
c. psychogenic amnesia.
d. anterograde amnesia.

12.115 c p. 479 Applied M

As a result of a picture in a newspaper, a local politician was recognized as a minister who had suddenly disappeared one day and never made further contact. The politician/minister did not recall his previous family or profession. This disorder is probably
a. somatoform disorder.
b. conversion disorder.
c. dissociative fugue.
d. schizoid personality.

12.116 d p. 479 Fact M PT/OLSG

When a person appears to have two or more distinct personalities, that person is said to have which disorder?
a. schizophrenic disorder.
b. somatoform disorder.
c. conversion disorder.
d. dissociative identity disorder.

12.117 c p. 480 Concept M

There is a controversy among mental health professionals as to the true existence of the
a. somatization disorder.
b. conversion disorder.
c. dissociative identity disorder.
d. dissociative fugue disorder.

12.118 d p. 480 Concept M

The major controversy relating to dissociative identity disorder involves the question of
a. how this disorder relates to schizophrenia.
b. what sorts of treatment are most effective.
c. what factors in a person's life lead to this disorder.
d. whether this disorder actually exists.

Sexual and Gender Identity Disorders

12.119 d p. 480 Fact M

Disturbances in sexual desire, sexual arousal, or the ability to attain orgasm are classified as
a. paraphilia.
b. transsexualism.
c. dissociative disorder.
d. sexual dysfunction.

Chapter 12 - Psychological Disorders: Their Nature and Causes 253

12.120 Which of the following refers to a lack of interest in sex or active aversion to sexual activities?
a
p. 480   a. sexual desire disorders
Fact   b. sexual arousal disorders
E   c. paraphilias
     d. paraphobias

12.121 The inability to attain or maintain an erection and the absence of vaginal swelling and
b   lubrication are classified as
p. 480   a. sexual desire disorders.
Fact   b. sexual arousal disorders.
M   c. paraphilias.
     d. dissociative fugue.

12.122 When sexual arousal requires the use of unusual or bizarre imagery or acts, it is characterized as
c
p. 481   a. sexual dysfunction.
Fact   b. orgasm disorders.
M   c. paraphilias.
     d. paraphobias.

12.123 Fetishes, frotteurism, pedophilia, sexual sadism, and sexual masochism belong to the
d   category of disorders called
p. 481   a. sexual dysfunction.
Fact   b. sexual desire disorders.
M   c. fugue.
     d. paraphilias.

12.124 Men who collect women's undergarments and obtain sexual pleasure from fondling them
a   have a problem called
p. 481   a. fetishism.
Applied   b. transvestism.
M   c. voyeurism.
     d. pedophilia.

12.125 Frotteurism is a type of paraphilia in which a person becomes aroused only by
d   a. inflicting pain on another person.
p. 481   b. watching a stranger get undressed.
Fact   c. sexual activity with young children.
M   d. rubbing against a nonconsenting person.

12.126 The disorder in which individuals report sexual urges and fantasies involving sexual
b   activity with children usually younger than thirteen is referred to as
p. 481   a. voyeurism.
Fact   b. pedophilia.
M   c. fetishism.
PT/OLSG   d. orgasm disorder.

12.127 Sexual masochism is a type of paraphilia in which a person becomes aroused only by
d   a. watching a stranger get undressed.
p. 481   b. exposing one's genitals to a stranger.
Fact   c. inflicting pain on another person.
M   d. receiving pain from another person.

12.128 Someone who gets sexual pleasure from being hurt by others exhibits sexual _____, while
b   someone who gets sexual pleasure from hurting others exhibits sexual _____.
p. 481   a. voyeurism; exhibitionism
Fact   b. masochism; sadism
M   c. fetishism; domination
     d. internalism; externalism

12.129   Individuals who believe they were born with the wrong sexual identity, are displeased with
d   their own bodies, and repeatedly request that they receive medial treatment that will alter
p. 481   their primary and secondary sexual characteristics are considered to have
Fact
    a.   sexual dysfunction disorder.
M
    b.   paraphilia disorder.
    c.   dissociative identity disorder.
    d.   gender identity disorder.

12.130   Which of these is not a symptom of gender identity disorder?
c   a.   A strong feeling that one is born with the wrong sexual identity.
p. 481   b.   Multiple requests for some medical procedure to correct one's gender identity.
Fact   c.   Strong sexual attraction to people of the same sex as one's self.
M   d.   An active dislike for the body that one is born with and a desire to change it.

12.131   Research indicates that most people who undergo sex change operations
b   a.   eventually want to become the original sex again.
p. 481   b.   feel happier and more comfortable with their "new" bodies.
Fact   c.   become depressed and often contemplate suicide.
M   d.   are not prepared for the changes that will occur.

Eating Disorders

12.132   Both bulimia and anorexia nervosa are related to
b   a.   an intense fear of becoming fat.
p. 483   b.   dissatisfaction with personal appearance.
Fact   c.   periodic bouts of extreme overeating.
M   d.   uncontrollable, unnatural sexual desires.

12.133   Starvation is to binge as
a   a.   anorexia nervosa is to bulimia nervosa.
p. 483   b.   bulimia nervosa is to anorexia nervosa.
Fact   c.   hypochondriasis is to somatoform disorder.
M   d.   somatoform disorder is to hypochondriasis.

12.134   When individuals are very fearful of gaining weight and fail to maintain a normal body weight, they have
b   a.   paraphilia nervosa.
p. 483   b.   anorexia nervosa.
Fact   c.   bulimia nervosa.
E   d.   neologism nervosa.
PT/OLSG

12.135   A disorder that involves alternating episodes of binge eating followed by various forms
c   of compensatory behavior designed to avoid weight gain is called
p. 483   a.   somatoform disorder.
Fact   b.   anorexia nervosa.
E   c.   bulimia nervosa.
    d.   dissociative disorder.

12.136   The bulimic's repeated purging results in
d   a.   no change in taste sensation.
p. 484   b.   shift in taste sensation only for sweet items.
Fact   c.   increased taste sensation.
E   d.   decreased taste sensation.

Chapter 12 - Psychological Disorders: Their Nature and Causes

12.137
d
p. 484
Fact
M

Social forces may contribute to the disorders of anorexia and bulimia by
a. constantly using images that are sexually arousing.
b. providing too many confusing kinds of food.
c. separating young people from their families.
d. creating too much pressure to be very thin.

Personality Disorders: Traits That Harm

12.138
d
p. 484
Fact
M

Disorders that are associated with collections of extreme and inflexible traits that cause distress and adjustment problems are
a. somatoform disorders.
b. conversion disorders.
c. anxiety disorders.
d. personality disorders.

12.139
b
p. 485
Applied
M

Ralph suspects that everyone is trying to take advantage of him. He also bears strong grudges against his neighbors who he believes are plotting against him. Ralph is most likely suffering from
a. a schizoid personality disorder.
b. paranoid personality disorder.
c. antisocial personality disorder.
d. borderline personality disorder.

12.140
c
p. 485
Applied
M

Lisa believes that her parents and her teachers are joined in a plot to make sure she fails school. In fact, she is convinced her fellow students are also involved in sabotaging her education. Lisa shows many symptoms of
a. multiple personality disorder.
b. schizoid personality disorder.
c. paranoid personality disorder.
d. dependent personality disorder.

12.141
c
p. 485
Fact
M

Individuals detached from the social world, showing little interest in friendships, love affairs, or any other kind of intimate contact with other persons are characterized as _____ personality.
a. paranoid
b. antisocial
c. schizoid
d. introvert

12.142
c
p. 485
Fact
M
PT/OLSG

A schizoid personality disorder is characterized by
a. physical symptoms that have no underlying cause.
b. a desire to alter primary and secondary sex characteristics.
c. social detachment and emotional coldness.
d. multiple personalities.

12.143
d
p. 485
Applied
M

Ralph has always been a loner, and has no interest in friends or family. He truly doesn't care whether other people like him or hate him, as long as they leave him alone. Ralph shows many symptoms of
a. narcissistic personality disorder.
b. paranoid personality disorder.
c. multiple personality disorder.
d. schizoid personality disorder.

12.144 An individual who shows a tremendous instability in his or her interpersonal relationships, moods, and
b self-image would probably be classified as having a
p. 485   a. paranoid personality disorder.
Fact   b. borderline personality disorder.
M   c. histrionic personality disorder.
    d. schizoid personality disorder.

12.145 A disorder involving dramatic, emotional displays, exaggeration of life events, and demands
d for constant reassurance is _____ personality disorder.
p. 485   a. antisocial
Fact   b. narcissistic
M   c. paranoid
    d. histrionic

12.146 People suffering from antisocial personality disorder typically display
a   a. total disregard for the rights and feelings of others.
p. 485   b. a belief that others are plotting to harm them.
Fact   c. a strong need to be the constant center of attention.
M   d. several different people living in the same body.

12.147 Which of the following are not among the origins associated with antisocial personality disorder?
b   a. disturbances in brain function
p. 486   b. fear of punishment
Fact   c. reduced emotional reactions to negative stimuli
C   d. inability to delay gratification

12.148 Gary Gilmore, the individual who murdered several individuals, including a service station attendant, was
d probably suffering from
p. 486   a. paranoid personality disorder.
Applied   b. histrionic personality disorder.
M   c. schizoid personality disorder.
    d. antisocial personality disorder.

12.149 A third major cluster of personality disorders described by the DSM-IV involves
a   a. fearful and anxious behavior.
p. 486   b. social and emotional behavior.
Concept   c. withdrawal and apathy behavior.
M   d. introverted and antisocial behavior.

Substance-Related Disorders

12.150 Disorders that involve maladaptive use of various substances or drugs that lead to
c significant impairment or stress are called _____ disorders.
p. 486   a. substance-reaction
Fact   b. substance-reduction
C   c. substance-related
    d. substance-recurrent

12.151 Ralph uses drugs and his use results in his missing many days of work, being arrested for
b driving under the influence, and neglecting to pay his bills. Ralph's problems would be
p. 487 classified as
Applied   a. substance dependence disorder.
M   b. substance abuse disorder.
    c. substance reaction disorder.
    d. substance risk disorder.

Chapter 12 - Psychological Disorders: Their Nature and Causes   257

12.152 A person who spends considerable amounts of time and money trying to acquire a specific
c   drug on a regular and increasing pattern has
p. 487   a. substance reaction disorder.
Fact   b. substance abuse disorder.
M   c. substance dependence disorder.
        d. substance risk disorder.

12.153 The proportion of adults who smoke has _____ in the U.S.; the proportion of teenagers
c   who smoke has _____ in the U.S.
p. 487   a. increased; decreased
Fact   b. increased; increased
M   c. decreased; increased
        d. decreased; decreased

12.154 Which of the following is not a factor that places teenagers at risk for substance abuse?
c   a. low degree of support from parents
p. 487   b. high level of stress in adolescent lives
Fact   c. increased number of problems
M   d. tendency to cope with problems in maladaptive ways

Schizophrenia: Out of Touch with Reality

12.155 The disorder characterized by profound distortions of thought, perceptions, and emotion is
c   a. somatoform disorder.
p. 487   b. psychogenic fugue.
Fact   c. schizophrenia.
E   d. dissociative disorder.

12.156 The term that refers to the jumbled and meaningless speech patterns shown by schizophrenics
d   who jump from one topic to the next with no organization is
p. 488   a. delusion.
Concept b. hallucination.
M   c. paraphilia.
PT/OLSG d. word salad.

12.157 Word salad produced by schizophrenics is most likely due to problems in
b   a. long-term memory.
p. 488   b. selective attention.
Concept c. iconic memory.
M   d. dissociative attention.

12.158 Believing that your basement has spiders the size of dogs is a _____; seeing the spiders
c   walking up the stairs is a _____.
p. 488   a. catatonia; paranoia
Concept b. paranoia; catatonia
M   c. delusion; hallucination
        d. hallucination; delusion

12.159 Beliefs by schizophrenics that they are extremely famous, important, or powerful are called delusions of
a   a. grandeur.
p. 488   b. omnipotence.
Concept c. ubiquitousness.
C   d. omniscience.

12.160   When schizophrenics believe they are under the control of outside forces they have delusions of
b
p. 488
Fact
E
PT/OLSG
a. grandeur.
b. control.
c. persecution.
d. power.

12.161   The most common perceptual distortions experienced by schizophrenics are _____ hallucinations.
b
p. 489
Fact
M
a. visual
b. auditory
c. olfactory
d. gustatory

12.162   Which of the following is not one of the major problems faced by individuals who suffer from schizophrenia?
c
p. 489
Fact
M
a. delusions
b. hallucinations
c. split personality
d. inappropriate emotions

12.163   One key symptom of schizophrenia involves
b
p. 489
Fact
M
a. gustatory hallucinations.
b. inappropriate emotional reactions.
c. social contagion.
d. two or more personalities.

12.164   One symptom of schizophrenia involves
a
p. 489
Fact
M
a. unusual actions.
b. social contagion.
c. multiple personalities.
d. gustatory hallucinations.

12.165   Symptoms involving the pressure of something that is not normally present, for example, hallucinations, are called
d
p. 489
Fact
M
a. transient symptoms.
b. neutral symptoms.
c. negative symptoms.
d. positive symptoms.

12.166   Symptoms involving the absence of something that is normally present, for example, absence of emotions are called
a
p. 489
Fact
M
a. negative symptoms.
b. positive symptoms.
c. transient symptoms.
d. neutral symptoms.

12.167   Patients with _____ generally have a _____ prognosis.
b
p. 489
Fact
M
a. positive symptoms, poorer
b. negative symptoms, poorer
c. neutral symptoms, better
d. negative symptoms, better

12.168   According to some researchers, the three phases of schizophrenia are
b
p. 490
Concept
C
a. excitatory, activity, resolution.
b. prodromal, acute, residual.
c. foundational, functional, refractory.
d. behavioral, cognitive, emotional.

Chapter 12 - Psychological Disorders: Their Nature and Causes   259

12.169 Schizophrenics who show marked disturbance in motor behavior, for example, alternating
d between total immobility and wild excited activity, are most likely _____ types.
p. 490 a. disorganized
Fact b. motor
M c. paranoid
  d. catatonic

12.170 Catatonic schizophrenia is a type of schizophrenia in which the patient alternates _____ with _____.
d a. deep feelings of depression; excitation and elation
p. 490 b. a strong need for love and caring; social distancing
Fact c. detailed delusions; detailed hallucinations
M d. long periods of immobility; wild, excited activity

12.171 A schizophrenic who has delusions of persecution and grandeur claiming to be Emperor
b Nero is most likely a _____ type.
p. 490 a. disorganized
Fact b. paranoid
M c. catatonic
  d. undifferentiated

12.172 A schizophrenic who shows disorganized speech, disorganized behavior, lack of
c affect, word salad, and fits of giggling, making faces, and other child-like behavior is
p. 490 most likely a _____ type.
Fact a. residual
M b. catatonic
  c. disorganized
  d. paranoid

12.173 The model that suggests that only when a genetically-inherited predisposition is coupled
b with stressful conditions does schizophrenia develop is called the
p. 491 a. family-factor model.
Fact b. diathesis-stress model.
M c. cognitive-stress model.
  d. sociobiological model.

12.174 According to the diathesis-stress model of schizophrenia, this disorder appears when which
c two factors are combined?
p. 491 a. A lack of fear and a lack of guilt.
Fact b. Delusions and hallucinations.
M c. Inherited predisposition and life stress.
  d. Drug abuse and poor family environment.

12.175 Which of the following family factors have not been proposed to be related to schizophrenia?
b a. situations where one parent has all the power
p. 491 b. low socioeconomic status
Fact c. confusing and inconsistent patterns of communication
C d. high levels of conflict between parents

12.176 Which of these is not a pattern of family interaction that has been claimed to cause schizophrenia?
b a. Extremely high levels of conflict between the parents.
p. 491 b. One or both parents sexually abuse the child.
Fact c. All social power in the family rests with one parent.
C d. Child is placed in a double bind.
PT/OLSG

12.177 c p. 491 Concept M
Ralph's mom often insists that he should give her a hug, but whenever he approaches she stiffens and turns away. This behavior is called a
a. dissociation.
b. delusion.
c. double bind.
d. deception.

12.178 a p. 491 Fact M
The cognitive functioning of schizophrenics who show positive symptoms shows a reduced ability to
a. ignore irrelevant or distracting stimuli.
b. notice changes in their environment.
c. repeat back a list of numbers.
d. form social bonds with other people.

12.179 b p. 491 Fact M
The cognitive functioning of schizophrenics who show negative symptoms shows a reduced ability to
a. ignore irrelevant or distracting stimuli.
b. notice changes in their environment.
c. form social bonds with other people.
d. control their emotional responses.

12.180 d p. 491 Fact M
One general way in which the brains of schizophrenics are different from the brains of others is that they show
a. higher levels of activity in all brain regions.
b. a smaller connection between the two hemispheres.
c. lower levels of activity in all brain regions.
d. enlarged ventricles (spaces filled with fluid).

12.181 c p. 492 Fact M
Which of the following has been proposed as a possible link to schizophrenia?
a. increased acetylcholine activity
b. decreased acetylcholine activity
c. increased dopamine activity
d. decreased dopamine activity

12.182 a p. 492 Fact C
An excess of the neurotransmitter _____ may be implicated in schizophrenia.
a. dopamine
b. serotonin
c. epinephrine
d. norepinephrine

12.183 a p. 492 Fact C
Which of these factors has not been blamed as a cause of schizophrenia?
a. Toxic chemicals in the environment
b. Inherited genetic predispositions
c. Abnormal levels of dopamine in the brain
d. families in conflict

12.184 d p. 492 Concept M
A problem brought on in part by drug therapy, which allowed chronically mentally ill patients to be released from hospitals, is
a. drug addiction.
b. increased crime.
c. higher incidence of schizophrenia.
d. increased homelessness.

12.185 c p. 492 Fact M
As many as one-third of all homeless people, according to some estimates, were previously
a. highly-paid employees who got laid off from work.
b. young children abandoned by their parents.
c. hospitalized for serious psychological disorders.
d. convicted for various violent crimes.

Chapter 12 - Psychological Disorders: Their Nature and Causes

12.186
a
p. 492
Fact
M

Some people who receive treatment for psychological disorders later wind up homeless on the streets, largely because
a. they have no psychological help outside the hospital.
b. drug treatments are unsuccessful for them.
c. they have been subjected to electric shock therapy.
d. they refuse to return to the hospital.

12.187
d
p. 492
Concept
C

If someone is released from a mental institution because drug treatment has reduced his symptoms, why does that person sometimes wind up on the street showing symptoms again?
a. Drug treatments become less effective with time.
b. The drugs produce too many unpleasant side effects.
c. Others actively prevent them from getting the drugs.
d. They may switch to using street drugs and alcohol.

12.188
b
p. 492
Applied
E

If someone talks about committing suicide, that person
a. is unlikely to commit suicide.
b. is likely to commit suicide.
c. is trying to see another's reaction.
d. is trying to get information about procedures.

12.189
c
p. 492
Fact
C
PT/OLSG

Which of the following statements about suicide is not true?
a. The majority of persons who commit suicide have told others about their intentions.
b. If you think someone is suicidal, bringing up the topic and talking to them about it can help.
c. Someone who is contemplating suicide should be left alone to think through the issues.
d. Giving away valued possessions and starting to come out of a deep depression are associated with suicide attempts.

CHAPTER 13

Multiple-Choice Questions

Psychotherapies: Psychological Approaches to Psychological Disorders

13.1
d
p. 498
Fact
M

Psychotherapies include which of the following?
a. Marital, drug, and surgical therapies.
b. Group, self-help, and spiritual therapies.
c. Social, school, and workplace therapies.
d. Individual, group, and family therapies.

13.2
b
p. 498
Concept
M
PT/OLSG

Procedures in which a trained person establishes a special relationship with an individual seeking help in order to remove or modify existing symptoms, change disturbed patterns of behavior, and promote personal growth are called
a. behavioral medicine.
b. psychotherapies.
c. psychobiological therapies.
d. psychopharmacological therapies.

13.3
a
p. 499
Fact
M

Which of the following are based on the assumption that abnormal behavior derives primarily from the complex imbalance of hidden, inner forces?
a. psychodynamic therapies
b. behavioral therapies
c. cognitive therapies
d. social cognition therapies

13.4
b
p. 499
Fact
C

The form of therapy devised by Freud is _____.
a. rational-emotive
b. psychoanalysis
c. counterconditioning
d. meta-analysis

13.5
b
p. 499
Concept
M

According to Freud, psychological disorders stem from conflicts between
a. ego versus superego.
b. id versus ego versus superego.
c. conscious versus preconscious.
d. sexual drives versus libidinal drives.

13.6
b
p. 499
Concept
M
PT/OLSG

Freud suggested that psychological disorders stem from _____ of id impulses.
a. interpretation
b. repression
c. transference
d. abreaction

13.7
d
p. 499
Concept
M

According to Freud, the ego is protected from anxiety by the use of
a. resistance.
b. counter-resistance.
c. unconditional positive regard.
d. defense mechanisms.

13.8
c
p. 499
Fact
M

According to Freud, the release of emotion obtained as a result of understanding unconscious conflicts is called
a. transference.
b. resistance.
c. abreaction.
d. relief.

Chapter 13 - Therapy: Diminishing the Pain of Psychological Disorders

13.9
a
p. 499
Applied
M

A therapist who has you relax on a couch and talk about anything that comes to mind, whether it seems to make sense or not, is using a psychoanalytic process called
a. free association.
b. empathy regard.
c. resistance.
d. transference.

13.10
c
p. 499
Fact
M

When a psychoanalyst tells a client what unconscious desires and motivations are behind the client's current behavior problems, it is
a. transference.
b. resistance.
c. interpretation.
d. free association.

13.11
b
p. 500
Concept
C

Avoid anxiety is to intense emotional feelings as
a. transference is to resistance.
b. resistance is to transference.
c. conscience is to ego ideal.
d. ego ideal is to conscience.

13.12
b
p. 500
Applied
M

When Lisa's therapist told her that her pattern of forming relationships with abusive men is based on her ambivalent feelings toward her father, she became very angry and refused to pay for the session. The therapist might regard Lisa's reaction as
a. transference.
b. resistance.
c. association.
d. interpretation.

13.13
b
p. 500
Fact
M

In psychoanalysis, intense emotional feelings of love or hate toward the analyst on the part of the patient is called
a. abreaction.
b. transference.
c. resistance.
d. counterconditioning.

13.14
a
p. 500
Concept
M
PT/OLSG

Which of the following is not one of the characteristics of psychoanalysis?
a. empathy
b. free association
c. transference
d. abreaction

13.15
d
p. 500
Fact
M

One major drawback of classical Freudian psychoanalysis is that it
a. does not take unconscious wishes into account.
b. puts too much emphasis on biological factors.
c. doesn't appeal to articulate, intelligent people.
d. is generally very time-consuming and expensive.

13.16
b
p. 501
Fact
M

A major criticism of classical Freudian psychoanalysis is that it
a. is more concerned with research than helping people.
b. applies best to verbal, intelligent, successful people.
c. ignores important theories of psychosexual development.
d. typically does not last long enough to be effective.

13.17
c
p. 501
Fact
M

Which of the following is not true with regard to classical psychoanalysis?
a. It is costly and time-consuming.
b. It is based on Freud's nonscientific theories.
c. It is supported by research findings that once insight occurs, mental health follows.
d. It requires that clients possess high verbal skills.

13.18 Research evidence contradicts the major assumption of Freud's psychoanalysis, which was
d
p. 501　　a. mental health was a condition of limited libido.
Concept　b. working toward mental health required a substantial amount of libido.
C　　　　c. transference was a fundamental part of therapy.
　　　　　d. once insight is acquired, mental health will follow automatically.

13.19 Which of the following contend that psychological disorders occur because the environment
b somehow interferes with personal growth and fulfillment?
p. 501　　a. psychoanalytic therapists
Fact　　　b. humanistic therapists
M　　　　c. behavioral therapists
　　　　　d. cognitive therapists

13.20 In therapy, facilitator is to director as
c
p. 501　　a. transference is to resistance.
Concept　b. resistance is to transference.
M　　　　c. humanistic is to psychoanalytic.
　　　　　d. psychoanalytic is to humanistic.

13.21 A form of therapy that tries to help people understand themselves and the world from their
d own personal, unique perspectives, without the therapist telling the client what to do or what
p. 501 it means, is
Fact　　　a. behavioral therapy.
M　　　　b. psychoanalysis.
　　　　　c. somatic therapy.
　　　　　d. client-centered therapy.

13.22 (Bonus) Which of the following is most often associated with client-centered therapy?
d
p. 501　　a. Sigmund Freud
Fact　　　b. Albert Ellis
E　　　　c. Alfred Adler
　　　　　d. Carl Rogers

13.23 According to client-centered therapy, psychological problems arise primarily from
a
p. 501　　a. a distorted self-concept.
Fact　　　b. conflicts between the id and ego.
M　　　　c. unconscious motivations.
　　　　　d. inappropriate reinforcers.

13.24 A warm and accepting environment, a high level of empathetic understanding, and
c unconditional positive regard are characteristic of
p. 502　　a. psychoanalytic therapy.
Fact　　　b. behavioral therapy.
M　　　　c. client-centered therapy.
　　　　　d. Gestalt therapy.

13.25 Which of the following is not one of the primary features of client-centered therapy?
b
p. 502　　a. unconditional acceptance
Concept　b. interpretation of dreams
M　　　　c. accurate reflection of clients' feelings
PT/OLSG　d. emphatic understanding

13.26 A therapist who communicates to a client a warm, personal attitude that the client is a good,
d worthwhile, loveable human being, no matter what the client says or does, is displaying
p. 502　　a. free association.
Fact　　　b. counterconditioning.
M　　　　c. emotional transference.
　　　　　d. unconditional positive regard.

Chapter 13 - Therapy: Diminishing the Pain of Psychological Disorders   265

13.27   Which of the following views suggests that psychological problems stem from not
a   consciously acknowledging key aspects of our emotions?
p. 502   a. Gestalt therapy
Fact   b. Psychoanalytic therapy
M   c. Client-centered therapy
             d. Cognitive therapy

13.28   Gestalt therapy is based on the belief that psychological problems occur when a person has
b   a. allowed the id to become a threat to the ego.
p. 502   b. tried to deny the reality of important feelings.
Fact   c. adopted unrealistic conditions of worthiness.
M   d. developed irrational, illogical thought patterns.

13.29   If asked to perform the two-chair technique -- moving back and forth between two chairs
c   playing themselves in one chair and the role of some other person in another chair --
p. 502   you are probably seeing which of the following therapists?
Applied   a. behavioral
M   b. client-centered
             c. Gestalt
             d. cognitive

13.30   Which of these is a belief common to all humanistic therapies?
d   a. Past traumatic experiences control our lives.
p. 502   b. Unconscious motivations control our lives.
Fact   c. People are basically evil.
M   d. People are basically good.

13.31   Which of the following is characteristic of humanistic therapies?
d   a. belief that unconscious motives are the source of psychological problems
p. 502   b. improving the relations between the ego and the superego
Concept   c. reliance on transference and resistance during therapy
M   d. eliminating flaws in the self-concept as a goal of successful therapy

13.32   Which of the following is not one of the assumptions of humanistic therapies?
d   a. People have control over their own behavior.
p. 502   b. Flaws in self-concept produce psychological distress.
Concept   c. People have the ability to make choices.
M   d. The therapist must force repressed urges from patients.
PT/OLSG

13.33   One important criticism of humanistic therapies is that they are
c   a. too time-consuming and expensive.
p. 502   b. based on outmoded theories of personality.
Fact   c. too vague about what happens in therapy.
C   d. overly optimistic about human potential.

13.34   Scientific research has supported the emphasis that humanistic therapy has placed on
c   a. unconscious urges and repressed desires.
p. 503   b. giving children unconditional positive regard.
Fact   c. the gap between the self-image and the "ideal self."
M   d. the principles of classical and operant conditioning.

13.35   Which of the following are considered to be lasting and important contributions of
a   humanistic therapies?
p. 503   a. discrepancies between the ideal self and self-image as a source of psychological
Fact   maladjustment
C   b. demonstrating the effectiveness of free association
             c. the belief that strengthening the superego can help reduce anxiety
             d. the recognition of the importance of learning principles in therapy

13.36 b
p. 503
Concept
M

In therapy, emphasis on past experience is to emphasis on current experience as
a. behavior therapy is to humanistic therapy.
b. humanistic therapy is to behavior therapy.
c. psychodynamic therapy is to humanistic therapy.
d. humanistic therapy is to psychodynamic therapy.

13.37 d
p. 503
Fact
E

Therapies based on the principles of learning are
a. person-centered therapies.
b. psychoanalytic therapies.
c. Gestalt therapies.
d. behavioral therapies.

13.38 c
p. 503
Fact
M

Which of the following suggests that psychological problems are the result of faulty learning, that is, the acquisition of maladaptive habits and reactions?
a. Gestalt therapy
b. client-centered therapy
c. behavioral therapy
d. neo-Freudian therapy

13.39 a
p. 503
Applied
M

Ralph's therapist says it doesn't matter what originally caused his violent fear of automobiles. All that matters is that this behavior is causing problems, and it needs to be changed. This therapist most likely practices _____ therapy.
a. behavioral
b. psychoanalytic
c. humanistic
d. Freudian

13.40 c
p. 503
Concept
M

Many behavior therapists believe that a client must engage in _____, which means practicing the skills acquired during therapy in daily life.
a. autonomous self-reinforcement
b. behavioral self-monitoring
c. guided self-care
d. intrinsic self-management

13.41 d
p. 503
Concept
M

Explaining phobias on the basis of the feared object actually being associated with a real danger is based on the principles of
a. transference.
b. unconditional positive regard.
c. operant conditioning.
d. classical conditioning.

13.42 a
p. 503
Fact
M

A procedure involving prolonged exposure to a fear stimulus under conditions where the client cannot avoid the fear stimulus may produce extinction of the fear response. This procedure is called
a. flooding.
b. transference.
c. resistance.
d. counterconditioning.

13.43 d
p. 504
Concept
M

The procedure of systematic desensitization involves using classical conditioning to
a. make a stimulus that once was pleasant become unpleasant.
b. teach people to avoid the behaviors that commonly lead to depression.
c. help give a person a chance to develop a more accurate self-concept.
d. develop a relaxation response to something that once produced fear.

Chapter 13 - Therapy: Diminishing the Pain of Psychological Disorders   267

13.44 Lisa's therapist helped her overcome her fear of enclosed spaces by having her imagine
c   being in gradually smaller and smaller rooms while she kept her body relaxed and her breathing
p 504 slow. Lisa was probably undergoing
Applied   a. flooding.
M   b. Gestalt therapy.
           c. systematic desensitization.
           d. aversive therapy.

13.45 Which of the following clinical procedures are based, in part, on classical conditioning?
b   a. transference
p. 504   b. systematic desensitization
Concept   c. two-chair technique
M   d. token economy

13.46 The basic goal of therapy based on the principles of operant conditioning is to change the
a   person's behavior by
p. 504   a. changing the reinforcements that control the behavior.
Concept   b. helping the person develop a clearer view of him/her self.
M   c. uncovering the unconscious motivation for the behavior.
           d. changing the way the person thinks about the behavior.

13.47 Which of the following approaches requires that maladaptive behaviors be clearly identified
b   along with the reinforcers that maintain the behaviors, as well as efforts to change the
p. 504 environment such that reinforcers for the maladaptive behaviors are no longer provided?
Concept   a. classical conditioning
C   b. operant conditioning
           c. client-centered
           d. aversion therapy

13.48 Which of these is not one of the important steps involved in applying the principles of
b   operant conditioning to therapy?
p. 504   a. Identifying the undesired behaviors.
Fact   b. Understanding what produced these behaviors.
M   c. Identifying the events that reinforce the behaviors.
           d. Removing the reinforcers from the environment.

13.49 In a token economy, the tokens (poker chips, gold stars, etc.) function to reinforce desired
b   behaviors because
p. 504   a. they have special, individual meaning for the client.
Fact   b. they can be used to buy other reinforcements (treats).
M   c. they are able to serve as a conditioned stimulus.
PT/OLSG   d. they are able to serve as an unconditioned stimulus.

13.50 Setting up a system in a clinical hospital that involves clients earning points for
b   appropriate behaviors that can be exchanged for privileges such as listening to the radio
p. 504 is an example of
Concept   a. systematic desensitization.
M   b. a token economy.
           c. counterconditioning.
           d. reciprocal inhibition.

13.51 The process through which behavior is affected by exposure to others' behavior is
c   a. a token economy.
p. 504   b. flooding.
Fact   c. modeling.
M   d. classical conditioning.

13.52 a p. 505 Fact E

Assertiveness training is sometimes taught through the process of
a. modeling.
b. extinction.
c. flooding.
d. counterconditioning.

13.53 d p. 505 Applied M

A therapist might use modeling to reduce a patient's phobia about dogs by
a. giving rewards when the patient approached a dog.
b. discussing where the patient's fear came from.
c. explaining that logically the patient should not fear dogs.
d. having the patient watch others playing with dogs.

13.54 b p. 505 Applied M

Ralph was afraid of dogs. His therapist never asked him to think about dogs or to go near them, but he let him watch other children who were having great fun playing with a puppy. The therapist treated Ralph's phobia using
a. counterconditioning.
b. modeling.
c. systematic desensitization.
d. extinction.

13.55 d p. 505 Concept M

Having children who show high levels of aggressive behavior watch films of children behaving in a nonaggressive manner is an attempt to change their behavior through
a. classical conditioning.
b. transference.
c. shaping.
d. modeling.

13.56 d p. 505 Applied M

Lisa has an extreme fear of snakes. Which of these situations would describe a therapist using modeling to reduce her fear?
a. Having her relax while thinking about snakes.
b. Putting her in a room of snakes until her fear weakened.
c. Giving her M&M candies when she saw a snake.
d. Having her watch someone handle snakes confidently.

13.57 b p. 505 Fact M

The belief that how we think strongly affects how we feel and what we do is most characteristic of
a. person-centered therapy.
b. cognitive therapy.
c. Gestalt therapy.
d. existential therapy.

13.58 a p. 505 Concept M

Which of the following therapists suggest that psychological disorders stem from faulty or distorted modes of thought?
a. cognitive therapists
b. behavioral therapists
c. modeling therapists
d. Freudian therapists

13.59 c p. 505 Concept M

According to Albert Ellis, the self-defeating cycle of many psychological problems starts with
a. unconscious conflict.
b. negative transfer.
c. irrational thoughts.
d. abreaction.

13.60 d p. 505 Fact M

A form of cognitive behavior therapy that focuses on developing logical, rational thoughts is
a. psychodynamic therapy.
b. obsessive-compulsive therapy.
c. aversive conditioning therapy.
d. rational-emotive therapy.

Chapter 13 - Therapy: Diminishing the Pain of Psychological Disorders

13.61
d
p. 506
Concept
M

Having a client recognize irrational views such as catastrophizing is characteristic of
a. person-centered therapy.
b. Gestalt therapy.
c. self-help group therapy.
d. rational-emotive therapy.

13.62
c
p. 506
Applied
C

Which of these would most likely be considered an irrational belief or assumption in rational-emotive therapy?
a. "A bad grade on this test will lower my average for the course."
b. "A bad grade in this course will not look good on my transcript."
c. "A bad grade on this test will mean I'll never get a decent job."
d. "A bad grade in this course will pull down my cumulative average."

13.63
a
p. 506
Concept
M
PT/OLSG

The main function of rational-emotive therapy is to persuade people to
a. recognize their own irrational beliefs and assumptions.
b. confront the people who have let them down in life.
c. get in touch with feelings they are trying to deny.
d. reach their full potential as human beings.

13.64
d
p. 506
Fact
M

According to Beck's cognitive therapy, depression is caused by
a. a discrepancy between the self-concept and reality.
b. unconscious conflicts created in early childhood.
c. a chemical imbalance in the cerebral cortex.
d. distorted thoughts that make a person feel worthless.

13.65
b
p. 506
Fact
M

In Beck's model of depression, seeing oneself as totally worthless because of one or two failures is an example of
a. absolutistic thinking.
b. overgeneralization.
c. exceptions to the rule.
d. selective perception.

13.66
c
p. 506
Concept
M

In cognitive behavior therapy, depression is assumed to be caused by
a. experiencing traumatic events in the past.
b. reinforcements for depressed behaviors.
c. illogical thinking about ourselves and the world.
d. a breakthrough of unconscious wishes and desires.

13.67
b
p. 506
Applied
M

If a depressed mother sees her child fall on the playground and start to cry, which of these thoughts would Beck's cognitive behavior therapy say is most likely?
a. I hope she hasn't knocked a tooth loose.
b. Only a bad mother would let her child get hurt.
c. If I don't act worried, he'll get up and play some more.
d. Now every pair of jeans has a hole in the knee.

13.68
d
p. 507
Applied
C

In Beck's Cognitive Behavior Therapy, the concept of _____ is emphasized, which indicates that a person's depression influences what is remembered and what kinds of thoughts are processed.
a. negative mood-negative thought interaction
b. mood-thought confound
c. mood-thinking procedure
d. mood-dependent memory

13.69 a p. 507 Fact M

Which of the following approaches emphasizes cooperation between the therapist and client in identifying an individual's assumptions, beliefs, and expectations and in formulating ways of testing them to modify inappropriate beliefs?
a. Beck's cognitive-behavior therapy
b. Ellis' rational emotive therapy
c. Rogers' person-centered therapy
d. Dollards' modeling therapy

13.70 b p. 507 Fact C

Cognitive behavior therapy attempts to change the illogical beliefs that cause depression by
a. forcing people to realize how irrational they are.
b. helping people identify and test their assumptions.
c. demonstrating how they relate to unconscious urges.
d. reinforcing people for changing their beliefs.

13.71 a p. 507 Applied M

When a cognitive behavior therapist helps a client decide how to test the assumptions that led to his depression, the therapist arranges the tests so that
a. the client is likely to notice and remember his successes.
b. they reinforce more positive, nondepressed behavior.
c. they uncover his unconscious wishes and desires.
d. they help the therapist make a specific diagnosis.

13.72 c p. 507 Fact M

Recent research has indicated that cognitive therapies may be highly effective in treating _____.
a. schizophrenia.
b. phobias.
c. depression.
d. anxiety disorders.

13.73 b p. 508 Applied M

It is very difficult to be both angry and laugh at the same time. This statement is reflective of the
a. comedic faces hypothesis.
b. incompatible response hypothesis.
c. opposites attract hypothesis.
d. laughter is the best medicine hypothesis.

13.74 d p. 508 Applied M

Nurse O'Flaherty presents information from the health practitioner area that
a. cognitive flexibility reduces depression.
b. social skills training reduces depression.
c. assertiveness training reduces depression.
d. humor reduces depression.

Group Therapies: Working with Others to Solve Problems

13.75 b p. 509 Fact M PT/OLSG

A type of therapy that involves several people all meeting together to receive psychological help is called
a. psychoanalysis.
b. group therapy.
c. humanistic therapy.
d. intermittent therapy.

13.76 d p. 509 Concept M

A form of therapy based on the _____ view in which group members act out their feelings in front of other group members is called _____.
a. rational-emotive; transference
b. rational-emotive; psychodrama
c. psychoanalytic; transference
d. psychoanalytic; psychodrama

Chapter 13 - Therapy: Diminishing the Pain of Psychological Disorders

13.77
a
p. 509
Fact
M

Role reversal and mirroring are techniques used with
a. psychodrama.
b. assertiveness training.
c. transference therapy.
d. humanistic therapy.

13.78
d
p. 509
Fact
M

Two forms of group therapy that are based on behavioral learning principles are
a. psychodrama and mirroring.
b. encounter groups and sensitivity training groups.
c. rational-emotive and cognitive behavioral therapy.
d. social skills training and assertiveness training.

13.79
b
p. 509
Concept
C

Assertiveness refers to the ability to
a. force other people to do things your way.
b. express your feelings and stand up for your rights.
c. be completely open and honest in dealing with others.
d. construct a reality that is consistent and accurate.

13.80
c
p. 509
Fact
M

Behavioral group therapies are helpful in teaching individuals
a. conflict insight.
b. cognitive flexibility.
c. self-control.
d. inner strength.

13.81
c
p. 509
Fact
M

Two humanistic group therapies aimed at helping people understand themselves better and become more open and honest with others are
a. psychodrama and role reversal.
b. social skills training and assertive training.
c. encounter groups and sensitivity-training groups.
d. systematic desensitization and aversive therapy.

13.82
d
p. 509
Fact
M

Which of these is not a form of group therapy?
a. Assertiveness training
b. Psychodrama
c. Social skills training
d. Cognitive behavior training

13.83
b
p. 509
Fact
E
PT/OLSG

Encounter groups and sensitivity-training groups are a product of
a. behavioral group therapies.
b. humanistic group therapies.
c. psychodynamic group therapies.
d. behavioral individual therapies.

13.84
a
p. 509
Fact
M

Self-help groups consist of
a. people who have a similar sort of problem.
b. troubled people and a trained group leader.
c. people with special skills for helping others.
d. those who are too weak to help themselves.

13.85
d
p. 509
Fact
M

Groups of people experiencing the same problems who meet to help each other in their efforts to cope with these difficulties, for example, Alcoholics Anonymous, are referred to as
a. psychodynamic groups.
b. person-centered groups.
c. humanistic groups.
d. self-help groups.

272   Test Bank - Essentials of Psychology (2nd Edition)

13.86 The main purpose of a self-help group is to provide people with an opportunity to
a
p. 509 a. find support from others who face the same problems.
Fact b. practice specific skills and behaviors they will need.
M c. interact with a professional trained to help them.
  d. confront their unconscious wishes and desires.

13.87 A basic assumption of self-help groups is that when you are facing a problem in your life
d
p. 510 a. it is generally caused by illogical thought processes that need to change.
Fact b. it is important to understand the basic cause of your problem from your past.
M c. you will need to find a caring, trained professional to help you deal with it.
PT/OLSG d. no professional can help as much as someone who has faced the same problem.

Therapies Focused on Interpersonal Relations: Marital and Family Therapy

13.88 The main assumption of interpersonal therapies is that personal problems are often the result of
a
p. 511 a. unsatisfying or ineffective relationships with important others.
Fact b. an unconscious struggle over repressed desires.
M c. the conditioning of maladaptive behaviors in the past.
  d. illogical or irrational thoughts and assumptions.

13.89 Which of these is not an example of interpersonal therapy?
b
p. 511 a. couple therapy
Fact b. Gestalt therapy
E c. family therapy
  d. marital therapy

13.90 Psychotherapy that focuses on relations between couples is called
d
p. 511 a. bilateral therapy.
Fact b. didactic therapy.
M c. family therapy.
  d. marital therapy.

13.91 One of the important goals of couple or marital therapy is to
d
p. 512 a. improve the sexual enjoyment in the relationship.
Concept b. give each person a more accurate self-concept.
M c. prepare young people for the realities of married life.
  d. teach couples to communicate more effectively.

13.92 Which of the following appears to be characteristic of couples that are poorly adjusted?
c
p. 513 a. adequate communication skills
Fact b. explaining negative actions on the basis of external causes
M c. explaining negative actions on the basis of internal causes
  d. use of flattering terms to explain their partners' behaviors

13.93 An important goal in couple or marital therapy is to make changes in
c
p. 513 a. how children of divorce cope with their situation.
Fact b. each person's subconscious motivations and desires.
C c. the explanations people give for their partners' behaviors.
  d. each individual's degree of personal growth.

13.94 If Lisa is happily married, which explanation is she most likely to give for why her husband
c never buys her flowers?
p. 513 a. "He never thinks very much about me."
Applied b. "There's no romance in his soul at all."
C c. "We don't have money to spend on that."
  d. "He's not very good at showing feelings."

Chapter 13 - Therapy: Diminishing the Pain of Psychological Disorders

13.95
b
p. 513
Fact
M

An important goal of family therapy is to make changes in
a. each person's individual self-concept.
b. patterns of interaction within the family.
c. the reinforcements that maintain behavior.
d. how people explain a partner's behavior.

13.96
b
p. 513
Fact
C

Which of the following approaches assumes that relations between family members are more important in producing psychological disorders than aspects of one's personality?
a. communications approach
b. family systems therapy
c. social interaction therapy
d. means-ends analysis therapy

13.97
a
p. 513
Fact
C

One of the main assumptions of family therapy is that when one member of the family displays inappropriate behavior, it means that this behavior
a. affects and is affected by everyone else in the family.
b. results from a personality disorder in that family member.
c. must be changed before anything else can be done.
d. should be ignored so the therapist can focus on other things.

13.98
a
p. 514
Fact
M
PT/OLSG

In general, the research that has been performed to evaluate the success of family therapy has led to the conclusion that after participating in family therapy
a. family members relate to each other better.
b. children become more intelligent.
c. unconscious urges are weaker.
d. people have more accurate self-concepts.

13.99
a
p. 514
Study
C

Henggler and colleagues (1992), in a study with juvenile offenders in South Carolina, found that
a. family therapy led to fewer subsequent arrests and crimes than the probation-officer approach.
b. probation-officer approach led to fewer subsequent felonies than family therapy.
c. probation-officer approach led to fewer subsequent arrests than family therapy.
d. family therapy led to fewer subsequent child maltreatment problems than the probation-officer approach.

13.100
c
p. 514
Concept
C

The application of the basic methods of experimentation to the study of the effectiveness of a specific form of therapy involves using an _____.
a. effectiveness study
b. ephemeral study
c. efficacy study
d. efficiency study

Psychotherapy: Some Current Issues

13.101
b
p. 515
Fact
C

Which of the following has not contributed to an increased use of psychotherapy?
a. a decrease in the negative attitudes about psychotherapy
b. fuller understanding of the implications for effectiveness of therapy
c. greater sophistication and effectiveness of psychotherapy itself
d. increase in the types of therapy that are applicable to a wider range of disorders

13.102
a
p. 515
Fact
M

Hans Eysenck criticized the effectiveness of psychotherapy in 1952, but it now appears that Eysenck was wrong in that he
a. overestimated the proportion who show spontaneous recovery.
b. underestimated the likelihood of spontaneous recovery.
c. overestimated the proportion who improve due to therapy.
d. conducted his studies with subjects who were diagnosed as malingers.

13.103
c
p. 515
Fact
C

Early research indicating that psychotherapy was no more effective than no treatment at all was based on
a. an incomplete and inaccurate definition of psychotherapy.
b. the opinions of physicians who did not practice psychotherapy.
c. inaccurate estimates of how many improve with and without therapy.
d. an outmoded theory of how such research should be conducted.

13.104
b
p. 516
Fact
M

Most research on the effectiveness of psychotherapy supports which of these conclusions?
a. People who receive no treatment improve most.
b. People who receive psychotherapy improve most.
c. Psychotherapy is just as effective as no treatment.
d. No general conclusions can be drawn from the research.

13.105
b
p. 516
Fact
M

Most research suggests that therapy is
a. equally effective as no treatment at all.
b. more effective than no treatment at all.
c. less effective than no treatment at all.
d. more effective than no treatment at all only for adults and not for adolescents.

13.106
c
p. 516
Fact
M

Research on the effectiveness of psychotherapy indicates that the more treatment individuals receive, the more
a. psychological problems they seem to develop.
b. positive their attitudes toward psychotherapy.
c. improvement in symptoms they show.
d. medications they require to function.

13.107
b
p. 516
Study
C

Martin Seligman (1995) advocated that rather than _____ research to test psychotherapy, _____ research should be used.
a. effectiveness, efficacy
b. efficacy, effectiveness
c. efficiency, effectiveness
d. efficacy, efficiency

13.108
a
p. 516
Applied
C

One of the difficulties in comparing efficacy studies with the actual practice of psychotherapy is that
a. in efficacy studies participants have a single disorder, while patients may have several disorders.
b. in efficacy studies several therapies are used, while in actual practice only one therapy is usually used.
c. in efficacy studies participants get the chance to choose the type of therapy, while in actual practice only one type is usually available.
d. in efficacy studies the focus is on general improvement, while in actual practice the focus is on improvement in one specific area of functioning.

13.109
b
p. 517
Study
C

In 1994, *Consumer Reports* conducted a study on the effectiveness of psychotherapy and found that improvements were greatest when therapy was received from
a. marriage counselors, physicians, and social workers.
b. psychiatrists, psychologists, and social workers.
c. physicians, psychologists, and marriage counselors.
d. physicians, ministers, and family therapists.

13.110
c
p. 517
Study
C
PT/OLSG

The *Consumer Reports* study on the effectiveness of therapy found that
a. the shorter the therapy sessions, the greater the improvement.
b. the more education provided about the disorder, the greater the improvement.
c. the longer therapy continued, the greater the improvement.
d. the more specific the disorder, the greater the improvement.

Chapter 13 - Therapy: Diminishing the Pain of Psychological Disorders   275

13.111 Which of these is one possible reason why all different forms of psychotherapy are equally effective?
a
p. 518   a. They have a common core that makes them effective.
Fact   b. Each works best for a particular ethnic group.
M   c. There are no meaningful differences between them.
            d. They are equal because none of them is effective.

13.112 All forms of psychotherapy have a common core of features that includes
b
p. 518   a. a belief in the importance of the unconscious.
Fact   b. an explanation for the client's problems.
M   c. an agreement on the causes of disorders.
            d. a desire to aid the client's personal growth.

13.113 An important common feature of all forms of psychotherapy is the belief that the client
a
p. 518   a. is doing something constructive about the problem.
Fact   b. could solve his or her problems without any help.
M   c. learns new ways of understanding him or her self.
            d. has a secret desire to maintain the problem.

13.114 In order for a therapeutic alliance to develop, a patient in psychotherapy must believe in
a
p. 518   a. the therapist's genuine desire to help.
Fact   b. accepting responsibility for his or her actions.
M   c. specific biological causes for a disorder.
            d. the knowledge and expertise of the therapist.

13.115 Which of the following is not one of the features held in common by the different therapies?
b
p. 518   a. therapeutic alliance
Concept   b. psychodrama
M   c. special kind of setting
PT/OLSG   d. suggestion of specific actions in order to cope with problems

13.116 Two of the major themes that are common to all effective therapies are
d
p. 518   a. education and interaction.
Concept   b. direction and direct help.
C   c. specific setting and specific actions.
            d. hope and personal control.

13.117 Which of the following is not a reason for seeking therapy for a psychological disorder?
c
p. 519   a. The psychological problem is causing you serious emotional discomfort.
Applied   b. If a psychological problem you have had in the past suddenly worsens.
M   c. If your friend says you have been acting weird and he cannot understand you.
            d. If you hear voices telling you what to do.

13.118 With regard to the relative effectiveness of various forms of psychotherapy, it is most likely
c   to be the case that
p. 520   a. some forms of therapy are consistently better than others.
Fact   b. classical psychotherapies are slightly better than humanistic therapy.
M   c. the form of therapy that is best depends on the type of problem being treated.
            d. biologically based therapies are more effective than any other research.

13.119 According to research comparing the effectiveness of different kinds of therapy,
c
p. 520   a. psychoanalysis is the least effective form of therapy.
Concept   b. behavior therapy is the most effective form of therapy.
M   c. various forms of therapy seem to yield equal benefits.
            d. humanistic therapy is more effective than cognitive therapy.

13.120   With regard to the relative effectiveness of various types of psychotherapy, research has
d   generally determined that
p. 520   a. behavioral therapy is the most effective.
Fact   b. person-centered is the most effective.
C   c. psychoanalysis is the most effective.
            d. various forms of therapy seem to be equally effective.

13.121   Since drugs are used to treat many psychological disorders, there is a controversy surrounding
c   the question of _____ for psychologists.
p. 520   a. medical training
Concept   b. hospital privileges
C   c. prescription privileges
            d. pharmacological training

13.122   One of the problems with giving psychologists prescription privileges is that
a   a. such privileges might make psychology be viewed as a "junior branch" of psychiatry.
p. 521   b. the drugs given by psychologists would be specific to the disorder.
Concept   c. the psychologists would continue to emphasize treating behavior.
C   d. such privileges might generate more money for psychologists.

13.123   Which one of the following does not account for the possible cultural insensitivity of
b   psychotherapy in general?
p. 521   a. Cultural biases in diagnosis exist.
Concept   b. Cultural biases in location exist.
M   c. Most therapies were developed with persons of European descent.
            d. Cultural gaps may inhibit communication between therapists and clients.

13.124   Which of these is not a likely reason for therapy to be less effective for people of varying
c   cultural and ethnic backgrounds?
p. 521   a. Therapists might have difficulty communicating with people very different from themselves.
Fact   b. Therapies were originally developed for middle-class people of European descent.
M   c. People of different racial backgrounds show different patterns of brain chemistry.
PT/OLSG   d. Therapists might be subject to subtle or unconscious forms of cultural bias.

13.125   As an example of cultural bias in diagnosis, it has been found that African-Americans are more likely to
b   be diagnosed as _____, and less likely to be diagnosed as showing _____ than persons of European descent.
p. 521   a. mood disorders, schizophrenia
Fact   b. schizophrenia, mood disorders
C   c. somatoform disorders, anxiety disorders
            d. anxiety disorders, somatoform disorders

13.126   A therapist who uses psychoanalysis with a client from a disadvantaged background would probably not be
d   responding to the issue of
p. 521   a. therapeutic alacrity.
Applied   b. societal awareness.
M   c. ethnic action.
            d. cultural sensitivity.

13.127   Which of these would be a culturally insensitive way to treat a young African-American
b   woman suffering from depression who never progressed beyond seventh grade in school?
p. 522   a. Discussing her beliefs and assumptions about the world and her role in it.
Applied   b. Asking her to keep a detailed written journal of her thoughts and feelings.
C   c. Asking her about the dreams she remembers and what they mean to her.
            d. Discussing her childhood and how she interacted with her family members.

Chapter 13 - Therapy: Diminishing the Pain of Psychological Disorders

Biologically Based Therapies

13.128
b
p. 522
Fact
M

Drugs that are prescribed for the purpose of treating psychological disorders are called
a. recreational drugs.
b. psychotropic drugs.
c. psychological drugs.
d. behavioral drugs.

13.129
d
p. 522
Fact
M

The major single reason for a dramatic drop in the number of patients in psychiatric hospitals from the mid-1950s to the mid-1970s is
a. psychosurgery.
b. an increase in the number of psychotherapists.
c. electroconvulsive therapy.
d. drug therapy.

13.130
a
p. 523
Fact
M

The major tranquilizers, for example phenothiazines, are used as
a. antipsychotic drugs.
b. antianxiety drugs.
c. antidepressant drugs.
d. bipolar mood inhibitors.

13.131
b
p. 523
Fact
M

Chlorpromazine (Thorazine) is in the chemical family of phenothiazines that are used to deal with the symptoms of
a. bipolar disorder.
b. schizophrenia.
c. major depression.
d. multiple personality.

13.132
d
p. 523
Fact
M

Antipsychotic drugs seem to produce their effects by
a. blocking acetylcholine effects in the brain.
b. facilitating acetylcholine effects in the brain.
c. facilitating dopamine effects in the brain.
d. blocking dopamine effects in the brain.

13.133
b
p. 523
Fact
M
PT/OLSG

The condition called tardive dyskinesia often occurs among patients who are maintained on ____ drugs.
a. antidepressant
b. antipsychotic
c. antimania
d. antianxiety

13.134
c
p. 523
Fact
M

A side-effect of prolonged antipsychotic drug treatments involves a loss of motor control, especially in the face resulting in involuntary muscle movements of the tongue, lips, and jaw is called
a. zoloft syndrome.
b. prosopagnosia.
c. tardive dyskinesia.
d. tertiary disorder.

13.135
d
p. 523
Concept
C

Which of the following arguments best characterizes the effects of antipsychotic drugs?
a. The symptoms disappear as a result of the drug eliminating the underlying cause.
b. They restore the depleted amount of dopamine necessary for normal functioning.
c. They treat neither the symptoms nor the underlying cause.
d. They relieve the symptoms but fail to eliminate the causes that underlie them.

13.136　Which of the following is true of antipsychotic drugs?
a
p. 523　　a. They do seem to relieve major symptoms of schizophrenia.
Concept　b. They do seem to eliminate the causes that underlie schizophrenia.
C　　　　c. They are not often associated with side-effects.
PT/OLSG　d. They are sometimes known as minor tranquilizers.

13.137　Monoamine oxidase (MAO) inhibitors, tricyclics, and Prozac are likely to be used for
b
　　　　a. mania.
p. 523　　b. depression.
Fact　　　c. schizophrenia.
C　　　　d. anxiety.

13.138　The neurotransmitter effects most likely to be modified by the use of antidepressant
b　　　drugs are those of
p. 523　　a. dopamine and acetylcholine.
Fact　　　b. serotonin and norepinephrine.
M　　　　c. substance P and glycine.
PT/OLSG　d. GABA and endorphins.

13.139　Shortcomings of both tricyclics and MAO inhibitors include
a
p. 524　　a. serious side effects.
Fact　　　b. delayed behavioral action.
M　　　　c. serious side effects and delayed behavioral action.
　　　　　d. neither serious side effects nor delayed behavioral action.

13.140　Lithium is used to treat
a
p. 524　　a. bipolar disorders.
Fact　　　b. schizophrenia.
M　　　　c. obsessive-compulsive disorders.
　　　　　d. paranoid delusions.

13.141　Which of the following drugs is helpful in treating bipolar disorders?
b
p. 524　　a. barbiturates
Fact　　　b. lithium
M　　　　c. valium
　　　　　d. fluoxetine

13.142　The minor tranquilizers, such as the benzodiazepines, Valium, Ativan, Xanax, and Librium
d　　　are given for
p. 524　　a. schizophrenia.
Fact　　　b. bipolar mood disorders.
M　　　　c. depression.
　　　　　d. anxiety disorders.

13.143　When antianxiety drugs (such as Valium) are used in combination with alcohol
a
p. 524　　a. their effects can be magnified.
Fact　　　b. their effects can be reduced.
M　　　　c. their effects can be unpredictable.
　　　　　d. their effects can be idiosyncratic.

13.144　Concerning cultural differences in reactions to antipsychotic drugs, physicians practicing
b　　　in _____ seem to prescribe _____ doses.
p. 525　　a. America; lower
Applied　 b. Asian countries; lower
C　　　　c. Asian countries; higher
　　　　　d. Asian countries and America; equal

Chapter 13 - Therapy: Diminishing the Pain of Psychological Disorders

13.145 Which of the following is considered a biologically based therapy?
c
p. 525 a. psychoanalysis as performed by a physician.
Concept b. Gestalt therapy as performed by a psychiatrist.
M c. electroconvulsive therapy performed by a psychiatrist.
  d. behavioral based therapy as performed by a psychologist.

13.146 Electroconvulsive therapy (ECT) is a biologically based treatment that involves
b
p. 525 a. using neuro-electrical stimulators to reduce seizure activity.
Fact b. triggering a seizure by applying electrical current to the brain.
M c. aversive counterconditioning with painful electrical shocks.
  d. controlling epilepsy with drugs that affect neurotransmitters.

13.147 Which of the following treatments produces body-wide muscle contractions lasting at
b least thirty seconds?
p. 526 a. prefrontal lobotomy
Fact b. electroconvulsive therapy
M c. lithium treatment
  d. benzodiazepine drug therapy

13.148 Electroconvulsive therapy should be used with caution. However, it appears to be effective
b with severe
p. 526 a. drug addictions.
Fact b. depression.
M c. dissociative disorders.
PT/OLSG d. alcohol addictions.

13.149 The Portuguese psychiatrist, Egas Moniz, received the 1949 Nobel Prize for Medicine for
d his work in the development of
p. 526 a. antianxiety drugs.
Fact b. antidepressant drugs.
M c. electroconvulsive therapy.
  d. prefrontal lobotomies.

13.150 The primary purpose of a prefrontal lobotomy was to
d a. improve the mood of depressed patients.
p. 526 b. reduce delusions and hallucinations.
Fact c. eliminate vivid, disturbing nightmares.
C d. control violent or unacceptable outbursts.

13.151 Of the following forms of treatment for psychological disorders, which is used least often?
b a. electroconvulsive therapy
p. 526 b. psychosurgery
Fact c. drug therapy
M d. biological therapy

The Prevention of Psychological Disorders: Bringing Psychology to the Community

13.152 Which of the following were designed to bring treatment for psychological disorders directly
b to where people lived?
p. 527 a. state mental institutions
Fact b. community mental health centers
M c. private mental hospitals
  d. milieu therapy centers

13.153 Which of the following were designed to deliver outpatient services for psychological disorders?
a
p. 527 a. community mental health centers
Fact b. state mental institutions
M c. private mental hospitals
 d. milieu therapy centers

13.154 Which of the following were designed to deliver emergency services for individuals
c suffering from psychological problems?
p. 527 a. state mental institutions
Fact b. private mental hospitals
M c. community mental health centers
PT/OLSG d. milieu therapy centers

13.155 Which of the following is not a primary function of community mental health centers?
c a. provide aftercare for persons newly released from the hospital
p. 527 b. provide emergency service during moments of crisis
Fact c. provide long-term care for chronic schizophrenics
M d. provide consultation services in dealing with psychological problems

13.156 Preventing psychological disorders from developing refers to _____ prevention.
a a. primary
p. 527 b. secondary
Fact c. tertiary
M d. milieu

13.157 Primary prevention refers to programs designed to
c a. assess the psychological damage of an event.
p. 527 b. detect psychological disorders early.
Fact c. prevent psychological disorders from occurring.
M d. ease the pain of psychological disorders.

13.158 Early detection and treatment of minor psychological disorders that prevents them from
b becoming major psychological disorders refers to _____ prevention.
p. 527 a. milieu
Fact b. secondary
M c. primary
 d. tertiary

13.159 Secondary prevention refers to programs designed to
b a. assess the severity of a psychological disorder.
p. 527 b. detect and treat psychological disorders in their early stages.
Fact c. prevent psychological disorders from occurring.
M d. ease the pain associated with a disorder.

13.160 Efforts to minimize the harm done to the individual and to society as a result of
c psychological disturbance refers to _____ prevention.
p. 528 a. secondary
Fact b. primary
M c. tertiary
 d. milieu

13.161 Tertiary prevention refers to programs designed to
d a. assess the severity of a psychological disorder.
p. 528 b. detect psychological disorders early.
Fact c. prevent psychological disorders from occurring.
M d. minimize the harm a disorder does to a person.

Chapter 13 - Therapy: Diminishing the Pain of Psychological Disorders

13.162
b
p. 529
Fact
M
PT/OLSG

A general guideline used in determining when you should expect to see some progress during therapy is about
a. three weeks.
b. three months.
c. ten to fourteen days.
d. six months.

13.163
b
p. 529
Fact
M

Which of the following is not a guideline you should follow when deciding if you should leave a particular therapist?
a. any suggestion that you engage in sexual relations of any type with the therapist
b. any lateness of billing or clarity of accounts
c. exaggerated claims and guarantees of cures and total happiness
d. indications from others that your problems are getting worse and these changes for the worse do not seem to be a temporary trend

282 Test Bank - Essentials of Psychology (2nd Edition)

CHAPTER 14

Multiple-Choice Questions

14.1
b
p. 533 Bonus
Fact
E

The branch of psychology that investigates all aspects of social thought and social behavior is
a. cognitive psychology.
b. social psychology.
c. attribution psychology.
d. dissonance psychology.

14.2
c
p. 534
Fact
M

The topics of attribution, prejudice, social influence, and love are most likely to be studied by _____ psychologists.
a. clinical
b. counseling
c. social
d. educational

14.3
b
p. 534
Fact
M

Social psychology is the field of psychology that focuses on
a. how people communicate their thoughts to others.
b. how people interact with and think about others.
c. what makes people do the things they do.
d. how children develop their attitudes toward others.

14.4
d
p. 534
Fact
M

Social behavior refers primarily to the ways in which we
a. understand and think about others.
b. grow into full and complete people.
c. decide what is morally right and wrong.
d. interact with others.

Social Thought: Thinking about Other People

14.5
a
p. 535
Fact
M

The study of attribution includes examining
a. why others act the way they do.
b. inconsistencies between attitudes of different individuals.
c. consequences of our actions in relation to others.
d. the tendency to pay attention to negative social information.

14.6
c
p. 535
Applied
M

When you are trying to decide whether your friend's lateness is due to carelessness or to a traffic accident, you are involved in the process of
a. categorization.
b. conformity.
c. attribution.
d. reciprocity.

14.7
a
p. 535
Applied
M

The process of attribution would apply most directly to which of these questions?
a. What makes my roommate open the window at night?
b. Who would make the best leader of this organization?
c. How can I get my neighbor to keep his dog leashed?
d. When do people fall in love, and what makes it last?

14.8
b
p. 535
Fact
M

The basic task of making an attribution is to determine if a behavior is caused by
a. consensus or consistency.
b. internal or external causes.
c. objective or subjective causes.
d. consistency or distinctiveness.

Chapter 14 - Social Thought and Social Behavior

14.9
c
p. 535
Applied
M

Suppose you see a mother grab her child and pull him back sharply. If you decide the mother has done this to protect the child from a passing car, you have made a(n) _____ attribution.
a. psychosocial
b. interactive
c. external
d. internal

14.10
d
p. 535
Applied
M

Suppose you see a mother grab her child and pull him back sharply. If you decide the mother has done this because she has poor control over her temper, you have made a(n) _____ attribution.
a. psychosocial
b. interactive
c. external
d. internal

14.11
c
p. 535
Concept
M

According to Kelley, attribution is influenced primarily by
a. cognitive, emotional, and behavioral aspects.
b. stimuli, behaviors, and outcomes.
c. consensus, consistency, and distinctiveness.
d. compliance, conformity, and obedience.

14.12
c
p. 535
Applied
M

Your roommate is nicknamed "old reliable." She acts pretty much the same regardless of whom she is with or the situation in which she is participating. She is considered to be high in
a. consensus.
b. conformity.
c. consistency.
d. distinctiveness.

14.13
d
p. 535
Applied
M

You don't put much faith in the movie reviews in the paper, but when everyone you talk to agrees that the picture is terrific you decide to see it. The factor that convinced you is
a. compliance.
b. consistency.
c. distinctiveness.
d. consensus.

14.14
b
p. 535
Concept
M
PT/OLSG

According to Kelley, if a person reacts the same way to a given stimulus or situation on different occasions (i.e., across time), he/she exhibits
a. low distinctiveness.
b. high consistency.
c. high consensus.
d. low covariation.

14.15
b
p. 535
Concept
C

Kelley suggests that we are most likely to attribute another's behavior to internal causes when
a. consistency and consensus are high, and distinctiveness is low.
b. consensus and distinctiveness are low, and consistency is high.
c. consensus and distinctiveness are high, and consistency is low.
d. consistency and consensus are low, and distinctiveness is high.

14.16
d
p. 535
Concept
C

Kelley suggests that we are most likely to attribute another's behavior to external causes when
a. consensus, consistency, and distinctiveness are all low.
b. consensus and distinctiveness are low, and consistency is high.
c. consensus and distinctiveness are high, and consistency is low.
d. consensus, consistency, and distinctiveness are all high.

Test Bank - Essentials of Psychology (2nd Edition)

.17
)
p. 535
Concept
C
PT/OLSG

According to Kelley, we tend to attribute behavior to external causes if consistency is _____, distinctiveness is _____, and consensus is _____.
a. high; low; low
b. high; high; high
c. low; low; low
d. low; high; high

14.18
a
p. 536
Fact
M

The fundamental attribution error refers to our tendency to
a. overestimate the role of internal causes in causing others' behavior.
b. overestimate the role of external causes in causing others' behavior.
c. give ourselves more credit for our success than we really deserve.
d. overestimate the role of situations in causing our own behavior.

14.19
a
p. 536
Concept
M
PT/OLSG

The fundamental attribution error is the tendency to explain the behavior of others in terms of _____ causes.
a. internal
b. external
c. stable
d. unstable

14.20
b
p. 536
Applied
M

When making the fundamental attribution error, we are most likely to blame a student's poor academic record on the basis of
a. a stressful home-life.
b. laziness.
c. difficulty of subject matter.
d. pressure from teachers.

14.21
c
p. 536
Fact
M

A consistent error people make when figuring out the causes of other people's behavior is the fundamental attribution error, in which people tend to
a. fail to make attributions when they are appropriate.
b. make attributions even when they are not appropriate.
c. overemphasize the importance of internal factors.
d. overemphasize the importance of external factors.

14.22
a
p. 536
Concept
M

One explanation for the fundamental attribution error is that
a. when we focus on others' behavior, we assume their actions reflect their underlying characteristics.
b. when we focus on others' behavior, we are not aware of the environment.
c. the environment is never as influencial as a person's actions.
d. the behavior always occurs first, then the environment intrudes.

14.23
b
p. 536
Concept
M

If an observer is made aware of the situational forces affecting disadvantaged groups, the _____ still operates, indicating its importance in social behavior.
a. false consensus effect.
b. fundamental attribution error.
c. self-serving bias.
d. self-handicapping effect.

14.24
d
p. 536
Fact
M

The tendency to take credit for our positive behaviors by attributing them to internal causes and blame negative ones on external causes is called the
a. fundamental attribution error.
b. self-monitoring bias.
c. automatic vigilance.
d. self-serving bias.

Chapter 14 - Social Thought and Social Behavior

14.25
d
p. 536
Fact
M
PT/OLSG

The tendency to interpret the causes of our positive behavior as a result of an internal cause is the
a. fundamental attribution error.
b. basis of most gender differences.
c. illusory correlation.
d. self-serving bias.

14.26
d
p. 536
Fact
M

The tendency to interpret the causes of our negative behavior as a result of external causes is the
a. fundamental attribution error.
b. basis of most gender differences.
c. illusory correlation.
d. self-serving bias.

14.27
a
p. 537
Applied
M

Which of the following seems to be determined by the need to protect and enhance our self-esteem?
a. self-serving bias
b. fundamental attribution error
c. false consensus
d. automatic vigilance

14.28
b
p. 537
Concept
M

One important reason why people demonstrate the self-serving bias is that it allows them to
a. make more accurate attributions.
b. feel better about themselves.
c. change themselves for the better.
d. become more successful in life.

14.29
c
p. 537
Applied
C

Ralph's performance won a prize in a music competition. According to the self-serving bias, what reason is Ralph most likely to give?
a. The judges happen to like my particular style.
b. There wasn't very much competition from other artists.
c. I must have a great deal of musical talent and skill.
d. I was having an unusually good day that day.

14.30
c
p. 537
Applied
M

Recent research has found that, in athletics, the self-serving bias is used most by _____, and by athletes who performed _____.
a. rookies; on teams
b. veterans; on teams
c. rookies; alone
d. veterans; alone

14.31
c
p. 537
Study
C

Roese and Amirkhan (1997), in a study of athletes and explanations for wins or losses, found that
a. wins were attributed to external factors.
b. losses were attributed to transient factors.
c. wins were attributed to internal factors.
d. losses were attributed to internal factors.

14.32
b
p. 537
Fact
M
PT/OLSG

An area of study concerned with understanding the processes through which we interpret, analyze, and thus use social information is called
a. social attribution.
b. social cognition.
c. cognitive perspective.
d. cognitive dissonance.

14.33
c
p. 538
Applied
C

Research on assigning blame for a rape presents evidence that _____ of a _____ rape were assigned more blame for the rape.
a. victims; stranger
b. rapists; stranger
c. victims; date
d. rapists; date

14.34 What is one explanation that accounts for the tendency to assign more blame to the victims
d of a rape than to the rapist?
p. 538 a. self-handicapping
Applied b. self-serving bias
C c. fundamental attribution bias
d. belief in a just world

14.35 Which is the best example of social cognition?
b a. Feeling sexually attracted to another person.
p. 538 b. Deciding how someone is likely to act in a situation.
Fact c. Confiding your feelings to a close friend.
C d. Conforming to the expectations of a group.

14.36 Cognitive rules-of-thumb we create for making judgements or decisions very quickly
c are called
p. 539 a. automatic vigilances.
Concept b. compliances.
M c. heuristics.
d. ingratiations.

14.37 When we wish to make a decision quickly based on information that is already available
a using minimum effort, we will generally use
p. 539 a. heuristics.
Fact b. dissonance.
M c. consensus.
d. recategorization.

14.38 In general, our skills at social cognition are
a a. very good, though we do make some errors.
p. 539 b. not as accurate as a well-programmed computer.
Concept c. effective only when applied to ourselves, not to others.
M d. innate to us and cannot be changed with experience.

14.39 The tendency to believe that other persons share our attitudes to a greater extent than
d is true is called the
p. 539 a. availability heuristic.
Fact b. forced compliance effect.
M c. fundamental attribution error.
d. false consensus effect.

14.40 The tendency to overestimate the extent to which we are similar to others is the _____ effect.
a a. false consensus
p. 539 b. priming
Fact c. illusory correlation
M d. self-serving bias
PT/OLSG

14.41 Thinking that most people are in favor of legalizing drugs as you are is most likely an
b example of the
p. 539 a. self-serving bias.
Applied b. false consensus effect.
M c. group polarization effect.
d. social norm effect.

14.42 One of the explanations for the false consensus effect is the
c a. representative heuristic.
p. 539 b. social contagion heuristic.
Concept c. availability heuristic.
C d. implicit correlation heuristic.

Chapter 14 - Social Thought and Social Behavior 287

14.43   The false consensus effect is fairly common, but it does not occur when _____ attributes
b   are under consideration.
p. 539
    a. highly undesirable
Fact
    b. highly desirable
M
    c. socially acceptable
    d. socially unacceptable

14.44   The false consensus effect does not operate in all situations, especially those involving
a
    a. highly desirable attributes.
p. 539
    b. highly negative attributes.
Concept
    c. highly social attributes.
M
    d. highly cognitive attributes.

14.45   Thinking that makes assumptions that don't hold up to rational scrutiny, but which are
b   nonetheless compelling, is called
p. 539
    a. social error thinking.
Fact
    b. magical thinking.
M
    c. counterfactual thinking.
    d. counterproductive thinking.

14.46   If someone with AIDS offers you a sweater that has been sealed in a plastic bag for a year
c   and you do not accept it, you have responded according to the principle of _____, which is
p. 540   part of magical thinking.
Applied
    a. proximity
M
    b. heuristics
    c. contagion
    d. similarity

14.47   The principle of _____ implies that if two objects touch they might pass properties between each other,
b   lasting longer than the original interaction.
p. 540
    a. social proximity
Concept
    b. social contagion
M
    c. social similarity
    d. social continuity

14.48   The principle of _____ implies that things that resemble one another share common properties.
c
    a. proximity
p. 540
    b. contagion
Concept
    c. similarity
M
    d. continuity
PT/OLSG

14.49   Lisa knows she did not study enough for the psychology exam and will probably get a low score on this
d   exam, so she believes that if she does not think about the exam, she will not get the low score. This type
p. 540   of thinking illustrates the
Applied
    a. social contagion principle.
C
    b. principle of self-handicapping.
    c. principle of counterfactual thinking.
    d. thinking-makes-it-so principle.

14.50   Rozin and colleagues (1992) asked participants to rate a sweater owned by a healthy person or a
c   person with AIDS, given that the sweater had been in a plastic bag and never touched by the owner.
p. 540   Consistent with the principle of _____, the sweater owned by the person with AIDS was rated _____.
Study
    a. contagion, higher
C
    b. proximity, lower
    c. contagion, lower
    d. proximity, higher

14.51 b p. 541 Fact M

The tendency to evaluate events by thinking about alternatives to them, that is, "What might have been," is called
a. diffusion of responsibility.
b. counterfactual thinking.
c. motivated skepticism.
d. realistic conflict.

14.52 c p. 541 Concept C

The prediction that negative outcomes that follow unusual behavior will generate more sympathy for the persons who experience them than negative outcomes that follow usual or typical behavior is based on
a. diffusion of responsibility.
b. motivated skepticism.
c. counterfactual thinking.
d. fundamental attribution.

14.53 d p. 541 Concept M

The finding that negative outcomes that follow unusual behavior, rather than usual behavior, will generate more sympathy for the experiencing person illustrates
a. social contagion.
b. self-handicapping.
c. self-serving bias.
d. counterfactual thinking

14.54 b p. 541 Concept C

If you were to list the three biggest regrets in your life - the things you wish most strongly you could change - you would tend to list those things that
a. you did do.
b. you did not do.
c. you wanted someone else to do.
d. you wanted someone else to not do.

14.55 d p. 541 Concept C

If you were to list the three biggest regrets in your life during the last week - the things you wish most strongly you could change - you would tend to list those things that
a. you wanted someone else to do.
b. you wanted someone else to not do.
c. you did not do.
d. you did do.

14.56 c p. 541 Concept M

One explanation offered for the "What might have been" effect is that people are quite good at
a. enhancement.
b. self-evaluation.
c. rationalizing.
d. self-handicapping.

14.57 b p. 542 Applied C

In counterfactual thinking, research by Gilovich and Medvec (1994) indicates that, for the short term, we tend to express regrets for _____, and for the long term, we express regrets for _____.
a. actions we took against others; actions others took against us
b. actions we took; actions we did not take
c. actions we did not take; actions we took
d. actions others took against us; actions we took against others

14.58 d p. 542 Concept C

A theory proposed by Roese (1997) to explain counterfactual thinking involves the idea that we engage in such thinking in situations where we experience
a. positive outcomes.
b. delayed outcomes.
c. ambiguous outcomes.
d. negative outcomes.

Chapter 14 - Social Thought and Social Behavior 289

14.59
b
p. 543
Concept
E

Lasting evaluations of various aspects of the social world are called
a. bystander effects.
b. attitudes.
c. traits.
d. false consensus.

14.60
b
p. 543
Fact
M

Attitudes are composed of three dimensions, which are
a. conscious, unconscious, and preconscious.
b. cognitive, affective, and behavioral.
c. internal, external, and conditional.
d. primary, secondary, and tertiary.

14.61
c
p. 543
Fact
M

The dimension of attitude that consists of feelings of liking and disliking is called the _____ dimension.
a. behavioral
b. interpersonal
c. affective
d. cognitive

14.62
d
p. 543
Fact
M

The dimension of attitude that consists of the beliefs that a person might have toward an object is called the _____ dimension.
a. behavioral
b. interpersonal
c. affective
d. cognitive

14.63
c
p. 543
Concept
M
PT/OLSG

The notion that our attitudes are formed on the basis of rewards delivered by our parents for expressing the "correct view" is based on
a. social contagion.
b. cognitive dissonance.
c. operant conditioning.
d. classical conditioning.

14.64
c
p. 543
Applied
C

Which of these situations indicates the effect of operant conditioning on the formation of attitudes?
a. Bret likes black cars because his family always took his father's black car on trips to the seashore.
b. Nancy enjoys football, everyone in her family always liked football and talked about it a lot.
c. When Lisa showed an interest in drawing, her father gave her art supplies and displayed her pictures proudly.
d. After Ralph took piano lessons for a year, he lost interest and switched to playing the drums.

14.65
b
p. 543
Applied
C

Which of these situations indicates the effect of classical conditioning on the formation of attitudes?
a. Bret hates broccoli, even though it is his mother's favorite vegetable.
b. Nancy dislikes lavender perfume because the meanest teacher she ever had wore it.
c. Lisa's parents made her tend her baby sister, so now Lisa earns money as a baby sitter.
d. After being caught and punished for cheating in third grade, Ralph is now very honest.

14.66
c
p. 543
Fact
C

Under what circumstances will attitudes be developed through observational learning?
a. When we have an innate, biological readiness to develop that attitude.
b. When something is paired repeatedly with a pleasant or unpleasant stimulus.
c. When we observe other people repeatedly expressing a certain attitude.
d. When we are repeatedly rewarded or punished for expressing a certain attitude.

14.67 The efforts to change attitudes are called
a
p. 543   a. persuasion.
Fact   b. dissonance.
E   c. contagion.
        d. modification.

14.68 When a fast food company makes a commercial showing a happy family having a great
b   time eating at their restaurant, which part of the situation is called the source?
p. 543   a. The fast food company
Applied b. The happy family
M   c. The fun they are having
         d. The person watching the ad

14.69 In general, a persuasive message about cancer produces more attitude change if the communicator is
b   a. a government official, rather than a common person.
p. 543   b. a medical professional, rather than a lay person.
Fact   c. a friend, rather than someone in the media.
M   d. a woman, rather than a man.

14.70 According to the traditional approach to persuasion, an ad is more likely to be effective in
b   changing your attitudes if
p. 543   a. the person giving the message speaks particularly slowly and distinctly.
Applied b. it appears that the message was not designed to persuade you.
C   c. you are a person who has higher self-esteem than most people.
         d. the person giving the message is not so attractive that you are distracted.

14.71 Which of the following speakers is most likely to change the attitudes of members of
a   an audience?
p. 544   a. one who speaks at a faster than normal rate
Fact   b. one who speaks at a slower than normal rate
M   c. one who speaks at a normal rate
         d. rate of speaking has no influence on attitude change

14.72 Lisa is making a presentation at a conference trying to persuade others of the value of recycling. Lisa will
b   be more effective in changing others' attitudes if she
p. 544   a. is organized.
Applied b. is attractive.
M   c. uses logic.
         d. speaks slowly.

14.73 Ralph is working on a difficult crossword puzzle while at the same time listening to a political speech
d   extolling the virtues of a certain candidate. Ralph will tend to favor this candidate because he has been
p. 544 _____ while listening to the speech.
Applied a. relaxed
M   b. actively thinking
         c. emotionally reserved
         d. distracted

14.74 When a Republican speaker is addressing a Democratic audience on some issue, that speaker
c   will be more effective using a/an _____, yet when a Democratic speaker addresses that same
p. 544 audience, that speaker should use a/an _____.
Applied a. assertive approach; aggressive approach
C   b. one-sided approach; two-sided approach
         c. two-sided approach; one-sided approach
         d. aggressive approach; assertive approach

Chapter 14 - Social Thought and Social Behavior

14.75 The _____ of attitude change concentrates on the question of what cognitive process are involved in determining attitude change.
c
p. 544
Fact
M
PT/OLSG
a. traditional approach
b. cognitive dissonance interpretation
c. cognitive perspective
d. persuasion model

14.76 Which of the following models suggests that when individuals receive a persuasive message, they think about it in terms of the arguments made and the arguments possibly left out?
d
p. 544
Fact
M
a. impression management model
b. counterfactual thinking model
c. repeated exposure model
d. elaboration likelihood model

14.77 The elaboration likelihood model attempts to explain attitude change by suggesting that
d
p. 544
Concept
M
a. attitudes have no objective reality, so there really is no such thing as attitude change.
b. most people want their attitudes to change, and just need an excuse to change them.
c. the most important factor is the psychological "fit" of the message and the audience.
d. attitude change can occur through either the central route or the peripheral route.

14.78 According to the elaboration likelihood model, the most important factor that leads to either attitude change or to resistance is
a
p. 545
Concept
M
a. our thinking about the message.
b. the message itself.
c. who presents the message.
d. the attractiveness of the communicator.

14.79 According to the elaboration likelihood model, high personal relevance is to low personal relevance as
b
p. 545
Concept
C
a. peripheral route is to central route.
b. central route is to peripheral route.
c. consensus is to consistency.
d. consistency is to consensus.

14.80 The central route to persuasion refers to
a
p. 545
Fact
M
PT/OLSG
a. the careful processing of arguments.
b. the impact of persuasion cues on attitude change.
c. attitude change that occurs because individuals recognize inconsistencies between their attitudes and their behavior.
d. persuasion induced by fear.

14.81 According to the elaboration likelihood model of persuasion, we are more likely to use the central route when
a
p. 545
Fact
M
a. dealing with very important issues.
b. dealing with issues of little importance.
c. the issue is not personally relevant.
d. we can't invest much mental effort.

14.82 According to the elaboration likelihood model, little cognitive activity is performed and attitude change involves a seemingly automatic response to persuasion cues through the
d
p. 545
Fact
M
a. transient route.
b. diffusion route.
c. central route.
d. peripheral route.

14.83
a
p. 545
Applied
M

Advertisements that are designed to sell by having a "star" endorse the products are using the
a. peripheral route to persuasion.
b. transient route to persuasion.
c. central route to persuasion.
d. diffusion route to persuasion.

14.84
a
p. 545
Concept
M

According to the elaboration likelihood model, a television commercial is most likely to appeal to the peripheral route when advertising
a. perfume.
b. medical insurance.
c. vitamins.
d. investments.

14.85
b
p. 545
Applied
M

When Ralph was buying a new pair of sneakers, he selected the brand that looked cool to him, and that was advertised by a sports star he really admired. According to the elaboration likelihood model, this illustrates the _____ route to attitude change.
a. central
b. peripheral
c. diffusion
d. transient

14.86
b
p. 545
Fact
M

A technique for changing attitudes in which individuals are somehow induced to state positions different from their actual view is called
a. diffusion of responsibility.
b. forced compliance.
c. false consensus.
d. impression management.

14.87
b
p. 545
Fact
M

When individuals engage in _____, their attitudes sometime change in the direction of what they were asked to do or say.
a. attitude-consistent behavior
b. attitude-discrepant behavior
c. attitude-consonant behavior
d. attitude-enhancement behavior

14.88
c
p. 546
Applied
M

The Fantasy Man was able to persuade females to have sex with him by describing fantasies that appealed to the females, and respond to him through the _____ of attitude change.
a. transitional route
b. central route
c. peripheral route
d. diffusion route

14.89
b
p. 546
Applied
M

One reason that the Fantasy Man was successful in his persuasive appeal to females is that the females
a. listened carefully to his arguments.
b. did not carefully analyze his arguments.
c. were impressed by his clothing.
d. were impressed by his credentials.

14.90
c
p. 547
Fact
M

The unpleasant state we experience when there is an obvious gap between our attitudes and our actions is called
a. self-denial.
b. counterfactual thinking.
c. cognitive dissonance.
d. false consensus effect.

Chapter 14 - Social Thought and Social Behavior

14.91 Cognitive dissonance is produced when we
b
p. 547 a. are persuaded to change our minds about something.
Fact b. discover we hold two contradictory attitudes.
M c. make decisions based on too little information.
  d. find ourselves sexually attracted to someone.

14.92 An unpleasant feeling that results from a conflict between two different attitudes or between
b an attitude and behavior is called
p. 547 a. social incentives.
Fact b. cognitive dissonance.
M c. elaboration likelihood.
  d. frustration aggression.

14.93 One way of reducing the unpleasant feelings associated with dissonance is to
a a. change our attitudes or behaviors so that they are more consistent with one another.
p. 547 b. evaluate the information given us when we formed the attitude.
Fact c. confirm our feelings with someone else who has gone through this same situation.
C d. deny that we have these unpleasant feelings.

14.94 One way of reducing the unpleasant feelings associated with dissonance is to
d a. deny that we have these unpleasant feelings.
p. 547 b. evaluate the information given us when we formed the attitude.
Fact c. confirm our feelings with someone else who has gone through this same situation.
C d. acquire new information that supports our attitude or behavior.
PT/OLSG

14.95 One way of reducing the unpleasant feelings associated with dissonance is to
c a. evaluate the information given us when we formed the attitude.
p. 547 b. conclude that the attitudes or behaviors involved are not important.
Fact c. confirm our feelings with someone else who has gone through this same situation.
C d. deny that we have these unpleasant feelings.

14.96 Considering the tactics that are available to reduce the unpleasant feelings associated with dissonance, the
b tactic that is probably used most often is
p. 547 a. the one that involves trivialization.
Fact b. the one that requires the least effort.
C c. the one that involves acquiring supporting information.
  d. the one that requires actually changing the attitude or behavior.

14.97 Suppose you have just said you like a certain brand of breakfast cereal, but you really
d hate it. According to cognitive dissonance theory, in which of these situations should
p. 547 your attitude toward the cereal change the least?
Applied a. You voluntarily said this to a friend.
C b. You were asked to say this to a stranger.
  c. You were told to write an essay about the cereal.
  d. You were paid a fee to say this in a TV commercial.

14.98 Someone who experiences cognitive dissonance is likely to respond by _____ that caused
d the dissonance.
p. 547 a. repeating the actions.
Fact b. forgetting the situation.
M c. strengthening the attitudes.
  d. changing the attitude or the action.

14.99 Which of these people is most likely to experience cognitive dissonance?
c a. Someone who loves Italian food but is allergic to it.
p. 547 b. Someone who is deeply religious but too ill to go to church.
Applied c. Someone who hates jazz but listens to all-jazz radio.
M d. Someone who loves stamps and collects many of them.

14.100 b
p. 547
Concept
M

The fact that the stronger the reasons for engaging in attitude-discrepant behavior, the weaker the pressures toward changing the underlying attitude is called the
a. embarrassment effect.
b. less leads to more effect.
c. forced compliance effect.
d. more leads to more effect.

14.101 d
p. 547
Concept
M

The finding that the weaker the reasons for engaging in attitude-discrepant behavior, the greater the pressure to change these attitudes is called the
a. embarrassment effect.
b. more leads to more effect.
c. forced compliance effect.
d. less leads to more effect.

14.102 a
p. 547
Fact
E

One of the major factors involved in the occurrence of the less-leads-to-more effect is that people must feel that they had _____ in performing the attitude-discrepant behavior.
a. a choice
b. no choice
c. adequate reason
d. inadequate reason

14.103 d
p. 548
Applied
C

To encourage a group of teenagers to practice safe sex, the research on practical uses of cognitive dissonance indicates you should
a. give them more information about the dangers of risky sexual behavior.
b. have them sign petitions urging other teens to use safe sexual behaviors.
c. ask them to think about their own sexual behaviors.
d. have them state the importance of safe sex and think about their own sexual behaviors.

14.104 b
p. 548
Fact
M

If you claim to believe in something, but your actions contradict this belief, it is referred to as
a. ingratiation.
b. hypocrisy.
c. compliance.
d. reciprocity.

14.105 c
p. 548
Study
C

Research by Stone and colleagues (1994), in looking at conditions encouraging safe sex, found that students in the _____ group purchased condoms more than students in the other groups.
a. information
b. mindfulness
c. hypocrisy
d. commitment

14.106 b
p. 548
Fact
E
PT/OLSC

Recent research indicates that we can sometimes change our attitudes by doing or saying things
a. out of character.
b. in line with what we believe.
c. we want to happen.
d. we want others to do.

Social Behavior: Interacting with Others

14.107 c
p. 549
Fact
M

A negative evaluation of an entire group based on a small amount of experience with members of that group is called
a. discrimination.
b. a stereotype.
c. prejudice.
d. an attitude.

Chapter 14 - Social Thought and Social Behavior

14.108 A negative attitude toward the members of specific social groups based solely on their
c   membership in that group is called
p. 549   a. counterfactual thinking.
Fact   b. racial identification.
M   c. prejudice.
        d. stereotypes.

14.109 The view of prejudice that suggests that prejudice stems from competition between social
a   groups over valued commodities or opportunities is the
p. 550   a. realistic conflict theory.
Fact   b. cognitive dissonance theory.
M   c. social learning theory.
PT/OLSG d. social categorization theory.

14.110 The realistic conflict theory proposes that prejudice is the result of
d   a. categorization conflict.
p. 550   b. egalitarian conflict.
Concept c. social conflict.
M   d. economic conflict.

14.111 According to realistic conflict theory, prejudice
a   a. is more evident in times of economic hardship.
p. 550   b. is less evident in times of economic hardship.
Concept c. is fairly consistent regardless of economic circumstances.
M   d. first decreases then increases during economic hardship.

14.112 Prejudice based on assigning negative terms to members of various outgroups while
b   assigning positive terms to members of one's ingroup is characteristic of which of
p. 550 the following theories?
Concept a. realistic conflict theory
M   b. social categorization theory
        c. social learning theory
        d. counterfactual thinking theory

14.113 We tend to divide the social world into "in-group" and "out-group." This tendency is the basis for the
c   theory of prejudice called
p. 550   a. group orientation.
Concept b. social grouping.
M   c. social categorization.
        d. realistic grouping.

14.114 Out-group members, in contrast to in-group members, are seen as being more _____.
d   a. active
p. 550   b. inactive
Fact   c. heterogeneous
M   d. homogeneous

14.115 In-group members, in contrast to out-group members, are seen as being having _____.
a   a. fewer undesirable traits.
p. 550   b. more undesirable traits.
Fact   c. more homogeneity.
M   d. more consistencies.

14.116 According to social categorization theory, the basis of prejudice is that individuals
c   a. compete for resources.
p. 550   b. learn prejudice through modeling.
Concept c. divide people into us and them.
M   d. are innately driven to be prejudiced.

295

14.117 c p. 550 Fact M

The key to the social learning view of prejudice is
a. competition for limited resources.
b. dividing people into us and them.
c. observing attitudes and behaviors of others.
d. contrasting personalities with those familiar to us.

14.118 b p. 550 Applied M

In the past, television has presented members of minority groups in unflattering ways. The impact that these portrayals might have on the prejudice of children can be explained through
a. social categorization.
b. social learning.
c. social contagion.
d. social facilitation.

14.119 d p. 550 Fact M

Cognitive frameworks consisting of knowledge and beliefs about specific social groups -- frameworks suggesting that by and large, all members of these groups possess certain traits are called
a. prejudices.
b. social norms.
c. social categorizations.
d. stereotypes.

14.120 d p. 550 Fact M PT/OLSG

This view of prejudice emphasizes the role of stereotypes.
a. realistic conflict
b. social categorization
c. social learning
d. cognitive

14.121 a p. 551 Fact M

Which of the following is not true about stereotypes?
a. Information relevant to a particular stereotype is processed more slowly than information unrelated to it.
b. Information consistent with the stereotype is usually given more attention.
c. Stereotypes may block our attention to information inconsistent with it.
d. We tend to remember more easily information consistent with the stereotype.

14.122 c p. 551 Fact M

Information that is _____ with a stereotype may be _____.
a. consistent, slowly processed
b. inconsistent, quickly processed
c. inconsistent, actively refuted
d. consistent, actively refuted

14.123 b p. 551 Study M

Recent research indicates that when individuals encounter others who behave contrary to stereotypes, these others are perceived as
a. an exception to the existing stereotype.
b. a new subtype of the existing stereotype.
c. an example of a new stereotype.
d. a prototype of conflicting stereotypes.

14.124 d p. 551 Concept M

Because of the processes maintaining a stereotype, a particular stereotype may be somewhat
a. self-actualizing.
b. self-aggrandizing.
c. self-enhancing.
d. self-confirming.

14.125 b p. 551 Fact M

One of the reasons that stereotypes exist and persist is that they allow us to make
a. complex decisions based upon information received from the behavior of the affected parties.
b. quick-and-dirty judgments about others without complex effortful thought.
c. emotional decisions about other individuals when cognitive information fails.
d. decisions about others based upon processing of several pieces of information.

Chapter 14 - Social Thought and Social Behavior

14.126
a
p. 551
Fact
M

A stereotype allows us to perceive all out-group members as possessing more negative traits than our own in-group, thereby bolstering our
a. social identity.
b. social awareness.
c. social grouping.
d. social interaction.

14.127
a
p. 552
Fact
M

According to the text, an important part of reducing prejudice in children is to
a. reduce the prejudice expressed by their parents.
b. provide formal discussion on reducing prejudice.
c. keep contact between groups to a minimum.
d. expose affluent White kids and poor Black kids.

14.128
c
p. 552
Concept
M

Increased contact between groups can sometimes reduce prejudice, especially if several conditions are met. Which of the following is not one of the conditions?
a. The groups are approximately equal in status.
b. Existing norms favor equality.
c. The persons involved view one another as atypical members of their respective groups.
d. The groups work toward shared goals.

14.129
b
p. 552
Concept
M

Which of the following factors increases the chances that intergroup contact will reduce prejudice?
a. Contact is formal between two groups.
b. The two groups are fairly equal in status.
c. The two groups are allowed to work on separate tasks.
d. The members of the two groups must be atypical of those groups.

14.130
c
p. 552
Concept
M

According to the contact hypothesis, which of the following proposals for Hispanic and Anglo third graders is best designed to help reduce prejudice between the two groups?
a. Gifted Hispanic students tutor Anglo students having problems in mathematics.
b. Hispanic and Anglo students attend a formal lecture on the virtues of world cooperation.
c. Hispanic and Anglo students work together on organizing a school recycling program.
d. Hispanic and Anglo students individually write essays on why people need to share with each other.

14.131
b
p. 552
Fact
M
PT/OLSG

Which of these situations represents intergroup contact that might actually increase prejudice between the groups?
a. Providing informal, one-to-one contact.
b. Having the groups compete for prizes.
c. Giving the groups equal status in the situation.
d. Creating norms that support group equality.

14.132
c
p. 552
Concept
M

Which of the following appears to reduce prejudice?
a. minimizing recategorization
b. increase group differences so that ingroups and outgroups can be more easily identified.
c. increase recategorization
d. increase individual productivity

14.133
d
p. 553
Applied
M

If a sports team is so divided by racial prejudice that the team can't compete well, research would indicate that it might help most to
a. have the two racial groups compete against each other.
b. discuss the history and social implications of racism.
c. schedule formal discussions between the races.
d. emphasize the functioning of the team as a whole.

14.134
b
p. 553
Applied
M

Many people were once prejudiced against left-handed people, believing that the left hand was associated with sin. We learned not to divide people up by handedness but, instead, to see both left- and right-handed people as equally "good," in a process called
a. cognitive dissonance.
b. recategorization.
c. racial identification.
d. attribution.

14.135
c
p. 553
Concept
M

Sexism is defined as
a. identification based on gender.
b. dissonance based on gender.
c. prejudice based on gender.
d. stereotype based on gender.

14.136
c
p. 553
Concept
M

One form of sexism involves the _____, which is a barrier against advancement of females to the top positions in some organizations.
a. locked door
b. executive washroom
c. glass ceiling
d. corner office

14.137
b
p. 553
Study
M

Research conducted by Ohlott and colleagues (1994), on the barriers to female advancement in organizations, found that while developmental opportunities for males and females were similar, females tended not to be given
a. assignments viewed as complex.
b. assignments viewed as crucial to their organizations.
c. assignments viewed as gender related.
d. assignments viewed as simple.

14.138
c
p. 554
Fact
E

In social psychology, social influence refers to
a. socioeconomic status.
b. leadership abilities.
c. how people change the behavior of others.
d. cultural effects on one's behavior.

14.139
b
p. 554
Fact
M

The three forms of social influence are
a. prosocial behavior, overhelping, and deindividualization.
b. conformity, compliance, and obedience.
c. conformity, prosocial behavior, and persuasion.
d. persuasion, compliance, and social contagion.

14.140
d
p. 554
Fact
M

Pressures toward thinking or acting like most other persons refers to
a. obedience.
b. deindividualization.
c. prosocial behavior.
d. conformity.

14.141
a
p. 554
Fact
E

Spoken and/or unspoken rules indicating how we should or ought to behave are referred to as
a. social norms.
b. automatic vigilance.
c. bystander effect.
d. prosocial behavior.

Chapter 14 - Social Thought and Social Behavior

14.142
b
p. 554
Applied
M

Driving on the right side of the road and the notion that one should never show up for a party exactly on time are examples of
a. bystander effects.
b. social norms.
c. rules of etiquette.
d. cultural biases.

14.143
c
p. 554
Concept
C

Norms that specify what most people do in a situation are called _____, and _____ specify what should be done in that situation.
a. social norms; situational norms
b. injunctive norms; descriptive norms
c. descriptive norms; injunctive norms
d. situational norms; social norms

14.144
b
p. 555
Fact
M

A form of social influence in which individuals attempt to influence others through direct requests is called
a. conformity.
b. compliance.
c. obedience.
d. consensus.

14.145
b
p. 555
Fact
M

Compliance is what occurs when we
a. are pressured to think and act like other people.
b. agree to a request someone has made.
c. follow the orders of an authority figure.
d. decide why someone has done what they did.

14.146
c
p. 555
Concept
M

The compliance principle of _____ involves complying with a request that focuses on the decreasing availability of an item.
a. consistency
b. reciprocity
c. scarcity
d. resistance

14.147
c
p. 555
Concept
M

We are generally more likely to comply with a request from someone who has provided a previous favor or concession to us, illustrating the compliance principle of
a. resistance.
b. scarcity.
c. reciprocity.
d. consistency.

14.148
b
p. 555
Applied
M

Lisa has agreed to volunteer her time to an organization that raises money for children. Because of the compliance principle of _____, she is now much more likely to donate money to that organization.
a. reciprocity/equity
b. commitment/consistency
c. authority/leader
d. friendship/liking

14.149
c
p. 556
Fact
M

An effort to increase one's appeal to a target person before asking that person to grant a request is called
a. foot-in-the-door.
b. compliance.
c. ingratiation.
d. interpersonal attraction.

14.150 Ingratiation is a technique of social influence that relies on
a
p. 556 a. making the other person like you more.
Fact   b. strengthening the social norms of compliance.
M   c. understanding why people do the things they do.
        d. asking for smaller favors first, and working up.

14.151 Which of these illustrates someone using the technique of ingratiation to borrow $20.00?
b
p. 556 a. "Could you let me have $50.00?"
Applied b. "My, you're looking lovely today!"
M   c. "Do you have a quarter I could borrow?"
        d. "May I sell you this book for $20.00?"

14.152 The ingratiating tactic of flattery is called
b
p. 556 a. a self-enhancing tactic.
Fact   b. an other-enhancing tactic.
M   c. a deception.
        d. an offensive technique.

14.153 Ralph is going for an interview for a desirable job. He gets his hair cut, buys a new shirt and tie, and
a   arrives a few minutes early for the interview. Ralph is engaging in
p. 556 a. self-enhancement tactic of compliance.
Applied b. occupational-enhancement tactic of compliance.
M   c. other-enhancement tactic of compliance.
        d. interaction-enhancement tactic of compliance.

14.154 Lisa is going for an interview for a desirable job. She puts on a powerful perfume, makes very flattering
c   comments to the interviewer, and talks as if she knows a lot about the company. These compliance tactics
p. 556 a. will help her in her relationship with the interviewer.
Applied b. will be very successful for her.
E   c. will more than likely backfire on her.
PT/OLSG d. will be powerful enough to make a positive impression.

14.155 After friends help you move your entertainment center you immediately ask them to help
c   you paint your living room. This is an example of what social psychologists call
p. 556 a. automatic vigilance.
Applied b. forced compliance.
M   c. foot-in-the-door technique.
        d. door-in-the-face technique.

14.156 The foot-in-the-door technique seems to be effective because people want to be
a
p. 556 a. consistent.
Fact   b. dissonant.
M   c. self-assured.
        d. self-confident.
PT/OLSG

14.157 Which of these illustrates someone using the foot-in-the-door technique to borrow $20.00?
c
p. 556 a. "Could you let me have $50.00?"
Applied b. "My, you're looking lovely today!"
M   c. "Do you have a quarter I could borrow?"
        d. "May I sell you this book for $20.00?"

Chapter 14 - Social Thought and Social Behavior 301

14.158
c
p. 556
Applied
C

The _____ is involved when a salesperson offers a good deal on a car to a customer, the customer accepts the deal, and then the salesperson comes back saying that the sales manager has required him to change the deal so that there will be extra expenses for the customer.
a. foot-in-the-door technique
b. door-in-the-face technique
c. lowball technique
d. that's-not-all technique

14.159
a
p. 556
Concept
C

The foot-in-the-door technique and the lowball technique are effective because of the pressure on individuals to
a. behave consistently.
b. behave rationally.
c. behave competently.
d. behave emotionally.

14.160
b
p. 556
Concept
M

Starting with a very large request and then asking for a smaller one if the large request is rejected is an example of what social psychologists call
a. foot-in-the-door technique.
b. door-in-the-face technique.
c. label technique.
d. that's-not-all technique.

14.161
a
p. 556
Fact
M
PT/OLSG

In the door-in-the-face technique, the first request is a _____ one and the second request is a _____ one.
a. large; small
b. small; large
c. large; large
d. small; moderate

14.162
a
p. 556
Applied
M

Which of these illustrates someone using the door-in-the-face technique to borrow $20.00?
a. "Could you let me have $50.00?"
b. "My, you're looking lovely today!"
c. "Do you have a quarter I could borrow?"
d. "May I sell you this book for $20.00?"

14.163
b
p. 556
Concept
M

The compliance principle of reciprocity is the basis for
a. the foot-in-the-door principle.
b. the door-in-the-face principle.
c. the lowball principle.
d. the fast-approaching deadline principle.

14.164
b
p. 557
Applied
M

If a beautiful individual creates the impression that she is very popular and very much in demand as a dating partner, she is laying the foundation for someone to comply with her request to get engaged. She is using the compliance technique of
a. foot-in-the-door.
b. playing hard to get.
c. door-in-the-face.
d. ingratiation.

14.165
c
p. 557
Concept
M

The playing-hard-to-get technique is based on the compliance principle of
a. reciprocity.
b. commitment.
c. scarcity.
d. consistency.

14.166 a p. 557 Fact E
A form of social influence where an individual orders another to behave in a specific way is called
a. obedience.
b. forced compliance.
c. impression management.
d. conformity.

14.167 b p. 558 Concept M
Milgram's studies of obedience indicate that if harm is to come to another
a. most people readily disobey commands made by authority figures.
b. most people readily obey commands made by authority figures.
c. women, but not men, generally obey authority figures.
d. men, but not women, generally obey authority figures.

14.168 c p. 558 Concept C
The major result of Milgram's studies in which people thought they were giving large electrical shocks to strangers was to demonstrate that
a. Americans are too independent to comply with inappropriate orders from authority figures.
b. people who obey dangerous orders from their leaders are psychologically unstable.
c. ordinary people are remarkably willing to obey the wishes of authority figures.
d. men are more likely to comply with the orders of an authority figure than women.

14.169 b p. 558 Applied M
A cult leader will be more successful in ordering members to turn over all of their belongings if the leader begins by
a. emphasizing the importance of personal responsibility.
b. asking for reasonable donations from the members.
c. denying that the leader has any special powers.
d. mentioning that others have refused to do this.

14.170 c p. 558 Fact C
Which of the following is not true about obedience?
a. Relieving participants of personal responsibility will increase obedience.
b. People are more likely to obey persons with visible signs of authority.
c. Obedience is less likely if commands are gradual in nature.
d. People are less likely to obey if someone else also obeys with them.

14.171 a p. 558 Fact E PT/OLSG
An important factor in getting participants to obey in the obedience studies is that the person in authority relieves the participant of
a. responsibility.
b. emotion.
c. awareness.
d. cognition.

14.172 d p. 558 Fact M
An individual is more likely to disobey an authority figure if the authority figure
a. is cordial and compassionate.
b. takes time to explain the actions.
c. takes complete responsibility for the actions.
d. is pursuing purely selfish goals.

14.173 b p. 558 Concept M
An important factor that will make people less likely to obey an authority figure occurs when
a. social norms support the authority figure.
b. we witness other people refusing to obey.
c. the orders gradually increase in strength.
d. the authority assumes all responsibility.

14.174 c p. 559 Concept M
Prosocial behavior is behavior that
a. makes us more attractive to other people.
b. obeys the orders of authority figures.
c. helps other people with no direct reward.
d. treats all ethnic groups with equal respect.

Chapter 14 - Social Thought and Social Behavior

14.175
b
p. 559
Fact
E

Behaviors that involve actions that benefit others without necessarily providing any direct benefit to the person performing them are called
a. compliance.
b. prosocial behavior.
c. cognitive dissonance.
d. self-serving bias.

14.176
c
p. 559
Concept
M

When we help someone because they are in need of our help, and not because of our own needs, this explanation is known as the
a. negative state relief hypothesis.
b. genetic determinism hypothesis.
c. empathy-altruism hypothesis.
d. behavior commitment hypothesis.

14.177
b
p. 559
Concept
M

When we see someone in need of help it increases our negative feelings, and when we then help in order to reduce these negative feelings, the explanation would be known as the
a. genetic determinism hypothesis.
b. negative state relief hypothesis.
c. empathy-altruism hypothesis.
d. behavior commitment hypothesis.

14.178
b
p. 559
Applied
M

Lisa saw an older lady fall in the street and spill her groceries. Lisa felt bad for the lady, helped her gather up the groceries, and felt better when the lady smiled and thanked her. This situation is an example of the _____ explanation of prosocial behavior.
a. empathy-altruism hypothesis.
b. negative state relief hypothesis.
c. genetic determinism hypothesis.
d. dissonant/action hypothesis.

14.179
b
p. 559
Concept
M

The hypothesis that explain prosocial behavior based on our own feelings is called _____, and the hypothesis that is based on others' feelings is called _____.
a. genetic determinism hypothesis, dissonant/action hypothesis
b. negative state relief hypothesis, empathy-altruism hypothesis
c. empathy-altruism hypothesis, negative state relief hypothesis
d. dissonant/action hypothesis, genetic determinism hypothesis

14.180
b
p. 559
Concept
M

When we help someone in need of help who is related to us, but not to strangers, the explanation would be the
a. negative state relief hypothesis.
b. genetic determinism hypothesis.
c. empathy-altruism hypothesis.
d. behavior commitment hypothesis.

14.181
c
p. 560
Applied
M

One way to resist compliance attempts is to
a. try to avoid contact with individuals who make requests.
b. ask for reasons for the request.
c. not reciprocate trivial concessions.
d. don't respond to emotional appeals.

14.182
b
p. 560
Applied
M

One way to resist persuasion attempts is to
a. use humor.
b. develop counterarguments.
c. become emotional.
d. not pay attention to the message.

14.183 It appears that the _____ has more support for explaining prosocial behavior than the other hypotheses.
d
p. 561
Fact
M
a. dissonant/action hypothesis
b. genetic determinism hypothesis
c. negative state relief hypothesis
d. empathy-altruism hypothesis

14.184 One reason that empathy may increase our willingness to help others is the idea that by helping, we
a
p. 561
Fact
M
a. experience an overlap of our self and the other person.
b. contribute to the other person's sense of worth.
c. assist in our own self-aggrandizement.
d. develop the sense of community.

14.185 The bystander effect indicates that when someone is in trouble, the people nearby (bystanders) will be
c
p. 562
Concept
M
a. more likely to help if the victim is similar to them.
b. frightened of the responsibility and will tend to leave.
c. less likely to help if they believe others are present.
d. confused by crowds and won't know what is happening.

14.186 A reduced tendency of witnesses at an emergency to help when they believe that there are other potential helpers present is called the
b
p. 562
Fact
M
a. self-serving bias.
b. bystander effect.
c. fundamental attribution error.
d. counterfactual thinking.

14.187 The bystander effect can be explained partly on the basis of
c
p. 562
Concept
M
a. self-serving bias.
b. fundamental attribution error.
c. diffusion of responsibility.
d. counterfactual thinking.

14.188 The phenomenon of diffusion of responsibility predicts that
b
p. 562
Fact
M
a. when more people witness a situation, each one is more likely to respond.
b. when more people witness a situation, each one is less likely to respond.
c. any behavior that contributes to the survival of the species will increase.
d. any behavior that contributes to the survival of the species will decrease.

14.189 Research on the bystander effect and diffusion of responsibility indicates that, if you are in trouble and need help, you will be better off if
c
p. 562
Fact
M
a. there are two potential helpers nearby.
b. there are many potential helpers nearby.
c. there is only one potential helper nearby.
d. there are no potential helpers nearby.

14.190 Research indicates that the higher the _____ in an area, the _____ the spontaneous helping in that area.
b
p. 562
Study
M
a. age of the population, higher
b. population density, lower
c. population density, higher
d. age of the population, lower

14.191 In most circumstances, people who are in a good mood are
a
p. 562
Fact
M
a. more likely to help someone in trouble.
b. less likely to help someone in trouble.
c. equally likely to help someone in trouble.
d. likely to help only those similar to themselves.

Chapter 14 - Social Thought and Social Behavior 305

14.192　　If someone is in a good mood, how does this affect their willingness to help someone else
d　　who is in trouble?
p. 563　　a.　They are always more likely to help.
Fact　　b.　They are always less likely to help.
M　　c.　They are more likely to help if the person is male.
　　d.　They are less likely to help if helping looks unpleasant.

14.193　　The text suggests that people who are in a good mood are less likely to help others if
b　　a.　they believe the world is a just place.
p. 563　　b.　they think it might spoil their mood.
Concept　　c.　they have an internal locus of control.
M　　d.　they feel that others would do the same thing.

14.194　　Which of the following is true concerning the effects of mood on the tendency to help others?
c　　a.　Being in a good mood will always increase the tendency to help others.
p. 563　　b.　Being in a negative mood will always inhibit the tendency to help others.
Fact　　c.　Mood and plight of the victims interact in determining the likelihood of helping others.
C　　d.　Mood has no real effect on helping; it is the severity of the situation that determines
　　　　the tendency to help others.

14.195　　When a person is in a bad mood, under what circumstances is this person more likely
d　　to help someone in trouble?
p. 563　　a.　When they are focusing on their own troubles.
Fact　　b.　When they are in a hurry to get someplace.
M　　c.　When the person in trouble is male.
　　d.　When they are trying to cheer themselves up.

14.196　　If you are in a position of needing help to finish a paper, why would you refuse to accept
b　　help on that paper from your roommate?
p. 563　　a.　Accepting help means that your paper is too complicated.
Applied　　b.　Accepting help puts you in an unfavorable or negative light.
M　　c.　Accepting help means that you will have to give her credit.
　　d.　Accepting help puts you in the position of having to tell your professor you received help.

14.197　　If someone wants to make you look bad while at the same time giving the impression that
c　　the help is freely given by a good person, that person is using the tactic of
p. 563　　a.　compliance helping.
Applied　　b.　situational helping.
M　　c.　overhelping.
　　d.　reciprocal helping.

14.198　　Gilbert and Silvera (1996) found that when participants rated strangers who were working on an anagram
b　　task, those strangers who had received lots of help, as compared to little help
p. 563　　a.　were rated higher on sociability.
Study　　b.　were downrated on ability.
M　　c.　were rated the same on ability.
　　d.　were rated higher on ability.

14.199　　The term that refers to the fact that interpersonal attraction is influenced by the physical
c　　closeness of people's living quarters is
p. 564　　a.　social comparison.
Fact　　b.　ingratiation.
M　　c.　propinquity.
　　d.　priming.

14.200 In which of the following situations was propinquity likely to have been an important factor?
b
p. 564   a. Lisa was hired as a junior executive by a national advertising agency.
Applied b. Lisa and Ralph become good friends after sitting next to each other in three of their
M   first semester courses.
         c. You loaned your roommate $20 even though he asked for $50.
         d. You refused to turn down your stereo when ordered to do so by your neighbor.

14.201 According to the repeated exposure effect, being exposed to some stimulus over and
d   over again usually has the effect of
p. 564   a. changing our attributional decision about it.
Fact   b. increasing our conformity to social norms.
M   c. making our attitudes toward it more negative.
         d. making our attitudes toward it more positive.

14.202 Which of these sayings is most strongly supported by research on interpersonal attraction?
c   a. Opposites attract.
p. 564   b. Absence makes the heart grow fonder.
Concept c. Birds of a feather flock together.
M   d. Beauty is only skin deep.

14.203 The most plausible explanation for why we are attracted to others who are similar to ourselves is that they
b   a. allow us to access the availability heuristic much more easily.
p. 564   b. provide validation for our own attitudes and behaviors.
Concept c. allow us to use stereotypes in our evaluation of others.
M   d. provide a basis for reduction of cognitive dissonance.

14.204 We are attracted to others who are similar to ourselves because they
a   a. make us feel good.
p. 564   b. reduce dissonance for us.
Concept c. permit easy comparison.
M   d. validate our stereotypes.

14.205 The proposition that we are attracted to physically attractive people because such a characteristic is
d   associated with good health and reproductive capacity, and therefore increases the probability that our
p. 565 genes will be contributed to the population comes from
Fact   a. attractive gene proposal.
M   b. hereditary contribution effect.
         c. genetic determinism hypothesis.
         d. evolutionary psychology.

14.206 Someone whose face is in most ways a "typical" face of that person's culture will usually
b   seem to be
p. 565   a. boring and not very attractive.
Fact   b. highly physically attractive.
M   c. younger and less well developed.
         d. older and more mature.

14.207 Judgments of attractiveness depend upon _____, as well as facial features.
c   a. head size
p. 565   b. height/weight correlation
Fact   c. physique
E   d. hair length

14.208 Gardner and Tockerman (1994), in a study of physique, found that individuals who were made to appear
d   _____, were rated as _____.
p. 565   a. normal weight, less attractive
Study   b. slim, less attractive
E   c. overweight, more attractive
         d. overweight, less attractive

Chapter 14 - Social Thought and Social Behavior

14.209
b
p. 566
Fact
M

An intense emotional state involving attraction, sexual desire, and deep concern for another person refers to
a. close relationship.
b. love.
c. propinquity.
d. compassion.

14.210
b
p. 566
Fact
M

This type of love emphasizes commitment and concern for the loved one's well-being.
a. passionate love
b. companionate love
c. romantic love
d. responsible love

14.211
d
p. 566
Fact
M

Which of these is not one of the components necessary for the experience of romantic love?
a. Intense emotional arousal
b. The cultural concept of romantic love.
c. Desire to be loved by the object of affection.
d. Commitment to another's well-being.

14.212
a
p. 566
Concept
E

One explanation for the powerful reaction from romantic love is that
a. infant attachment is a forerunner of love.
b. emotions are stronger than thought.
c. emotions occur without the tempering of cognition.
d. physical attractiveness is the foundation of the emotion.

14.213
b
p. 566
Concept
E
PT/OLSG

According to evolutionary theory, _____ enhances the tendency to engage in sexual intercourse and to commitment to provide long term child care.
a. lust
b. love
c. cognition
d. emotion

NOTES

NOTES

NOTES

NOTES

NOTES

NOTES

NOTES